To Right These Wrongs

To Right These Wrongs

THE NORTH CAROLINA FUND

AND THE

BATTLE TO END POVERTY AND INEQUALITY

IN 1960S AMERICA

Robert R. Korstad and James L. Leloudis

With photographs by Billy E. Barnes

THE UNIVERSITY OF NORTH CAROLINA PRESS

CHAPEL HILL

This book was published with the generous assistance of the
Mary Reynolds Babcock Foundation and the Z. Smith Reynolds Foundation.

Change Comes Knocking: The Story of the NC Fund (DVD) © 2009 Video Dialog Inc.

The paper in this book meets the guidelines for permanence and durability of the Committee on
Production Guidelines for Book Longevity of the Council on Library Resources. The University of
North Carolina Press has been a member of the Green Press Initiative since 2003.

Library of Congress Cataloging-in-Publication Data
Korstad, Robert Rodgers.
To right these wrongs : the North Carolina Fund and the battle to end poverty and inequality in
1960s America / Robert R. Korstad and James L. Leloudis ; with photographs by Billy E. Barnes.
p. cm.
Includes bibliographical references and index.
ISBN 978-0-8078-3379-7 (cloth : alk. paper) — ISBN 978-0-8078-7114-0 (pbk. : alk. paper)
1. North Carolina Fund—History. 2. Economic assistance, Domestic—North Carolina—
History. 3. Poverty—Government policy—North Carolina—History. I. Leloudis, James L.
II. Barnes, Billy E. III. Title.
HC107.N83P634 2010
362.5'80975609046—dc22
2009052890

cloth   14 13 12 11 10   5 4 3 2 1
paper   14 13 12 11 10   5 4 3 2 1

FOR JACQUELYN AND DIANNE

I still think today as yesterday that the color line is a great problem of this century. But today I see more clearly than yesterday that back of the problem of race and color, lies a greater problem which both obscures and implements it: and that is the fact that so many civilized persons are willing to live in comfort even if the price of this is poverty, ignorance, and disease of the majority of their fellowmen.

—W. E. B. DU BOIS,
The Souls of Black Folk (1953)

If it may be said of the slavery era that the white man took the world and gave the Negro Jesus, then it may be said of the Reconstruction era that the southern aristocracy took the world and gave the poor white man Jim Crow. . . . And when his wrinkled stomach cried out for the food that his empty pockets could not provide, he ate Jim Crow, a psychological bird that told him that no matter how bad off he was, at least he was a white man, better than the black man. . . . And when his undernourished children cried out for the necessities that his low wages could not provide, he showed them the Jim Crow signs on the buses and in the stores, on the streets and in the public buildings. And his children, too, learned to feed upon Jim Crow.

—MARTIN LUTHER KING JR.,
"Our God Is Marching On!" (1965)

There can be no question but that in the South in general (or in the nation as a whole, of course) only an interracial movement of the poor can dig deeply into the root causes of poverty and exert the pressure necessary to alleviate and cure these causes—and develop a genuinely democratic society.

—JOHN SALTER,
community organizer in northeastern
North Carolina, 1968

Contents

To Right These Wrongs

INTRODUCTION

This book is about the politics of race and poverty in America. It tells the story of the North Carolina Fund, a pioneer effort to improve the lives of the "neglected and forgotten" poor in a nation that celebrated itself as an affluent society. Governor Terry Sanford created the Fund in 1963, at a time when the United States stood at a crossroads. A decade of civil rights activism had challenged the country to fulfill its promise of equality and opportunity. Not since the Civil War and Reconstruction had reformers raised such fundamental questions about the political and social foundations of the republic. But it was by no means clear how Americans would answer. Alabama governor George C. Wallace spoke for one possibility. In his inaugural address, delivered on the steps of the Alabama statehouse in January 1963, he pledged to defend "Segregation now! Segregation tomorrow! Segregation forever!" Those words made Wallace the point man for a politics of fear and resentment, which eventually spread to communities across the land.[1]

In North Carolina, Governor Terry Sanford offered a dramatic alternative. On July 18, six months after Wallace's swearing-in, Sanford announced the establishment of the North Carolina Fund, a unique five-year effort to stamp out the twin scourges of discrimination and economic deprivation. "In North Carolina there remain tens of thousands whose family income is so low that daily subsistence is always in doubt," he explained. "There are tens of thousands who go to bed hungry. . . . There are tens of thousands whose dreams will die." That anguish cried out for "institutional, political, economic, and social change designed to bring about a functioning, democratic society." This, the governor proclaimed, "is what the North Carolina Fund is all about." With those words, Sanford positioned the private nonprofit corporation and the state as the "advance guard" in what would soon become a national, federally funded war on poverty.[2]

The Fund was overseen by a board of directors that included civic leaders — men and women, black and white — from across the state. It began its work with $2.5 million in financial backing from two local philanthropies, the Z. Smith Reynolds and Mary Reynolds Babcock Foundations, both of which were tied to influential banking and tobacco interests. The Ford Foundation, which had been investing in projects of social reconstruction in urban America, gave an additional $7 million. After passage of the Economic Opportunity Act and creation of the Office of Economic Opportunity (OEO) in 1964, the Fund also became the primary conduit for the flow of federal antipoverty dollars into North Carolina. By 1968, it had received just over $7 million from the OEO and the Departments of Labor; Housing and Urban Development; and Health, Education, and Welfare. The Fund's total five-year budget of $16.5 million roughly equaled the state of North Carolina's average annual expenditure for public welfare during the mid-1960s.[3]

The Fund's reliance on a combination of private and federal dollars was a calculated political tactic designed to ensure its independence. It allowed Sanford and his allies to bypass conservative state lawmakers and challenge the entrenched local interests that nourished Jim Crow, perpetuated one-party politics, and protected an economy built on cheap labor and racial antagonism. The Fund's purpose, explained executive director George Esser, was "to *create* the possible" by mobilizing like-minded reformers at the community level and promoting new approaches to antipoverty work that would have gone nowhere had they been proposed to the state's welfare bureaucracy. That intrepid but pragmatic strategy was the Fund's greatest strength and, in time, its most serious liability. During an intense five years of experimentation, the Fund served as a laboratory for Lyndon Johnson's Great Society and became a site of conflict for the forces that tore that effort apart.[4]

The battle against poverty—in North Carolina and in other communities across the nation—has been seen too often as the economic extension of the civil rights movement. There is truth in that characterization, but only if one places the black freedom struggle in the context articulated by Martin Luther King Jr. at the conclusion of the 1965 voting rights march from Selma to Montgomery, Alabama. In a remarkable speech, King told listeners that their campaign for the right to vote exposed "the very origin, the root cause, of racial segregation." He took them back to the biracial politics of Reconstruction and Populism, explaining that Jim Crow was something more than a simple expression of racial hatred. It was instead a "political stratagem" employed by white elites "to keep the southern masses divided and southern labor the cheapest in the land." As a system of power, white supremacy terrorized blacks and saddled ordinary whites with poverty as part of the bargain for racial privilege. On the basis of that historical understanding, King argued that poor and politically marginalized Americans—more whites than blacks—would never be free until they joined forces to dismantle Jim Crow and fulfill the nation's democratic promise. United, they could "build a great society: a society of justice where none would pray upon the weakness of others; a society of plenty where greed and poverty would be done away; a society of brotherhood where every man would respect the dignity and worth of human personality."[5]

Taking our cue from King, we begin the story of the North Carolina Fund with a flashback to the economic and political turmoil of the late nineteenth century, for it was there that the stage was set. In the 1880s and 1890s, the spread of sharecropping and the rapid commercialization of agriculture spawned a farmers' revolt that found its political voice in the People's Party, the largest third-party movement in American history. To varying degrees, Populist insurgents across the South experimented with biracial politics. Writing in the *Arena*, a national journal of reform, Tom Watson, one of Populism's most eloquent spokesmen, made the case: "The People's Party says to these two [races], 'You are kept apart that you may be separately fleeced of your earnings. You are made to hate each other because upon that hatred is rested the keystone of the arch of financial despotism which enslaves you both. You are deceived and blinded that you may not see how this race antagonism perpetuates [an economic] system which beggars both.' . . . The conclusion, then, seems to me to be this: the crushing burdens which now oppress both races in the South will cause each to make an effort to cast them off. . . . They will become political allies. . . . And on these broad lines of mutual interest, mutual forbearance, and mutual support the present will be made the stepping-stone to future peace and prosperity."

Watson's vision of a New South underestimated the hold that racial fear had on white people's imaginations and the willingness of elites to resort to brute force in defending the color line. By the opening years of the twentieth century, virulent white supremacy movements across the South had crushed any hope for biracial democracy and secured a regime of racial capitalism that relied on segregation, black disfranchisement, and antiunionism to concentrate the region's wealth in the hands of the few. That new order demonstrated a remarkable capacity to discipline apostate whites and to subordinate material interests to racial phobias. It contaminated the minds of even the most ardent egalitarians, to say nothing of the vast majority of white dissidents who had never been comfortable with interracialism. Tom Watson was again a case in point. Once a fierce democratic crusader, he ended his career as a raging anti-Semite, racial bigot, and champion of the Ku Klux Klan.[6]

When Terry Sanford became governor in 1961, he inherited the bitter legacies of an economy built on cheap labor and white supremacy. The state's factory workers earned some of the lowest industrial wages in the nation, more than a third of families lived below the poverty line, half of all students never finished high school, and a fourth of all adults were functionally illiterate. Those conditions had once given North Carolina's industries—textiles, tobacco, and agriculture—a competitive edge at the bottom of America's economy, but in the decades after World War II even that advantage was rapidly becoming a liability. Automation in the textile and tobacco factories and the mechanization of farming cost thousands of men and women their jobs and drove them onto the welfare rolls or out of state. The population loss was particularly acute among the young, who potentially had the most to contribute to North Carolina's prosperity. At the same time, a generation of black citizens who had defended democracy in battles abroad demanded freedom at home. They built a reinvigorated civil rights movement through the National Association for the Advancement of Colored People, the Southern Christian Leadership Conference, and the Congress on Racial Equality; they rallied to fresh efforts at biracial unionism; and their children turned the world's attention to places such as Greensboro, North Carolina, where the sit-in phase of the black freedom struggle began in 1960. In the face of those challenges, die-hard segregationists fought to defend the crumbling kingdom of Jim Crow. Others, like Terry Sanford, saw in the upheaval the white South's last best chance to reconstruct itself.

A year before President Lyndon Johnson declared a national war on poverty, Sanford and his allies in the liberal wing of the state Democratic party set out to awaken North Carolinians to poverty's social costs.[7] The governor aimed to diversify the economy, improve public education, and reduce the state's dependence on low-wage manufacturing. He and his supporters even signaled a willingness—indeed, an eagerness—to surrender segregation, so long as they could control the pace and direction of change. As much as they understood poverty as a structural problem, they also worried about the values that deprivation appeared to instill in those they called the "people of poverty." Sanford and his associates embraced the notion of a "culture of poverty," which was well established in scholarly literature and had been popularized in 1962 by Michael Harrington's best-selling exposé, *The Other America.* The poor were "pessimistic and defeated," Harrington wrote. "They tend to be hopeless and passive, yet prone to bursts of violence; they are lonely and isolated, often rigid and hostile. To be poor is not simply to be deprived of the material things of this world. It is to enter a fatal, futile universe, an America within America with a twisted spirit." Worse yet, these characteristics seemed to be self-perpetuating, for "the children of poverty [became] the parents of poverty and [began] the cycle anew."[8]

Like other reform-minded Americans who snatched Harrington's book from the shelves, Governor Sanford saw in the sufferings of the poor a dark vision of the future. He reasoned that North Carolina would remain outside the economic mainstream so long as it was burdened by men and women who lacked the motivation, work ethic, and skills to participate successfully in the labor force and in the lives of their communities. It was necessary and *right*, Sanford and Fund officials insisted, for the state to develop new strategies to "reverse trends, motivate people, re-orient attitudes, supply the education and the public services and the jobs that will give all our people the chance to become productive, more self-reliant, and able to compete in the complex but dynamic, exciting but perilous world of today and tomorrow."[9]

The Fund's initial efforts adhered closely to a traditional, top-down model of social change. In the fall of 1963, it called for proposals from local social service agencies and private charities that were interested in working together to "analyze their [communities'] poverty problems, and come up with some ideas for solving them." Fifty-one groups responded, and from that number the Fund chose eleven projects spread across the state and with "a good balance between large cities and smaller ones, rural communities and industrial areas." Most of the proposals emphasized the deficiencies of the poor and, to that end, called for educational initiatives—kindergartens, tutoring, bookmobiles, and vocational training—that encouraged self-improvement. The petitioners also stressed a dire need for additional teachers and social welfare workers. A long history of underfunding had left welfare agencies and the schools ill-equipped to meet their basic responsibilities, much less take on bold new ventures. The Fund responded by hastily organizing a volunteer program for North Carolina college students during the summer of 1964, a moment when hundreds of young people, mostly from outside the South, were traveling to Mississippi to take part in the Freedom Summer campaign for civil rights and black voter registration. Students in the North Carolina Volunteers came from nearly three dozen campuses across the state and were assigned to racially integrated teams of men and women to work for each of the eleven community action programs. They served in a wide variety of roles, from camp counselors to tutors, library assistants, and aides to public health nurses. In 1965, the Fund drew on its experience with the Volunteers program to train the first participants in President Johnson's "domestic Peace Corps," Volunteers in Service to America.[10]

The student volunteers served as canaries in the coal mines: they were the first to confront the challenges that would soon beset the Fund and the larger national antipoverty movement. The fact that they worked and lived together—black next to white, women alongside men—horrified most whites in the communities they went to serve. Every team suffered racial taunts; many endured social ostracism; and in several cases, the volunteers were fired upon by members of the Ku Klux Klan. Those experiences alarmed and unsettled the students. They were disappointed by the resistance they encountered, frightened by the rage they provoked, and shocked by the conditions they discovered in poor people's homes. Some simply soldiered on, trying as best they could to put scenes of misery out of mind, but most could not avoid asking hard questions about themselves and their society. White volunteers confronted their own prejudices in the angry faces of those who scorned them, while their black peers wrestled with the possibility that whites might be trusted allies. Together, black and white students came to understand that charity and self-help would never be enough to alleviate poverty. That task, one Fund veteran explained, required something different: a "radical strategy" to "stop the exploitation of the poor by the more economically well off."[11]

Just such a strategy erupted from the unpaved streets and ramshackle houses in poor communities, where residents struggled to pay the rent, feed and clothe their children, keep warm through the winter, and stay healthy without indoor plumbing and safe drinking water. When members of Congress crafted the Economic Opportunity Act, they included a requirement that all antipoverty efforts promote the "maximum feasible participation" of the poor. To most lawmakers, that meant little more than consulting poor people as the clients of community action programs and finding ways to improve their access to government services. But as the North Carolina Fund began to organize in locales across the state, men and women who had long been denied the basic rights of economic and political citizenship were emboldened by their inclusion in a national crusade. That was particularly true of blacks in Durham, a tobacco manufacturing town, and in "North Carolina's Mississippi," the cluster of counties in the northeastern corner of the state dominated by tenant farms and plantation agriculture. In these places, poor residents drew strength from a long local history of struggle against white supremacy as well as from recent agitation for civil rights. When offered the opportunity, they stepped forward and insisted on serving as officers, not just foot soldiers, in an ever-broadening battle for economic justice and political equality. That mobilization frightened whites up and down the social ladder. But, as one activist explained, the goal of poor people was at once less sinister and more profound than usurping the authority of whites: "We weren't trying to take over; we were just trying to have a participatory democracy."[12]

That democratic impulse transformed the War on Poverty's agenda. By 1966—two short years after the call to battle—both the North Carolina

Fund's George Esser and OEO director Sargent Shriver had adopted a new vocabulary. Esser, who had devoted his early career to the study of public administration and the promotion of bureaucratic efficiency, now explained that his agency's purpose was to "strengthen and expand the democratic process itself at all levels, so that all our people can play an active part in the shaping of their own, and the nation's, destiny." In testimony before a Senate committee, Shriver echoed that view. "Democracy," he explained, "means more than giving every man a vote, because many of the problems we face today will never appear on a ballot: welfare regulations; code enforcement; garbage collection; police brutality. . . . Beyond the formal ballot comes the larger mandate of democracy—to give the poor an effective voice in reshaping our cities. To give the poor a role, an opportunity to contribute to the rebuilding of our society."[13]

Democratic aspirations also rose up from predominantly white communities in the hills and hollows of Appalachia. One of the Fund's most ambitious community action projects was sponsored by Watauga, Avery, Mitchell, and Yancey Counties in the northwestern corner of the state. Here, as in other sites, women were among the most effective grassroots organizers, and they, along with Fund-supported staff, connected local antipoverty efforts with a broader regional uprising that first emerged from the coal towns of Kentucky and West Virginia. White Appalachian activists drew inspiration from the black freedom struggle and set out to duplicate the victories won with the Civil Rights Act of 1964 and the Voting Rights Act of 1965, which cut the legs from under a century-old system of legal discrimination. "The time for action is now," they declared. "Never again can Americans take pride in their 'democracy,' for the basic facts of the denial of human rights to one-third of [the] people have been exposed. True democracy can and will be realized through the use of 'Poor Power.' . . . Thirty-four million Americans can, by uniting around their poverty, exert the necessary pressure . . . to change the present structure of power which has for so long denied the opportunity to rise to the standard the other two-thirds of the nation enjoys."[14]

Implicit in this call for poor power was a recognition that impoverished "white[s] . . . and the Negroes [had] problems that [were] alike" and that by "fight[ing] together" they might win "opportunities that [had] been denied them." The Fund made its most concentrated effort to realize that possibility in Durham. There, for a brief moment, it managed to organize poor whites and to draw them into a coalition of black neighborhood councils. But building that effort into a meaningful political alliance was a Herculean task. It cut against the grain of hundreds of years of history, in which race had been inscribed as the fundamental organizing principle of southern—indeed, American—life, and in which poor whites, as subordinate partners in the regime of white supremacy, had been unable to accumulate the social assets necessary to press their economic self-interests. Establishing a biracial alliance of the poor also required time, the one resource that was in shortest supply.[15]

By late 1968, when the Fund closed the doors on its five-year experiment, a resurgent politics of race had gained the advantage on the battlefield. In North Carolina, as elsewhere in the South, the Republican Party, decimated at the beginning of the twentieth century by its openness to biracialism, reinvented itself as a standard-bearer for free enterprise, states' rights, and opposition to a civil rights agenda that positioned the federal government as a counterweight to local and private power. From the ashes of Barry Goldwater's failed presidential bid in 1964, a new generation of conservative politicians, led in North Carolina by Congressman Jim Gardner and soon joined by disaffected Democrats such as television editorialist Jesse Helms, rewrote the political narrative of Lyndon Johnson's Great Society. They colored antipoverty efforts black, charged that "community action" and "maximum feasible participation" were little more than covers for "radical intrigue," and warned that life was a zero-sum game in which any gain by blacks came at the expense of poor and working-class whites.[16]

Once more, the Fund was at the center of national debates over poverty and politics. Its efforts to mobilize the poor and to demand accountability from elected officials and government agencies generated "intense public hostility" that was "responsible in significant part" for the dismantling of the War on Poverty. In 1967, conservative southerners in Congress—Republican and Democrat—forged an alliance with big-city mayors who resented the way that federal antipoverty programs sidestepped their political machines by providing direct funding to grassroots organizations. Together, they sought to quash the democratic potential of the War on Poverty by requiring that federal grants be administered through local governments rather than through community action agencies or nonprofits such as the North Carolina Fund and by banning recipients of those grants from any form of political activity, including voter registration drives. Two years later, that alliance spearheaded tax legislation designed to shackle private philanthropies, especially the Ford Foundation, in similar ways. The Tax Reform Act of 1969 gave the Internal Revenue Service power to rescind the tax-exempt status of foundations whose grants were used for political purposes, broadly construed; required foundations to police their grant recipients' behavior; and authorized "harsh penalties" for abuses. The IRS could fine foundations up to 100 percent of the value of offending grants and could assess individual officers and directors up to 50 percent of that value. Officials from the Ford Foundation and other philanthropies worried about the effect of those regulations. The foundations would continue to support programs to fight poverty, but there was now a danger that they would become overly cautious and "tip the balance against new commitments to experimentation, originality and creativity."[17]

In the decades that followed, conservatives undertook a persistent campaign to dismantle the institutions and programs of the Great Society. That effort took place on several fronts. As they gained political power in Washington, Republicans replaced the senior leadership at the OEO, curtailed its spending on community action, and eventually shuttered the command center of the War on Poverty. Politicians and intellectuals also worked aggressively to steer public debate away from the political economy of poverty to concerns about the effectiveness of welfare and the behaviors of the poor. In many respects, they brought the conversation around full circle to a preoccupation with a culture of poverty. The counterassault culminated in 1996 with sweeping welfare reform that returned money and control to the states. That move significantly compromised key principles of the Great Society. The federal government was made a less effective ally of the dispossessed, and antipoverty programs lost much of their force as a vehicle for social and economic change. As these shifts took place, fundamental questions all but faded from view: where does poverty come from, and why does it persist?

In his 1988 State of the Union address, Ronald Reagan heaped scorn on the Great Society. "Some years ago, the federal government declared war on poverty," he quipped, "and poverty won." That misguided campaign left behind "a massive social problem," Reagan continued. Rather than helping the poor, it created "a poverty trap" and made dependency its "one enduring heirloom, passed from one generation to the next." The president's solution was to get the federal government out of the poverty-fighting business and to return responsibility for the poor to state and local governments and private charities. "It's time for Washington to show a little humility," he declared. "There are a thousand sparks of genius in 50 states and a thousand communities around the nation. It is time to nurture them and see which ones can catch fire and become guiding lights."[18]

Reagan offered localism as a way to enforce work, reduce welfare rolls, and regulate the lives of the poor. But had he looked more carefully at the history of the War on Poverty, he would have found an alternative legacy, one less interested in disciplining the poor than in ameliorating their condition. In North Carolina, that inheritance is the social learning amassed by the hundreds of volunteers, staff, community activists, and ordinary men and women the North Carolina Fund called to battle. As they took up arms against the scourge of poverty, they came to understand that their enemy was neither a paradox in a land of plenty nor a misfortune the poor had brought upon themselves. They discovered that poverty is political; it is the product of decisions — made by the few rather than the many — about the distribution of power, wealth, and opportunity. To fight poverty is to struggle for democracy — to give voice to those who have been excluded from civic life, to transcend divisions that breed anger and distrust, and to balance individual responsibilities to society with social responsibilities to one's fellow citizens. The challenge, George Esser wrote in 1968, is to "reinstate human freedom and human dignity and genuine justice as major goals in American society." That work remains largely undone and calls on new generations to right the wrongs of the past.[19]

BATTLE LINES

We often think of the poor as inhabiting the margins of our world, but that image misses something important. In North Carolina, the poor might better be imagined as the foundation upon which the state's modern social and economic order was built. That structure first took shape during the last quarter of the nineteenth century, as North Carolinians struggled over the organization of wealth and power in the new commercial economy that arose from the death of slavery. Change came about at a frenzied pace. Between 1880 and 1900, the state and private investors financed the construction of more than five thousand miles of new railroad that snaked through the countryside, linking once isolated communities to regional and national webs of trade. On the outskirts of small towns and cities, merchant entrepreneurs built cotton and tobacco factories that turned farmers' crops into profitable commodities, primarily cigarettes, thread, and cloth. But alongside a host of opportunities, this new world also produced dislocation and want. For black North Carolinians, the cruelties of tenancy and debt peonage destroyed emancipation dreams of independence on the land; white farmers, too, slid into sharecropping as they moved from subsistence to commercial agriculture; and in textile and tobacco factories, rural folk, seeking refuge from hardships on the land, worked sixty-six-hour weeks for wages that made child labor a necessity of life. In all of this, two fundamental questions begged to be resolved: who would reap the bounty of this age, and by what principles would that abundance be shared?[1]

Struggle over these questions reached a flash point in the election of 1894, which set white elites united in the Democratic Party against a broad but uneasy alliance among African Americans, middling white farmers, and a nascent class of industrial workers. Black Republicans and white Populists joined forces behind a "fusion" slate of candidates and captured two-thirds of the seats in the state legislature. Two years later, they extended their legislative majority and elected Republican Daniel L. Russell as governor. While similar insurgencies erupted in other southern states, only in North Carolina did a biracial Republican-Populist alliance seize such extensive control of state government.

Fusionists used their newfound political power to enact a program of reforms designed, in the words of a former Democrat, to secure "the liberty of the laboring people, both white and black." They capped interest rates on personal debt, increased expenditures for public education, shifted the weight of taxation from individuals to corporations and railroads, and made generous appropriations to state charitable and correctional institutions. To expand political participation among the 36 percent of the population who could neither read nor write, Fusionist lawmakers required that party symbols be printed on all ballots. And most important, they gave ordinary North Carolinians a voice in local affairs by replacing a system of county government based on legislative appointments with elected boards of county commissioners and city aldermen. The Fusionists' goal was nothing short of a "revolution in [state] politics."[2]

Democrats were stunned by the Fusion victories. Their party had held and exercised power primarily through local networks of kinship and patronage. They were therefore initially ill prepared to counter the Fusionists' appeal to shared economic interests and issues of equality that undercut those networks and had the capacity to mobilize voters across even the deep divide of race. By 1898, however, Democrats had begun to organize themselves around a new strategy centered on what political economist Kent Redding has described as a "fully politicized white identity." In past campaigns, Democrats had addressed race as one among many issues, and when they dismissed black voters, they most often did so by arguing that poverty and ignorance made former slaves the dupes of scheming carpetbaggers and scalawags. The appeal in 1898 was different. Under the leadership of young party chairman Furnifold M. Simmons and Raleigh newspaperman Josephus Daniels, Democrats made race their primary issue, and they spoke of blacks as fundamentally "other," sharing with whites no commonality of interest or intention. The result was a white supremacy campaign of unprecedented focus and ferocity.[3]

Playing on the racial mistrust that was slavery's lasting residue, Democrats sought to pry apart a biracial alliance that, at its best, was tenuous, contested, and fragile. They dodged the economic and class issues that held together the Fusion coalition and emphasized instead the specter of "negro domination." At the heart of their appeal were warnings of miscegenation and sexual danger. Democrats insisted that having secured the ballot, black men would soon claim another prerogative of white manhood: access to white women. In an effort to whip up race hatred, party newspapers created a black-on-white rape

The *Raleigh News and Observer*'s depiction of black political participation as a monster sprung from the Fusion ballot box, September 27, 1898. Courtesy of the North Carolina Collection, Wilson Library, University of North Carolina at Chapel Hill.

scare and accused white Fusionists of sacrificing their wives and daughters on the altar of biracial politics.[4]

This sharpened rhetoric of race was a potent weapon, but Democrats understood that words alone would not restore them to power. In the closing days of the 1898 campaign, party leaders turned to violence and intimidation. They organized White Government Unions throughout the state and encouraged the party faithful to strip down to their red undershirts, a symbol of the Confederacy's sacrifice and the late-nineteenth-century equivalent of the hooded robes worn by the Ku Klux Klan during Reconstruction. The Democrats' determination to defeat their challengers at any cost was revealed most starkly in the coastal city of Wilmington, where white paramilitaries under the command of former congressman Alfred Moore Waddell staged the only municipal coup d'état in the nation's history. They marauded through the town's black district, set ablaze the print shop of the local black newspaper, murdered as many as thirty black citizens, and drove from office a biracial board of aldermen.[5]

Democrats won the 1898 election by a narrow margin. They claimed only 52.8 percent of the vote, but that was enough to oust most Fusionists from the legislature. The victors moved immediately to silence black and white

A postcard produced by local photographer Henry Cronenberg documented the destruction of Love and Charity Hall, which housed the *Daily Record*, Wilmington's black newspaper. Courtesy of the New Hanover County Public Library, Robert M. Fales Collection.

dissenters. In the 1899 legislative session, Democrats drafted an amendment to the state constitution that aimed to end biracial politics once and for all by stripping from black men the most fundamental privilege of citizenship: the right to vote. The Fifteenth Amendment to the federal Constitution, adopted at the height of Reconstruction, forbade the states from denying the ballot to citizens on the basis of race. North Carolina Democrats, like their counterparts elsewhere in the South, got around that prohibition by adopting a literacy test. In order to vote, citizens first had to demonstrate to local election officials that they could read and write, upon command, any section of the Constitution. That gave Democratic registrars wide latitude to exclude blacks and large numbers of poor whites from the polls. The literacy test was thus designed to achieve the very thing the federal Fifteenth Amendment expressly outlawed.[6]

In 1900, Democratic gubernatorial candidate Charles Brantley Aycock put the disfranchisement amendment before voters for approval. On the stump, he promised the white electorate a new "era of good feelings" in exchange for racial loyalty. The hour's need, Aycock declared, was "to form a genuine

Members of the Wilmington Light Infantry, a unit of the state militia, pose with a machine gun purchased by the city's white business leaders. The gun squad used the weapon to quell black resistance during the race riot and coup d'état. Courtesy of the Cape Fear Museum of History and Science, Wilmington.

white man's party. Then we shall have peace everywhere. . . . Life and property and liberty from the mountains to the sea shall rest secure in the guardianship of the law. But to do this, we must disfranchise the negro. . . . To do so is both desirable and necessary — desirable because it sets the white man free to move along faster than he can go when retarded by the slower movement of the negro — necessary because we must have good order and peace while we work out the industrial, commercial, intellectual and moral development of the State." For those who still harbored doubts about supporting a Democratic candidate and the disfranchisement amendment, the party's Red Shirts offered their own brand of persuasion. On election eve, Alfred Moore Waddell encouraged a white crowd in Wilmington to "go to the polls tomorrow and if you find the negro out voting, tell him to leave the polls and if he refuses, kill him, shoot him down in his tracks." The beleaguered remnants of the Populist and Republican opposition could hardly counter such tactics. With a turnout of nearly 75 percent of qualified voters, Aycock and disfranchisement won by a 59 to 41 percent margin.[7]

The Democrats' triumph cleared the way for a system of racial capitalism characterized by one-party government, segregation, and cheap labor. With the removal of black men from politics, North Carolina's Republican Party became little more than an expression of regional differences among whites that set the western mountains, the party's surviving stronghold, against the central Piedmont and eastern coastal plain. The political contests that mattered occurred not in general elections but in the Democratic primaries, where party leaders exercised tight influence over the selection of candidates and electoral outcomes. Under such circumstances, many North Carolinians found no reason to cast a ballot. Only 50 percent of the newly constrained pool of eligible voters turned out for the 1904 gubernatorial election, and by 1912 the number declined to less than 30 percent. This system of one-party rule sharply circumscribed debate and dampened enthusiasm for the kinds of social investment that Fusionists had championed at the turn of the century. In the state's cities and larger towns, white middle-class merchants and professionals taxed themselves willingly in order to provide their children with the benefits of education, but spending for rural areas lagged far behind. At the same time, a great gulf opened up between black and white schooling. In 1880, North Carolina had spent roughly equal sums per capita for black and white children, but by 1915 state allocations favored white students over black by a margin of three to one.[8]

Having asserted that race, not class, was the fundamental dividing line in North Carolina society, the state's self-styled redeemers set about normalizing imagined racial hierarchies — making them seem natural and self-evident. Since such notions needed to be established anew with each generation, the work of race making was unending. Over time, the architects of white privilege developed an elaborate system of discriminatory law and custom known commonly as Jim Crow, a name taken from the familiar black-face characters in nineteenth-century minstrel shows. Lawmakers passed North Carolina's first Jim Crow law in 1899, during the same session in which they crafted the disfranchisement amendment to the state constitution. The law required separate seating for blacks and whites on all trains and steamboats. The aim of that and other such regulations was to mark blacks as a people apart and, in doing so, to make it psychologically difficult for whites to imagine interracial cooperation. Segregation also divided most forms of civic space — courthouses, neighborhoods, and public squares—that might otherwise have been sites for interaction across the color line. In Charlotte, soon to be North Carolina's largest city and the hub of its new textile economy, neighborhoods in 1870 had been surprisingly undifferentiated. As historian Thomas Hanchett has noted, on any given street "business owners and hired hands, manual laborers and white-collared clerks . . . black people and white people all lived side by side." By 1910, that heterogeneity had been thoroughly "sorted" along lines of race and class. In communities large and small across the state, this process played out a thousand times over as white supremacy erected a nearly insurmountable wall between the blacks and poor whites who had risen in the late 1890s to challenge Democratic power.[9]

Jim Crow also worked to relegate the majority of black North Carolinians to the countryside and to create, in effect, a bound agricultural labor force. Jobs in the textile industry, which in the early twentieth century would become North Carolina's leading employer, were, with few exceptions, reserved for whites only. The industry's boosters promised that factory jobs would free poor whites from want by teaching them the virtues of thrift and insulating them from economic competition with blacks. But segregated employment was far less of a boon than textile promoters claimed. Jim Crow held black earnings to near-subsistence levels, dragged white wages downward by devaluing labor in general, and advanced industrial employers' interests by tempering white workers' efforts at organization with concern for the protection of racial privilege.

In all of these ways, the triumph of white supremacy set the stage for an extended period of economic development and wealth accumulation bound up with enduring poverty. Between 1880 and 1900, investors built an average of six new cotton mills a year in North Carolina. The pace quickened in the opening decades of the twentieth century, so that by the late 1930s the state claimed 341 mills and had displaced Massachusetts as the world center of cotton textile production. At its peak, the cotton goods industry in North Carolina employed more than 110,000 people. The story of tobacco, although different in its particulars, followed a similar trajectory. By the 1920s, two North Carolina firms—R. J. Reynolds in Winston-Salem and American Tobacco in Durham—dominated the industry. Their combined market influence enabled them to set prices along the entire production chain, from the purchase of raw tobacco to the sale of cigarettes.[10]

Together, tobacco and textiles transformed crossroads towns into cities and built some of the great fortunes of the early twentieth century. In Durham, James B. Duke used his family's tobacco wealth to endow Duke University and to establish the Southern Power Company (today, Duke Energy), which brought electricity to and quickened development in much of North Carolina's central Piedmont region. The Reynolds family, connected by banking and business partnerships with the Gray and Hanes families, anchored the wealth of Winston-Salem, which in the 1930s one journalist described as a city of "one hundred millionaires." Greensboro's Cone brothers, Caesar and Moses, first entered the textile industry as cotton brokers for southern mills and later built an empire on the production of denim. In nearby Burlington, J. Spencer Love consolidated a handful of family mills into Burlington Industries, which eventually became the world's leading textile firm, and in Kannapolis, Charles A. Cannon oversaw the state's largest company town. Located thirty miles southwest of Kannapolis, Charlotte, which claimed its own share of textile firms, fed industrial North Carolina's hunger for investment capital. Between 1897 and 1927, more than ten new banks opened offices in the city, including a branch of the Federal Reserve. The legacy of that development remains apparent today. Charlotte is home to several of the nation's largest banks, including Bank of America, and ranks second only to New York as a financial center.[11]

Despite the scope of this economic development and the wealth it generated, North Carolina remained a poor state. In 1938, deep into the Great Depression, President Franklin D. Roosevelt's National Emergency Council issued its *Report on Economic Conditions of the South*, which explained how circumstances in North Carolina and elsewhere in the region produced poverty that was "self-generating and self-perpetuating." The average annual industrial wage in the South was $865, as compared to the $1,219 earned by workers outside the region. Southern factory hands' wages were so low primarily because the workers competed for jobs with a virtually limitless pool of desperately poor rural folk. On southern farms in general, per capita income was only $314, slightly more than half of the $604 earned by farmers elsewhere in the nation. For tenant families—white and black—who owned no land of their own, that figure plummeted to an average of only $74 per person. Those families, the *Report* observed, were "living in poverty comparable to that of the poorest peasants in Europe."

Such deprivation left southern states with limited means and even less incentive to invest in education and the development of what economists call human capital. Local tax bases were shallow, which made raising revenues for public education far more difficult than in other parts of the nation. Large landowners and manufacturers also saw no compelling reason to invest in schooling beyond the elementary grades. In low-wage enterprises, possession of a high school diploma was unlikely to improve laborers' productivity. Odds were that it would instead encourage them to leave their home communities in search of better prospects. Added to all of this, the South was also a region of "sickness, misery, and death. . . . Wage differentials bec[a]me in fact differentials in health and life; poor health, in turn, affect[ed] wages." And so poverty fed upon itself from one generation to the next. In his letter accompanying the *Report*, President Roosevelt minced no words in characterizing the situation. "It is my conviction," he wrote, "that the South presents right now the Nation's No. 1 economic problem."[12]

The *Report* was prepared for the National Emergency Council by an ad hoc group of southern New Dealers working in federal agencies. They recruited as their chairman Frank Porter Graham, president of the University of North Carolina. Graham was a natural choice. Having helped draft the Social Security Act of 1935, he enjoyed close personal ties to the White House. He also had a long record of association with progressive causes. In the late 1920s, he responded to labor unrest in North Carolina's cotton mills by calling on employers to adopt an "Industrial Bill of Rights," and during the 1930s, as president of the Southern Conference for Human Welfare, he spoke boldly for improved race relations. In Chapel Hill, Graham led a faculty whose members had created a distinct body of regional scholarship, art, and literature that turned a critical eye on the South and its social ills. Most notable were sociologist Howard Odum, whose graduate students took up taboo subjects such as lynching, and playwright Paul Green, whose 1927 Pulitzer Prize–winning play, *In Abraham's Bosom*, explored the forbidden topic of white-on-black sexual violence and the tragic human costs of racial bigotry. Green's work was so controversial that it was never performed on his own campus or, for that matter, anywhere below the Mason-Dixon Line.[13]

Graham and his colleagues, at home and in Washington, called for reform in the South with considerable moral authority. But they confronted a political machine determined to shore up rather than change the status quo. From the late 1920s through the late 1940s, a close-knit group of Democrats known as the Shelby Dynasty kept a tight rein on political power in North Carolina. They took their name from the small cotton mill town of Shelby, west of Charlotte, which was home to lawyer and textile manufacturer O. Max Gardner, elected governor in 1928. Gardner wielded political influence from the county courthouse to Congress. His endorsement of candidates in the Democratic primaries could make or break party hopefuls, so much so that North Carolina voters usually knew the likely winners well in advance. In 1932, when Gardner left North Carolina to practice law in Washington, D.C., his hand-picked successor, John C. B. Ehringhaus, replaced him in the governor's office. Four years later, Gardner's brother-in-law, Clyde R. Hoey, also of Shelby, succeeded Ehringhaus.[14]

North Carolina's New Deal governors embraced a progressive image and sought to share Franklin Roosevelt's popularity among voters, but, as historian William Chafe has observed, that public stance often "acted as camouflage, obscuring [darker] social and economic realities." At home and in Washington, North Carolina's leaders fought hard to restrain the New Deal's capacity to make change. They were particularly concerned to limit the scope of federal jobs programs such as the Works Progress Administration. Where those programs made inroads, they tended to put significant upward pressure on agricultural and manufacturing wages. For that reason, the North Carolina legislature consistently refused to budget the matching funds required for federal expenditures in the state. In 1934, the Roosevelt administration called the lawmakers' hand by threatening to withdraw all federal grants. Governor Ehringhaus reluctantly agreed to provide half of the $3 million federal officials demanded, all of which he earmarked for highway construction. Even then, North Carolina continued to rank last or next to last among the states for per capita spending on work relief. New Deal reforms often appeared momentous, historian Carl Abrams has written, but it was remarkable "how little North Carolina's society, economy, and politics had changed by the end of the decade." O. Max Gardner captured that paradox most succinctly when he observed that North Carolina was a "conservative, progressive State."[15]

SUCH WAS THE WORLD in which Terry Sanford came of age. He was born in 1917 to Cecil and Betsy Sanford in the cotton mill and farming town of Laurinburg, southwest of Fayetteville near the South Carolina border. In 1898, Democrats had come there to launch their statewide white supremacy campaign with a rally on Confederate Memorial Day, May 10. Sanford's father ran a family-owned hardware store until the Great Depression forced him into bankruptcy. He then worked a series of odd jobs until landing a secure position as bookkeeper for a local oil company. Sanford's mother was an elementary school teacher. He recalled that his family lived "on the downside of average"; they were respectable, but not closely tied to the large landowners and manufacturers who ran the town. As a schoolboy, Sanford delivered newspapers and telegrams and sold vegetables in Laurinburg's mill villages and its black neighborhood, New Town. He was struck by the plight of residents in both communities, and even though he had no ready explanation for what he saw, he never felt comfortable with the notion that such deprivation was simply a part of the natural order of things. That unease reflected the influence of his parents, who were drawn to progressive causes. As a child, Sanford's father had seen the Red Shirts ride through Laurinburg; thirty years later, while working as a Democratic registrar, he signed up the first black citizens to vote in local elections since the turn of the century. In the same year, 1928, young Sanford joined his mother in a parade down Laurinburg's main street to support Al Smith, the Democratic Party's Catholic candidate for president. The state as a whole showed less religious tolerance and, in a singular breech of Democratic loyalty, went for Republican Herbert Hoover.[16]

After finishing high school, Sanford enrolled in a small Presbyterian college in nearby Maxton, ever mindful of his family's limited resources. But the quality of the teaching disappointed him, and in 1935 he transferred to the University of North Carolina in Chapel Hill. Sanford quickly fell under the sway of the university's charismatic president, Frank Graham. He remembered Graham's lasting influence: "I would say that I probably would have followed a different path and probably been a different kind of person if I hadn't gone to Chapel Hill. I always saw [Graham] as . . . representing the ideals that I thought were proper and I would like to have as my ideals. I think Frank Graham woke people up to the fact that we could do something about some of our problems. He woke them up to the fact that it wasn't so bad to champion the cause of the sharecropper and the black, and the working man that wasn't unionized and was being pretty much treated as chattel." As a student, Sanford also began to test his talent for politics. He joined the University Party, one of several competing political organizations on campus, managed a friend's (unsuccessful) bid for student body president, and sought out ways to involve himself in state campaigns. In the 1936 gubernatorial race, he and his father stumped for Democratic Party maverick Ralph McDonald, a professor at Salem College who ran against the machine politics of the Shelby Dynasty and denounced disingenuous state officials who "boast[ed] loudly of their loyalty to FDR and [sought] to destroy the policies of the New Deal."[17]

Sanford graduated in 1939 but stayed on in Chapel Hill to begin law school. World War II interrupted his studies. After the Japanese bombing of Pearl Harbor, he signed up for national service, first as a special agent for the FBI and then as a paratrooper in the U.S. Army's 517th Parachute Combat Team. Sanford saw action in five campaigns in Europe. He won a Bronze Star and, for wounds he suffered in the Battle of the Bulge, a Purple Heart. At the war's end, he returned to Chapel Hill, where he completed his law studies in 1946.[18]

Sanford came home as part of a generation made impatient by the experience of global war. The defeat of fascism seemed to open up new opportunities for peace and prosperity that would at last bring relief from more than a decade of economic depression. Veterans also returned less parochial in their views, less content with ways of life they had once taken for granted. Clint Newton, a former fighter pilot and friend of Sanford, recalled that he and his classmates "came back with a lot of confidence. We had gotten the job done.... Here you have all these people coming back, having been ... exposed to France, Italy, Sicily, North Africa, England—you name it. We found our respective towns were not the center of the universe. We wanted to make North Carolina better."[19]

That restlessness for change was evident all around, most especially among black North Carolinians. During the war, they had embraced a national "double-V" campaign for victory against fascism abroad and racism at home. In Durham, which claimed one of the South's most vibrant African American business communities, black leaders from ten southern states met in 1942 at the North Carolina College for Negroes (later, North Carolina College at Durham, and today, North Carolina Central University) to declare their opposition to "the principle and practice of compulsory segregation." They issued the "Durham Manifesto," which demanded voting rights and equal educational and job opportunities for black citizens. A year later, black tobacco workers in Winston-Salem seized the promise of the 1935 Wagner Act, a critical piece of New Deal legislation that established the National Labor Relations Board (NLRB) and charged the agency with safeguarding labor's right to collective bargaining. Thousands of black workers joined with several hundred whites to organize a local of the Food, Tobacco, Agricultural, and Allied Workers (FTA) union, and in 1944 it won a contract and an immediate wage increase from the R. J. Reynolds Tobacco Company, long known for its staunch antiunionism. That victory was, in the words of one participant, "like being reconstructed again." The Reynolds workers drew on their newfound strength to register hundreds of voters and in 1947 helped elect a black city alderman, the first local candidate in the South to defeat a white rival since the turn of the century.[20]

White liberals of Sanford's generation also chafed at the racial status quo. The campus at Chapel Hill was a center of political ferment. In 1945, respected and outspoken Presbyterian minister Charles (Charlie) M. Jones, pastor of Frank Graham's church, led his congregation in defying denominational authorities and local custom by opening their sanctuary to blacks. "We do not close our doors or discriminate against ... any sincere worshipper who may present himself," the church's board of deacons declared. That same fall, student leaders touched off a political firestorm by calling publicly for the admission of black students to the university and the repeal of Jim Crow laws. Sanford's sister, Helen, also joined the fray. As a representative of Woman's College in Greensboro (today, the University of North Carolina at Greensboro), she proposed that the statewide student legislature endorse a similar resolution insisting on the removal of Jim Crow from the statute books.[21]

In 1948, many liberal-minded students and veterans pushed even harder against the political status quo by organizing local chapters of the Progressive Party and backing the presidential candidacy of Henry Wallace, one of Franklin Roosevelt's vice presidents and secretary of commerce under Harry Truman. In Chapel Hill, they published a party newsletter, the UNC *Wallace Weekly*. Supporters rallied around Wallace's advocacy of world peace, enthusiasm for the newly chartered United Nations, and unwavering call for racial equality. A Wallace campaigner wrote to the campus newspaper: "After a war against fascism, the fascist philosophy of racism still mars our own democracy. Equal opportunity is still an unfulfilled promise for our Negro citizens, especially on the campus." Members of the Progressive Party pursued that principle through an active alliance with black workers, particularly those who labored in the tobacco factories of Winston-Salem and Durham. Their slogan was direct and unequivocal: "Jim Crow Must Go!" Wallace's campaign failed in North Carolina, as did those of others on the local Progressive Party ticket: gubernatorial candidate Mary Watkins Price; U.S. Senate candidate W. T. Brown, a black pastor from St. George's Methodist Church in Maxton; and nominee for state attorney general Conrad O. Pearson, a black lawyer from Durham. Even so, the very presence of a woman and African Americans on the ballot suggested just how unsettled politics had become in the immediate postwar years.[22]

The chief beneficiary of that disquiet was populist gubernatorial candidate W. Kerr Scott, an Alamance County farmer and former state secretary of agriculture. He bested Democratic Party power brokers by defeating their favored candidate, Charles M. Johnson, whom O. Max Gardner had appointed state treasurer in 1932. Scott won by tapping into grassroots support for the reformist principles of the New Deal and by building a coalition of liberal urban voters and rural backers. He called the latter group his "branch-head boys," a reference to the fact that many lived far removed from the state's commercial centers, in the backwoods along small creeks and streams. On the stump, Scott promised to "Go Forward" with New Deal programs that had done much to improve life in the countryside: the construction of farm-to-market roads, rural electrification, and the expansion of telephone networks. Scott also appealed to white industrial workers with a pledge to raise the state's minimum wage and to repeal an antiunion right-to-work law passed in 1947. North Carolina's growing number of black voters responded to his moderate stance on race. Scott endorsed funding equalization for black and white schools and soon after his election appointed the first black member of the State Board of Education. "I am going to follow through to see that the minority race has a fair opportunity and gets the training to fit into the state's growth," the new governor explained.[23]

Terry Sanford later remembered that Kerr Scott "liked to stir things up." That he did with great flare in 1949, when he appointed University of North Carolina president Frank Graham to complete the term of U.S. senator J. Melville Broughton, who had died in office. A year later, Graham ran for election to a full six-year term of his own. There were three other contenders in the Democratic primary, the most prominent of whom was Raleigh lawyer Willis Smith. Smith chaired the board of trustees at Duke University and was past president of the American Bar Association. He had also served as speaker of the North Carolina House of Representatives from 1931 to 1932. As the 1950 campaign season approached, Smith showed little interest in opposing Graham, but conservative Democrats—led by Clyde Hoey, former Depression-era governor and now North Carolina's senior senator— implored him to add his name to the ballot. They were troubled, the editor of the *High Point Enterprise* explained, by Graham's "pink-tinted" politics. They also saw in opposing Graham an opportunity to settle a score with Governor Scott, who had undertaken a wholesale purge of Democratic regulars in the state bureaucracy. Once Smith announced his candidacy, the battle lines were clearly drawn. The 1950 Senate race would be a struggle for control of North Carolina's Democratic Party, pitting old-guard conservatives against a "Scott-Graham liberal insurgency."[24]

Sanford and other progressive Democrats of his generation flocked to Graham's campaign. In 1948, Sanford had moved from Chapel Hill to Fayetteville, where he opened a law practice, joined a variety of civic organizations, and began to position himself as a rising star in the Democratic Party. A year later, he won election as president of the Young Democrats Club, thanks largely to friendships within a statewide network of fellow veterans. That position demanded that Sanford maintain a measure of neutrality in the primary, but there was never any doubt that he considered himself one of Graham's "boys." He consulted with Scott and Graham on the selection of a campaign manager and canvassed door-to-door for Graham in Fayetteville's white working-class neighborhoods.[25]

In the hard-fought primary, Graham won 303,605 votes (48.9 percent) to Smith's 250,222 (40.5 percent). Under North Carolina law, the leader's lack of a majority entitled the runner-up to call for a runoff. Smith hesitated. He was unsure that he could raise the necessary money or that he had the stamina for another contest. Then, on June 5, just days before the deadline for Smith's decision, the U.S. Supreme Court handed down rulings that affirmed black students' right to equal access to publicly funded graduate education and banned segregation on railroad cars. The court's actions galvanized Smith's supporters. On the afternoon of June 6, Jesse Helms, a young news director for WRAL radio in Raleigh, made arrangements to air at fifteen-minute intervals a plea for Smith backers to rally at his home and urge him to demand a runoff. The crowd that gathered on Smith's lawn was persuasive. The next morning, Smith called for a second primary.[26]

The political battle that followed was the rawest since the white supremacy campaign of 1898–1900, and like that earlier contest, it would cast a shadow over North Carolina politics for many years to come. In the closing weeks of the first primary, Smith supporters had targeted what they described as Graham's leftist political leanings. They suggested that he had imbibed socialist principles during a year of graduate study at the London School of Economics, faulted his support for President Truman's plan for national health care, and criticized his leadership of the Southern Conference for Human Welfare, which not only had been interracial but had included members of the Communist Party. In the second primary, the Smith camp brought race front and center. They focused particularly on Graham's service in 1946–47 on President Truman's Committee on Civil Rights, which issued the first federal report on race relations and laid the groundwork for Truman's desegregation of the military a year later. The report, titled *To Secure These Rights*, called for an immediate end to Jim Crow in all aspects of American life.[27]

Smith and his supporters directed their harshest criticism at the report's call for establishing a permanent Fair Employment Practices Commission (FEPC), which would have been charged with eliminating discrimination in the workplace. Graham recognized the value of such an agency as a forum for airing racial grievances, but he flinched at granting it enforcement power. Like other white gradualists, he argued that job opportunities for black Americans would be advanced more effectively through education and moral suasion rather than federal intervention. The Smith camp found little comfort in that

WHITE PEOPLE
WAKE UP
BEFORE IT'S TOO LATE
YOU MAY NOT HAVE ANOTHER CHANCE
DO YOU WANT?

Negroes working beside you, your wife and daughters in your mills, and factories?

Negroes eating beside you in all public eating places?

Negroes riding beside you, your wife and your daughters in buses, cabs and trains?

Negroes sleeping in the same hotels and rooming houses?

Negroes teaching and disciplining your children in school?

Negroes sitting with you and your family at all public meetings?

Negroes Going to white schools and white children going to Negro schools?

Negroes to occupy the same hospital rooms with you and your wife and daughters?

Negroes as your foremen and overseers in the mills?

Negroes using your toilet facilities?

> Northern political labor leaders have recently ordered that all doors be opened to Negroes on union property. This will lead to whites and Negroes working and living together in the South as they do in the North. Do you want that?

FRANK GRAHAM FAVORS MINGLING OF THE RACES

HE ADMITS THAT HE FAVORS MIXING NEGROES AND WHITES — HE SAYS SO IN THE REPORT HE SIGNED. (For Proof of This, Read Page 167, Civil Rights Report.)

DO YOU FAVOR THIS — WANT SOME MORE OF IT?
IF YOU DO, VOTE FOR FRANK GRAHAM

BUT IF YOU DON'T

VOTE FOR AND HELP ELECT

WILLIS SMITH for SENATOR
HE WILL UPHOLD THE TRADITIONS OF THE SOUTH

KNOW THE TRUTH COMMITTEE

A handbill circulated by Willis Smith's supporters warned that Frank Graham favored "mingling of the races." Courtesy of the Southern Historical Collection, Wilson Library, University of North Carolina at Chapel Hill, Daniel Augustus Powell Papers.

distinction. In campaign press releases, Smith warned white voters that under the proposed FEPC "a man's job [could be] claimed by another man just because he is of another race or color." Handbills distributed primarily in rural and white working-class neighborhoods raised the alarm more shrilly. "White People Wake Up Before It's Too Late," one exclaimed. "Frank Graham Favors Mingling of the Races." That appeal was powerful in its simplicity: Frank Graham posed a threat to white privilege and the racial division of labor from which it was derived. By contrast, Smith promised to "Uphold the Traditions of the South."[28]

The Graham campaign's response was largely ineffective. In a broadside widely circulated in the state's textile towns, Graham supporters warned white millhands that Smith would roll back the hard-won economic gains of the New Deal. Then they insulted those very same voters. "Are you ignorant

Frank Graham's backers argued that votes for Willis Smith would reverse the economic gains white cotton mill workers had enjoyed under Franklin Roosevelt's New Deal. Courtesy of the Southern Historical Collection, Wilson Library, University of North Carolina at Chapel Hill, Daniel Augustus Powell Papers.

or prejudiced?" a pro-Graham newspaper ad asked. "If so, you are the person at whom the phony race issue is aimed." In communities that had supported Graham in the first primary, he encountered in the second men and women who refused to shake his hand. Some even spat at him.[29]

Graham scored a clear victory only in North Carolina's western mountain counties, where resentment over regional exclusion from political influence ran deep. In the rural east, where the state's black population was concentrated and the issue of race had particular resonance, he suffered a stunning reversal, surrendering to Smith seventeen of the counties he had won in the first primary. Results in the Piedmont, North Carolina's central industrial region, were only slightly better. Graham prevailed, but by a diminished margin. On the second ballot, many white working-class and urban professional voters defected to Smith. Most in the latter group expressed admiration for

Graham as a man of character. Their wariness of his politics, however, revealed something basic about their self-styled liberal views on race. They had no taste for demagoguery of the sort displayed in the Smith campaign's handbills, but neither did they embrace the prospect of racial equality—certainly not in the near term. That distinction was critically important. When ballots were tallied in the second primary, Smith outpolled Graham by more than 19,000 votes.[30]

Graham's defeat was one of a cluster of setbacks for progressive forces in North Carolina. Just a few months before the second primary, black tobacco workers and their white allies in Winston-Salem had been defeated in a similar campaign of intolerance. Picking up on Cold War anticommunism and racial distrust, R. J. Reynolds forced a new vote on certification of the FTA. The company pointed to the presence of Communist Party members among the union leadership and played to fears of racial leveling in an industry that had traditionally reserved higher-skilled, better-paying jobs for whites. For most white workers at Reynolds, as for most white Americans in general, the two issues seemed inseparable. Indeed, FBI director J. Edgar Hoover and other leaders on the right had been insisting for some time that communists were behind rising black agitation for equality. The stage was set for a dramatic turnabout in the FTA local's prospects. During the early 1940s, the National Labor Relations Board had intervened in Winston-Salem to ensure a fair vote on unionization, but in 1950, in the context of growing Cold War anxieties and Joseph McCarthy's assault on domestic dissent, federal officials demurred, lest they be perceived as soft on communism. The NLRB sided with Reynolds's request to exclude several thousand black seasonal workers from the union election. That change of policy tipped the scales in Reynolds's favor, cost FTA activists their jobs, and took from black workers and their fellow white unionists the right to negotiate a fair wage and decent conditions on the factory floor.[31]

Race also bore heavily on organizing efforts among white textile workers. Between 1946 and 1953, the Congress of Industrial Organizations (CIO) fielded a massive union campaign in the South. Called Operation Dixie, it aimed to bring the benefits of collective bargaining to southern workers, to increase their earnings, and to protect their northern counterparts against interregional wage competition. Architects of the campaign made a calculated decision to focus on textiles, the whites-only industry that formed the foundation of the South's manufacturing economy, and in order to avoid the red taint of communism, they moved early in the crusade to distance themselves from the biracialism and civil rights activism advocated by FTA and other more radical unions within the CIO. At one level, that strategy seemed practical and realistic. A direct confrontation with white supremacy would have required daring and a breadth of vision that many would have been unable to muster and that others would have read as naive and overly idealistic, even in the relatively fluid context of the immediate postwar years. In the end, however, pragmatism was ineffective. It offered white workers little leverage within the regime of one-party politics, where the terms of participation and the police power of the state were controlled by the employers from whom they sought concessions. The end results were disastrous. Opponents of Operation Dixie denounced the campaign as a covert civil rights crusade, smeared and red-baited organizers as outside agitators, and mobilized state militias to face down striking workers. In 1953, its resources depleted, the CIO closed the organizing effort.[32]

The losses of the early 1950s underscored the resiliency of the South's system of racial capitalism and the extraordinary capacity of that social order to thwart the dreams and cramp the imaginations of so many who inhabited it. Conservative push-back chilled political debate; isolated and undercut the credibility of outspoken leaders, black and white alike; and narrowed the range of ideas that might be marshaled in critique of Jim Crow. In North Carolina, many white progressives worried that racial tensions had been so whipped up as to overshadow all other concerns. Soon after Willis Smith's victory over Frank Graham, D. Hiden Ramsey, an Asheville newspaperman and member of the State Board of Education, shared with colleague Louis Graves at the *Chapel Hill Weekly* his concern that the "evil genii of racial prejudice" had been set free from their bottle. "The chances are that we will not get them back into the bottle ... for a long time," Ramsey warned. "I fear we are in for a modified version of Bilboism." His reference was to the white supremacist demagogue Theodore G. Bilbo, governor and later senator from Mississippi. In the U.S. Senate, Bilbo had introduced bills to fund the deportation of blacks to Africa, an idea he championed in his 1947 book, *Take Your Choice: Separation or Mongrelization*.[33]

Events in Chapel Hill and on the campus of Frank Graham's university suggested just how constrained the discussion of race and class—and of the connection between the two—had become. In 1950, the University of North Carolina's board of trustees named Gordon Gray to succeed Graham as president. Gray, scion of Winston-Salem's leading family, was the publisher of the *Winston-Salem Journal* and in that capacity had led the newspaper's attack on tobacco workers' FTA local. Two years later, state leaders in the Presbyterian Church defrocked Chapel Hill's liberal minister Charlie Jones. The official charge was heresy, but what was really at issue was simmering anger over Jones's public stance on race. At the same time, the University of North Carolina became the target of congressional investigations of the purported link between civil rights agitation and the communist threat. In 1953, the Senate Internal Security Subcommittee subpoenaed Milton Abernathy, who had run a leftist bookshop in Chapel Hill during the 1930s and 1940s. Abernathy had also edited a journal of political dissent called *Contempo* and had helped host campus visits by such notable black artists as Langston Hughes, James Weldon Johnson, and Richard Wright. Abernathy's inquisitors, including newly elected Senator Willis Smith, accused him of running an underground press and distributing propaganda on behalf of the Communist Party.[34]

Even more sensational was the prosecution of university alumnus and political activist Junius Irving Scales, the son of one of Greensboro's oldest and most respected families. As a student during the 1930s, Scales had been drawn to the Communist Party's affirmation of the fundamentally American notion of equal rights, and he had involved himself in the struggles of North Carolina's industrial workers, black and white. Scales served four years in the army. At the end of World War II, he, like many of his generation, returned with great optimism for the future. He picked up his old affiliations with the Communist Party and, while a history graduate student in Chapel Hill, served as the only white officer of the Southern Negro Youth Congress, which had been founded in 1937 by black Communist Party activists to challenge Jim Crow. Such affiliations made Scales a target for FBI scrutiny. The agency tracked his movements throughout the early 1950s, and in 1954 it arrested him on charges of advocating overthrow of the United States government. After seven years of trials and Supreme Court affirmation of his conviction, Scales went to prison in 1961. He was the first person to be jailed for violating the Smith Act of 1940, which de facto made a felony of Communist Party membership. Scales served fourteen months before President John F. Kennedy commuted his sentence.[35]

For most white southerners — indeed, for most white Americans — the red menace and the black menace had become one and the same. The right had captured the issue of race as its own and had once again made it a tool to divide. For any moderate white politician with serious aspirations to office, the lesson was clear: matters of race were to be addressed only through inference or indirection, never head-on. Blacks, of course, did not have that option. Theirs would be the burden of sustaining the battle for racial equality and economic justice.

THE IMPLICATIONS OF FRANK GRAHAM'S defeat and mounting political intolerance were not lost on Terry Sanford. Throughout the 1950 campaign he had been disappointed — sometimes angered — by Graham's reluctance to confront his opponent. Preference for the high road was fine as a matter of moral principle, but in practice it simply gave the advantage to Willis Smith's supporters. Sanford watched as Graham was vilified and resolved that such a thing would never happen to him. He jotted in a small notebook thoughts for running a more successful campaign:

Never get on the defensive.
Be aggressive with a positive program in the beginning.
Don't give them any quarter.
Counter-attack on another issue.
Don't let somebody drag you into something you don't want to do.

Sanford kept his notebook close to hand throughout the 1950s, as he responded to black citizens' unyielding call for civil rights and set about piecing together his own political career.[36]

In 1952, Sanford took time away from his legal practice in Fayetteville to run for a seat in the state senate. He cared little for the office itself, but he understood that before he could make a career in politics he would need firsthand experience with the backroom workings of life in the state capital. At the time, Fayetteville was a small outpost of change in American race relations. The military base at nearby Fort Bragg had begun to dismantle Jim Crow soon after President Harry Truman ordered the desegregation of the armed forces in 1948. Schoolchildren on the base studied in integrated classrooms, and the officers' club was the one restaurant in town where blacks and whites could eat together. As a former army officer, Sanford had many opportunities to dine at the club, but on one significant occasion he demurred. Through legal and veterans circles, he had made the acquaintance of Harry Groves, a former second lieutenant in the Judge Advocate General's Corps, Fayetteville's only black attorney, and the convener of a group of black professionals who met regularly to discuss race and politics. With a nod to larger civic aspirations, the group called themselves the Townsmen. During the 1952 campaign, Groves invited Sanford to join them for dinner at Fort Bragg. Sanford hesitated, and then sent word that he would meet the men but not share a meal with them. The political risk was simply too great.[37]

In 1954, after finishing his two-year term in the state legislature, Sanford returned briefly to the bar and then signed on as manager of Kerr Scott's campaign for a seat in the U.S. Senate. The job was too attractive to turn down. For one thing, it gave Sanford access to Scott's "branch-head boys," who he understood would be essential to his own aspirations. "They were people, by and large, that I would not have been involved with," Sanford later explained. "They were people that I might have had some difficulty reaching. They particularly were valuable to have on my side when racism became a big thing . . . because they were out in the rural areas where they, by being for me, would dispel a great many of those fears." Working for Scott also offered an opportunity to settle a political score. Scott was vying for the Senate seat left empty by Willis Smith, who had died in office in 1953. Years later, Sanford confided to an ailing Frank Graham that he read that turn of events as a sign of divine retribution. Sending Scott to Washington, he believed, was a way for Graham supporters "to get even, to rectify [the] injustice" of their earlier defeat.[38]

Scott's opponent was Alton A. Lennon, a lawyer, former state legislator, and Smith loyalist whom Governor William B. Umstead had named to fill Smith's seat until a special election could be held. As the race tightened, Lennon worked to undermine Scott with the tactics that had been so effective against Frank Graham. On May 17, just twelve days before the primary vote, the U.S. Supreme Court ruled in a set of cases known collectively as *Brown v. Board of Education* that "separate educational facilities [were] inherently unequal" and thus unconstitutional. Lennon immediately pointed a finger of blame at Scott, telling newspapers that the former governor and "certain of his top advisers" had "encouraged the abolition of segregation in our public schools for many years."[39]

Scott tried to deflect the attack by positioning himself as neither a white supremacist nor an integrationist. He told the *Raleigh News and Observer* that he hoped to "avoid stirring up fear and bad feeling between the races." He reminded blacks of his support for their schools and reassured whites that "no candidate would favor the end of segregation." The moment's need, Scott argued, was for restraint rather than hasty reaction. He urged "all fellow citizens, regardless of race, color or creed, [to] remain calm and work together in an orderly fashion while machinery is being set up to avoid disruption of our pattern of school life." The Lennon camp would have none of it. On the eve of the election, handbills turned up in white precincts publicizing an ad that appeared to have been placed in the *Winston-Salem Journal* by the Scott campaign; it bore the signature of a prominent black leader who praised Scott's "interest in our race" and support for desegregation.[40]

Mindful of the lessons he had recorded in his notebook, Terry Sanford responded with strong-arm tactics of his own. Through contacts in Winston-

Salem, he confirmed that the ad was a fake and had been planted by the city's mayor. He then sent an undercover Scott supporter to the Lennon camp to retrieve a fistful of handbills and instructions for their distribution. On the morning before election day, those materials and the man's story made the front page of the *News and Observer*. A banner headline exclaimed, "Alton Lennon Forces Flood State with 'Phony' Race Issue Leaflets." Sanford's quick thinking paid off—just barely. Scott won the primary by a margin of 51 to 49 percent of the vote and went on to claim the contested Senate seat.[41]

Across the state, early reactions to *Brown* echoed Scott's concern to avoid open confrontation and racial hostility. On the night after the decision, Greensboro's city school board declared its willingness to comply. "It was unthinkable," said superintendent Benjamin Smith, "that we would try to abrogate the laws of the United States of America." Three days later, Winston-Salem attorney Irving Carlyle advised delegates to the state Democratic Party convention that "as good citizens we have no other course except to obey the law laid down by the United States Supreme Court." His audience applauded and adopted a resolution affirming that view. Most political insiders had no interest in the massive resistance that soon erupted in Virginia and Deep South states. They feared that such a stance would tarnish North Carolina's progressive image, provoke direct federal intervention, and unleash racial hard-liners within the Democratic Party who might steer the state down a self-destructive road. Top party leaders sought instead to manage the situation, to maintain a "tone of moderation" while limiting the pace and scope of change in race relations.[42]

In August 1954, Governor Umstead appointed an advisory committee on education to study the implications of *Brown*. The group quickly became know as the Pearsall Committee, after its chairman, Thomas J. Pearsall of Rocky Mount. By North Carolina standards, Pearsall was a moderate on race issues. He ran a large tenant farming operation that spread across four eastern counties. Pearsall approached his tenants with a strong sense of noblesse oblige. He employed a nurse to watch after their health and built a cannery to encourage them to put away wholesome food. Sixteen prominent whites and three blacks served with Pearsall. The black committee members included two presidents of state-supported colleges and a home demonstration agent, all of whom depended heavily on political favor from whites. The group's report, delivered in December, concluded that "the mixing of the races forthwith in the public schools throughout the state" risked violence and "should not be attempted." The report reasoned that North Carolina could avoid that danger and at the same time comply with *Brown* by removing references to segregated education from state statutes and delegating to city and county school boards the authority to desegregate at whatever pace and by whatever means best suited local conditions. State legislators made those recommendations into law with passage of the Pupil Assignment Act of 1955, which encouraged foot-dragging and delay. Civil rights activists who wished to force immediate desegregation no longer had legal grounds for suing the State Board of Education. Their only option was to challenge each of North Carolina's 175 school districts one by one.[43]

In April 1955, the U.S. Supreme Court heard arguments regarding implementation of the *Brown* decision. North Carolina's assistant attorney general, Harvard-educated I. Beverly Lake, joined his counterparts from five other southern states in petitioning for local control over the process of desegregation. A staunch defender of Jim Crow, Lake acknowledged grudgingly that the court was within its rights in ruling that segregated schooling violated the Fourteenth Amendment, but he insisted that the justices had no authority to dictate the terms of remedy. After all, no federal law required that the states provide public education, and even Congress lacked "the authority to assign children to this or that [school]." The court accepted the gist of that argument. On May 31, in a decision known as *Brown II*, the justices ordered that desegregation be undertaken with "all deliberate speed." That vague mandate, devoid of any clear plan of action, assured that the process of dismantling educational Jim Crow would be drawn out and fiercely contested for many years to come.[44]

Within a few weeks of *Brown II*, Luther Hodges, North Carolina's former lieutenant governor who had replaced William Umstead after his death in office in late 1954, appointed a second Pearsall Committee. This time, the group was comprised solely of white legislators. In response to *Brown II*, they proposed a constitutional amendment that would allow local communities to close their schools by public referendum if desegregation was forced upon them and in such places would authorize the State Board of Education to provide white students with vouchers to attend private schools. A special session of the state legislature gave the amendment overwhelming approval in July 1956 and made arrangements to submit it to voters in September. Hodges and Pearsall campaigned vigorously for what quickly became known as the Pearsall Plan. They argued that the plan charted a "middle way" between potential white violence and the *"intemperance"* of black activists in the National Association for the Advancement of Colored People (NAACP). With obvious reference to white fears of race mixing, the governor warned blacks against the danger of losing "their identity in complete merger with [whites].... [The NAACP] has used every means at its command to convince you that you cannot develop your own culture within your own race and therefore that you must be ashamed of your color and your history by burying it in the development of the white race." In open defiance of the governor, the state's black teachers association rejected his logic. *Brown*, they said, was "just, courageous, and timely." But whites thought otherwise. In September's special referendum, voters approved the constitutional amendment by a margin of four to one.[45]

Terry Sanford campaigned enthusiastically for the Pearsall Plan, repeating the often-heard promise that it offered a safety valve for local communities. He advised the members of a women's club in eastern North Carolina that they should not "approach this question of the Supreme Court's decision by screaming, crying, or in sullen despair. The Supreme Court may be just as wrong as Corrigan [an American aviator who, in 1938, departed from New York, aimed for California, and ended up in Ireland], but [our] response must be calm, quiet and deliberate.... The people of North Carolina have reasoned their way out of many difficult situations, and we will reason our way out of this one." Years later, Sanford reaffirmed that view. He described the Pearsall Plan as "a brilliant piece of strategy" that had calmed the state and provided some protection from hot-headed legislators. "It satisfied people . . . on both sides of the issue," archsegregationists who were reassured that desegregation could be delayed indefinitely and moderate whites who found comfort in the fact that when change came, it would be gradual and on their terms. During the run-up to the referendum on the plan, Governor Luther Hodges thanked Sanford for his support: "It would have been too bad to have had a factional split up on this important school matter." As it had so many times since the turn of the century, a gentlemen's agreement on the necessity of white unity within the Democratic Party had carried the day.[46]

Only three families ever requested funds under the Pearsall Plan, and in only one instance did the State Board of Education issue a voucher. The plan's architects had understood from the outset that it could never be implemented on any meaningful scale, since the state had neither the financial resources nor an adequate number of private schools to provide for large numbers of white students fleeing public education. But that was not the point. Together with the Pupil Assignment Act of 1955, the Pearsall Plan did its work by mobilizing moderate white opinion behind a strategy of postponement and delay and by erecting nearly insurmountable barriers to anything more than token desegregation. At the beginning of the 1958–59 school year, only 10 of North Carolina's 322,000 black students attended formerly white schools. The lesson was not lost on observers elsewhere in the South. School officials from Little Rock, Arkansas, where white resistance to desegregation had forced President Dwight Eisenhower to use troops to restore order, complimented their North Carolina colleagues on the effectiveness of the state's more deliberate response to *Brown*: "You . . . have devised one of the cleverest techniques of perpetuating segregation that we have seen. . . . Why if we could be half as successful as you have been, we could keep this thing to a minimum for the next fifty years."[47]

In the midst of the crisis over school desegregation, Terry Sanford had been calculating his own political future. He thought seriously about running for governor in 1956. On the last day for candidates to declare their intentions, he traveled to Raleigh with his filing fee in his pocket. But at the last moment, he changed his mind. The circumstances surrounding the upcoming elections seemed too treacherous. For one thing, Luther Hodges would be running as an incumbent. That advantage was rare for North Carolina governors, who were forbidden by the state constitution from succeeding themselves. As in Hodges's case, it became available only when a lieutenant governor was called on to complete the term of a deceased predecessor. Sanford also understood that race was likely to be the central issue in the campaign, especially if an ardent segregationist entered the Democratic primary. In such a situation, Hodges would have prior claim to the middle ground, leaving Sanford or any other moderate contender with no option but to defend the Supreme Court and *Brown*. Sanford understood that allowing himself to be boxed-in in that way would amount to political suicide. "I knew if I got beat," he said, "I would probably be through." A block short of the offices of the State Board of Elections, Sanford folded the money in his pocket and decided to return to Fayetteville. Over the next three years, he bided his time and worked to expand his political networks through veterans and civic organizations across the state.[48]

ON FEBRUARY 4, 1960, Sanford announced a decision that he had been contemplating since his student days in Chapel Hill. He would be a candidate for governor. Speaking before a hometown audience in Fayetteville, he called for a "New Day" in North Carolina. He took his cue, in part, from Kerr Scott's 1948 and 1954 campaigns, in which the populist Democrat had urged voters to "go forward." "The time has come," Sanford declared, "to quit holding back. I call on you to join with me to build a better North Carolina. Let's quit holding the line. The object of the game is not to defend the goal but to score a touchdown. The touchdown for North Carolina is expanding, growing, developing and building."[49]

Sanford aimed his remarks at voters of his generation who had come out of wartime with great confidence, an eagerness to escape the past, and determination to build new lives for themselves and their children. The old men of North Carolina politics were, for the most part, now offstage. Willis Smith had died in office, as had Kerr Scott; Luther Hodges was contemplating a run for vice president; and Frank Graham was in political exile in New York, where he labored as the United Nations' special envoy to India and Pakistan for the resolution of their dispute over Kashmir. Eli Evans, who had been student body president at the University of North Carolina during the late 1950s, recalled the promise of the moment: "I remember being excited that someone that young and dynamic could be governor. It was so revolutionary that someone was going to try to assemble the World War II veterans and this was going to be a new generation."[50]

Sanford also tapped into a broad spirit of boosterism among business leaders and middle-class voters who were determined to modernize the state and integrate it fully into the national economy. They had begun in the late 1940s with the Good Health Campaign, a crusade motivated by persistently high rates of disease and untimely death in North Carolina, along with the fact that during World War II more North Carolinians were rejected for military service than citizens of any other state. In 1947, the health crusaders won the legislative votes and appropriations necessary to build a new state hospital and establish a four-year medical school on the university campus in Chapel Hill. During the following decade, state and local leaders also scoured the nation and the globe to attract $1 billion worth of new industrial investments. That effort culminated in 1959 with the founding of the Research Triangle Park in what was then rural Durham County. The park was a bold idea for its time, designed to leverage the strengths of three neighboring universities — the University of North Carolina at Chapel Hill, North Carolina State University in Raleigh, and Duke University in Durham — to make the state a player in new fields of scientific research and technological innovation. As Sanford observed in the announcement of his candidacy, such efforts grew from an honest — sometimes painful — assessment of North Carolina's shortcomings and optimistic engagement with new possibilities. "I have been impressed, in traveling across the state," he told attentive supporters, "that our people are becoming more and more . . . determined that now is the time when something must be done. . . . This is a New Day in North Carolina,

On the campaign trail in rural Bertie County, Terry Sanford added a down-home touch to his call for a "New Day" in North Carolina. Photograph by Laura F. Harrell, courtesy of the North Carolina State Archives, Governor Terry Sanford Photograph Collection.

when we are facing opportunities unsurpassed, unprecedented, unequaled in all of the sweep of the state's history."[51]

Sanford worried from the outset that one issue—race—could derail his ambitions. But try as he might, he could not make the issue go away. Three days before he announced his candidacy, four black students from North Carolina Agricultural and Technical College in Greensboro sat down at the lunch counter of the local Woolworth's and demanded service. In doing so, they ushered in the sit-in phase of the modern civil rights movement. Similar protests erupted in Raleigh, High Point, Charlotte, and Winston-Salem. On February 16, Martin Luther King Jr. visited Durham to encourage student demonstrators. "If the officials threaten to arrest us for standing up for our rights," he advised them, "we must answer by saying that we are willing and prepared to fill up the jails of the South." Two months later, King was again in North Carolina, this time on the campus of Shaw University in Raleigh for the founding of the Student Nonviolent Coordinating Committee, which would spread the sit-in movement throughout the South and lead the struggle

Martin Luther King Jr. (center) intensified the national focus on civil rights protests in North Carolina when he visited the Woolworth lunch counter shut down by sit-in demonstrators in Durham and later returned for the founding of the Student Nonviolent Coordinating Committee at Shaw University in Raleigh. Photograph by Jim Thornton, courtesy of the *Durham Herald-Sun*.

to reclaim for black citizens the voting rights that had been stolen from them more than a half century earlier. Terry Sanford recognized the capacity of that activism to provoke white backlash and the challenge that the two together posed for self-styled moderate politicians. He was therefore alarmed when former assistant attorney general I. Beverly Lake, who had emerged during the debate over *Brown* as one of the state's leading defenders of white supremacy, announced that he, too, intended to seek the Democratic Party's nomination. The campaign was shaping up to be just the sort of contest that Sanford had most hoped to avoid.[52]

Before joining the state attorney general's office, Lake had been a law professor at Wake Forest College, then a small Baptist institution located in the town of the same name. He was born in Wake Forest in 1906 and received his undergraduate degree from the school where he taught. In 1950, Lake had supported Frank Porter Graham's senatorial campaign, but *Brown* hardened his racial views. Soon after his appearance before the U.S. Supreme Court in 1955, he infuriated Governor Hodges by making a speech in which he denounced the NAACP as white North Carolinians' sworn enemy and suggested that the wisest means of resisting desegregation might be to follow the lead of more strident southern states and close the public schools. "We shall fight the NAACP," Lake exclaimed, "county by county, city by city, and if need be, school by school as long as possible while organizing and establishing other methods of educating our children." In October 1955, when Hodges passed him over for appointment as attorney general, Lake left state service to join the law practice of conservative Raleigh broadcaster A. J. Fletcher, who, along with his young radio reporter and protégé Jesse Helms, had played a critical role in defeating Frank Graham and sending Willis Smith to Washington.[53]

Lake returned to private life but did not surrender the public stage. When the second Pearsall Committee began its work in the summer of 1955, he attempted to steer its recommendations toward a hard-line defense of segregation. Lake worked closely with two committee staffers, his former law student W. W. Taylor Jr. and Tom Ellis, also a lawyer and a key supporter of Willis Smith in the 1950 Senate race. Thomas Pearsall was so angered by Lake's effort at intervention that he furloughed Ellis as the committee prepared its final recommendations for the legislature. Lake refused to back down. When the Pearsall Committee's report reached the state senate, Robert B. Morgan, another Lake student, introduced a competing bill that quickly became known as the Lake Plan. It proposed that the requirement to provide public education be struck from the state constitution and that legislators rather than local voters be granted the authority to close existing schools, locality by locality or, if necessary, in one summary action. Lake and his associates believed that such drastic options were necessary to stave off a civil rights movement whose ultimate aims reached far beyond the schoolhouse. "The eventual goal," said Taylor and Ellis, "is racial intermarriage and the disappearance of the Negro race by fusing into white."[54]

Lake failed to redirect the Pearsall Committee, but the very public fight he provoked in the state legislature positioned him as a leader of die-hard segregationists. He embraced that role and continued to speak out. In 1957, Lake accepted an invitation from WRAL-TV to address viewers on the civil rights situation. He urged continued resistance to *Brown* and hammered away at a familiar theme as he sought to expose the sinister aims of the NAACP. That organization, he warned parents, was "trying to condition [their] children, even before they [were] old enough to be conscious of sex, to accept integration, not only in the classroom, but in the living room and the bedroom as well." Lake's strident opposition to *Brown* attracted the attention of Wesley C.

Terry Sanford confronts I. Beverly Lake during the Democratic gubernatorial campaign, May 1960. Courtesy of the *Raleigh News & Observer* and the North Carolina State Archives.

George, professor of anatomy in Chapel Hill and founder of the Patriots of North Carolina, a well-heeled white supremacist organization. George and other leaders of the Patriots urged Lake to consider a bid for the governor's office. They promised access to the group's roster of twenty thousand members, who could be counted on to bankroll Lake's candidacy and to work their local communities on his behalf. When Rocky Mount physician Clarence W. Bailey offered Lake a $10,000 campaign contribution, the decision was sealed. Lake announced his candidacy on March 1, 1960.[55]

In a four-way race in the Democratic primary, Lake surprised political pundits and the Sanford campaign by winning 27.8 percent of the vote compared to Sanford's 41.3 percent. He immediately called for a runoff, setting the stage for a replay of the 1950 senatorial election. Sanford still had the notebook of lessons learned in that contest, and he managed his campaign accordingly. When Lake accused him of being an integrationist, Sanford denied the charge. He later recalled how important that move had been. "I fudged . . . when I said Dr. Lake knows I'm not an integrationist. I grant you that I knew at the time that I was [being] mildly hypocritical. But . . . I was being very, very careful not to be over-labeled." As one of Sanford's friends observed, he felt "deep down" that the race issue "was going to have to be settled if . . . we were to grow as a state." That's why he and his wife, Margaret Rose, chose to send their two children to an integrated public school soon after Sanford was sworn into office. But in the heated circumstances of the campaign, he was determined to prevent Lake from defining the terms of debate. "An integrationist? What the hell did that mean? I wasn't going to let him put that title on me," Sanford explained. "You can't let those words be used. You've got to talk about what you stand for. . . . So I deliberately wouldn't let them put that title on me."[56]

Sanford answered Lake by changing the subject and turning Lake's apocalyptic rhetoric to his own advantage. Early in the campaign, Sanford's college friend and pollster Lou Harris encouraged him to steer clear of direct engagement with the race issue. He should focus instead on education, how it might be improved and the ways that it might enlarge opportunities for all North Carolinians. That advice sat well with Sanford. His mother had been a schoolteacher, and his attendance at a public university had opened doors that otherwise would have been closed to him. Education was an issue that Sanford could embrace. It also appealed to a growing population of white middle-class suburbanites, many of whom had taken advantage of the college tuition benefits of the GI Bill and understood schooling as a critical factor in their own upward mobility. Sanford's promise to employ more teachers, raise their pay, reduce class size, and improve the quality of instruction played particularly well with white women, a constituency Harris identified as key to winning the election. They were deeply concerned for their children's future and their families' ability to pass newfound prosperity from one generation to the next. One woman Harris polled neatly summarized the views of many others like her: "I'm not concerned with integration. I think if we keep moderate, things will work out. The big thing is to improve the schools. . . . I, for one, would be willing to pay higher taxes. . . . I'd be for Terry Sanford. . . . He is in sympathy with the views of Frank Graham and Kerr Scott. . . . He is a moderate on integration, not like Lake."[57]

Sanford played to those sensibilities and warned that Lake's strident defense of white supremacy would ultimately consume white middle-class "hopes and aspirations . . . in racial bitterness." "The people of North Carolina do not want integration and we cannot afford to close our schools," he said to voters, "but this is where the professor would lead us. If Professor Lake keeps up his present approach he is inadvertently leading North Carolina down the road to complete integration, to federal troops, to closed schools. We do not want that — we cannot have it." "I take my stand for keeping the schools open and improving them," he declared. "And I stand for moving forward with a positive program—not holding the tight line against economic progress in North Carolina." To underscore the cost that a hard-line defense of segregation might impose, Sanford's campaign ran television spots in which civic leaders in Little Rock, Arkansas, reported that new businesses had steered clear of the city since 1957, when its schools closed in defiance of *Brown*. "We do not need that kind of climate in North Carolina," Sanford told voters. "We need a continuation of the sunny, bright climate to build for tomorrow." The *Charlotte Observer* sounded a similar theme shortly before election day. The paper advised that voters faced a stark choice between a candidate "full of vigor and hope, enthusiasm and confidence and . . . a man wedded to the status quo, obsessed with false fears, who had pandered to the basest and rawest of human emotions." Decisions made at the ballot box would determine whether North Carolina continued to go forward or followed the path of "some other southern states" that had shackled themselves with "bitter racial hatred and gloomy economic pessimism."[58]

Sanford's appeal persuaded a majority of white voters. They expressed little outright enthusiasm for civil rights, but by the same token, they were not willing to sacrifice their children's future on the altar of massive resistance. Sanford offered them a comforting middle way. If managed carefully, desegregation would occur slowly. There would be time to work things out, either by adapting or, as would eventually be the case for a significant minority, moving to private and church school alternatives. Sanford polled 56 percent of the vote in the second Democratic primary and went on to defeat his Republican opponent handily in the general election. In a reversal of the ordinary coattail effect, his victory helped carry North Carolina for Democratic presidential candidate John F. Kennedy, whose nomination Sanford had seconded at the party's national convention. As a gesture of gratitude, the president's brother and sister-in-law, Robert and Ethel Kennedy, traveled to North Carolina to attend Sanford's inauguration.[59]

Sanford opened his inaugural address by summoning the memory of Charles Brantley Aycock, whose portrait he would later hang above his desk in the governor's office. Aycock had come to power in 1900 on a platform of white supremacy and better schools. To the end of his political career, he never voiced regret for the violence his party had visited upon Fusionist opponents—in his view, that had been the necessary means of wresting power from black pretenders and apostate whites—but he did insist that "permanent white supremacy" could not be established by force and repression alone. Such a policy would surely set in motion a black exodus from North Carolina, he warned, and it might also provoke federal meddling with

Terry and Margaret Rose Sanford celebrating victory in the second Democratic primary. Courtesy of the North Carolina State Archives, Governor Terry Sanford Photograph Collection.

the literacy test on which disfranchisement and white rule depended. To Aycock's way of thinking, what the state needed was a more adroit racial policy, one that joined the active subordination of blacks with an effort to cultivate among them some measure of collaboration and consent. The challenge was to craft a system of managed race relations that would provide the "good order and peace" required for economic development and that would make room for whites and blacks to work out their separate destinies. "We are confronted with a condition," Aycock advised fellow Democrats, "which demands statesmanship and not passion and prejudice."[60]

Sanford shared none of Aycock's racial animosity, nor did he accept the permanence of racial separation. But like Aycock, he affirmed the value of statesmanship and was confident that he understood how to manage race relations for the benefit of blacks and whites alike. In his inaugural address, he championed education as the means to that end. "We must give our children the quality of education which they need to keep up in this rapidly advancing, scientific, complex world," Sanford declared. "They must be prepared to compete with the best in the nation and I dedicate my public life to the proposition that education must be of a quality which is second to none. A second-rate education can only mean a second-rate future for North Carolina." Sanford also challenged his audience to imagine improving the quality of education as an inclusive enterprise: "We are not going to forget, as we move into the . . . demanding years ahead, that no group of our citizens can be

In October 1961, President John Kennedy thanked Terry Sanford for his political support by delivering the keynote address at the annual celebration of the University of North Carolina's founding. Here, Kennedy and the governor share the stage with university president William C. Friday. Courtesy of the North Carolina Collection, Wilson Library, University of North Carolina at Chapel Hill, William Clyde Friday Collection.

denied the right to participate in the opportunities of first-class citizenship. Let us extend North Carolina's well-known spirit of moderation and good will, of mutual respect and understanding, in order that our energies and our resources, our abilities and our wills, may be directed toward building a better and more fruitful life for all the people of our state."[61]

Those words sent a stir through Sanford's audience, who answered with sustained applause. Few other public officials in the South were bold enough to endorse equal opportunity for blacks, not even in Sanford's carefully crafted language. But there were limits to the new governor's approach. He aimed his remarks primarily at white, middle-class North Carolinians, and he spoke to them not about reordering privilege but enshrining the kind of opportunity they valued and knew firsthand in their own lives. In that sense, Sanford stood at some distance from the New Deal liberalism that had inspired his parents with its concern for economic reform and the use of government to broker a more equitable distribution of the nation's abundance. Throughout the campaign, he had employed to good effect Kerr Scott's admonition against "hold[ing] the line" on progress, but unlike his mentor, he seldom spoke to what progress might mean for existing arrangements of wealth and power. There was little by way of political or economic critique built into Sanford's message. He sought instead to frame a positive appeal, one cast in more universal terms that could bridge political constituencies and that white middle-class voters would find palatable. The New Day in North Carolina would begin not with social upheaval but with the opening of opportunities for individual citizens to realize their full potential. Supporters greeted Sanford's speech with enthusiasm much like that accorded John F. Kennedy's inaugural address two weeks later, when he took the presidential oath and called on a new generation to assume the mantle of leadership. For the moment, the optimism of those inauguration days energized the state and nation, but it would soon be tested as an emboldened citizenry took up the call to action and exposed deep incongruities between political ideals and the realities of American life.

SANFORD DEVOTED THE FIRST months of his administration to pushing through the state legislature a bold plan for school improvement. He had long opposed the trickle-down approach to social investment that characterized North Carolina through much of the twentieth century. The Hodges administration, in particular, had made the recruitment of new industry its priority, arguing that more money for schools would have to wait until efforts at economic development began to improve state revenues. In Sanford's view, that policy was backward and "dangerously wrong." North Carolina would not attract new employers — certainly not employers that paid better wages — until the state faced up to the educational challenge and began to make the investments necessary to prepare its citizens "to compete in a national market." "We are not going to lift ourselves by our bootstraps," he had told supporters on the campaign trail, "if we wait for increased income from new businesses before we fulfill our responsibility to the public schools."[62]

To that end, Sanford made common cause with United Forces for Education, a coalition of educators that included the American Association of University Women, the state Congress of Parents and Teachers, the Federation of Women's Clubs, the State School Boards Association, the State Grange, and the North Carolina Education Association. He included in his 1961 budget their call for $100 million worth of new investments in North Carolina's public schools. To pay for that expanded appropriation, Sanford turned to the state sales tax. Governor Ehringhaus had first imposed that levy in 1933 as a means of balancing North Carolina's Depression-era budget. From the outset, opponents had criticized it as the most regressive of many options for raising new revenues. Ehringhaus's own State Tax Commission characterized the sales tax as "unsound, unfair, and unwise," and the state commissioner of revenue called it a "tax on poverty." Sanford revived the controversy by proposing that all exemptions to the sales tax be repealed, including those for food and medicine. Even the governor's closest allies reeled at that suggestion; they warned that it would be the undoing of the Democratic Party, which had always "been the party of the poor and oppressed." But Sanford refused to yield. He insisted that, just as in 1933, "there simply wasn't any other place to find the money"—not in increased property or income taxes, which the wealthy would surely oppose, and, in a tobacco state, not in a higher tax on cigarettes. In June, after months of intense lobbying and backroom deal making, lawmakers approved Sanford's school program. The results were immediate and impressive. Overnight, North Carolina rose from thirty-ninth to thirty-second place among the states in average teacher salaries and jumped from forty-fifth to thirty-eighth in per pupil expenditures.[63]

Shortly before the legislative session ended, Sanford traveled to the National Governors' Conference in Hawaii, where he was hailed as a champion of public education. Invitations soon followed from all over the country for him to visit and speak about his program of reform. As biographers Harold Covington and Marion Ellis have observed, the summer months of 1961 were a heady time for Sanford and his staff. They sensed that the possibilities were limitless in their quest to "make things better." "We could do anything," recalled Sanford aide Hugh Cannon. "I mean we could try anything, anything that wasn't illegal." But civil rights—the one issue that Sanford had sought so carefully to head off during the campaign—threatened at every turn to upset the game plan.[64]

In February 1960, the Greensboro sit-ins initially attracted little press attention. Few observers at the time recognized the larger significance that, in retrospect, seems so obvious. But as the months wore on, civil rights demonstrators made clear that they had no intention of retreating. Sit-ins spread from Greensboro to towns large and small across North Carolina and throughout the South. By August 1961, those protests had mobilized more than seventy thousand participants regionwide. In May of that same year, the Congress on Racial Equality (CORE) organized Freedom Rides that sent busloads of civil rights activists through the South to test enforcement of U.S. Supreme Court rulings against segregation in interstate transportation. CORE had sponsored the first demonstration of that kind in 1947. In that instance, Freedom Riders met stiff resistance as they traveled through North Carolina. In Chapel Hill, they escaped two carloads of angry white men when activist minister Charlie Jones intervened and sheltered them at his home. Several of the riders were later arrested, including one of CORE's founders, Bayard Rustin, who served twenty-two days on a North Carolina chain gang. The Freedom Rides of 1961 passed through North Carolina and other Upper South states with little trouble, but in Anniston, Alabama, one of the buses was firebombed, and in Birmingham and Montgomery, Freedom Riders were viciously beaten when state and local authorities stood aside and gave free rein to white mobs.[65]

The violence in Alabama shocked the nation and stiffened the resolve of civil rights organizers. In North Carolina, Durham lawyer Floyd McKissick established a local chapter of CORE. McKissick was born in Asheville in 1922. He studied at Morehouse College in Atlanta and served during World War II as a sergeant in the army. In 1951, he was one of three black students admitted by federal court order to the University of North Carolina School of Law. McKissick later opened a practice in Durham and became heavily involved in the civil rights struggle through the NAACP. He promoted union organizing among black tobacco workers and defended student sit-in demonstrators in court. In 1962, McKissick and CORE director James Farmer decided to focus a new protest effort on North Carolina, in large part to test Governor Sanford's reputation as a moderate. The campaign was called Freedom Highways, and like the earlier Freedom Rides, it targeted segregation in restaurants, motels, and other public services along the South's major transportation routes. This time, white North Carolina's response resembled 1947 more than 1961. In Raleigh, local officials ordered that fire hoses be turned on demonstrators, and in Statesville, police called in a truck used for mosquito control and dispersed a crowd of more than six hundred protesters by spraying them with pesticide.[66]

Sanford was ill prepared to address the rising tide of civil disobedience. He had come into office with little to say about civil rights, other than to wish privately that the issue would go away; he had no meaningful relationships with black leaders; and to the extent that he had addressed the race issue, it was primarily as a matter of disagreement among whites. The 1960 campaign had asked little more of him. Few black North Carolinians could vote, and those who managed to register were unlikely to cast their ballots for I. Beverly Lake. The challenge for Sanford the candidate had been to maintain support from a broad cross-section of white voters, and in order to do that, he consistently steered clear of the one issue that was sure to divide them. Sanford protégé Jim Hunt remembered that any other strategy would have amounted to political suicide. Critics often asked why Sanford had not been more forthright in 1960, but had they been the ones campaigning, Hunt declared, "those people would have lost." Perhaps Hunt was right. But once elected, something different was required of Sanford. The risk of violence and bloodshed was mounting; lives were on the line, as was the legacy of Sanford's generation. The time for campaigning had passed; the question now was how well Sanford would govern.[67]

Sanford recognized that distinction, if only dimly at first. Soon after his inauguration, he began to bring black professionals into state government. He explained his reasoning in a memoir written shortly after he left office. "We have often heard it said that the Negro race was not furnishing leadership," Sanford wrote. But "leadership . . . comes . . . mostly from being tried in positions of leadership. Consequently we cannot expect adequate amounts of leadership unless we put Negroes in positions of leadership." To that end, the governor made more than three dozen black appointments to state boards, ranging from the Medical Care Commission to special committees on educational television and atomic energy.[68]

Sanford also sought the counsel of black business and community leaders. He relied on John Larkins, a sociologist in the state Department of Welfare, to scout the issues in local civil rights disputes. In Durham, John Wheeler, president of the Mechanics and Farmers Bank, provided a link to the city's influential black middle class. And in Raleigh, Sanford aides recruited John Winters, a black construction contractor and recently elected member of the city council. Winters had perhaps the most notable influence on Sanford. He came from a working-class background and could speak about the indignities of Jim Crow from the perspective of the porters, laborers, and domestics whom whites most often passed by as nameless figures on the landscape. He was also forthright in his dealings with Sanford. When the governor's aides complained about outside agitators who stirred up racial troubles, Winters corrected their error. "You don't understand," he said. "We're the outsiders. We've been outsiders and [now] we're trying to get in." On another occasion, Winters was with Sanford as he spoke over the phone with a white hotel manager and attempted to convince the man to make rooms available to a group of visiting African diplomats. At the end of the call, he suggested that perhaps Sanford was working the problem the wrong way around. "Governor," he said, "if you make arrangements for John Winters to go to that hotel and be accommodated . . . then you wouldn't have to worry about these Africans."[69]

The lessons that John Winters sought to teach Sanford stayed with the governor as he traveled the state to promote his program of school improvement. Out on the hustings, he "stumbled [upon] the whole confusing pattern of poverty"; he began to recognize Jim Crow's cruelty in the blighted hopes of black children; and — tentatively at first — he started to draw connections between the two. As one of the governor's aides later reported, Sanford realized that "these children have so many distractions — hunger, sickness, crowded living and poor studying conditions — coming between them and their lessons that they can't take advantage of what the school has to offer." At a tender age, they were already caught up in a "cycle of tragedy and failure."[70]

Black students cheered when Sanford visited their schools. It was, after all, unheard of that a governor should spend so much time in black communities. Sanford, in turn, offered his customary advice on the importance of hard work and good grades. "I told the students across the state, white and Negro," he later recalled, "that this is not the age for the common laborer; you must have a skill and you must work here and now to get it. Education is your future." But as the governor repeated those words in one school after another, they began to haunt him. On one occasion, he finished a meeting with black children feeling too distressed to eat his dinner. "I had the sickening feeling that every time I talked to them I was saying words that were a mockery," Sanford remembered, "that I was talking about opportunities that I knew, and I feared they knew, didn't exist, no matter how hard they might work in school. All of my words [came to have] a shallow sound, at least to me." The "improvement of schools wasn't enough," he concluded. "Not nearly enough."[71]

Time spent with black schoolchildren worked a change in Sanford. It began to pull back the cloak of caution that he had wrapped so snugly around himself during the 1950s. It also prodded him to reassess his understanding of discrimination, deprivation, and the connections that drew the two tightly together. In his unpublished memoir, Sanford reflected on this experience of discovery and his confrontation with the banality of racial injustice:

> I was not in years past always understanding of [the Negro's] bitterness and despair brought about by the discrimination he faced in all his life. I grew up in Laurinburg, at the time mostly a farming town, and people who know this town will agree that it is one of the best in the state. Its [white] people are civic minded . . . decent and fair. Not many [of them] believed their attitudes were those of prejudice. They just hadn't thought much about it, one way or the other. I am sure that I generally shared these sentiments as I came up in the community. This wasn't anything vicious and mean. It was mostly an accommodation of thought, adjusting to the realities in order to avoid unpleasant topics. Not many of these good people would be intentionally insulting, and not many could have brought

Governor Sanford visiting a black elementary school in Jacksonville, March 1962.
Courtesy of the North Carolina State Archives, Raymond Stone Photograph Collection.

themselves to believe that they had any part in visiting injustice upon the Negro race. That is just the way things were, and every person just had to make the most of the Presbyterian circumstances that befell them.

Jim Crow had done its job: it had naturalized racial subordination and, for most whites, had placed such matters well beyond active thought or questioning. Indeed, the majority of white North Carolinians assumed that "the Negro was content and satisfied with his 'place in life.'" But, as Sanford recalled, the social unrest of the early 1960s had revealed to him a different truth. As springtime demonstrations in Raleigh continued into the summer, he asked "who . . . was sending in the money" to keep black college students in town beyond the end of the academic year. "I was amazed to discover," he wrote, "that their support came from the local older Negro, the janitor, the truck driver, the garbage man, the elevator operator. . . . Incredibly, these older Negroes had been dissatisfied all the time . . . and they were intensely, if secretly, proud of the young Negroes who were militantly insisting on change." That insight transformed Sanford's thinking. It replaced ignorance and misapprehension with a measure of empathy and understanding, and it set the governor on a decidedly new course.[72]

In the end, what distinguished Sanford from so many of his contemporaries around the region was not simply a matter of temperament—although that was surely important. Something deeper and more profound was at work: a willingness to attend to dissenting voices, a capacity to learn life lessons from outside his own circle of experience, and the courage to reconsider the moral foundation of his actions. Sanford recalled later in life that there were any number of ways that he might have responded to the social unrest of the early 1960s: "I could have reacted to all of this by defensive measures, by adding to the insults, by giving them a wide berth and staying away from the strife[,] by suggesting that these were only radicals, outside agitators . . . and making veiled suggestions to show the Communists were behind all of this mean business of stirring up our good Negro citizens." The governor, however, wanted something different for himself, his state, and the region. "I wasn't foolish enough to think I could correct all wrongs, in all places, for all people, in four years in the Governor's Mansion. [But] I did want to do my part, in my time. I wanted to live up to [the] . . . high hopes and lofty ideals of the American Dream [and] I believed that North Carolina should lead the nation."[73]

How was that to be accomplished? Sanford had no clear answer, but in late 1962, he began to test ideas. In October, he appeared before a group of Methodist laymen in rural Rutherford County and suggested that economic prospects for white and black North Carolinians were closely linked. His administration was working hard to improve per capita income in the state, but it would not accomplish that goal without confronting the issue of racial inequality. The governor explained: "A major reason, as Census Bureau figures show, for North Carolina's low per capita standing is that Negroes do not have adequate economic opportunities. If we counted the per capita income of white citizens only, North Carolina would rank 32nd in per capita [income] rather than 42nd." For the governor, the implications of that fact seemed obvious and compelling. If whites hoped to improve their own lot, they first would have to address the "difficult problems of race" in a new "spirit of Christian fellowship." "In these days in America," Sanford argued, "we need to show living proof that people of different backgrounds and races can work together. If we are true to our religious Good Samaritan, we should help those in need of help. It is as simple as that. But it is powerful in its capacity to achieve broader opportunities for everyone, the helped and the helpers alike." That appeal received a lukewarm response from the Methodist laymen and the state press. Even the *Raleigh News and Observer*, one of the governor's most ardent supporters, buried the story.[74]

Sanford pressed on with a sense of urgency. The North Carolina Constitution forbade sitting governors from running for reelection; halfway through his term, Sanford was acutely aware that time was running out. "I knew . . . before I left office," he later said, "that I had to make a firmer determination of where we were headed." In late November 1962, he reminded a meeting of the Southern Association of Colleges and Schools that the end of slavery had opened up new opportunities for the South, and he called on members to undertake a similar reimagining of the region's future: "We need our own and a new kind of Emancipation Proclamation, which will set us free to grow and build, set us free from the drag of poor people, poor schools, from hate and demagoguery. It has to be a bold dream for the future, realistic in terms of our country, and aware that the South is entering the mainstream of American life. . . . The South, and the rest of the nation for that matter, needs to take a long, hard look at itself to see where it stands now and to see where it hopes to stand twenty years from now." Implicit in that message, and in the choice of the plural first-person pronoun, was a remarkable recognition of the common fate of all southerners, black and white, rich and poor alike.[75]

With every iteration, Sanford sharpened his understanding of the challenges at hand and, in turn, focused his message. Perhaps he recalled the advice of his mentor, Frank Graham, who had encouraged students to clarify their thinking by pausing to ask, what are the problems? In early January 1963, Sanford invited John Ehle, one of his aides, to join him in the library at the governor's mansion. He wanted to share some notes that he had scrawled on a legal pad under the heading "Observations for a Second Century." Ehle immediately recognized the significance of what Sanford had written: the governor was planning to make a forthright endorsement of "Negro rights."[76]

Over the next few weeks, Sanford circulated his draft to more than one hundred friends and supporters. Most encouraged him; others were horrified by what his actions would mean for the Democratic Party. Then, on January 18, 1963, Sanford traveled to Chapel Hill, where as a young man he had first begun to recognize that racial discrimination was "absolutely wrong and immoral." He spoke in the afternoon to the North Carolina Press Association gathered at the university's Carolina Inn. He began with a personal aside to men and women he knew well and respected as opinion makers. "I wanted to take this occasion, talking to [you] to say something . . . that I have long wanted to say, that I believe we must say." Then he read his prepared statement, once again invoking the one hundredth anniversary of emancipation on January 1, 1863. It was a date that black North Carolinians, and blacks across the South, had long celebrated as Jubilee, but that whites, if they took any notice at all, mostly chose to ignore.

> The American Negro was freed from slavery one hundred years ago. In this century he has made much progress, educating his children, building churches, entering into the community and civic life of the nation.

> Now is the time in this hundredth year not merely to look back to freedom, but forward to the fulfillment of its meaning. Despite this great progress, the Negro's opportunity to obtain a good job has not been achieved in most places across the nation. Reluctance to accept the Negro in employment is the greatest single block to his continued progress and to the full use of the human potential of the nation and its states.

> The time has come for American citizens to give up this reluctance, to quit unfair discrimination, and to give the Negro a full chance to earn a decent living for his family and to contribute to higher standards for himself and all men.

> We cannot rely on law alone in this matter because much depends upon its administration and upon each individual's sense of fair play. North Carolina and its people have come to the point of recognizing the urgent need for opening new economic opportunities for Negro citizens. We also recognize that in doing so we shall be adding new economic growth for everybody.

> We can do this. We should do this. We will do it because we are concerned with the problems and the welfare of our neighbors. We will do it because our economy cannot afford to have so many people fully and partially unproductive. We will do it because it is honest and fair for us to give all men and women their best chance in life.

The governor's audience at first sat silent, and then rose to give him an ovation.[77]

By the beginning of his third year in office, Sanford was rediscovering connections between poverty and racial justice that tobacco workers in Winston-Salem had exposed in the 1940s, that the biracial Fusion alliance had grasped during the late 1890s, and that black and white Republicans had identified as the central concerns of Reconstruction. He argued that North Carolina could not join the American economic mainstream until it invested in developing the full potential of its people and guaranteed equal rights for all. Sanford stated that point most clearly in April 1963, when he visited North Carolina

Agricultural and Technical College. He was there to receive the Omega Psi Phi fraternity's Citizen of the Year Award. "Facts cannot be denied," he said in his acceptance speech, "and in North Carolina today they can be stated simply. We must move forward as one people or we will not move forward at all. We cannot move forward as whites or Negroes. . . . We can only move forward as North Carolinians."[78]

With that declaration, Sanford turned his back on the principles that had defined his party and the white South since the turn of the century. He rejected the segregationist legacy of Charles Brantley Aycock, whose advocacy on behalf of public education he so deeply admired. In 1901, Aycock had admonished an audience at the Colored State Fair that progress and prosperity required "that each race should remain distinct, and have a society of its own." That arrangement, he insisted, "is well for you; it is well for us; it is necessary for the peace of our section." Sanford had come to understand that no social vision could have had more disastrous consequences for the state and its people. In the positions that he staked out during the winter of 1962–63, he began to close in on ways to act upon that realization and to exercise the kind of leadership that he had long imagined for himself and the state. Sanford was positioning North Carolina at the forefront of what soon would become known as the nation's War on Poverty.[79]

ALLIANCES

As Sanford grappled with North Carolina's political and economic challenges, he joined a newly invigorated discussion of poverty in America. During the 1930s, the poor had been the nation's most visible citizens, and Franklin Roosevelt's New Deal had set out to relieve their suffering, to string beneath all Americans a social safety net, and to curb the worst imbalances of wealth and power. A decade later, World War II and the United States' global ascendancy ended the Great Depression and ushered in a new era of prosperity. Overnight, it seemed, America had become a nation of upwardly mobile suburbanites, living in comfortable single-family homes financed by GI loans and enjoying all of the conveniences of a burgeoning consumer economy. At the same time, the Cold War stifled dissent in the name of national security and choked off the politics of class. Intellectuals proclaimed the end of ideology and the triumph of what John Kenneth Galbraith called "the affluent society," characterized by abundance and the absence of want. But true to biblical prophecy, the poor remained. When television began to beam fresh images of the poor into suburban living rooms, middle-class Americans were shocked to rediscover such deprivation in their midst. In 1960, they watched as newsman Edward R. Murrow exposed the plight of migrant farmworkers in the documentary "Harvest of Shame." That same year, they saw stark images of desperate poverty in Appalachia as television news crews followed presidential candidate John F. Kennedy on the campaign trail in West Virginia. One of the most talked-about new books of 1962 was Michael Harrington's *The Other America*. Harrington told the story of millions of men and women, "politically invisible" and largely "unknown to suburbia," who had been left behind by industrial automation and the mechanization of agriculture, who lacked the education and skills to compete in a modern economy, and who were now "neglected and forgotten" in decaying urban slums and dying rural hamlets.[1]

Any of these images could have come from North Carolina. In 1960, census data revealed that 37 percent of all North Carolinians lived on less than

$3,000 per year in family income, a full $1,000 below the national poverty threshold defined by multiple studies between 1959 and 1963 and later adopted by President Johnson's Council of Economic Advisers. Half of all students dropped out of school before obtaining a high school diploma, and of adults twenty-five years of age and older, one-fourth had less than a sixth-grade education and were, for all practical purposes, illiterate. An astonishing 73 percent of North Carolina families lived on $6,000 or less a year, a figure that by national standards defined a condition of deprivation.[2]

In the 1930s, policymakers and students of American society had understood such conditions as the products of class inequality and structural failure in the economy. But to most observers during the 1950s, poverty's causes seemed to lie primarily within individuals rather than institutions. That changed perspective was, in large measure, the product of a behavioralist turn in the social sciences. With knowledge of the murderous power of Nazi ideology still fresh in their minds and, in the context of the Cold War, concerned about warding off the influence of Soviet totalitarianism, American academics turned from normative questions of justice and equality to the study of human behavior. They sought to understand the origins of prejudice, criminality, and other forms of social deviancy and, in so doing, to discern the means by which individual and collective behavior might be steered most effectively toward the common good. From that line of investigation emerged the notion of a culture of poverty. The concept had its origins in the work of two influential scholars: Edward Banfield, who studied Italian peasant communities and in 1958 published *The Moral Basis of a Backward Society*, and anthropologist Oscar Lewis, a student of poverty in rural Mexico and among Puerto Rican immigrants in New York. Banfield and Lewis argued that poverty was not simply a condition of deprivation, but also "a way of life . . . passed down from generation to generation along family lines." Michael Harrington adapted this idea for a popular audience. Once marginalized by structural changes in the economy, he argued, the poor tended to develop dysfunctional "attitudes of defeat and pessimism" that, over time, bound them and their children to lives of misery. They became, in effect, "immune to progress."[3]

Such notions fit neatly with Terry Sanford's passion for education. Soon after leaving office, he published an assessment of his administration in which he laid out his understanding of schooling's critical role in "human progress." The book was titled *But What about the People?* and in it Sanford indicted North Carolina and the nation for their failure to "protect the greatest of America's assets, her people, all of them." The consequences of that neglect were most apparent in the fate of poor children. "Like silt in a great river washing out to form a useless marshland," Sanford declared, their "potential for . . . development" was being "swept away in wasted lives." Only education could stop that erosion. In Sanford's view, it was *the* "vital tool for the creation of new jobs, for the development of a more substantial and diversified economic structure, for the elimination of the causes of poverty, the easing of prejudices and racial discrimination, the fulfillment of individual aspirations, and the cultivation of all human capacities."[4]

By late 1962, Sanford was juggling the policy implications of these many notions of education's benefits. During the summer, he had brought John Ehle into the governor's office as his ideas man and coordinator of "good works." Ehle was an Asheville native, a novelist and professor of communications at the University of North Carolina. Sanford left his first meeting with Ehle "considerably impressed" and later used funds from the Smith Richardson Foundation in Greensboro to buy a year of the professor's time away from teaching and writing. Ehle's great strength was that he had limited ties to government bureaucracies and party politics; he was open to new ideas and largely unconcerned with the political fallout from unorthodox means of getting things done. Together, the two men began working on a host of projects, ranging from a state film board to an arts conservatory, a summer academic camp for schoolchildren, and studies of social and economic development in poor rural communities. Sanford recalled that he and Ehle soon had "numerous ideas, concepts, doubts, and approaches floating around the Capitol. Now we needed precipitation to get them down to earth."[5]

That process began when Ehle encouraged Sanford to look to private foundations rather than the state legislature to finance his most ambitious and unconventional ideas. The advice struck a cord with the governor. Sanford's educational hero, Charles Brantley Aycock, had done the same when he partnered with the Rockefeller-financed General and Southern Education Boards to promote a school-building campaign of staggering proportions: during the period 1902–10, the state erected on average more than one new schoolhouse a day.[6]

In November 1962, Ehle and Sanford followed the well-worn path of their turn-of-the-century predecessor. They traveled to New York, in this instance for a round of meetings with officials of the Carnegie Corporation and the Ford Foundation, two of the nation's wealthiest philanthropies. The staff at Carnegie did not quite know what to expect. As Ehle explained in his briefing for Sanford, they had "never had a governor come to call before" and were somewhat concerned that their guest might arrive "with motorcycle cops and a lot of aides." Sanford's charm and informality quickly put his hosts at ease. He established a warm rapport with the corporation's president, John Gardner, and in the months that followed, Carnegie provided seed money for Sanford's new Governor's School, a summer program designed for intellectually gifted students. Gardner, however, was not interested in proposals aimed at poverty, which did not fit the corporation's focus on education. More fertile conversations on that topic began that same afternoon in the offices of the Ford Foundation.[7]

Sanford had set the stage for his visit in a letter to Ford president Henry Heald. "We have a great many needs down here," the governor had begun. "Sometimes, sitting at this desk in this particular office, they seem to mount up to almost comical proportions, but we are going about them as best we can." He then listed a mishmash of initiatives that he hoped would "help take North Carolina into the mainstream of American life." Sanford noted first his concern for the economic and educational needs of the state's black citizens, which he proposed to address through a summer program for "the training of exceptional Negro students" and an employment bureau that would move those young people into rewarding jobs. Next, he jumped to the arts, describing for Heald his vision of a state conservatory and repertory theater. With a nod to the disjointed character of his shopping list, Sanford tried to summarize: "I have mentioned the plight of the Negro, and our hopes in the arts, and in between and around these two interests are many other concerns." Sanford was still searching for direction. Even so, his letter and November visit captured Heald's attention. Heald and Paul Ylvisaker, director of Ford's Division of Public Affairs, recognized at once the resonance between Sanford's catalog of needs and the foundation's own priorities.[8]

Henry Ford and his son, Edsel, established the Ford Foundation in 1936 with a cash gift of $25,000. Over the next fourteen years, additional gifts followed, and in that period the foundation gave away a total of $19 million. The grants went to the Detroit Symphony, the Henry Ford Hospital, and a variety of institutions devoted to the preservation of Americana, including Independence Hall in Philadelphia, the birthplaces of Noah Webster and the Wright brothers, and Thomas Edison's laboratory. This rather conventional approach to philanthropy began to change in a big way with Edsel's death in 1943 and Henry's passing in 1947. Ford Motor Company was America's largest privately owned firm, and the Ford family had always been secretive about its business practices and the extent of its wealth. That guardedness followed Henry to the grave. Lawyers arranged his estate so that 10 percent of Ford Motor stock passed to family heirs; the remaining 90 percent — plus responsibility for paying the $42 million that the family owed in inheritance taxes—went to the Ford Foundation. The arrangement protected the heirs from the need to sell stock in order to cover their tax liabilities and preserved the cloak of secrecy that shielded Ford Motor Company's financial affairs from public scrutiny. This windfall posed an immediate and daunting challenge for the Ford Foundation: what to do with "all that money"?[9]

In 1948, Henry Ford II appointed a study committee to answer that question. The committee was comprised of eight leading academics, including Thomas H. Carroll, incoming dean of the School of Business Administration at the University of North Carolina. Carroll and his colleagues traveled extensively across the country to consult with civic leaders and scholarly experts on the social, economic, and political challenges before America and the world. In those conversations, the study committee kept in mind a critique of philanthropy best articulated by Edwin R. Embree in a 1949 *Harper's* article titled "Timid Billions." Embree had been the director of the Julius Rosenwald Fund, which during the 1920s had invested much of the Sears executive's fortune in the construction of African American schools in the South. He drew on that experience to chastise American philanthropies for their lack of vision and focused purpose. Most made their gifts to "conventional" recipients — hospitals, universities, and welfare agencies. "Instead of pouring brains and money into frontal attacks on fresh problems," Embree complained, "they tend[ed] toward . . . 'scatteration' — that is the sprinkling of little grants over a multiplicity of causes and institutions." The study committee's final report addressed that critique head-on. It was short on specifics, emphasizing instead a five-point global program for the advancement of peace, the strengthening of democracy, the promotion of economic development, the improvement of education, and the study of "individual behavior and human relations." It was a blueprint for a "save-the-world foundation" guided by "big men with big ideas."[10]

By the mid-1950s, the Ford Foundation had the deep pockets to match that ambitious agenda. In 1956, the foundation sold one-fifth of its Ford Motor Company stock in a public offering. That sale brought in $643 million. Other sales followed, and Ford was soon giving away annually more than four times as much money as America's second-largest foundation, Rockefeller, and more than ten times as much as the third largest, the Carnegie Corporation. Its gifts accounted for roughly one-fourth of the total spending by all American foundations. That wealth and the influence it bought provoked suspicion, especially as the Ford Foundation involved itself in foreign affairs. Congressional committees held hearings on the foundation's activities on two occa-

Paul Ylvisaker, director of the Ford Foundation's Public Affairs Division. Photograph by William Simmons, courtesy of the Ford Foundation.

sions between 1952 and 1954 in which right-wing Republicans closely allied with Joseph McCarthy denounced Ford's peace initiatives as soft on communism.[11]

Despite the study committee's call for big thinking, many of the Ford Foundation's programs remained scattershot well into the late 1950s. That was particularly true of the work of its Public Affairs Division, which had responsibility for domestic initiatives. In 1955, then Ford vice president Dyke Brown, who had served as assistant director of the study committee, recruited Paul Ylvisaker to take charge of the division and energize its staff. Ylvisaker had grown up in Bethany, Minnesota, where his father was a minister and president of Bethany Lutheran College. He earned his bachelor's degree from Mankato State University, began graduate work at the University of Minnesota, and then completed a Ph.D. in political science at Harvard. When the call came from Brown, Ylvisaker was teaching at Swarthmore and serving as an aide to former Philadelphia mayor and now U.S. senator Joseph S. Clark Jr. A young man in his midthirties, Ylvisaker had just suffered a heart attack. He saw in the offer from Ford an opportunity to escape the pressure of balancing an academic career with politics. The challenges he faced at the foundation were nonetheless daunting. As Ylvisaker later remembered, the organization was balkanized and its grant making was often unimaginative. Public Affairs continued to direct the bulk of its awards to "community do-good [agencies] and academic research." In his first eighteen months, Ylvisaker resigned three times on account of frustration, but on each occasion was convinced to stay.[12]

By 1961, Ylvisaker had finally prevailed. The Public Affairs Division stopped funding multiple small grants, cut back on its support for academic research—which Ylvisaker believed was too often satisfied with talk in the place of action—and focused its resources on a new program that financed wide-ranging demonstration projects in five American cities: Boston, New Haven, Oakland, Philadelphia, and Washington, D.C. Known as the "Gray Areas" project, its title reflected the influence of the Chicago School of Sociology, whose founders in the 1920s and 1930s had described the processes of assimilation and upward mobility by which immigrant communities were incorporated into the American middle class. The gray areas themselves were residential rings that separated urban central business districts from outlying suburbs. In the late nineteenth and early twentieth centuries, those neighborhoods had been inhabited by families from eastern and southern Europe. Now, in the post–World War II period, they were home to a rapidly expanding population of native migrants, including large numbers of black and white southerners and new arrivals from the American territory of Puerto Rico (thus the characterization of the communities as gray).[13]

Ylvisaker and other students of the American city worried that for these populations old processes of upward mobility and middle-class assimilation no longer functioned. The new migrants were isolated physically by white flight to the suburbs and economically by their lack of the education and skills necessary for success in the modern workplace. In Ylvisaker's view, "19th-century notions of service and charity" were inadequate to correct that situation and to relieve the human suffering and the "wastage of manpower" that it produced. The Gray Areas initiative promised to substitute instead large-scale experiments in social engineering that approached poverty not as a matter of individual relief but as the challenge of synchronizing education, job training, and social services. Through its grants, Ford encouraged coordination among schools, welfare agencies, churches, and private philanthropies, all with an eye to making more efficient and effective the "adjustment of the citizenry of the Gray Area." The ultimate objective, Ylvisaker explained to Ford trustees, was "to show that urban growth and change can take place in a climate of hope, respect, and social stability."[14]

Ford was eager to take the Gray Areas approach to the small towns and rural communities of the South, where it could address problems of migration and social dislocation at their source. But foundation staff worried that the investment risk was prohibitively high in a region wracked by racial violence and in which most political leaders were determined to defend white supremacy at any cost. In that context, Sanford was the kind of ally that Ford had been seeking. He shared Ylvisaker's conviction that in successful campaigns for social improvement "ideas and perspectives—not money—are the scarcest commodity, and of all instruments of social action, the most powerful." Sanford was also a moderate who had disavowed racial demagoguery and demonstrated considerable skill in managing social change. Ylvisaker remembered that "when Terry came along to the foundation one day, boy, what a breath of fresh air he was. . . . When Heald and I took him to the elevator, when he pushed the button and let them descend, Heald turned to me and said, 'Have you still got your wallet?' That was a time when we were really happy to be took." Soon after his return to Raleigh, Sanford followed up with a letter to Heald in which he invited Ford staff to visit North Carolina. He also emphasized the point that he understood had most excited his New York hosts. "We have some very old problems, as you know," Sanford wrote, "and they need good thinking and new approaches. We have a climate here which permits new work now. I am not sure it encourages it—I am not sure the climate anywhere encourages new ideas and activities—but it permits it, so we are in a good position to get some things done."[15]

Even before the New York trip, Sanford and his aides had begun exploring what might be done with Ford Foundation funds. They turned first to the University of North Carolina's Institute of Government, where Sanford had served briefly as associate director after his graduation from law school. The institute had been established in 1931 to provide educational, advisory, and research support for state and local governments. Sanford's key contact there was George H. Esser Jr., a Virginia native and graduate of Harvard Law School. Esser had been the institute's point man on urban issues and municipal government since joining the faculty in 1948, and in that capacity he had gotten to know Paul Ylvisaker. He participated in a Ford-financed study of urban development in North Carolina's central Piedmont region and worked for the foundation as a site visitor for grants in half a dozen cities, mostly in the Midwest. Through those activities, Esser became familiar with Ford's shifting priorities, particularly its desire to move away from small grants and support for academic research toward large-scale demonstration projects such as Ylvisaker's Gray Areas initiative. In early November 1962, he drew on that knowledge to sketch a plan for what he described as a "North Carolina Foundation." He encouraged Ford to consider a grant of several million

George Esser at a North Carolina Fund staff retreat. Photograph by Billy E. Barnes, courtesy of the North Carolina Collection, Wilson Library, University of North Carolina at Chapel Hill, Billy Ebert Barnes Collection.

dollars, matched by funds from local philanthropies, that would be spent on the state's economic, social, and educational needs. Ford "would hardly be in a position to set up such a foundation in every state," Esser continued, but "some state must be in the vanguard when pilot projects are selected. North Carolina, it seems to me, has all those qualities desirable for a pilot project — a state in transition economically, committed to education, responsive to change, and seeking to lift itself by its bootstraps."[16]

In an effort to convince Ford of North Carolina's readiness to tackle the problem of poverty, Sanford's aides organized a whirlwind tour of the state for foundation officials from January 15 to January 18, 1963. The Ford delegation, led by Ylvisaker, began its visit in Burnsville, a small mountain town just north of Asheville, where they met with a group of businessmen, educators, and civic leaders from communities across western North Carolina. Conversation centered on the decline of the timber and mining industries, which for nearly a century had been mainstays of the region's economy, and on the plight of mountain farmers whose small holdings made it increasingly difficult for them to compete in the marketplace. The group also toured a number of particularly hard-hit communities, where scenes of deprivation overwhelmed Ford officials. "Rural poverty was an eye-opener," remembered Henry Saltzman, one of Ylvisaker's staffers. "I was familiar with the South in the sense of the Depression and all the Roosevelt programs. But seeing it firsthand was really impressive and depressive, and it was exciting to think that we were shaping an instrument that had a shot at making things better."[17]

At the end of their day in the mountains, the Ford entourage boarded two state-owned planes and flew to Greenville, a small town in the heart of the state's eastern tobacco belt. There, they learned about the mechanization of agriculture and the dramatic loss of population in eastern counties as families displaced by tractors and mechanical harvesters left in search of jobs and new economic opportunities. On the morning of the seventeenth, the delegation traveled to Raleigh for a meeting with representatives of major cities in the state's central Piedmont region. Those cities were being inundated by new arrivals from the countryside who often lacked the education and skills necessary for urban employment. The discussion that day focused primarily on what the state's public schools might do "to stop the cycle of cultural, educational poverty which handicaps many of our people." On the fourth and final day of their visit, Ylvisaker and the Ford team traveled to Chapel Hill, where they met with Esser and others at the university's Institute of Government to brainstorm ways that North Carolina and the foundation might collaborate to develop new approaches to alleviating poverty, in the South and as a model for other communities around the nation.[18]

DURING THE MONTHS THAT FOLLOWED, Sanford continued his conversations with Ford against a backdrop of deepening social crisis. The civil rights movement reached fever pitch during the spring of 1963. Demonstrators filled city streets by day and dominated evening newscasts; they gave notice of an urgent need for action to redress racial grievances. At the same time, loudening calls for justice provoked white anger that constrained political options, particularly at the state level. Under those circumstances, Sanford and his aides placed ever greater stock in their emerging alliance with private philanthropy. By summer, they came to realize that the promise of such collaboration stretched far beyond simple augmentation of existing government services. It had even greater value as an alternative to conventional politics. Sanford recognized in the relationship with Ford a means of "slipp[ing] around" his adversaries and advancing a social agenda that otherwise would have been beyond his political reach.[19]

An incident in late January revealed how flammable the situation had become and how important leadership would be in keeping the state from exploding. A group of four hundred supporters of the North Carolina Defenders of States' Rights converged on the Caswell County courthouse to proclaim their opposition to school desegregation. A century earlier, Klansmen had gathered at the same spot, where they murdered state senator John "Chicken" Stevens, a local white leader of the biracial Republican Party. Speakers at the 1963 rally drew a connection between the two eras when they denounced Sanford as "a carpet bagger" (an odd label, given the fact that he was a North Carolina native) and characterized his liberal views on race as a thinly veiled plan to "make [black] bedfellows for our sons and daughters." Once more, the time had come to fight for "the preservation of the white race," they exclaimed. "Unless we take a firm stand and use the word 'never,' and that's what they're using in Alabama and Mississippi, we're not going to lick this thing." Such incendiary rhetoric alarmed Sanford, who understood from experience that only the slimmest of electoral margins had kept North Carolina from following the path of its Deep South neighbors. His challenge, he believed, was to preserve that fragile balance by managing black protest on one front and, on the other, warding off white fury.[20]

By 1963, more than a decade of civil rights protests had illuminated a central principle of social change: movement toward racial justice would occur only to the extent that activists created sufficient public disorder to expose the contradictions of American democracy. With this in mind, Martin Luther King Jr.'s Southern Christian Leadership Conference (SCLC) mobilized young people, trained them in nonviolent tactics of confrontation, and demanded once and for all the dismantling of Jim Crow. The SCLC's aim was to provoke a crisis that would force the Kennedy administration to back federal civil rights legislation. In the view of SCLC strategists, nothing less would counter the determination of southern whites to resist change.

Birmingham, Alabama, became the flashpoint in the SCLC's campaign. In April, King wrote his now-famous "Letter from Birmingham Jail," in which he sought to educate liberal white churchmen about the moral purpose of civil disobedience. "Nonviolent direct action seeks to create such a crisis and establish such creative tension that a community that has constantly refused to negotiate is forced to confront the issue," King explained. "Just as Socrates felt that it was necessary to create a tension in the mind so that individuals could rise from the bondage of myths and half-truths to the unfettered realm of creative analysis and objective appraisal, we must see the need of having nonviolent gadflies to create the kind of tension in society that will help men to rise from the dark depths of prejudice and racism to the majestic heights of understanding and brotherhood."[21] In the weeks that followed, Birmingham's black public school students took to the streets in protest and filled the local jails in what became known as the Children's Crusade, designed to overwhelm a judicial system dedicated to the defense of white privilege. White Birmingham's response was swift and brutal. In May, national television audiences watched in horror as Commissioner of Public Safety Eugene "Bull" Connor ordered his men to unleash attack dogs on demonstrators and to blast marchers with fire hoses so powerful that they peeled the bark off of trees. Four months later, a Klan bombing took the lives of four young girls attending Sunday school at the city's Sixteenth Street Baptist Church.

In North Carolina, from the industrial cities of the Piedmont to the small towns of the agricultural east, local folk joined seasoned student protesters in marches and sit-ins that became part of a regionwide uprising. Some of the most intense confrontations took place in Greensboro and Raleigh. Throughout much of May and into early June, student body president Jesse Jackson and his North Carolina A&T classmates, along with women from Bennett College, led nightly demonstrations outside Greensboro's downtown restaurants and movie theaters. The marches attracted hundreds, sometimes thousands, of participants. The young people were boisterous and insistent. They took possession of the city's central square, blocked traffic, and sang freedom songs outside the offices of Greensboro's banks and insurance companies. Downtown merchants felt the consequences in their tills. The presence of such large black gatherings in the city center frightened white customers and encouraged many of them to do their shopping elsewhere. Jesse Jackson made it clear that there would be no relief until white Greensboro conceded to black demands. "No doubt about it," he exclaimed, "we're not going to stop. We'll be there tomorrow and tomorrow and tomorrow."[22]

Protesters in Raleigh squared off with the state's power brokers as well as local business owners. Students from the city's black colleges, Shaw University and St. Augustine's, staged "suitcase sit-ins" at the Sir Walter Raleigh Hotel, a favorite lodging place for out-of-town legislators, and picketed outside the nearby S&W Cafeteria, a segregated establishment where many of the lawmakers dined. The demonstrators, complained Secretary of State Thad Eure, were "the motliest Negro group you ever saw." Equally disturbing to Eure and his colleagues was the presence of white students and faculty from North Carolina State University and nearby Chapel Hill. They represented the interracialism that white supremacists had sought to silence since the late nineteenth century; they threatened to give the civil rights struggle a measure of credibility that opponents could more easily deny an all-black movement; and, above all else, they seemed to confirm the role of left-wing faculty and Chapel Hill liberalism in fomenting social unrest. "If I hadn't already signed the university appropriations bill," snarled state senator Clarence Stone, "I'd be holding back my pen."[23]

The young activists in Raleigh and Greensboro further antagonized public officials by adopting tactics that the SCLC had used so effectively in Birmingham: they provoked mass arrests and filled the jails. At the height of the Greensboro marches, police held more than twelve hundred people in custody, and in Raleigh, officials packed young women thirty at a time into cells designed to hold no more than six. Such circumstances placed all involved—protesters and police alike—under severe physical and emotional strain. There was increasing danger that events might spiral out of control. Governor Sanford relieved the tension in Greensboro by cleverly outmaneuvering the demonstrators. He prevailed upon local authorities to release the students and send them back to their campuses. It was, said Congress on Racial Equality (CORE) director James Farmer, "the first and only jail lock-out in the movement." Sanford saw his action as "just a good bit of strategy." It took the pressure off of local officials and business leaders but also acknowledged, at least implicitly, that the demonstrators had a valid claim against the injustices of Jim Crow.[24]

On May 10, a group of students who had been freed from the Raleigh jail under similar circumstances marched across town to the governor's mansion. They were unwilling to go home without being heard. Sanford was hosting a black-tie fundraiser for the North Carolina Symphony. While his guests waited for a star from the Metropolitan Opera to perform, the young people on the lawn began singing gospel hymns and freedom songs. Sanford instructed his Highway Patrol bodyguard to stay behind as he stepped outside to speak to the crowd. After several tense minutes in which the students booed and shouted insults at the governor, he attempted to defuse the situation. "I'll be glad to talk to you about any of your problems," he assured the young people, "any of your grievances, any of your hopes." Black businessman and Raleigh city councilman John Winters, who had often advised Sanford on race matters, was with the protesters. He recalled that they were not satisfied with the governor's response, but at the same time felt grudging respect for the fact that he had offered to hear their demands. "That in itself," Winters said, "was a memorable thing. A southern governor—who had [state troopers] on the premises that he could call and say, Get rid of these students because they are trespassing—took a different tact. He talked with them."[25]

Sanford's efforts to mollify the protesters neither diminished their insistence on change nor held back a rising tide of white anger. That hostility reached a fever pitch in mid-June, after President Kennedy nationalized the

Alabama National Guard and forced Governor George Wallace to step aside as two black students, Vivian Malone and James Hood, registered for classes at the state university. On the evening of that confrontation, Kennedy addressed the nation with a call for racial justice. He echoed sentiments that Governor Sanford had expressed six months earlier in his second-emancipation speech in Chapel Hill:

> One hundred years of delay have passed since President Lincoln freed the slaves, yet their heirs, their grandsons, are not fully free. They are not yet freed from the bonds of injustice. They are not yet freed from social and economic oppression. And this Nation, for all its hopes and all its boasts, will not be fully free until all its citizens are free.
>
> We preach freedom around the world, and we mean it, and we cherish our freedom here at home, but are we to say to the world, and much more importantly, to each other that this is the land of the free except for the Negroes; that we have no second-class citizens except Negroes; that we have no class or caste system, no ghettoes, no master race except with respect to Negroes?
>
> Now the time has come for this Nation to fulfill its promise. The events in Birmingham and elsewhere have so increased the cries for equality that no city or State or legislative body can prudently choose to ignore them.

The president closed by announcing that he would ask Congress for new civil rights legislation to ensure "all Americans the right to be served in facilities which are open to the public—hotels, restaurants, theaters, retail stores, and similar establishments." Unless Congress acted, he warned, black Americans' "only remedy" would be "in the street." On June 12, the day after Kennedy's speech, a Klansman in Jackson, Mississippi, answered his call to conscience by assassinating Medgar Evers, a field secretary for the National Association for the Advancement of Colored People (NAACP).[26]

The week's events unsettled Hargrove "Skipper" Bowles, a Greensboro native who served in Sanford's cabinet as secretary of the state Department of Commerce and Development. He wrote to the governor on June 13, warning that the situation in Greensboro and across the state was "worsening by the hour. People who were [once] sympathetic with the Negro . . . are now very outspoken in their disgust for the entire race, plus the Kennedys and Governor Sanford. . . . The phrases you hear most now are: arrogant—too demanding—pressure from Washington and the damned Kennedys and their stooge, Sanford—let's put them in their place—filthy, ignorant, irresponsible—they've gone too far. From all sides we hear, 'save the white race.'"[27]

On June 18, as protests continued unabated, Sanford appeared on the state's public television network in an attempt to redirect a "situation [about] to degenerate to the point of mob against mob, citizen against citizen, force against force." He opened by affirming the legitimacy of protesters' demands. "The Negro citizen by his demonstrations has delivered the message that he is not content," Sanford said, "that he has a burning desire to break down the barriers which prevent his normal passage and patronage in places open to the public, that he has a determined discontent with a situation which denies him many of the opportunities, freedoms of choice, and privileges which are afforded as a matter of course to other citizens. Anyone who hasn't received this message doesn't understand human nature." "But," the governor added in rebuke of civil rights activists, "we have had sufficient demonstrations." Further agitation would only "breed disorder, endanger lives, establish animosity, and serve no good purpose." "I will take whatever steps are necessary to preserve the peace," he warned. Sanford demanded that he be allowed time to work the issues politically: "It is necessary that all mass demonstrations stop and deliberations start." To that end, he announced his intention to convene a meeting of "protest leaders from around the State." "This is the positive and constructive way for reaching a solution for problems," Sanford told his viewers. "It is imperative that we try it."[28]

On June 25, 150 civil rights leaders gathered in the old house chamber of the state capitol building. They included CORE activist Floyd McKissick; Jesse Jackson, leader of the student demonstrations in Greensboro; Golden Frinks, SCLC secretary and organizer in eastern North Carolina; and state NAACP president Kelly Alexander of Charlotte. Sanford joined the group in the morning for opening remarks. Once again, he acknowledged their grievances. "The demonstrations have shown just how unhappy and discontent you are," Sanford conceded. "How anxious you are to remove, and remove right now, the indignities and injustices which have been visited upon your parents and their parents. . . . Your enemy and mine is a system bequeathed us by a cotton economy, kindled by stubbornness, intolerance, hot-headedness, north and south, exploding into war and leaving to our [generation] the ashes of vengeance, retribution and poverty." But, as in his television address, Sanford insisted that the time for demonstrations was over. Protests "have been followed by progress for you," he lectured the civil rights leaders, "but you would be making a mistake to assume that the demonstrations alone . . . brought you progress. The demonstrations brought the message, and the message, in its truth and fullness, stirred the action which brought you progress. This may be a subtle distinction, but it is an important distinction, and it has great meaning for your future." Arguing that further change would come not in the streets but in quieter negotiations with whites of goodwill, Sanford urged his audience to defer to his Good Neighbor Council, formed several months earlier to promote equal employment opportunities, and the new Mayors' Co-operating Committee, through which local communities would identify solutions to their particular civil rights challenges.[29]

Despite the governor's assurances, neither of those ad hoc committees delivered on the promise of change. They functioned more as forums for white pronouncements of good intentions than as instruments of decisive action. Sanford's civil rights adversaries had predicted as much. At the end of the June 25 meeting, Floyd McKissick expressed their dissatisfaction. "We fear the governor misunderstands the situation," he told his compatriots. "It is utterly necessary that the people see the point of the demonstrations, not just the governor. And every indication is that the majority of the white people in North Carolina have not begun to grasp [that] point." John Brooks, a representative of the NAACP, agreed. Sanford's speech amounted to little more than an attempt at "brainwashing." The way forward was not quiet diplomacy but for the assembled organizers to "go home and plan bigger and better demonstrations."[30]

Sanford had asked civil rights activists to put their faith in the prestige of his office and his capacity for statesmanship. But in fact, he was operating from a position of rapidly diminishing political clout. By early 1962, statewide polls revealed that 60 percent of voters disapproved of his job performance. Many resented the food tax that underwrote Sanford's program of educational reform; others were uneasy with his stance on civil rights. Those disgruntled voters rejected a $61 million state bond referendum for schools, prisons, and hospitals in November 1961. A year later, Republicans increased their representation in the state legislature from seventeen to twenty-five seats, the party's largest gain since 1928, when North Carolina had lined up behind Herbert Hoover in opposition to the Democrat's Catholic presidential candidate, Al Smith. The most startling upset came in Greensboro and surrounding Guilford County, where voters rejected the entire slate of Democratic candidates for the state legislature and local county offices. Joe Hunt, former speaker of the house and a candidate for the senate, read the vote as a "protest . . . against [Sanford's] administration."[31]

Despite those setbacks, early impressions from the 1963 legislative session seemed auspicious. Lawmakers began the term by celebrating the opening of a new legislative building designed in modernist style by nationally acclaimed architect Edward Durell Stone. The building spoke to the state's progressive aspirations, as did one of the legislature's most significant actions: repeal of the last of North Carolina's Jim Crow laws. But more reactionary undercurrents also coursed through the new statehouse. Angry lawmakers tried but failed to eliminate appropriations for the University of North Carolina's public television network when they learned that one of its employees had been a regular participant in civil rights demonstrations. The legislature approved without debate measures increasing the penalties for trespassing and contempt of court. No discussion had been necessary, one lawmaker observed, because the laws' purpose was obvious. Conservative House and Senate leaders also proposed a resolution calling on Congress to establish a new "Court of the Union" to review rulings by the U.S. Supreme Court. Then, on June 25—the last day of the session and as Sanford's civil rights conference was meeting in the old capitol—lawmakers blindsided the governor with a speaker ban law, which threatened to hold the University of North Carolina hostage to the defense of white supremacy.[32]

The speaker ban was the handiwork of Secretary of State Thad Eure and a small group of influential lawmakers who had heard enough from campus dissenters. Just days before the ban's passage, Eure had telegraphed his counterpart in Ohio to request a copy of similar legislation under consideration in that state. He had learned of the measure from Jesse Helms, general manager of WRAL-TV in Raleigh, who praised Ohio lawmakers in one of his daily editorials at the end of the evening news. Their good judgment and fortitude, Helms suggested, provided "a lesson for the rest of us who have been too timid, or too disinterested, or both, to take a stand." Legislative leaders in North Carolina rushed their version of a speaker ban to approval within an hour of its introduction in the state house of representatives. Along the way, they paid little heed to the rules of debate. On the final vote in the senate, President Pro Tem Clarence Long, known for his poor eyesight, removed his glasses as he called for a show of hands. Seeing no opposition, he gaveled the bill into law. The ban prohibited state-supported universities and colleges from hosting speakers who were members of the Communist Party, who had advocated overthrow of either the federal or state constitution, or who had ever invoked the Fifth Amendment. Its broader purpose was to stifle students and faculty—particularly those at white campuses in Chapel Hill, Raleigh, and Greensboro—who in alarming numbers were joining the call for racial justice. As one state representative acknowledged to a Raleigh newspaper, "The Speaker Ban Law was originally passed more to curb civil rights dem-

CORE activists rally outside the Chapel Hill post office.
Courtesy of Jim Wallace, Falls Church, Virginia.

onstrations than to stop Communist speakers on state campuses." Sanford, denied the veto by the state constitution, was powerless to block the legislation.[33]

Things only got worse for the governor in the months that followed. During the winter of 1963–64, CORE leaders James Farmer and Floyd McKissick targeted Chapel Hill for an intensified sit-in movement aimed at convincing local officials to outlaw racial discrimination in all public establishments. In August, more than two hundred thousand Americans, black and white, had gathered for the March on Washington, where they pressed a national civil rights agenda. CORE was now eager for a victory that might break the white South's resistance to open accommodations and dislodge President Kennedy's civil rights bill from a deadlocked Congress. Chapel Hill seemed to be the opportune place to strike, and one where CORE expected to meet minimal resistance. Black high school students had already built a strong foundation with protests stretching back to 1959, and the University of North Carolina in Chapel Hill had a long-standing reputation as a liberal oasis. McKissick had special reason to think that Chapel Hill might lead the South as an "open city." In 1951, when a federal court ordered that he and two other black students be admitted to the university's School of Law, campus officials did not resist, and thus the University of North Carolina became the South's first public institution of higher education to desegregate.[34]

Chapel Hill's black community embraced the CORE initiative. Responding to the oft-repeated claim that civil rights protests were the work of outside agitators, they publicly underscored the local roots of their discontent. "We Chapel Hill Negro citizens are not pawns in the hands of the professional civil rights movement," wrote Mrs. W. P. Dolliver in a letter to the *Chapel Hill Weekly*. "This is OUR fight; this is OUR hurt; and this is OUR town." As Mc-Kissick and Farmer sought to ratchet up the demonstrations in Chapel Hill, they also turned to a small but supportive cast of university activists. Chief among these were Pat Cusick and John Dunne, white students at the University of North Carolina, and Quinton Baker from Durham's North Carolina College, the state's leading publicly funded black campus. Cusick was a native of Gadsden, Alabama; his great-grandfather had been one of the state's wealthiest slaveholders and a founder of the Alabama Klan. Baker grew up in Greenville, North Carolina, and was president of the state's youth chapter of the NAACP. Dunne had been lured to Chapel Hill from Ohio by one of the university's prestigious John Motley Morehead Scholarships, which he renounced soon after his arrival because of its namesake's segregationist views. During the spring of 1963, Dunne traveled to Birmingham with a group of student journalists. He stayed on to join the demonstrations and spent time in jail with SCLC activists. Dunne drew on that experience to explain CORE's decision to concentrate on Chapel Hill. "Chapel Hill, as a symbol of the enlightened South, was different from and perhaps more important than Birmingham," he said. "If a dozen pickets went out on the streets in Birmingham, there was a riot and forty arrests and all sorts of angry, hateful confusion . . . [but] that would not be the way in Chapel Hill. . . . Chapel Hill [had the capacity] to move . . . forward and to show other towns the way." CORE director James Farmer agreed. "Chapel Hill," he said, "is a key to the South and the nation."[35]

Dunne and others soon learned how misplaced their faith in Chapel Hill liberalism had been. Many whites lived up to the town's reputation and endorsed CORE's demands. But a number of leading business owners and a majority on the town council opposed the idea of a local civil rights ordinance on grounds that it would violate private property rights and the state constitution. Their response to the protests quickly turned nasty. One businessman used a mop to douse demonstrators outside his store with a mixture of

Protesters point accusingly at one of Chapel Hill's segregated businesses.
Courtesy of Jim Wallace, Falls Church, Virginia.

bleach and ammonia; in another instance, a restaurant owner hiked her skirt and urinated on students demanding that she serve black customers. The protests ground on from December until mid-April, when the local county attorney and superior court judge Raymond Mallard used the power of the law to quash dissent. Two hundred and seventeen demonstrators, mostly students, were brought to trial on nearly fifteen hundred indictments. Mallard denounced them in open court as dupes who were being "used by an international conspiracy that [was] threatening to destroy America." He lectured them about their responsibilities as loyal and law-abiding citizens, and then for most let their charges be dropped. The remaining dozen whom he considered to be ringleaders received either active jail time or an unusual punishment Mallard called "one of my special types of sentences." The latter was a suspended conviction that the court, at its discretion, could activate if, at any time during the next two to five years, the young activists took part in "any demonstrations for any cause on any public street, highway, or sidewalk." Student editors of the campus newspaper denounced the judge's rulings as "Mississippi Law." For Sanford aide John Ehle, the entire affair brought to mind an earlier observation by philosophy professor and Pulitzer Prize–winning playwright Paul Green. "The university [at Chapel Hill]," Green had said, was often "like a lighthouse which throws a beam out to the far horizons of the South, yet [remains] dark at its own base." Despite months of unrelenting protest, Chapel Hill gained only one newly desegregated business — a gas station that surrendered its Jim Crow toilets.[36]

For Sanford, the confrontation in Chapel Hill could not have been more poorly timed. In the spring of 1964 he was struggling to keep his agenda alive within the Democratic Party by orchestrating the election of his chosen successor, Greensboro native L. Richardson Preyer. Like Sanford, Preyer was a decorated World War II veteran who returned from service with his mind set upon moving North Carolina into the national mainstream. The two men, however, came from very different social backgrounds. Preyer was the grandson of Lunsford Richardson, inventor of the Vicks VapoRub cold remedy and founder of the Vick Chemical Company. His uncle, H. Smith Richardson, ran the firm through the early 1970s. Preyer attended Woodberry Forest, an elite boarding school in Virginia, and went on to Princeton and Harvard Law. He worked briefly in private practice in Greensboro before being appointed a city magistrate in 1953 and then a judge on the North Carolina Superior Court. In 1961, Sanford encouraged President Kennedy to name Preyer to the United States District Court for the Middle District of North Carolina, a post that Preyer resigned after two years in order to run for governor.[37]

Preyer's chief opponents in the 1964 Democratic primary were I. Beverly Lake, whom Sanford had narrowly defeated in 1960, and Dan K. Moore, also from the conservative wing of the party. Moore, a native of Asheville, earned his law degree at the University of North Carolina and served during the 1950s as a judge on the North Carolina Superior Court. At the time of his candidacy, he was corporate counsel for the Carolinas division of Champion Papers, Inc., in the western part of the state. From the outset, the election shaped up as a referendum on Sanford's handling of black protest. John H. Jones, Grand Dragon of the North Carolina Klan, made that clear at a rally of more than seven hundred supporters who gathered on the outskirts of Chapel Hill as the town's civil rights protesters awaited trial. "Federal judges belong on the bench and not in the Statehouse," he exclaimed. "[And] thank God that governors spend only four years in office because four years of Terry Sanford is too much." Lake and Moore also linked Preyer to Sanford's conciliatory response to civil rights protests, as did news commentator Jesse Helms. Shortly before election day, Moore told a cheering white audience in Wilmington that "violence or chaos by a minority" should be "dealt with by the rule of law, not by fuzzy-minded liberals who have confused civil rights with anarchy."[38]

The vote on May 30 came just weeks after Judge Mallard handed down the last of his sentences in Chapel Hill. Preyer won only 37 percent of the votes, which entitled second-place finisher Dan Moore to call for a runoff. Moore initially had tried to carve out a middle ground for himself between Lake and Preyer, but in the second primary he turned to the right in order to gain Lake's endorsement and make the most of anti-Sanford sentiment. Shortly before the second primary in June, Lake went on WRAL-TV in Raleigh, the station operated by his law partner A. J. Fletcher and general manager Jesse Helms, to share his views on the remaining candidates' qualifications for office. Then, on June 26, the day before the election, he published his remarks in a paid newspaper advertisement. Lake told the 217,000 voters who had cast their first ballot for him that they now had the awesome responsibility of deciding North Carolina's future. Preyer, he conceded, was an "honorable man," but that was not enough. Voters also needed to look behind the candidate to the puppet masters who would pull the strings in his administration. There they would discover Governor Sanford and his advisers; Kelly Alexander, head of the state NAACP; and a small but threatening bloc of black voters who were "captive pawns in the hands of Bobby Kennedy and Martin Luther King." "Last and least," Lake added with sarcasm, "there [was] that small but noisy clique of professional Liberals at Chapel Hill who are a red and festering sore upon the body of a great university." If voters wanted "the government of North Carolina to be administered for four more years by one sympathetic to the Sanford administration," then Preyer was their man. Invoking memory of the last great challenge to white supremacy in North Carolina, Lake urged a wiser choice. "Our next Governor will direct our State government through the most critically dangerous four years since 1900," he said. "Because that is true, I asked you to vote for me in the First Primary and you did. Because that is still true, I am going to vote now for Judge Moore and I hope you will do the same."[39]

The second primary in 1964 bore striking resemblance to the match between Frank Graham and Willis Smith in 1950 and Sanford's own battle with Lake in 1960. But in this instance Sanford was not in control, and even he had to concede that it was much too late to stuff the genie of race back into the bottle. He tried to shelter Preyer from Lake's attacks by working quietly behind the scenes. He refused to comment on the election in his meetings with reporters and waited until the day before the second primary vote to offer Preyer his public endorsement. But that gave cold comfort to the broad cross-section of white North Carolinians who, in the words of one Lake supporter, saw the contest as "a race between the white people and the colored people." On election day, 62 percent of voters cast their ballots for Moore and handed Preyer and Sanford a resounding defeat. Preyer lost all but seven of the state's one hundred counties. Toward the end of his first year in office, Governor Moore paid his political debt to Lake. He appointed Sanford's old nemesis to a seat on the North Carolina Supreme Court. That, for Sanford, was perhaps the cruelest turn of all.[40]

PREYER'S DEFEAT WAS THE LAST engagement in a battle of attrition that characterized the second half of Sanford's term in office. Despite early successes, the governor lacked the political capital to achieve the ambitious goals that he had set for himself and the state. From early 1963 onward, he was checked at every turn by a conservative legislature and a skittish white electorate that had no stomach for even moderate racial advances or the kinds of public investments necessary to realize a "New Day." By all rights, the governor should have finished his term as a lame duck. But he and his young lieutenants refused to surrender the battlefield. They fought on, rallied new allies, mustered new resources, and opened a second front outside of conventional politics. In doing so, they demonstrated the same dogged determination that Sanford had exhibited in his earlier battle against I. Beverly Lake. At the end of a particularly long and grueling day during that campaign, Sanford had opened a note from a friend who asked why he was willing to suffer Lake's attacks and "stay in this business." Sanford scrawled his answer: "To keep the S.O.B.s out."[41]

In early 1963, as Sanford's team continued their efforts to convince the Ford Foundation that North Carolina was the right place to launch a new antipoverty initiative, they turned for assistance not to lawmakers in Raleigh but to wealthy white philanthropists in Winston-Salem and black power brokers in Durham. Sanford had limited options for securing the private matching funds that would satisfy Ford. North Carolina was home to only a handful of charitable foundations. The wealthiest was the Duke Endowment, established in 1924 by James B. Duke, architect of his family's vast fortune in tobacco, textiles, and electric power. But under the terms of its indenture, the endowment was restricted to investments in higher education, health care, and the rural ministry of the United Methodist Church. Sanford therefore turned to Winston-Salem and two smaller foundations spawned from the wealth of tobacco magnate Richard Joshua (R. J.) Reynolds. The Z. Smith Reynolds Foundation had been chartered in 1936 (the same year as the Ford Foundation) after the death of R. J.'s second son, Zachary. The foundation's sole purpose was to undertake "charitable works" in North Carolina. It made its first grant in 1937 to support efforts by the North Carolina State Board of Health to combat venereal disease. The second Reynolds charity, the Mary Reynolds Babcock Foundation, was established in 1953 after the death of R. J.'s elder daughter. It had a broad mandate to support the "betterment of mankind" and the furtherance of "the public welfare." By the early 1960s, both foundations were controlled by interlocking boards comprised primarily of Reynolds family members, including Charles (Charlie) H. Babcock, Mary Reynolds's husband; R. J. Reynolds Jr.; and Anne Reynolds Forsyth, Z. Smith's daughter from his first marriage.[42]

There was obvious irony in turning to the Reynolds heirs to underwrite an assault on poverty. The family fortune, after all, had been derived from the system of racial capitalism that impoverished tens of thousands of African Americans who labored in the various branches of the tobacco industry, including both the sharecroppers who grew the golden leaf and the factory hands who fashioned it into chewing plugs and cigarettes. Executives at the R. J. Reynolds Tobacco Company were among the state's most fervent opponents of labor unions, as witnessed in the late 1940s by their successful use of race-baiting and Cold War anticommunism to quash workers' effort to organize. But by the 1960s, the Reynolds wealth had passed into the hands of a second generation of family members who were far removed from the political and economic struggles of the workplace. They played no role in the day-to-day management of Reynolds Tobacco. They took their cues instead from the culture of mid-twentieth-century American philanthropy, which put its faith in social engineering and the use of private wealth to advance the common welfare. That was particularly true of Charlie Babcock, who came to North Carolina from Indiana and had no ties to the state's fraught history, and R. J. Reynolds Jr., who as mayor of Winston-Salem advocated the construction of public housing for the city's poor residents, black and white. Reynolds was also an ardent supporter of Franklin Roosevelt, and during the 1940 campaign had bankrolled the president's fireside chats.[43]

Sanford courted the Reynolds foundations for several months. Most of the negotiations were carried on face-to-face, primarily with Charlie Babcock, who was eager to have Ford invest in North Carolina. By early May, those talks had produced the desired result. Sanford wrote to Babcock thanking him for his assistance: "I have felt that you have recognized from the start the importance of [the problems of poverty] and that there has been a healthy agreement about how we might best move [forward]." Sanford sent a similar letter to R. J. Jr. and expressed to both men his hope that the Mary Reynolds Babcock and Z. Smith Reynolds Foundations would "be as generous as possible." He suggested a combined gift of $2.5 million over five years.[44]

Sanford's other key ally in securing a partnership with Ford was John H. Wheeler of Durham, a logical choice, even if a surprising one to most white North Carolinians. Wheeler was a leader in the large black community that had grown up around the city's tobacco industry. A native of Vance County, North Carolina, he spent his childhood in Atlanta and was educated at Morehouse College. In 1929, with an honors degree in hand, he moved to Durham. The city was home to the North Carolina Mutual Life Insurance Company, the largest black-owned business in the nation, and the Mechanics and Farmers Bank, where Wheeler took his first job as a cashier. Studying at night, he earned a law degree from North Carolina College, and by 1952 he had risen through the ranks to become the bank's president. During the late 1950s and early 1960s, he played the role of civil rights protagonist. As chairman of the Durham Committee on Negro Affairs, he gave voice to black demands — often couched in strident terms that opened up room for more traditional black leaders to negotiate compromise. In 1960, Wheeler joined Thurgood Marshall and Floyd McKissick as co-counsel for the plaintiffs in a lawsuit that challenged the Durham school board's refusal to assign black students to white schools. Wheeler also served on the executive committee of the Southern Regional Council from 1950 to 1964, at which time he was elected president. The council was the South's oldest and most influential interracial civil rights organization, and it gave Wheeler access to the nation's white political establishment. In 1961, John F. Kennedy appointed him to the President's Committee on Equal Employment Opportunity. Wheeler developed a close relationship with the committee's chairman, Vice President Lyndon Johnson, and worked closely with him on a number of civil rights issues, most notably improved job opportunities for blacks.[45]

Wheeler had been an early confidante of Terry Sanford. Soon after the governor's inauguration, he sent a fifteen-page letter detailing the need to improve job opportunities for black North Carolinians. He urged Sanford to act for economic reasons — unemployed blacks were a drain on the economy — and for the sake of the Democratic Party. Wheeler reminded the governor that "a large number of present officeholders owe[d] their margin of election day victory" to the state's small but committed corps of black voters. That support, he insisted, deserved "recognition and representation beyond the point of mere praise and lip-service."[46]

The Durham banker was equally forthright in encouraging Sanford to deliver his Emancipation Day address in January 1963. John Ehle recalled that Wheeler was a masterful tactician. When Sanford circulated a draft of his speech at a breakfast meeting in the governor's mansion, Wheeler immediately objected that it was too moderate. The governor would do better, he advised, to "lean somewhat more heavily on the law" rather than "goodwill and persuasion." Others in the room, particularly a number of conservative white party leaders, disagreed, and a lengthy discussion of the wording of Sanford's remarks ensued. At that point, Ehle recognized the brilliance of Wheeler's intervention: "by attacking the statement . . . [he] had got the group past the point of debating whether a statement [of any sort] ought to be released."[47]

Sanford's initial consultations with Wheeler and other black leaders were undertaken in private and with an eye toward securing their endorsement of policy decisions made by whites. But by the summer of 1963, ongoing civil rights protests had so altered the political balance of power that the governor could not go forward without the backing of men such as Wheeler. That support was particularly important to officials at the Ford Foundation, who were concerned that Jim Crow not hobble their plans for new work in the South. In July 1963, Ford president Henry Heald and members of his staff made their last pre-grant visit to North Carolina. At the end of the day, they called on Wheeler and asked for his frank assessment of Sanford's plans for battling poverty. Paul Ylvisaker recalled the significance of that meeting. It was, he said, "the first time anybody from the foundation's top echelon had gone to a black man." George Esser later wrote that had Wheeler's answers "not been satisfactory," Ford would have withdrawn from negotiations with the governor and his staff. "Wheeler had to say, 'This looks like a good thing to me.'"[48]

That night, while dining at the governor's mansion, Heald assured Sanford that Ford would commit $7 million to a statewide antipoverty campaign. Two weeks later, on July 18, with additional commitments in hand from the Z. Smith Reynolds and Mary Reynolds Babcock Foundations, Sanford, Charlie Babcock, John Wheeler, and C. A. (Pete) McKnight, editor of the *Charlotte Observer*, incorporated the North Carolina Fund. As newspapers reported the following day, the Fund would operate as a "special non-governmental corporation" responsible for "launch[ing] a Statewide program against poverty and educational deficiencies." Its charge was to "find new and better ways to improve education, economic opportunities, living environment, and general welfare of the people." Charlie Babcock suggested the name as encouragement for the new organization to model itself after the Commonwealth Fund, a New York–based philanthropy that from its founding in 1919 had led the nation in improving the health and welfare of the disadvantaged.[49]

The establishment of the North Carolina Fund was a trademark maneuver for Sanford. When confronted by I. Beverly Lake in 1960, he had refused to

speak directly to the issue of race. He changed the subject, insisted that education was the state's most pressing challenge, and, in doing so, held on to
white middle-class support and kept hard-core segregationists at bay. Now,
when faced with his weakened influence as chief executive, he moved the
fight into a new arena. In partnership with private foundations, he created
outside of electoral politics a competing source of legitimacy, influence, and
financial leverage. His North Carolina Fund would be "independent [and]
not subject to . . . political control" at either the state or local level. That arrangement would maximize the organization's ability to "reach down . . . into
the local areas and impose new challenges on them." For a time, it would also
shield the Fund against opposition to Sanford's progressive agenda. Decades
later, Paul Ylvisaker still marveled at this skillful gamesmanship. "Here was a
governor who had used up his equity in a one-term situation with the legislature, who knew he couldn't get blacks into decision-making in the short
run," and who, rather than conceding ground to his opponents, embraced
"philanthropy . . . as an alternative route and an accelerating device." For
Ylvisaker and his senior colleagues at the Ford Foundation, that was the key
to Sanford's appeal. We "knew instinctively," Ylvisaker recalled, that he "was
smart enough politically to do it."[50]

IMMEDIATELY AFTER THE FUND'S FORMATION, its incorporators named
a board of directors. The list of appointees reflected Sanford's shrewd political judgment and provided, in varying measure, regional, racial, and political
balance. In addition to Sanford, Wheeler, and McKnight, the board included
the following:

> James A. Gray Jr., a member of one of Winston-Salem's wealthiest and
> most influential families. His uncle, Bowman Gray, had taken the helm
> of the R. J. Reynolds Tobacco Company after its founder's death in
> 1918, and his father, James A. Gray Sr., served as company president and
> chairman of its board of directors. From 1959 to 1963, the younger Gray
> had been the publisher of the Winston-Salem Journal.[51]
>
> Samuel E. Duncan Jr., president of Livingstone College, a private institu-
> tion in Salisbury established in 1879 by the African Methodist Episcopal
> Zion Church. Duncan received his B.A. from Livingstone and went
> on to earn an M.A. and a Ph.D. in education from Cornell Univer-
> sity. As president of his alma mater, he developed close ties to Charlie
> Babcock and the Z. Smith Reynolds Foundation, which in 1959 and
> 1960 contributed $100,000 toward the construction of new dormitories

at Livingstone. Compared to his counterparts at publicly funded black campuses, Duncan had much greater latitude to speak his mind.[52]

Thomas Pearsall, architect of the state's response to *Brown v. Board of Education*. Pearsall represented large landholders in eastern North Carolina and centrists within the Democratic Party. He would eventually distance himself from the Fund as its antipoverty projects began to encourage political organizing among black sharecroppers and laborers in his home town of Rocky Mount and in nearby communities.

Wallace C. Murchison, a Wilmington attorney, who knew George Esser from their time together at Harvard Law School and their work with the Episcopal Church. He had campaigned for Terry Sanford in 1960 and later for Richardson Preyer, his college classmate at Princeton. Murchison had a reputation as a racial moderate in a city with a horrific racial past.[53]

J. Gerald Cowan, a retired senior vice president of Wachovia, one of the state's leading banks, and a former director of the Charlotte branch of the Federal Reserve Bank of Richmond. Cowan lived in Asheville and represented western North Carolina. He had worked briefly for the Emergency Relief Administration, a New Deal agency, from 1933 to 1935, and in the late 1950s served on a Ford Foundation–sponsored study commission on social and economic development in Appalachia.[54]

Anne Reynolds Forsyth, daughter of Z. Smith Reynolds, and *A. Hollis Edens*, former president of Duke University and executive director of the Mary Reynolds Babcock Foundation. Together with Charlie Babcock, they watched over the interests of the Winston-Salem philanthropies whose financial backing played a critical role in bringing the Fund into being.

Rosa May Blakeney Parker, former governor Luther Hodges's sister-in-law, a retired high school principal, and an influential operative in the state Democratic Party. As a member of the board of trustees of the Consolidated University of North Carolina, she provided a link to the state's leading publicly funded white colleges, including her alma mater, the University of North Carolina at Greensboro (formerly Woman's College), North Carolina State University in Raleigh, and the flagship campus at Chapel Hill.[55]

Skipper Bowles, a member of Sanford's cabinet, and *W. Dallas Herring*, a member of the Pearsall Committee and chair of the State Board of Education from 1957 to 1977. During the late 1950s and early 1960s, Herring played an influential role in establishing North Carolina's system of

The North Carolina Fund's board of directors and Sanford advisers pose for a portrait in the governor's office, July 1963. Included are (standing left to right) W. Dallas Herring, James A. Gray Jr., John Ehle, George Esser, A. Hollis Edens, John H. Wheeler, C. A. (Pete) McKnight, Samuel E. Duncan Jr., Thomas Pearsall, Fund attorney Robinson O. Everett, (sitting left to right) Rosa May Blakeney Parker, Anne Reynolds Forsyth, Terry Sanford, and J. Gerald Cowan. Not shown are Skipper Bowles and Wallace C. Murchison. Courtesy of the North Carolina State Archives, Governor Terry Sanford Photograph Collection.

two-year community colleges. Despite opposition from Luther Hodges and others who disapproved of his populist approach, Herring succeeded in requiring that the new schools offer comprehensive curricula, so that students might add to their vocational training more traditional instruction in the liberal arts.[56]

By mutual consent, Sanford served as the board's chairman. That was a particularly audacious move for a sitting governor, who, as his official authority waned, positioned himself to exercise far-reaching influence over public policy well beyond his term in office.

In June, a month before the formal incorporation of the Fund, George Esser had agreed to take a leave of absence from his faculty post at the University of North Carolina so that he might serve as executive director of the new agency. His first task in his new position was to prepare a formal proposal to the Ford Foundation, which he completed within a matter of weeks. The document was remarkable for its analytic clarity and rhetorical force. "We sense," Esser declared, "that the Ford Foundation wants to do throughout the country what we want to do in North Carolina." To that end, his proposal invited Ford to anchor an "all-out assault on poverty," the first of its kind in the nation.[57]

Esser cataloged the challenges that progressives confronted as they sought to move North Carolina into the mainstream of America. The rapid mechanization of agriculture was driving tens of thousands of people off the land. Whether they arrived in the cities of the Piedmont or "pass[ed] on to New York and Detroit and Ohio," few were equipped "to accept the jobs that [were] available, that more and more require[d] technical skill rather than manual labor." North Carolina's public schools were ill prepared to address the needs of this displaced population. One of every four adults who applied for a driver's license in the state could not read the written test and needed to have an examiner administer it orally. On the other hand, the state could not hold onto those citizens it did educate. Out-migration was robbing North Carolina of "brains as well as youth." The problem was particularly pronounced in African American communities. Two-thirds of black students "who ever stud[ied] in high school" left North Carolina for employment elsewhere, and one-third of those with some measure of college education followed close behind in an effort to escape the limitations of a low-wage, Jim Crow economy.[58]

When set beside the magnitude of these difficulties, the response of public officials appeared to reflect a wholesale abdication of responsibility and disregard for the social good. Esser's critique was scathing: "We find no evidence that any one agency, public or private, is looking at the problems of these people in their totality. We find no evidence that our community service agencies, public or private, are seeking to find new approaches, practical and successful approaches, to the dilemma of the poor. As our society has become more affluent . . . it seems to have come to be accepted that the 'poor will always be with us.' But the human costs, and the social coasts, are great. We cannot look at the evidence of school dropouts, and substandard housing, and submarginal wage rates, and illiteracy and illegitimacy, without remembering that these have a relationship, a direct relationship to crime and juvenile delinquency, to increasing welfare rolls, to rising governmental costs, and low per capita income." Such complacency posed as great a social danger as poverty itself. "We salve our consciences with charity," Esser warned, "when we had best be supplying opportunity."[59]

Esser understood his friend Paul Ylvisaker's impatience for action and dis-appointment at the tendency within government and the academy to study rather than to do. He spoke directly to that concern by championing a prag-matic approach to reform. "We must be willing to experiment," he asserted, "not half-heartedly but boldly. We must . . . act today on what we already know rather than to spend more years in research that never seems to reach the marketplace." Esser also made clear just how daring the Fund's architects were willing to be in their efforts to sidestep a recalcitrant legislature and to build new alliances in their statewide attack on poverty. They had already in-vited onto an advisory committee the heads of every state agency that dealt with some aspect of the poverty issue, and they had opened an independent channel of communication with the U.S. Department of Health, Education, and Welfare (HEW). While most southern politicians eschewed any form of federal involvement in local affairs, the Fund's board was eager "to ex-pedite the role that departments of the Federal Government might play" in reshaping public policy at the state and local level. Esser reported that in June, at Governor Sanford's invitation, HEW had sent a delegation to review planning for the Fund and to make recommendations for ongoing collabo-ration with a variety of federal agencies. This was the first step in building a relationship that within a year's time would involve Fund leaders in drafting the Economic Opportunity Act of 1964, establishing the federal Office of Economic Opportunity (OEO), and launching President Lyndon Johnson's national war on poverty.[60]

The operational model that Esser sketched for the Ford Foundation fol-lowed closely the plan of action that he had begun to lay out for Sanford as early as November 1962. He imagined the North Carolina Fund as an inter-mediary organization responsible for re-granting monies supplied by Ford, North Carolina foundations, and—eventually—the federal OEO. The Fund would manage those resources as a pool of social venture capital, which was to be invested in proposals that percolated up from local communities. That idea, Paul Ylvisaker remembered, stirred up "a hornet's nest of opposition in the Ford Foundation partly because they said, 'this would be a classic abdica-tion of responsibility,' you know, you'd give to somebody else to give." With the Senate investigations of the mid-1950s fresh in their memories, some of Ylvisaker's colleagues worried that pursuing that course of action was cer-tain to embroil the philanthropy in political controversy. That concern later proved to have been prescient, but for the moment, Esser and Ylvisaker suc-cessfully defended their approach as the kind of fresh idea that was required to "spur and goad" public officials to action. At their meeting on September 26–27, the Ford Foundation's trustees awarded the North Carolina Fund $7 million to be spent over a period of five years. By prior arrangement, the Z. Smith Reynolds and Mary Reynolds Babcock Foundations in Winston-Salem had earlier committed gifts of $1,625,000 and $875,000, respectively, in order to satisfy Ford's requirement of substantial local investment.[61]

On September 30, Governor Sanford officially launched the North Carolina Fund at a news conference in Raleigh. In his prepared statement, the governor thanked John Ehle, George Esser, and the many others who had provided leadership in planning "the first massive statewide effort in our country to find ways to break the cycle of poverty and dependency." As he described the principles that would guide the Fund's work, Sanford revealed how his own thinking had developed over the past year. "I have come to believe that charity and relief are not the best answers to human suffering," he explained, "that the schools are not the answer so long as only a third or a half of our students finish [high] school, that the wealth of America is not the answer if many families have fifty-some cents a day per person for all expenses, that it is not enough to have here the most powerful nation in the world and then to admit that we are powerless to find ways to give our young people training and job opportunities." In the publicity surrounding the Ford Foundation's decision to invest in North Carolina, Sanford and his allies also made clear that race would figure centrally in their battle against poverty. The *Raleigh News and Observer*, for example, took note of estimates that "racial discrimination alone [cost] the South between $5,000,000,000 and $6,000,000,000 in income each year." The newspaper's editors acknowledged that the "problem of poverty, of course, is not confined to the Negro in the South. There are too many poor white people, too. But any realistic appraisal of the problem cannot overlook the fact that . . . Southern Negroes still have less than half the income of whites. And nothing should be clearer than that North Carolina and the South will not approach equality with other regions unless all the people now dragging down this State and region share in any new opportunities."[62]

The state press welcomed the Ford grant announcement. In the east, the *Goldsboro News-Argus* named Sanford its man of the year, and in Raleigh, the *News and Observer* compared the North Carolina Fund to President Kennedy's commitment to conquering the new frontier of outer space. "In [the Fund] are possibilities not equaled by any experiments designed to put a man on the moon," the editors crowed. "Here is the fantastic project to make men happy in the fulfillment of their powers and their hopes on the earth." The *Greensboro Daily News* said of the Fund: "Idealistic it may seem, but . . . in it are embodied Terry Sanford's high hopes for North Carolina. Critics have dubbed him a cold-blooded political leader. But surely this climactic program of the final years of his administration reflects above all else warm-heartedness and a compassion for the least of these." Such praise was gratifying, but perhaps none more so than the accolades offered by Durham attorney and former state legislator Reuben O. Everett, born in 1879, who compared the Fund to the turn-of-the-century public school campaign led by Charles Brantley Aycock. After attending a briefing on the North Carolina Fund, he shared his enthusiasm in a letter to George Esser: "The meeting reminded me of the days . . . when in the midst of ignorance and poverty . . . Aycock . . . inspired us with the determination to [build a] school house a day and to train teachers. . . . I think now I see signs of a renaissance under a new inspired leadership."[63]

In the month before formal approval and announcement of the Ford grant, Esser busied himself with setting up an office, hiring a staff, and preparing guidelines for a call for proposals to be issued to communities large and small across the state. Esser had hoped that the Fund might locate its offices in Chapel Hill, but Sanford and the directors decided otherwise. They wanted to avoid associating the agency with political turmoil on campus. They were also eager to avoid Raleigh, which would have put the Fund within easy reach of the state legislature. The board settled instead on nearby Durham, a choice that signaled John Wheeler's influence and the Fund's commitment to engage issues of race and civil rights. On August 26, Esser opened the Fund's headquarters on Parrish Street, in the heart of Durham's black business district. Esser's goal was for the Fund to operate "with a small staff and a broad purpose," thus keeping itself nimble and responsive to creative opportunities. To that end, he began the agency's work with only four additional employees: an assistant to the director, a director of research, and two office support staff.[64]

Esser hired as research director a young man named Michael P. Brooks, who was working on a Ph.D. in urban social policy in the University of North Carolina's Department of City and Regional Planning. Brooks had not heard of the North Carolina Fund, but he saw great opportunity when Esser asked, "How would you like to help me spend $9 million?" "George was hiring me to [evaluate] the kinds of programs that would occur . . . to see what kinds of things worked and what sorts of things did not work," he recalled, "and as a young [graduate student], that was very exciting, that was very heady, so I was delighted to join with it." Brooks's first assignments were to prepare a statistical profile of poverty in North Carolina and to help formulate guidelines

As the North Carolina Fund grew, it relocated its headquartres to a building
formerly occupied by a Durham automobile dealership. Photograph by Billy E.
Barnes, courtesy of the North Carolina Collection, Wilson Library, University
of North Carolina at Chapel Hill, Billy Ebert Barnes Collection.

for community action programs (CAPs) that would promote policy innova-
tion at the local level. "The whole Ford Foundation philosophy," he remembered, was "that the problems of poverty in the past had been dealt with in
too fragmented a fashion. . . . They also had the sense that there had to be
. . . creative ideas out there that could be brought into action if some funds
were available to enable these ideas to bear fruit." That, of course, had been
Governor Sanford's thinking as well. In simplest terms, the Fund conceived
of community action programs as a mechanism for "get[ting] the best minds
in [local] communities around the table and see[ing] what kinds of creative
ideas [they could] come up with to solve" the problems of poverty.[65]

In late November 1963, just after Thanksgiving, the Fund distributed across
the state seven thousand copies of a pamphlet titled *The North Carolina Fund:
Programs and Policies*, known in-house as the "Red Book" for the color of its
binding. The publication invited politicians, civic and religious leaders, and
other concerned citizens to propose pilot projects for addressing the needs
of the poor. As local groups shaped their applications for funding, they were
to keep three guiding principles in mind. First, they should focus on experi-

Michael Brooks. Photograph by Billy E. Barnes, courtesy of the North Carolina Collection, Wilson Library, University of North Carolina at Chapel Hill, Billy Ebert Barnes Collection.

mental efforts rather than enhancement of existing programs. In practice, this would require addressing the conditions of poverty — "inadequate education, low or nonexistent income, limited job opportunities, dilapidated and over-crowded housing, poor physical and mental health, an inclination towards delinquency and crime" — not in isolation but through comprehensive approaches that recognized that each was cause and effect of the other. Second, projects seeking Fund support should represent broad community involvement that included members of the "target group" — the poor themselves. "No program designed to help our people break out of the cycle of poverty . . . will be successful," the Red Book warned, "if it is designed and carried out alone by community agencies, civic leaders, and informed consultants. . . . If we are to have significant results, each community must seek to understand life as do those living under conditions of poverty, and plan its program to take these facts into consideration." Finally, an effective attack on poverty would require coordination among agencies and institutions that too often competed rather than collaborated with one another: "There is little chance for a successful project if, for example, the schools are unwilling to participate, or if the county commissioners show no interest or assurance of financial support, or if the public welfare department does not assist. . . . Traditional functional boundaries and approaches must be subordinated to the total community effort."[66]

The Red Book made clear that Fund officials were intent upon a departure from business as usual. They challenged the authority of established welfare agencies, public and private, and the effectiveness of the men and women who provided conventional services to the poor. Indeed, the Red Book declared flatly that "existing techniques are not getting the job done." That stance was certain to provoke wariness and suspicion—what one member of the Fund's board of directors described as "friction between the old breed and the new breed." Nevertheless, the Fund did not—it could not—begin with a clean slate. Particularly in this initial presentation, it remained bound in its own way by the life experiences of those who shaped it and the intellectual framework within which academics and public officials thought of poverty.[67]

The Red Book attributed poverty as much to the character of the poor as to structures of economic and social inequality. To be sure, North Carolina needed to continue to strengthen its economy, "provide more jobs with wages that can compete with those of the other states," improve public education, and pull down the barriers of racial discrimination. Governor Sanford had devoted his administration to such reform. But, the Red Book cautioned, "this effort alone [was] not sufficient." It would do little to benefit the thousands of young people who dropped out of school each year. Those students, the Fund explained, came from homes "where the level of education, as well as of income and of general living environment, ha[d] been low for generations." Escaping such circumstances required that children cast off the behaviors and attitudes of their parents. For that reason, the Fund sought to study and understand the "motivations of the poverty stricken," to replace their despair with hope, and, in so doing, "upgrade the people" of poverty so that they might participate in the promise of American prosperity.[68]

By February 3, 1964, the deadline for proposals, the Fund had received fifty-one submissions representing sixty-six of the state's one hundred counties. Esser reported to his board that "some contained over 100 pages of illustrated material wedged into impressive bindings. Other proposals consisted of three or four pages of mimeographed material held together with a staple. All of the proposals represented considerable depth of thought and candid analysis, in a spirit of determination to do something about the miserably poor families found in [the applicants'] communities." The appeals for Fund support came from hurriedly assembled local committees, convened in most instances by a mayor or county commissioner. The committees included elected government officials, officers of civic clubs and charities, ministers, educators, leaders from local chambers of commerce, and the directors of social welfare agencies. For Esser, it was particularly gratifying "to see [these] public officials and private citizens," many of whom he had worked with professionally over the years, "sit down together and look hard at the problems of [poverty]." "From county after county," he wrote to Albert Coates, his mentor at the Institute of Government, "the same refrain comes through: 'We have learned so much, and we have found so many ways in which we can work together, that we are going to continue this effort whether or not we receive a grant.'"[69]

Responsibility for coordinating the review of the community action proposals fell primarily to the Fund's research director, Michael Brooks, and to three new employees, Billy E. Barnes, William H. Koch Jr., and William A. Darity. Barnes was a Winston-Salem native and a 1957 graduate of the University of North Carolina with a degree in radio, television, and motion pictures. He made his early career as a photojournalist working for McGraw-Hill Publishing Company. As Atlanta bureau chief, Barnes provided stories and photographs to several dozen McGraw-Hill magazines. In late 1963, Sanford aide John Ehle put in a midnight call to Barnes, who had been a student of his in Chapel Hill. "We are calling our people back," Ehle said. "We've got this antipoverty thing going, and it's the N.C. Fund and we would like [you] to come up here and talk to us about it." Ehle and newspaperman Pete McKnight believed that it was crucial to hire a public relations specialist to "[get] the word out" and begin "building community interest and support across the state." For Barnes, the invitation could not have been more perfectly timed. He was in his midthirties and already wondering, "Am I doing anything I can look back on fifty years from now and say 'I did something that made a difference'?" He had also been deeply moved by witnessing firsthand civil rights demonstrations in Atlanta and, in his capacity as a reporter, "attending the funeral of those children who were bombed in the Birmingham church." Barnes began work for the Fund in mid-January, just as the community action proposals began pouring into its Durham office.[70]

William Koch came to the North Carolina Fund from New York. He was a native of Springfield, Massachusetts, with a broad background in social work. Koch began his career as a caseworker in New York and in the mid-1950s joined the staff of the World Council of Churches. He served that organization as director of migrant ministries in Arizona and then, in Chicago, as director of a migrant citizenship project. Before moving south, Koch returned briefly to New York for an assignment in the council's Division of Home

Billy E. Barnes. Courtesy of
Billy E. Barnes, Chapel Hill,
North Carolina.

Missions. When he joined the Fund in January 1964 as director of community development, he was completing a doctorate in education at the University of Chicago. He based his thesis on firsthand insights into "aspirations of the migrant worker."[71]

Like Koch, William Darity also brought extensive field experience to the Fund. He was a native of Flat Rock, a small town in North Carolina's southwestern mountains. He had earned a B.S. from Shaw University in Raleigh, the state's oldest independent black institution of higher learning, and a master's degree from North Carolina College. Darity's interest and experience in health education landed him a post in the United Nations' World Health Organization in 1953. He served as an adviser to seventeen African and Middle Eastern nations, taught at American University in Beirut, and assisted with the training of Peace Corps volunteers in Pakistan. When he joined the North Carolina Fund in March 1964, he had just completed a Ph.D. in public health at the University of North Carolina. He was the first black student to earn a doctorate in any field at Chapel Hill. As director of program development, he teamed with Koch to provide technical assistance to the community action programs selected for Fund support.[72]

Over the course of five weeks in February and March, Fund staff and a subcommittee of the board of directors toured the locations from which the

William Koch. Photograph by Billy E. Barnes, courtesy of the North Carolina Collection, Wilson Library, University of North Carolina at Chapel Hill, Billy Ebert Barnes Collection.

Fund had received proposals. Esser felt strongly that they "owed each partici-pating community a personal visit" as a sign of respect and "as a vote of confi-dence." He also wanted an opportunity to "size-up the local leadership" face-to-face. The travel schedule was grueling. As one reporter noted, the teams "covered the state, sometimes making three meetings a day in as many com-munities. Some nights, a team left a smoke-hazed meeting room at 10:30 p.m. facing prospects of another meeting in another town the very next morning at 9:00." For the Fund staff, these journeys across the state were at once frustrat-ing, harrowing, and exhilarating. In a handful of communities, local leaders revealed how little they grasped the Fund's objectives. The Onslow County commissioners, for instance, "were on a kick about mental health." "One of them," the site evaluation reported, "thinks that mental health is the key to all poverty problems. He is of the opinion that high school dropouts, members of the unemployed ranks, etc., are suffering from mental illness rather than an environmental disadvantage. So the entire session consisted of an attempt . . . to explain to them why a mental health clinic in Jacksonville, N.C. is not the kind of comprehensive experimental program that The North Carolina Fund plans for these communities." As they traveled from site to site, the teams also encountered local lawmen who revealed a different sort of misunderstanding.

William Darity. Photograph by
Billy E. Barnes, courtesy of the
North Carolina Collection, Wilson
Library, University of North
Carolina at Chapel Hill, Billy
Ebert Barnes Collection.

Michael Brooks remembered that on a number of occasions the teams "were
stopped . . . on the highway . . . because they had an interracial group in the
car, and so there was some kind of suspicion that they must be troublemakers." Such experiences never diminished conviction that the Fund was "on the
cutting edge of some major change." The vast majority of local leaders and
townsfolk who turned out to meet the evaluation teams shared that sense of
possibility. In Wilson, an eastern tobacco town, the local newspaper cheered
the fact that the Fund, "without spending a cent of its [millions] in resources,"
had already "trigger[ed] a vast self-study effort on the local level across the
state."[73]

The Fund's board of directors met twice in early April to review proposals
and identify the projects they would support. After Governor Sanford's announcement of the winners, George Esser explained the logic of their selection. "From the Fund's earliest days," he said, "its board of directors realized
the importance of selecting a group of communities that would represent a
true cross-section of the state's poverty problems. There had to be projects
in the mountains, in the Piedmont, and in eastern North Carolina. There
had to be projects exploring solutions to rural poverty problems in sparsely-
populated areas. And there had to be projects working with the huge numbers

George Esser and Governor Sanford name the first communities to receive North Carolina Fund grants, April 1964. Photograph by Billy E. Barnes, courtesy of the North Carolina Collection, Wilson Library, University of North Carolina at Chapel Hill, Billy Ebert Barnes Collection.

of the poverty-stricken living in large cities, many of whom have migrated from the state's rural areas." In accordance with those principles, the Fund began its work by investing in eleven community action projects — seven announced in April plus another four added shortly thereafter. "We are confident," Esser told the press, "that these action proposals are the foundations of a great, general movement against poverty."[74]

In the western mountains, the Fund partnered with three projects: WAMY Community Action (or WAMY), a cooperative venture involving Watauga, Avery, Mitchell, and Yancey Counties; the Opportunity Corporation in Buncombe County and Asheville, the county seat; and in Macon County, the Macon Program for Progress. Proposals from each of the areas addressed the rising incidence of poverty caused by a loss of employment in the extractive industries that had been mainstays of the local economy. Mining and logging had provided what authors of the WAMY proposal described as "a brief period of prosperity," but by the 1950s, the mountain region's natural resources were

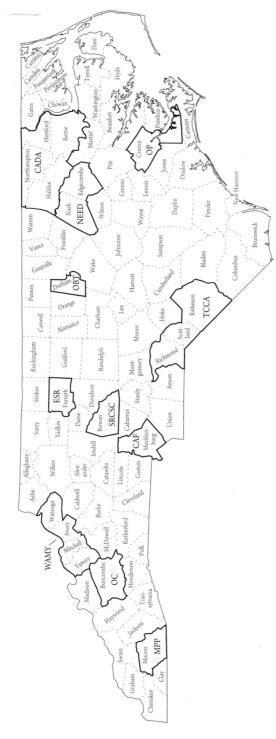

The eleven community action programs supported by the North Carolina Fund, from west to east: Macon Program for Progress, Opportunity Corporation, WAMY Community Action, Charlotte Area Fund, Salisbury-Rowan Community Service Council, Experiment in Self-Reliance, Tri-County Community Action, Operation Breakthrough, Nash-Edgecombe Economic Development, Choanoke Area Development Association, and Operation Progress. Courtesy of the Southern Historical Collection, Wilson Library, University of North Carolina at Chapel Hill, North Carolina Fund Records.

largely depleted and the jobs they supported were "dwindling away." In the past, mountain families might have sought refuge in farming, but that option had also become less viable. The rocky hillsides of the southern Appalachians resisted easy introduction of the large machinery that was transforming agriculture elsewhere, thus placing mountain producers at a distinct competitive disadvantage.[75]

These changes fueled a quickening cycle of decline. As incomes and property values stagnated, so, too, did local tax revenues available for investment in education and other social services. In the WAMY region, only two of fourteen secondary schools met the basic requirements for accreditation. Many students in those schools had no choice but to cut their education short in order to go to work and help their families earn much needed income. Others, as soon as they had a high school diploma in hand, set off in search of better prospects far from home. Between 1950 and 1960, population loss in the mountain counties seeking assistance from the Fund ranged from 19 to 28 percent. That exodus made it more difficult than ever to recruit new industry. "The 'big ones,'" local boosters complained, "continue[d] to get away, being caught downstream, below the mountains." Meanwhile, western counties became ever more tightly "trapped on the treadmill of poverty." Census data from 1960 revealed that Macon County and the nearby WAMY counties all had 50 percent or more of resident families living below the Fund-designated poverty line of $3,000 a year.[76]

Asheville and its surroundings managed, in some respects, to avoid the worst of the region's misfortune. Since the arrival of the railroad in 1880, the city had been a popular resort destination for wealthy vacationers from points up and down the East Coast. After World War II, the area enjoyed an even larger boom in tourism as newly affluent middle-class families piled into their station wagons and headed west to enjoy the mountain splendor. They cruised the winding path of the Blue Ridge Parkway, built in the late 1930s and early 1940s as a New Deal work relief project; they visited Biltmore House, the fabulous 250-room chateau built in the early 1890s by George W. Vanderbilt II, heir to the railroad fortune of his grandfather, Cornelius Vanderbilt; and in the evening, they filled Asheville's strip developments of motels, restaurants, and shops.

Asheville enjoyed a condition of relative prosperity during the early 1960s, but it could not shield itself entirely from the miseries of the larger mountain region. The same economic forces that brought a new breed of tourists to the city also attracted working people freshly displaced from sawmills, mines, and farms. Poor families constituted 30 percent of Buncombe County's population, a figure that might have been cause for optimism by comparison to other western counties. But the sheer number of those families—totaling more than ten thousand—provoked alarm rather than hope. As homegrown migrants crowded into deteriorating enclaves around Asheville's inner core, well-to-do residents worried openly about the strangers in their midst. Civic leaders explained to the Fund that the new arrivals were "largely unemployable"; their neighborhoods were breeding grounds for juvenile delinquency and "anti-social behavior"; and, most worrisome of all, they constituted a "'subculture of poverty' which [did] not share the values and aspirations of the more prosperous majority." Alleviating the deprivations of the mountain poor, it seemed, would require not only job training and aggressive industrial recruitment, but also a wide-ranging program of "social rehabilitation."[77]

Concern over the habits and attitudes of the poor was even more pronounced in eastern counties, where the Fund invested in four antipoverty initiatives: the Choanoke Area Development Association (CADA), representing Northampton, Halifax, Hertford, and Bertie Counties in the state's northeastern corner; Nash-Edgecombe Economic Development, which included those two counties and the city of Rocky Mount; Operation Progress in Craven County and New Bern, the county seat; and, along the South Carolina border, Tri-County Community Action, representing Richmond, Scotland, and Robeson Counties. Plantation slavery had dominated this region prior to the Civil War, and a century later its economy still depended heavily on the production of cotton, tobacco, peanuts, and corn. The eastern counties also claimed the state's largest African American populations. In no county did blacks constitute less than a third of local inhabitants; in several, including Edgecombe and all of the CADA counties, they were a majority. Small cities such as Rocky Mount, New Bern, and Governor Sanford's hometown of Laurinburg served the region as merchandizing, banking, and transportation centers. In Rocky Mount, the tracks of the Atlantic Coast Railroad bisected the downtown business district, marked the boundary between Edgecombe and Nash Counties, and divided the city's white and black neighborhoods. From late summer through midwinter, the sweet smell of tobacco scented the air as farmers and seasonal laborers crowded into the city's tobacco warehouses and processing plants. Rocky Mount and nearby Wilson boasted of having two of the world's busiest tobacco markets.[78]

By the late 1950s, eastern North Carolina was in the throes of an agricultural revolution. Landowners were investing heavily in machinery to replace human labor, and in the process, they were also dismantling the system of sharecropping and tenantry that for the better part of a century had provided a livelihood, however meager, to tens of thousands of farm families, black and white. In the CADA counties, for instance, the harvesting and curing of peanuts had been almost completely mechanized and more than 50 percent of the cotton crop was picked by machines. Tobacco lagged behind, but even there new pesticides and herbicides reduced the need for workers who walked the fields daily, hoeing weeds, plucking hornworms from the plants, and snapping off the side shoots, or suckers, that otherwise stunted the growth of the valuable tobacco leaves. As the cultivation process became less labor intensive, landlords dismissed their renters and turned to seasonal workers whom they employed only at the peak times of planting and harvest. Those displaced by these changes constituted a vast "surplus population" that either remained stranded in the countryside or flocked to nearby towns. In either case, lack of education left these men and women with few options for gainful employment. The result was "rampant poverty." In all of the counties selected by the Fund, no fewer than 40 percent of families lived on less than $3,000 a year. In Robeson, Northampton, and Bertie, that figure soared above 60 percent. The statistics for black families were even grimmer. In no county did the median income for that group rise to the $3,000 level.[79]

The Fund's petitioners acknowledged that curing poverty demanded economic development, job creation, and the expansion of existing social welfare programs. But like their counterparts elsewhere in the state, they found it difficult to imagine approaches outside of existing social hierarchies. The proposal from Nash-Edgecombe suggested that the counties might simultaneously address community health needs and put the brakes on rising medical costs by building a new — segregated — school to train black nurses. Civic leaders in the CADA region staked their hopes on recruiting new industries and developing the area's potential for tourism. They saw great promise in teaching the poor "some craft such as basket weaving, rug weaving, bead making, [or] leather work . . . which would produce merchandise for sale to tourists." Similarly, the proposal from Craven County sought to address high rates of unemployment and juvenile crime by establishing a job referral service for domestic workers that would match black women with white households, and by operating a "youth reclamation project" that would help young people stay in school by finding for them part-time jobs such as "car wash[ing], yard services, and catering."[80]

As they laid out these ideas for combating poverty, local leaders expressed deep concern that the poor would fail to embrace — and might even reject — new opportunities set before them. "The values of the poor in our area, as elsewhere," explained the Tri-County Community Action proposal from

Richmond, Scotland, and Robeson Counties, "appear to be characterized by a marked non-acceptance of those middle class values which the bulk of our population holds. . . . Our poor are often described as lazy, unstable, unreliable, irresponsible, immoral, apathetic, and absolutely disinclined to change." Thus it seemed to middle-class reformers that a major obstacle in breaking the "cycle of poverty" was the poor's own "self-imposed barrier to an improved condition." Craven County officials spoke of the less fortunate in much the same way. "The poor," they wrote, "are in a 'lock-step' situation from which they do not escape, because their motivation to attempt to rise above their condition is steadily eroded by the hopelessness and helplessness with which they see the future. They have the poverty habit . . . [and] become more addicted to it day by day, year by year, and generation by generation." One member of the Craven committee saw this habit expressed most vividly in the fact that poor people seemed unembarrassed by their threadbare clothing. "This says with remarkable perception," the Craven proposal concluded, "that the people in the hard core of poverty are so completely without hope or incentive that they will make no small effort to help themselves." The Fund's eastern partners worried that unless addressed head-on, these attitudes would derail the entire antipoverty effort. Without a change of outlook and values, the poor were likely to meet offers of assistance with "snarling defiance" and a "pitiful posture of fragile pride."[81]

This moral language of poverty made it possible for the Tri-County petitioners and those of like mind across the state to put aside difficult questions of equity and justice — questions made all the more dangerous by a civil rights insurgency now at high tide. As they understood the world around them, poverty appeared to arise from the confluence of disembodied economic forces — the mechanization of agriculture, or the urban migration of the displaced — and poor people's own incapacity to accommodate modern economic life. From that perspective, the liberally inclined could, with little sense of inconsistency, call for an end to poverty — for job creation, economic development, improved education, and expanded welfare services — while remaining largely silent on matters of privilege and inequality. There was, indeed, a certain comfort in the conviction that breaking the cycle of poverty required social adjustment and moral rehabilitation more than engagement with issues of power, subordination, and exploitation.

In the Piedmont, North Carolina's urban and heavily industrial central region, the Fund invested in the last four of its initial programs: the Charlotte Area Fund, the Salisbury-Rowan Community Service Council, the Experiment in Self-Reliance in Winston-Salem and surrounding Forsyth County, and Durham's Operation Breakthrough. Each community opened its proposal with a boosterish account of itself as a "progressive . . . modern city." Charlotte, with a population of three hundred thousand, was the largest of the lot. It served as the banking and transportation hub for a vast manufacturing belt that stretched from the Piedmont region of North Carolina through South Carolina and Georgia into northern Alabama. That region was the world center for cotton textile production. Together, the city and surrounding Mecklenburg County boasted of "more jobs and . . . a higher median income" than any other place in the state. Fifty miles to the north, Salisbury was a much smaller town but enjoyed similar good fortune. It had a number of textile manufacturing plants and was strategically located along the Southern Railway, one of the arteries that linked Charlotte and its hinterland to national markets. Salisbury and surrounding Rowan County ranked eleventh in the state for median family income. At the northwestern and northeastern corners of the Piedmont, Winston-Salem and Durham were world centers of tobacco manufacturing, made famous by their signature cigarette brands, Camel and Lucky Strike. Both cities also had a thriving textile sector, and they were home to some of the state's largest private fortunes. Winston-Salem and Forsyth County ranked second in the state for median family income; Durham and the surrounding county of the same name ranked seventh.[82]

In these cities, affluence existed side by side with some of the state's worst poverty. Fourteen thousand poor families—totaling more than sixty-nine thousand persons—lived in Charlotte-Mecklenburg. There, as in the other urban communities, they were confined to "dismal neighborhood[s]." They lived in run-down rental houses with "inadequate heat and toilet" facilities, and in poor parts of town the streets were "narrow, dirty, and very often unpaved." It was hardly surprising that Charlotte-Mecklenburg had "a higher crime rate, more public assistance cases . . . more cases of illegitimacy, more cases of tuberculosis, more cases of venereal disease, and more cases appearing in Juvenile Court than any other county in the state." In Salisbury, civic leaders warned that these problems were "an onerous drain on the economy" of the "whole community." "Paying a minimum of taxes," the poor drew "heavily on the resources of . . . Welfare, Health, Police and Fire Departments." The simplest social accounting, Salisbury's proposal concluded, made clear that it "would behoove all local public agencies" to work "toward alleviating this distressing problem."[83]

The Piedmont communities' analysis of poverty's causes echoed explanations offered in proposals from the mountains and eastern coastal plain. The economic vitality of these urban communities made them magnets for farm families turned off the land by machines and desperate to find a new livelihood. The problem, as city leaders explained it, was that first-generation rural migrants—white as well as black—had limited "knowledge of how to handle [a] pay check, pay rent, [or] do business on a cash basis." Because they possessed "little education and little or no training in any skill," they tended to find work only "in jobs that no other segment of society want[ed]." "In essence," authors of the Charlotte proposal observed, "they [were] marginal in their ability to produce, and thus the wages they receive[d] [were] marginal." In the end, these families missed out on the promise of the cities. They were once again "left behind" to sink even deeper into despair. At the same time, automation in manufacturing, particularly cotton textiles and tobacco, released thousands of men and women from jobs that had long been reliable, albeit meager sources of income. Again, the Charlotte proposal explained: "The percentage of jobs requiring unskilled labor" was declining at a dizzying rate. The irony of the situation was that while the "unskilled [were] finding jobs harder to get," scores of "other kinds of jobs requiring specific skills" went begging. Civic boosters identified this mismatch as a worrying drag on economic development.[84]

What was the solution? The Piedmont proposals echoed now-familiar themes. They suggested a settlement house approach in which neighborhood community centers would provide one-stop access to social services. The poor would find in these centers school readiness programs for young children, literacy classes for adults, recreational programs, instruction on homemaking and nutrition, and vocational counseling for high school dropouts and the unemployed. Like their counterparts across the state, Piedmont civic leaders put a premium on the coordination of existing antipoverty efforts. Those activities, the Charlotte proposal noted, were "as fragmented as they [were] earnest." As a corrective, Piedmont communities proposed the formation of "Rehabilitation Committee[s]" composed of social welfare professionals and volunteers from civic clubs, churches, and PTA councils. These committees would work intensively with a select group of troubled families "to diagnose [their] total problems" and to triage them to "appropriate health, recreational, welfare, cultural and educational resources." Poverty was a stubborn disease, and as such required strong medicine. Officials in Salisbury insisted that only a program of coordinated intervention would succeed in creating among the poor "a desire for more education and training," which "would eventually ameliorate the cycle of poverty."[85]

BY THE END OF OCTOBER 1964, the North Carolina Fund had awarded the eleven CAPs individual grants ranging from $10,000 to $40,000. As the agencies began their work and started to spend that money, they confronted difficult questions of purpose and authority that had simmered just beneath the surface during the initial round of consultation and grant making. In the call for proposals and in their discussions with CAP boards, Fund staff had emphasized the importance of involving the poor in program planning. The Red Book advised "that in each experimental project area, a special effort must be made to enlist the interest, participation and understanding of those who need hope and motivation." Fund evaluation teams judged each proposal against that standard. They responded to the Charlotte submission with particular delight. "One striking feature of the proposal," they noted, was "a strong statement concerning the importance of involving the residents of poverty-stricken neighborhoods in participating in their own improvement." In practice, however, the Fund and its local partners did not fully comprehend what it might mean to promote such engagement. They tended to equate poor people's involvement with minority representation. That ordinarily meant the inclusion of one or two black professionals whom white power brokers felt comfortable inviting onto the CAP boards. In the case of poor whites, the Fund operated on an unspoken assumption that their interests were best articulated by the staff of social welfare agencies.[86]

In a blistering letter to George Esser, Reginald Hawkins, a Charlotte dentist and civil rights activist, suggested how misguided such thinking could be. He charged that "Negro citizens in *true* leadership positions and/or the people directly caught up in the cycle of poverty were not consulted" in development of the Charlotte proposal "for fear that the cause of poverty would have been [exposed]" (emphasis added). Case in point: the proposal's utter silence on the most pressing issues of the day, resistance to school desegregation and ongoing job discrimination. Hawkins insisted that decisive action on both counts was "vital to breaking the cycle of poverty." Esser gently brushed off the complaint. He assured Hawkins that all proposals would be evaluated according to "objectives which I am sure you support," and he reiterated the Fund's commitment to the "participation of those who most need help and assistance." Years later, reflecting on this early stage of the Fund's work, Esser acknowledged the inadequacy of his reply. He and his colleagues were not at that time advocates of "citizen power." There was "paternalism in believing that you [could solve the poverty problem] by improving service delivery," Esser explained. "That was certainly Ford's initial impulse. It was Terry [Sanford's]; it probably was mine. It was only as we got to know more about the black point of view"—and more generally, the perspective of the poor—"that all of us, Terry included, understood that you had to involve people in more than making better services available. You had to involve and include them in the process."[87]

Remarkable commentary, tucked away in the Salisbury appeal, hinted at the challenge lurking within that proposition. The local group organized to answer the Fund's call for proposals included a subcommittee charged with investigating the question, "What is the church doing for the people in [poverty]?" Wiley Lash, chair of Salisbury's Negro Civic League, led the subcommittee, which included roughly equal numbers of black and white ministers, educators, welfare workers, and concerned citizens. What they discovered was disheartening. "The Protestant Christian Church in our community, as elsewhere, appears to be middle-class in its attitude," the subcommittee reported. "There is no direct interest in lower income people as *persons* and little desire to involve them in [mainline] congregations. . . . The ministry that is offered . . . if it exists at all, is likely to be quite limited and *paternal* in character, an attitude that can well keep low-income people at a distance."

The subcommittee took note of the "attitude of poverty" among the downtrodden—the frustration, apathy, and despair so familiar to those who wrote and spoke of a culture of poverty—but suggested that an even greater challenge was posed by the "*attitude of poverty*" among those more fortunate who considered themselves upright and pious. Too many members of mainline churches—black and white—lived by "an incredibly narrow image of morality," Lash's group argued. For them, the "Christian life consists of the cultivation of private purities and acts of kindness to the poor. Christian love is read as 'charity,' not justice." Such were the middle-class Christians who "[took] advantage of people by paying [the] lowest possible wages and providing only sub-standard working conditions," who "fear[ed] the entry into their congregations of low-income persons," and who, in doing these things, "refuse[d] to recognize [the poor] as the children of God."

Changing such attitudes was, in the subcommittee's view, the first and most important task at hand. Fighting poverty required more than charity, and more than the efficient delivery of social services. It demanded instead that men and women of faith search their hearts and set to work in the world to address issues of justice, power, and the distribution of wealth and opportunity. To them fell responsibility for ending job discrimination, guaranteeing access to adequate housing, and registering the poor to vote, so that they might participate as equals in a campaign for "community achievement." This was a prescient message, made all the more compelling by its use of a moral language with deep resonance for southerners, black and white alike, who inhabited what the Salisbury group called "the most pious and church-going section of the nation." As the Fund and its community partners set about their work in earnest, the issue of justice pressed heavily upon them, eventually demanding that they reconsider the assumptions, tactics, and alliances that they brought to bear on the "monstrous problem" of poverty.[88]

CITIZEN SOLDIERS

In mid-June 1964, Susie Powell, a native of Whitakers, a small town in eastern North Carolina, and a student at Bennett College, scribbled a brief note in her diary. She was one of a group of student volunteers—100 in 1964, followed by another 250 in 1965—selected by the North Carolina Fund as foot soldiers in the battle against poverty. Powell and her compatriots in the North Carolina Volunteers, dubbed the "First One Hundred" by the state's press, had just finished a three-day orientation at Duke University. They had spent their days in classrooms, listening to professors and public officials describe to them the poor and the causes of poverty, and in the evenings they had discussed with a mix of excitement and apprehension the work that lay ahead. Now they were packing their bags and preparing to board buses that would take them out across the state for a summer of service with the community action programs selected in the spring for Fund support. Powell paused amid all of the activity to record her thoughts about an adventure that she knew would be a defining moment in her life. "That day of the last session," she wrote, "I stepped from the air conditioned, well lit, cheerful looking, modernized [classroom] into the sultry heat of a determined sun. As I did so, I felt that I had moved from the idealism of the [seminar], where ideas are conceived and born, into a blunt world of reality which necessitates action. This was the world of poverty where I would meet [what the professors had called] 'these people.' At this point, I still did not know what I'd be doing specifically. I did know that I was a lucky American who had been accepting so much for so many years that I felt it was about time I gave back to the world and North Carolina what it had given me."[1]

Susie Powell and her fellow volunteers represented nearly every college campus in the state—small and large, public and private, black and white. A handful were themselves poor, but most came from middle-class households—economically secure but not particularly prosperous. Women outnumbered men three to one, reflecting the gendered character of social ser-

Members of the First One Hundred board a bus for their assigned communities across North Carolina. Photograph by Billy E. Barnes, courtesy of the North Carolina Collection, Wilson Library, University of North Carolina at Chapel Hill, Billy Ebert Barnes Collection.

vice and the fact that Fund recruiters targeted college majors that tended to enroll large numbers of women: education, psychology, sociology, and English. Racial representation in the group roughly mirrored the general population. The presence of African American students—thirteen in 1964 and fifty in 1965—flaunted the authority of Jim Crow and signaled the Fund's determination to confront the role of racial discrimination in the perpetuation of poverty.[2]

For the most part, the volunteers had grown up as beneficiaries of the expanding affluence of the 1950s. Theirs was an America that claimed to abide by principles of democracy and fair play and promised prosperity for all who worked to earn it. But as the volunteers began their service in communities across North Carolina, they discovered a starkly different reality. There, in the other America, they met men, women, and children who had gained little from playing by the rules and whose lives had been broken by promises unfulfilled. The students also came to see that poverty was not simply the product of bad personal choices, but was inextricably bound to the affluence from which they themselves benefited.[3]

The volunteers explained their motives for service in lengthy letters of application, and once in the field, they recorded their experiences, doubts, and discoveries in detailed daily activity logs. Together, those sources provide insight into the role young people played in shaping the Fund's antipoverty agenda, and they reveal that work's potential for expanding the boundaries of participatory democracy. In ways that none of the students anticipated, the Fund offered its volunteers an opportunity to rethink the meaning of citizenship, both for themselves and for the people they set out to help. The volunteers' challenge was not simply to serve the poor, but to model an inclusive notion of public life that otherwise had little currency in the segregated South.[4]

THE NORTH CAROLINA FUND did not invent the idea of a youth service corps. That concept dates back at least as far as the New Deal, when Franklin D. Roosevelt's administration created the Civilian Conservation Corps (CCC) and the National Youth Administration (NYA). The CCC took unemployed young men off the streets, put them in federal labor camps, and set them to work on a variety of construction projects in the national parks and national forests. Corps members received $30 a month plus room, board, and medical care, with the requirement that they send $25 a month home to their families. In that way, the CCC offered direct relief to the unemployed and indirect relief to thousands more who were never on the federal payroll. The National Youth Administration focused primarily on keeping young people in school. It provided high school and college students with work-study jobs on and off campus that relieved some of the financial pressure for them to quit school and take up full-time employment to aid their families. Students in the NYA did everything from farm chores to assembling radios for the armed forces, staffing libraries, and repairing run-down school facilities. The Depression-era programs had an obvious humanitarian purpose, but they were also guided by grittier concerns. Providing employment for young people helped offset the potential for social unrest, schooled a rising generation in participatory citizenship, and reinforced the ideals of democratic capitalism. Set against the rise of fascism in Europe and the appeal of Soviet communism, this was political work of the first importance. Eleanor Roosevelt underscored that point in an interview with the *New York Times*. "I have moments of real terror when I think we may be losing this generation," she said. "We have got to bring these young people into the active life of the community, and make them feel that they are necessary."[5]

With the emergence of the Cold War in the late 1940s and 1950s, political leaders began to adapt New Deal work and public service programs to the challenges of international conflict. In the years after World War II, weakened European empires confronted nationalist liberation movements throughout Africa and Asia. The colonial territories were, for the most part, desperately poor, and they became battlegrounds for the influence of the postwar super-powers, the United States and the Soviet Union, which competed to carve up the globe into opposing spheres of influence. On both sides, political leaders recognized that this cold war would be not only a military contest (fought primarily through small-scale proxy wars in the developing world), but also a battle of competing ideologies. To that end, Senator Brien McMahon, liberal Democrat of Connecticut, proposed recruiting college students as "mission-aries of democracy" who would carry abroad the gospel of the American way of life. In the 1960 contest for the Democratic presidential nomination, Sena-tor Hubert H. Humphrey of Minnesota suggested the creation of a youth peace corps to take up that task, and in June he proposed legislation to cre-ate such an organization. John F. Kennedy, who defeated Humphrey in the primaries, quickly made the idea his own. By championing an overseas ser-vice corps, he strengthened his appeal to young voters and underscored his determination to engage the struggle between freedom and communism on all fronts. Kennedy offered assurance that America could prevail in the Cold War through the power of its ideals, not simply the weight of its military might. In March 1961, he established the Peace Corps by executive order, and in September of that year, Congress fully authorized the new agency. Two years later, more than seventy-three hundred American volunteers were serving in forty-four countries around the globe.[6]

John Kennedy came into office without a well-developed domestic agenda. Foreign affairs had long been his chief interest. But by 1963 uprisings at home were testing the Kennedy administration's capacity for leadership. World War II had set in motion a domestic civil rights movement in much the same way as it had unleashed liberation struggles in former European colonies. Returning black servicemen and -women insisted that they be accorded the democratic rights for which they had risked their lives overseas. At the same time, the mechanization of agriculture in the South was replenishing the mi-grant stream that had been flowing from the region since the 1910s. Between 1940 and 1965, more than ten million displaced southerners — whites as well as blacks — left their homes in search of work and opportunity. They arrived in the cities of the North and West just as industrial automation was decreasing the need for their labor. As a result, America's great urban areas became powder kegs as unemployment, overcrowding, inner-city decay, and increasing pressure on social services strained the capacities of local governments.[7]

The new urban poor were part of the "other America" that Michael Harrington and like-minded social commentators discovered during the early 1960s. Even to those sympathetic observers, the poor appeared to be a people apart. "Whether a child comes from the city slum, the tenant farm or the mountain slope," North Carolina Fund director George Esser noted, "it seems clear that the child of poverty does not understand the world in which we live. He and his parents live in a different culture. Their values as individuals and families conflict with . . . those of middle-class America." On that much, liberals and conservatives often saw eye-to-eye. Where they differed was on how to cure the problem. Harrington offered an admittedly partisan characterization of the disagreement. Conservatives, he wrote, "condemn[ed] the poor" for their moral failings, while liberals approached the "personal ills of the poor as a social consequence, not a bit of biography," and sought to redeem the less fortunate from the circumstances that perpetuated their faults.[8]

Esser elaborated on the liberal perspective in an address to a group of federal, state, and foundation officials gathered in Raleigh to brainstorm strategies for battling poverty. Why, he asked, should middle-class Americans trouble themselves with the poor? "Why is it important that we be concerned with breaking the cycle of poverty? Why should we have any responsibility for those who cannot find or make opportunity? There are several answers. We know that we must develop more talent to compete with Soviet technology. We want to prove that we are not blind to human suffering. We want to counter the rising costs of juvenile delinquency and public welfare. [These answers] strike close to the issue of national survival. One of the greatest threats to this country, or to any democratic nation, is ignorance, discontent arising from ignorance, and the concentration of ignorance and discontent under the leadership of demagogues, whether Communist or Nazi in persuasion." In Esser's view, an all-out assault on poverty was essential to safeguarding democracy at home and promoting it abroad. "When we look into history," he continued, "we find that a nation is [only] as strong as its people. The seeds of decay were sown in Rome when the poor were fed corn instead of jobs. The seeds of decay were sown in Europe when absolute monarchs oppressed the poor to maintain their preferred position. So, today, Democracy is on the battle line in Latin America, and in Africa, and in Southeast Asia because there is no broad base of understanding and support for democratic government from a majority of the people." A similar fate, Esser implied, might yet overtake America at home.[9]

In 1963, the Kennedy administration sought to address its domestic challenges with new legislation. As a senator from Massachusetts, Kennedy had been a reluctant supporter of President Dwight D. Eisenhower's 1957 Civil Rights Act, but in mid-June 1963, after weeks of racial violence in Birmingham and a showdown with Governor George C. Wallace over the enrollment of two black students at the University of Alabama, he sent to Congress a civil rights bill of his own. A month earlier, the Kennedy administration had also proposed legislation to create a national service corps, or, as some described it, a "domestic peace corps." The recommendation for such an organization came from a special study committee chaired by the president's brother, U.S. attorney general Robert F. Kennedy. In congressional hearings, committee member William R. Anderson, retired commander of the uss *Nautilus*, the navy's first nuclear-powered submarine, spelled out the need for volunteers who would deliver assistance to the poor and bolster overburdened social service agencies. He appealed directly to concern for national security. Militarily, the nation was "in extremely good shape" for its stand-off with the Soviet Union, Anderson assured lawmakers. But on the domestic front—in areas "economic, human, [and] inspirational"—the situation was grim. America, the navy veteran argued, needed to fight as vigorously for hearts and minds at home as it did abroad. That was compelling testimony, but it failed to sway congressional skeptics. By autumn, both of Kennedy's bills were stalled in committee; they had been blocked by a coalition of conservative Republicans and white southern Democrats who opposed an activist role for the federal government in rearranging American racial and economic relations.[10]

The idea of a domestic peace corps languished in Washington, but in Raleigh it captured Terry Sanford's imagination. In July 1963, he scribbled a handwritten note to his staff suggesting that the North Carolina Fund consider organizing its own youth service corps. Someone in the governor's office then contacted James Beatty, a former track star from the University of North Carolina, who had expressed an interest in working in some capacity with college and high school students. At the time, Beatty was living in southern California, where he did public relations work for an insurance company. By late fall 1963, Beatty had "sold his house, quit his job, and moved [back] to North Carolina"—and George Esser found himself with a new staff member whom he had not planned on hiring. Beatty, he recalled, "was the only employee ever 'dumped on' the Fund by Terry Sanford." Unsure of what to do with his new colleague, Esser steered Beatty toward one of the governor's pet concerns: lowering the high school dropout rate. The track star soon opened negotiations with college and public school leaders in Guilford County to establish a tutoring program that would help struggling students stay in school and earn a diploma. Beatty modeled the scheme on similar initiatives at Yale and Columbia Universities, both of which he had visited. His idea was to recruit a tutoring corps from six local colleges, including two black institutions, Bennett College and North Carolina Agricultural and Technical College.[11]

Beatty prepared a grant proposal for the tutoring program, which Esser shared with Fritz Ianni, director of research for the Office of Education in the U.S. Department of Health, Education, and Welfare (HEW). Ianni had little enthusiasm for such a narrowly defined effort, but he told Esser, "I'll give you some money to experiment with the use of college students in a summer program." Ianni's aim was to use the North Carolina Fund to test ideas for the national service corps that HEW officials still hoped to create. Esser saw in that offer a happy confluence of interests. The Fund was wrapping up its review of proposals from counties across the state, and it had identified in that process two serious challenges for the projects it would endorse later in the spring. The community action programs would not be incorporated and fully operational until late 1964 or early 1965, and even then they would lack the staff necessary to implement the new initiatives they had imagined. In that context, a summer volunteer program seemed like an ideal way to jump-start the Fund's campaign against poverty. Esser quickly submitted a revised proposal to HEW, in which he sketched plans for a volunteer corps that would "channel constructive student activity at the roots of the problem of poverty." Ianni's office awarded a one-year grant of $49,000, which the Fund matched with $50,000 of its own to establish the North Carolina Volunteers.[12]

Sanford announced the Volunteers program on March 16, the same day that Lyndon Johnson sent to Congress the legislation that would become the Economic Opportunity Act of 1964. That was a fitting coincidence. These two white southerners shared a conviction that their region must face up to the destructive legacy of racial injustice. Only then could the South hope to join the national mainstream. Unlike so many of their predecessors, Johnson and Sanford were no longer willing to sacrifice the future "for the sake of hating." It was their responsibility, they believed, to step forward and provide the leadership that would take the South and the nation forward into a new day. In Johnson's words, their task was "to finish what Lincoln had begun."[13]

Over the next few months, Sanford worked closely with the Johnson White House as the president looked for models for his war on poverty and as the governor sought to carry the story of the North Carolina Fund to a national audience. Sanford testified before Congress on behalf of Johnson's poverty bill; he assigned George Esser to work with the president's task force on poverty, which was already planning the new federal antipoverty agency called for in the legislation; and, in April, he conferred with Johnson and White House staff at a strategy session in West Virginia. A month later, Sanford hosted the president on a visit to Rocky Mount, where they met with the Marlows, a white tenant-farming family who lived just outside of town in an "unpainted, four room house." William Marlow, like Johnson and Sanford, was a World War II veteran. He and his wife, Doris, had seven children, ranging from seven to eighteen years of age. When William became disabled by a back injury, the older children dropped out of school to help on the farm. The family earned $1,500 a year growing cotton and tobacco. At the end of his day in Rocky Mount, Johnson explained to the press that it was for people like the Marlows that he was launching his war on poverty. "Some people say if these Americans are poor, it's their own fault," he exclaimed, thumping and pounding the podium. "I have even heard people say that God ordains poverty for the poor. I don't believe them. I believe the reason most people are poor is that they never got a decent break. They never had a fair chance when they were young and they never got it later on." The president also heaped praise on Governor Sanford. "You have already started your own war on poverty to show that something can be done to help forgotten Americans get a decent break," he said. "I commend you on the leadership and progressive spirit that North Carolina has shown."[14]

Josh Horne, editor of the *Rocky Mount Evening Telegram*, took a different view. He complained that the governor had embarrassed the Marlows — and, more to the point, had humiliated the town — by taking the president to visit a family whose children had no shoes. Sanford replied that the Marlows were "good, proud people. They have nothing to be ashamed of, and they deserve a chance to break out of their circumstances. That was, I believe, the point the President wanted to make." Far from shaming Rocky Mount or the state, the president's trip had held up the North Carolina Fund and the Nash-Edgecombe community action program as models for the nation. "There are many places in the nation where the President could have found some poor people," he reminded the editor, "but not many which have planned a comprehensive community project to overcome the problems of the poor." *Business Week* agreed. In its coverage of Johnson's trip, it proclaimed the North Carolina Fund to be the "advance guard in [the] war on poverty."[15]

In the shadow of Sanford's politicking, George Esser was scrambling to

President Lyndon Johnson and Governor Sanford visit with William and Doris Marlow and their family. Photograph by Billy E. Barnes, courtesy of the North Carolina Collection, Wilson Library, University of North Carolina at Chapel Hill, Billy Ebert Barnes Collection.

pull together the Fund's volunteer program. He remembered March and April 1964 as the "wildest two months" of his life. At the suggestion of White House aide Richard Boone, Esser hired Curtis Gans to assist James Beatty. Gans was a graduate of the University of North Carolina, a former Peace Corps recruiter, and, at the time, a journalist with the *Miami Daily News*. Esser hoped that Gans would "supply the administrative skill Beatty lacked," but both men turned in a disappointing performance. By April 5, the deadline for student applications to join the North Carolina Volunteers, they had managed to identify only three hundred recruits, fewer than one hundred of whom had submitted the full dossiers requested by the Fund, and no concrete plans were in place for deploying the volunteers in the upcoming summer. At this point, Esser and Sanford intervened by convincing North Carolina's Methodist bishop to assign the Reverend Jack P. Mansfield to the Fund. Mansfield had been working on faith-based programs for migrant workers

President Johnson, accompanied by Senator Sam J. Ervin Jr. familiarizes himself with the Nash-Edgecombe Economic Development project. Photograph by Don Sturkey, courtesy of the North Carolina Collection, Wilson Library, University of North Carolina at Chapel Hill, Don Sturkey Photographic Negatives, 1951–1989.

sponsored by the North Carolina Council of Churches, and he had extensive experience with the use of lay volunteers. Under Mansfield's direction, the Fund extended its recruiting deadline to April 22, by which time a fresh blitz of the state's campuses had yielded a pool of five hundred applicants.[16]

Mansfield pulled the Volunteers program back from the brink, but his leadership and experience would have been far less effective had the idea of service not struck a nerve among American college students. Those young people were part of the post–World War II baby boom; they belonged to the single largest generation in American history. That fact alone nurtured among the young a powerful sense of their own "'history-making' presence." In his televised debate with Richard M. Nixon and again in his inaugural address, John Kennedy spoke to that self-assurance, reminding a new generation of Americans that before them lay a "rendezvous with destiny." Theirs would be the work of ridding the world of the "common enemies of man: tyranny, poverty, disease, and war itself." The children of the baby boom had also grown up in relative affluence, for the most part free of the financial insecurity that had plagued their parents during the Depression. That, too, bred a special feeling of optimism and possibility that propelled young people into the public sphere, where they began to insist that America live up to the democratic principles professed in school textbooks, civics lessons, and the rhetoric of political campaigns.[17]

The students who answered the North Carolina Fund's call for volunteers were very much a part of that confident, idealistic youth culture. Nearly all of them were actively involved in some form of community service work, primarily through their churches and campus organizations, and they pursued an enthusiastic interest in political matters, foreign and domestic, through organizations ranging from the Young Democrats Club to the Congress on Racial Equality. In those ways, they resembled their peers elsewhere in the country who were swelling the ranks of the Peace Corps or who in 1964 joined the Student Nonviolent Coordinating Committee's (SNCC's) Freedom Summer campaign, which sent one thousand volunteers—most of them white students from the North—to Mississippi and Alabama to teach "freedom schools" for black children and to register adults to vote. One member of the North Carolina Volunteers, who had been "looking for something interesting and exciting to do," signed up for Freedom Summer before hearing about the Fund's antipoverty project. Another recalled that when she "graduated from high school, under my picture in the year book, it said 'ambition—Peace Corps.' That's what I wanted to do." In the end, though, these students and others like them opted for a different path. They elected to remain close to the places where they had been born and raised, and to grapple with injustice in the part of the South they called home.[18]

STUDENTS GAVE A VARIETY OF reasons for joining the North Carolina Volunteers. In their application essays, they spoke most frequently of their religious faith and a desire to practice the principles of Christian brotherhood. A junior from Catawba College believed that it was his "duty to help those who are oppressed by poverty and ignorance." "I don't mean to sound pious," he explained, "but this is the way I think the Christian can . . . fulfill the work of Christ in today's world." Another white volunteer echoed those sentiments and suggested how the North Carolina Volunteers might undercut a lifetime of racial indoctrination. "Here in the South," she wrote, "most of us have been taught to think poorly of the Negro. When I look into the eyes of a white child [and a Negro child] I see no great difference. I see a human being in both." Those sentiments convinced her that the time had come "to do something about the problem of the underprivileged people instead of just thinking about them."

For religious students and the more secular-minded alike, a campaign against poverty also offered an opportunity to reclaim a sense of purpose in a world that on many fronts sacrificed individuality to the conformity of mass society. The volunteers had come of age in the immediate aftermath of World War II and at the height of the Cold War. In their classrooms and through the media they learned of totalitarian regimes — fascist and communist — in which ideology subordinated individual moral choice to the collective will and ultimately became an instrument of mass murder. At home, efforts to defend America against enemies real and imagined, from within and without, gave rise to McCarthyism and a wholesale assault on political dissent. A "nation whose first principle was freedom of speech" became in short order "a nation of people who [were] afraid to speak up." The volunteers were also children of the atomic age. They had learned in grade school to "duck and cover" to protect themselves from nuclear weapons, a triumph of technology that had the capacity to annihilate humankind. In the fall of 1962, that threat had become real as the United States and the Soviet Union faced off over missiles in Cuba; for thirteen days, the world teetered on the brink of nuclear Armageddon.[19]

As college students, the volunteers had begun to question the world they were inheriting. In their studies and through the popular culture, they searched for a sense of authenticity that American society otherwise seemed to deny them. They embraced the nonconformity of the Beats, the rebelliousness of rock and roll, and the existentialism of European intellectuals and liberal theologians. Young women, in particular, experienced the restlessness and longing of a generation on the cusp of change. In many instances, their mothers had ventured from the home into the public sphere during World War II, only to be pushed back in a postwar quest for "normalcy." For the daughters, college offered an entrée into the male world of work and public affairs, yet much on campus and in the general culture affirmed the value of an "Mrs." over a B.A.

In the midst of this turmoil and uncertainty, how was the individual to live a purposeful life? For answers, most volunteers turned first to the religious faith that as southerners they shared across the lines of race and class. In Sunday school and around the family dinner table, adults had impressed upon them an obligation to do good works. Hollis Miller, a sociology major at Lenoir-Rhyne College in Hickory and later a Lutheran minister, reflected on the centrality of Christ's example in his own quest for meaning. "I became more and more fascinated by the person of Jesus while I was in college," he explained, "and as I became more and more acquainted with the Bible (particularly the New Testament) and ... how so much of [Jesus'] life and work were spent talking to, helping what we would call 'the poor' or 'the down and out.' . . . All of that played a part in the mix, I think, of what was making me, by the time I finished my junior year in college, keenly interested in doing something that would directly have me helping people. . . . And then [the War on Poverty] gave me an opportunity. . . . I just saw Jesus as a role model there. . . . [I wanted] to experience, even in some small way, what he experienced. . . . That's a big part of the motivation out of which I was coming." Julie Habich, a Woman's College (now the University of North Carolina at Greensboro) student from Black Mountain, later spoke of similar considerations. Before joining the North Carolina Volunteers, she was naive about the political dimensions of poverty. "I was driven directly from the roots," she remembered, "my southern roots in the Southern Baptist church. We used to sing this song in Sunday school, 'Red and yellow, black and white, we are precious in his sight; Jesus loves the little children of the world.' Well, I internalized those things in a very literal way." To Habich, joining the War on Poverty "seemed appropriate and reasonable." "I was motivated by the desire to do something to make other people's lives better," she explained. "And in that, I felt powerful. . . . I felt that I had the ability to do that."[20]

In their writings, volunteers characterized acts of charity as existential gestures that affirmed the possibilities of human agency and the value of the committed individual. Rachel Stein, a sophomore from Duke University, pointed to her reading of Paul Tillich. The popular theologian defined God as "ultimate concern" and argued that human beings could know the divine only by living a compassionate life. That idea connected service to the intensity with which Stein and her peers were searching for "meaning and understanding of [themselves]." Other volunteers sounded variations on that theme. "I am twenty years old and I am tired of being useless," explained Rose Sims, a student at St. Mary's Junior College in Raleigh. "I feel that I have done very little to justify my existence, and I yearn for the opportunity to give back something of what life has given me." "There is a pressing feeling that you must do something," added a junior from Chapel Hill, "and it doesn't matter that what you can do is only an infinitesimal step toward all that should be done." Hollis Miller explained that point with a familiar parable about a "little boy who was picking up handfuls of starfish" on the beach. "Some man came along and asked the little boy what he was doing. He said he was throwing the starfish back into the ocean. And the man said, 'Oh, my goodness, lad. Why are you doing that? Look up and down this beach, miles of beach. Look at all these starfish! I mean, the job's impossible. You can never throw all these back. What difference will it make?' And the little boy picked up one, and threw it back into the ocean. And he said, 'I made a difference to that one.'" The tale's lesson was simple yet profound: giving of one's self to others affirmed a personal capacity to act and make a difference in a world that otherwise threatened to reduce the individual to insignificance.[21]

That was the answer that Hugh Jones, a freshman history major from Gastonia, gave to friends and family who were puzzled by his decision to spend his summer in a poor black community near the coast. "I have been asked— Why? Why do it?" he wrote. "Why have you spent two months [t]here, when you could have been sailing forth now toward a nice, secure, white, middle-class life? I have been told — Fool!, why have you squandered your time, when an easier life was so close to your grasp? My only answer has been this: No man really lives, if he lives in security. No man really grows, if he closes his mind. No man can receive anything at all in this world, of value, unless he gives, unless he works, unless he searches, unless he is challenged. I could not have let this summer go by, living in security, unchallenged and closed. There were too many people to seek out, for that. There were too many people mistreated and downtrodden, for that." Jones had organized people in his host community to demand equal access to education and public services, to press their rights as citizens, "to stand up straight and shout to the world . . . 'I am proud of my community, I am proud of myself.'" In the process, he, too, came to feel like more of "a proper man." The experience so focused his sense of purpose and identity that he pledged to carry a commitment to service forward into the rest of his life. "I cannot [do otherwise]," Jones explained. "There is something within me, eating on me, pushing me, that won't let me."

Many of the volunteers experienced their summer of service as a critical moment in their transition to adulthood. For the first time in their lives they felt capable of steering their own course in the world rather than being swept along by its currents. That experience was so intoxicating that it motivated nearly a quarter of the First One Hundred to reapply in 1965. Rose Sims was one of those veterans. In her 1965 application essay, she returned to questions of life's meaning and connected them to lessons learned as a participant in the North Carolina Volunteers. "All of my life I have yearned to do something to justify my existence," she confessed. "I have been brought up to believe that service and giving of yourself are the only things that give life any meaning, that you are not judged by what you get from this world but by what you give to it. Last summer I felt that I was really living for the first time. Finally I was able to render more than lip service to humanitarian principles. Not only did I have a deep sense of the importance of what we were doing, but I came to appreciate more fully the wonder and magnificence of people, all sorts of people. I knew that the only life for me would be one that would allow me to be deeply involved in humanity."

As prospective volunteers wrestled with these issues of meaning in their personal lives, they made direct connections to the civil rights movement and struggles over the nation's values and moral purpose. Black students saw in the Fund an opportunity to build on the political activism that they had taken up in high school or on their home campuses. Darrin Parker, a sophomore at the historically black Elizabeth City State College, was a member of the National Association for the Advancement of Colored People and had been arrested in a number of hometown civil rights demonstrations. He came from a family of eight children; his father was a janitor and his mother, a homemaker. "I was reared in poverty," Parker wrote in his application essay, "and to a large extent still live in it. I know what it is to be among the have-nots and to be faced with the fore knowledge of defeat and rejection."

Brenda Johnson, a student at Greensboro's North Carolina Agricultural and Technical College (A&T), was also a civil rights veteran. Her family belonged to a black Episcopal congregation and she had become involved in interracial protests through the Episcopal Young Churchmen. "We participated in a lot of demonstrations," she recalled. "We would team up into integrated couples, and we'd go to a restaurant that we knew would not let the black kids in. As soon as we walked through the door, you could hear forks just hit the table. You know, we were just creating problems." The Fund's volunteer program appealed to Johnson as an opportunity to continue her activism and to step from under the protection of a family that had sheltered her from the worst insults of Jim Crow. She came from a small, relatively privileged black middle class in Greensboro. Johnson's father was a photographer with Lockheed Aircraft, and she often spent summers with him in Ohio. Her mother was a county home demonstration agent, and her stepfather, with whom she and her mother lived, was a professor at A&T who taught agricultural economics and had traveled extensively in Africa and elsewhere in the world. Johnson's parents allowed her to join the Fund with great reluctance. "The summer of 1965 was the summer I ran away," she boasted. "I had never been allowed to work in high school or college. Daddy said, 'Your job is to get an education, I'll handle everything else.' So, in the summer of '65, I heard about the NC Volunteers; I submitted an application; I was accepted; school closed; and I called Daddy and I said, 'I'm not coming home this summer.' And he said, 'What!' I said, 'I've got a job.' He said, 'No, you don't.' I said, 'Yes, I do and I'm going to take it.'" Service as a volunteer allowed Johnson to "strike at independence." It also introduced her to members of the black community whom she viewed as strangers. She admitted to being frightened of poor blacks who lived "on the other side of town," but for that very reason embraced the "opportunity to really interact with a class of people that [she] had never had much interaction with before."[22]

For white students, too, the Volunteers program offered a chance to bear witness to racial justice. Neither the North Carolina Fund nor Lyndon Johnson's Great Society programs sought to tie antipoverty efforts directly to the black freedom struggle. Mindful of the political dangers of such a stance, they sought to downplay the association. Even so, prospective volunteers read the Fund's work in the vocabulary of race. In the South of the mid-1960s, how could they have done otherwise?

Many students came to the Fund as inheritors of the progressive tradition in North Carolina politics. Sandra Johnson, a Duke University freshman from Lillington, a small town in the southeastern section of the state's black belt, had grown up with her parents' stories of disappointment over the 1950 Senate race and Frank Porter Graham's defeat. They raised her "to think that there was something not right about two water fountains." In Chapel Hill, the campus YMCA nurtured the liberal heritage of Graham's university and served as a hub for student social activism. David Entin, a history graduate student from Jacksonville, Florida, regularly attended the Y's speaker series, where he met the likes of Michael Harrington and Malcolm X. At the Y, he also learned of SNCC's plans for Freedom Summer and signed up to join the hundreds of white college students who were preparing to travel to the Deep South.[23]

Entin changed his mind when he heard about the North Carolina Volunteers. His reasons were personal as well as political. The Volunteers program offered Entin and his girlfriend, Audrey Bunce, an opportunity to work together on a summer project, and it allowed them to do so while staying close to home, where they could draw inspiration from "a progressive southern governor" and invest themselves directly in improving the communities in which they lived. As it turned out, Entin and Bunce's relationship came to be framed by their era's call to democratic action. "Our first date was in November of 1963, on the day that John Kennedy was assassinated," Entin remembered. They married in February 1965, six months after their first tour as members of the North Carolina Volunteers and shortly before returning to eastern North Carolina to work for the Fund as full-time community organizers.[24]

Sandra Johnson, David Entin, and Audrey Bunce would have been the first to acknowledge that, in some respects, their stories were not the best examples with which to paint a portrait of the volunteers. The majority of their peers grew up in more conservative homes where parents, while not objecting, viewed with wariness their children's involvement with the Fund. "As a child, I was always taught that I had to respect every person," one volunteer reported. "What my parents didn't understand when they taught me this is that I would take that seriously." Students related a variety of experiences that transformed childhood morality into a stimulus for action. For Margaret Clark, a student at East Carolina College, the catalyst was a 1961 CBS News special report on the Peace Corps. In her application essay, she remembered "a little song that two of the volunteers used in trying to teach small children the English language. It went something like this: 'The ink is black, the page is white. Together we learn to read and write, to read and write.' That night, while only a sophomore at Rockingham High School, I took a line from that simple song and made it a motto — together we learn." When Clark applied to the Fund four years later, that dream was still with her. "This is my primary reason for wanting to become a part of the North Carolina Volunteers," she wrote, "because here I believe that together we could learn — I, how to understand people better; to broaden my horizons and to increase my knowledge of the world, my state, and myself; and 'they' (whoever 'they' may be) because of their having come in contact with me, may in some small way have been benefited by my experience."

For others, awareness sprang from a moment of confrontation that stripped away the "naturalness" of Jim Crow. Martha Watson, a student at Queens College in Charlotte, recalled that "my high school in Greensboro, North Carolina, attempted integration when I was a student there. One black girl attended and was 'egged' by our students. I was outraged — I don't know why — I just knew racism was very wrong." In incidents of this sort, the contradictions of southern — and, for that matter, American — life became painfully obvious, especially for white students who came from religious homes and had been taught to think of themselves and their neighbors as upright, moral people. Hollis Miller viewed the violence of disrespect and abuse "as a violation of the Bible, a violation of somebody's human dignity and human rights — all those were religious issues for me. I find it amazing that anybody who truly claims to be a Christian could have ever supported segregation."[25]

Whatever their source of insight, the students who spoke most eloquently of race often understood best the equally pressing need to bridge the class divide that separated the poor — black and white alike — from middle America.

Martin Anderson, a native of Rock Hill, South Carolina, and a music major at Duke University, addressed that issue at length in his application essay. "I will be the first to admit that my background is middle-class," he wrote, "but, since coming to college, I have had some contact with the 'lower-class world,' partly through organizations such as the Methodist Student Center and the Christian Interracial Witness Association, and partly by my own initiative. I am amazed and appalled at the lack of ability of the average middle-class person to even conceive of how other people live, and the tendency of the lower classes to misunderstand the middle class, to pay no attention to it, to even hate it. There are two completely different worlds with little if any communication between them. This lack of communication seems to me to be one of the major obstacles to overcoming poverty. I hope that by working in this program, I can help set up channels of communication and, therefore, understanding." Anderson and his peers took up that project with optimism and confidence. "I feel that, if given this opportunity," he declared, "I can do a great deal in the fight against poverty."

Each volunteer brought to antipoverty work a unique blend of motivations, but one theme resounded in nearly all of the students' writings. It was a conception of citizenship defined by President John F. Kennedy's call for patriotic self-sacrifice. In a nation threatened by communism abroad and social strife at home, the volunteers felt a responsibility to uphold American ideals. "Because I am a concerned American, I think to be able to help others is more than an opportunity; it is a duty that is part of the democratic form of government which we have," asserted Hugh Jones. Battling poverty became a way of advancing the cause of "social progress," achieving justice at home, and strengthening the nation for the global confrontation with communism. "The Fund was giving us a sort of knowledge that helped us be better citizens and to build a better America," recalled Penn Szittya. Guided by those concerns, the student volunteers dubbed themselves "citizen soldier[s]" in "President Johnson's challenge to eliminate poverty."[26]

THE VOLUNTEERS OF 1964 and 1965 began their summer of service in early June, when they gathered at Duke University to get to know one another and to prepare for their work among the poor. Roughly half of their orientation program was devoted to lectures by Fund staff and visiting speakers—sociologists, lawmakers, and social service professionals—who outlined the purposes of the Volunteers program and described the problems of poverty in the state. Most of the students found the presentations to be overly theoretical and abstract. For some, the approach was intimidating. Julie Habich remembered that during the classroom presentations everyone seemed to know "so much more [than I did]. They had all these ideas, and they had read all these books, and they had philosophies and were driven by beliefs about things." She, on the other hand, was "just saying, 'I want to help people. I want to do something good. I want to see some poor kid go to college.'" Other volunteers simply viewed the lectures as tedious. "To tell you the truth, I recall being quite bored," said one young man. The speakers "droned on like endless night bug[s]," wrote another.[27]

The volunteers responded more enthusiastically to the small-group discussions designed to expose their prejudices and test their convictions. In 1965, students were affected "most profoundly" by a screening of *A Patch of Blue,* starring black actor Sydney Poitier. The film told the story of a blind white girl who lived with an abusive mother and drunken grandfather. She periodically escaped the hardships of home by fleeing to a nearby park, where she met and fell in love with a gentle stranger portrayed by Poitier. Because of her blindness, the girl could not "see" race, and as a result, she was able to develop what Julie Habich described as "a relationship of affection and love. She even — heavens to Betsy — kissed somebody of another race right there on the silver screen. We explored that, we delved into it, we talked about what that meant, ad infinitum." Habich was appalled by the racial bigotry that the film stirred in her own mind, and equally pleased by the way that the ensuing discussion challenged her and others "to understand how we could relate to people of different races and socioeconomic backgrounds in ways that we hadn't before."[28]

Such exercises went a long way toward exposing the prejudices of race and class, but that was not the same as questioning the idea of a "culture of poverty," which was the underlying premise of the Fund's work. In fact, the training sessions reinforced the notion that volunteers had a moral obligation to redeem the poor. Students noted that orientation speakers "constantly commented about 'these people'" and kept a tight focus on the ways that poverty worked to "twist and deform" the human spirit. As one young woman wrote in 1964, "I was told that [the poor] were a people who needed to be given a sense of dignity and pride which was absent from their lives. . . . We, the Volunteers, were . . . to provide the atmosphere that could foster ambition, dissatisfactions, and ultimate change." She felt "resentful" of that attitude. "It was the way [the lecturers] separated one part of the world from the rest. I guess [the poor] were considered very much beneath them, and we were supposed to lift them up." Looking back on her experience years later, another volunteer made a similar point: "I think that perhaps the administrators of

Volunteers relax during their training session at Duke University. Photograph by Billy E. Barnes, courtesy of the North Carolina Collection, Wilson Library, University of North Carolina at Chapel Hill, Billy Ebert Barnes Collection.

the program, even though they might have had good intentions, really didn't have that much empathy for the people that they were going to help."[29]

At the end of orientation, the volunteers piled into cars and buses and made their way to their host communities. In 1964, the students were divided into nine teams and assigned to seven of the Fund's initial community action programs. The Tri-County Community Action project in the south-central part of the state (Richmond, Scotland, and Robeson Counties) and the WAMY Community Action (or WAMY) program in the mountains (Watauga, Avery, Mitchell, and Yancey Counties) each received two teams. The remaining groups were assigned to the Charlotte Area Fund, the Experiment in Self-Reliance in Winston-Salem and Forsyth County, Durham's Operation Breakthrough, the Nash-Edgecombe Economic Development project in Rocky Mount, and Craven County's Operation Progress in New Bern. A year later, in 1965, the Fund made volunteer teams available to these same communities (with the exception of Rocky Mount) and another eleven locations scattered across the state. Local community organizations applied to host teams of volunteers based on a vague promise from the Fund that the students would serve as extenders for professional relief workers and would help fill gaps in

Volunteers in Durham meet to plan a summer literacy program. Photograph by Billy E. Barnes, courtesy of the North Carolina Collection, Wilson Library, University of North Carolina at Chapel Hill, Billy Ebert Barnes Collection.

the delivery of existing social services. Such an arrangement appealed to city and county agencies that, regardless of location, struggled with staffing levels that were "totally inadequate . . . when equated with the vastness of the job expected of them."[30]

Once in the field, volunteers lived and worked together under the guidance of team directors. The Fund sought, whenever possible, to employ married couples for the supervisory positions. Team directors were generally in their late twenties, and most were enrolled in graduate studies, usually theology, education, or social work. A significant number had served previously with the Peace Corps. In fact, the Fund collaborated with officials in Washington to recruit directors as part of a reentry program for returning Peace Corps volunteers. All of the team leaders were white in 1964. In 1965, a third of the twenty-one teams were led by African American couples. The Fund made this change at the recommendation of William Darity, its director of program development. He insisted that "some of the teams [be] headed by Negro supervisors." Otherwise, black communities were likely to conclude that the

Fund was less than fully committed to civil rights as a part of its battle against poverty.[31]

Mixed-race living arrangements raised hackles from the very beginning. Governor Sanford penned an irate objection to George Esser when he first learned of plans to have black and white men and women living under the same roof. The Fund announced its plans in the middle of the runoff campaign that pitted Sanford's chosen successor, Richardson Preyer, against the more conservative Dan Moore, who wasted no time in making "political capital of the Volunteers program because of the integrated team approach." For Sanford, the situation stirred old fears of defeat at the hands of racial demagogues. "It has come to my attention that there are plans to house all of the Volunteers together in the various communities," the governor growled. "This is not the kind of detail which should be considered by the Board [of Directors], but I want you to know that I am violently opposed to it. It is the kind of thing that will wreck this program and damage the North Carolina Fund. We need to use much discretion, and I am distressed this early decision is so faulty in judgment. I am not one bit interested in giving these students any kind of 'life experience.' I would rather see the whole project abandoned now." Sanford closed with words of reassurance and warning for his friend. "I am sorry to write this letter, and you know you have my complete backing," he said to Esser, "but I don't want to see you cut to ribbons by the opponents."[32]

Esser eventually calmed the governor, but he and other Fund officials were less successful with the city leaders of Rocky Mount. When Jack Mansfield wrote in early May 1964 to ask about the community's preparations to receive its team of volunteers, he was surprised to learn that local project directors had set out to preempt the team that the Fund had promised them. W. W. Shaw, president of Rocky Mount's leading bank and chairman of the newly funded community action program, explained that they had recruited a volunteer force of their own from among white students at North Carolina Wesleyan College, a small Methodist school with a new campus on the outskirts of town. Mansfield's threat to investigate the irregularity convinced the Rocky Mount committee to reaffirm their original agreement to host a Fund-sponsored team. Even so, city leaders remained defiant. When they finally submitted their plans for placement of the volunteers, they insisted that the students should live and work on a segregated basis.[33]

Uncertain of how best to respond to this second rebuff, Mansfield passed the issue on to the students in the Rocky Mount team, who were then in the middle of their orientation in Durham. As other volunteers went into the field, they stayed behind debating among themselves. Was it better to concede the prerogatives of Jim Crow and carry on with their work among the poor, or would such concessions serve only to shore up the practices of inequality that produced poverty? Members of the Rocky Mount team eventually decided that they would not compromise their commitment to civil rights. Hollis Miller recalled their disappointment at local whites' unyielding loyalty to segregation: "We got word back that Rocky Mount was not going to take us—at first they said 'yes,' now they said 'no.' Interracial living? Rocky Mount was not ready for that. I don't know if they are now—but they certainly weren't in '64." After several days of idle waiting in Durham, Miller and his teammates received word that the Fund had reassigned them to join another group of volunteers already in Winston-Salem.[34]

As they arrived at their posts, the volunteers shared one common experience: they encountered social service agencies that had little idea of who they were or of what to do with them. In large measure, this was a result of the haste with which the Volunteers program was fielded in 1964 and again in 1965. The community action projects that received the first volunteers in June 1964 had been granted Fund support only two months earlier. Most were not yet fully incorporated, and few had staff on hand to coordinate volunteer placements. While they had general ideas about how they might use the student "helpers," specific details had to be worked out more or less on the spot. A similar situation prevailed in 1965. Financial support from the federal Office of Economic Opportunity did not arrive until late spring, and once again, the Fund scrambled to put its volunteers into the field. Making matters worse, the agency more than doubled the size of its volunteer corps and assigned students to eleven additional communities. This meant that more often than not, Fund administrators were starting afresh with local contacts and host agencies rather than building on relationships from the previous summer.

The first days—sometimes weeks—on the job disappointed many volunteers. They arrived to help the poor but discovered that they had been placed in libraries or recreation centers that served mostly white, middle-class children and were "in no way connected to poverty." In many communities, the volunteers also encountered social service professionals who "resented . . . neophytes" or worried that the students had been sent to "check up on them." They complained regularly that their supervisors viewed them "as simply a task force—there only to relieve [local welfare workers] of some of the burdens of their jobs." Responsibility for sorting out this confusion fell largely to the team directors, who spent days negotiating with local officials to identify new placements that matched the volunteers' desire for something other than "appendage jobs." In many locales, this process consumed the first week or more of the ten-week programs, and in no community was the tension ever fully resolved.

As the volunteers settled into their host communities, they took up a variety of predictable tasks. A majority spent their summer of service working with children in educational and recreational programs. In many cases, these interactions in the classroom or on the playground led the volunteers into the homes and neighborhoods of their young charges, where they became immersed in the lives of individual families. They tutored adults as well as children, counseled high school dropouts, served as advocates for access to health care and better housing, and, in the process, became increasingly aware of the complex causes of poverty. Other students took temporary positions in county health departments, where they worked with public health nurses to conduct dietary surveys, assisted in clinics, renovated homes, installed sanitary privies, and helped develop community water systems. In rural mountain communities, volunteers drove the bookmobiles that provided residents with their only access to public libraries and assisted with establishing craft cooperatives to provide employment and supplement family incomes.[35]

The most enterprising volunteers—and those fortunate enough to be in communities where local officials allowed them some latitude—managed to identify projects that satisfied their creativity and desire to work according to their own initiative. In 1965, the team assigned to New Bern arrived to discover that the local community action agency had made no formal plans for their summer; in fact, the executive director of the organization was not even in town to welcome them. Undeterred, the students quickly launched a project of their own in the New South Front Street area, a black enclave near the city's small business district. They began by going door-to-door, "listen[ing] to the neighborhood [and letting] the people who live[d] there tell what they need[ed] and want[ed]." The students soon discovered that residents were "so overwhelmed by their own needs from day to day" that they were "not likely to think in terms of what [was] happening to the rest of the people on their street." Local folk had little sense of themselves as a community or awareness of the leadership potential within their own ranks. The situation would have to change, the volunteers realized, before the community would "be ready to organize for a great deal of action." With that objective clearly in mind, the young people started homemaking classes for local women, first in the churches and then in the kitchens of individual participants. The gatherings offered "a chance for the women to get to know

Local leaders often found it easiest — and judged it politically safest — to assign the North Carolina Volunteers to recreational programs. Photographs by Billy E. Barnes, courtesy of the North Carolina Collection, Wilson Library, University of North Carolina at Chapel Hill, Billy Ebert Barnes Collection.

each other, to become aware of their common interests and problems, and [to] have the experience of working together to find out what to do about the things they would like to see changed." The volunteers expected that in the long run, the homemaking clubs "could be used as a channel of communication" between the neighborhood and municipal agencies and might function as "the moving force behind many community projects."

At the other end of the state, Alan Fairbank had a similar experience working for the WAMY project in Mitchell and Yancey Counties. His original assignment was to help staff the local library's bookmobile, which "would go out, way out in the remote parts, up the hollows and up the creeks." The experience, however, "was not that positive." Fairbank and his fellow volunteers had little meaningful work to do. "We would just basically stand around," he remembered, "while the librarian would check books in, check books out." Dissatisfied with that situation, Fairbank began to look for alternatives. Each day, as he drove to his assignment, he took the opportunity to stop at local country stores, where he met "pillars of the community" and tapped into social networks of people who had lived in the area for decades. The objective, he explained, was "to get their support, tell them what you want[ed] to do and why you [were] there. And they told me, 'You need to go see this person, you need to go see that person, check in with them, get their support, and then take it from there.'"[36]

Through that process, Fairbank made his way to the tiny rural hamlet of Price's Creek, to which WAMY officials agreed to assign him. A WAMY representative introduced him to the husband and wife who ran the community store. They were "receptive, friendly, supportive and said, 'Yes, we'd love to have your help, love to have you here all summer. To get started you need to go see this family, you need to talk to that family; if you want to work with the kids, go around and find out who has kids, and tell them what you want to do.'" Fairbank did just that and was surprised that he did not always receive a warm welcome. "There were people who were just suspicious of outsiders," he explained. "There were people who were suspicious that I wasn't telling them the truth, that I had some other agenda." But Fairbank persisted, and within a week or so, twenty or more children were regularly showing up to participate in the recreational activities that he organized.[37]

Through the children, Fairbank made the acquaintance of a relatively well-to-do tobacco farmer who owned a one-room schoolhouse that had been sitting empty for years. "The school was in not particularly good shape," he reported. "The front steps were rotten, a lot of windowpanes were broken, and the place was quite dirty—but the place had potential." With the owner's permission, Fairbank and a small group of fellow volunteers "organized the kids to clean it up. We put windowpanes in, fixed the front steps, and ultimately got electricity back to it." By midsummer, the building was functioning as a full-scale community center. Children played baseball in a nearby field, and they gathered inside for tutoring and remedial reading instruction. In the evenings, Fairbank and his coworkers "showed travel documentaries about Canada and things like that." "We got the big attendance from the movies," he recalled, when parents joined their children to learn and relax.[38]

As the volunteers settled in and began their work among "the people of poverty," they witnessed scenes of misery that stunned them and defied understanding. One young woman recoiled at the deprivation and abuse she witnessed in a run-down house not far from the campus of the University of North Carolina. She recounted the situation in her daily log: "Only five of the children were home. We read to them and played with them. Those children do not know how to even look at a book—Sophia, who is 6 [and] starts to school next year, picked up a book upside down and turned the pages from back to front. . . . The place has a sickening smell—The children have sores and whelps from beatings all over them—They also have protruding stomachs." David Entin encountered a similar scene on the outskirts of Durham. Years later, he described a "picture impressed indelibly" in his mind. "We had to drive a while and it was difficult to find the house. It was really a wooden shack without any paint, [with] broken windows, and just a few rooms. There was a large family, nine children, and the mother was in the hospital, and there were two teenage daughters—one I think had a child of her own—taking care of the whole family. The refrigerator was practically empty. I didn't see food around, and there were just flies on the kitchen table. One of the children, four or five years old, maybe she had polio, was crippled and couldn't quite walk. That was absolutely shocking for me that people were living in this condition." Entin subsequently devoted his career to working with poor communities elsewhere around the world. Even so, he recalled the Durham household he visited in 1964 as one of "the most extreme examples of abject poverty" he had ever seen.[39]

When faced with such suffering, most of the volunteers turned, at least initially, to familiar explanations. While they never quite blamed the poor for their plight, they did locate the causes of poverty within a cluster of social and psychological inadequacies. The poor, it seemed, "believed in nothing and [had] little faith in their own capacities." Early in the summer of 1964, Fund staff cataloged volunteers' insights from their first contact with poor communities in Craven County. "V[olunteer]s have noticed a very interest-

A child plays along a pathway in one of Durham's poor neighborhoods. Photograph by Billy E. Barnes, courtesy of the North Carolina Collection, Wilson Library, University of North Carolina at Chapel Hill, Billy Ebert Barnes Collection.

ing thing," the staff observed. "The poverty people are very pessimistic about life and their ability to control it. They are fatalists in a sense. In the V's eyes, 'I can see that the cycle of poverty must be largely due to this unenthusiastic plodding.'" Such views provided emotional distance from hardship and assured the students that they could "fix" the people they encountered. "All we had to do was clean up this one generation," a volunteer recalled later in life, "educate these people and lift them up, and it would be over with. We really believed that."[40]

A significant minority of the volunteers never escaped this way of thinking. In Chapel Hill, for instance, Robert Seymour, pastor of a liberal white congregation and director of the local summer program in 1965, commented on the "immaturity" of several volunteers "and also their lack of understanding of what constitutes cultural poverty." The students had expressed "deep resentment" over their assignment to tutor children "in whose homes there were television sets." "They fully expected to see all of these children in rags," Seymour explained, "and seemed to be disappointed when this was not the case." Such a response was not uncommon among the volunteers. Another student spoke honestly of his initial impressions. "When I first started my work," he wrote, "I thought my heart would go out to . . . these poverty-stricken people. Today I didn't feel sorry for anyone! These homes were sickening, literally nauseating at times—filthy, run down, smelly; children half-naked, flies! Yet all these so-called homes had T.V. sets, some stereos with piles of records. The mothers smoked cigarettes. I don't feel sorry for people in such situations. If the homes hadn't had these unnecessities perhaps I'd have felt differently." That the poor would "buy a TV rather than food or clothing" affirmed for this volunteer and others a belief that poverty reflected more a failure of judgment than a lack of resources. That assumption, in turn, shaped the way they conceived of their work. Poor people's "most urgent need," one volunteer observed, "is for self-esteem, self-interest, and initiative." The students believed that those qualities could be imparted only through "extensive rehabilitation work with individuals." "The people of poverty," they concluded, "need twenty-four hours of attention every day in order to make a complete transformation from the listlessness which sometimes surrounds them."[41]

Over time, face-to-face encounters made it difficult for most of the volunteers to continue that sort of typecasting. As they went about their work, they began to recognize that their own "middle-class environment . . . insulate[d] them from a knowledge" of poverty's origins and "the way the other half lives." What they thought they understood came primarily from newspaper accounts, popular stereotypes, and scholarly abstractions. During their ten weeks in the field, students wrestled with the tension between those "previously-held opinions and recently-gained impressions." One of the most striking features of their daily logs is how characterizations of the poor move grammatically from the third to the first person. As poverty came to have a human face, its afflictions could no longer be ascribed simply to "those people." They were instead the troubles of Pete, a teenager whose anger got him into fights and often landed him in jail, or the struggles of the Townsends, a couple known by social workers as the "worst case" in their county but who were in fact desperate for their children to have an education and the chance of a better life. By summer's end, the volunteers' characterizations of the poor were colored less by pity than by growing respect for "rather brave people who have warm family lives despite the continuing struggle that survival is for them." "I have realized how deep a personal pride many of these people have," admitted a junior from Atlantic Christian College in Wilson. "My attitude is now more patient in understanding and love with prejudice almost erased."[42]

Through personal interaction, the volunteers moved—often haltingly—toward thinking about themselves and the poor in ways that were new and emancipating. Rose Sims found it difficult to "explain to . . . friends and classmates . . . that there is so much more to life than the narrow, sterile, prejudiced world that they know and accept." After two months in the North Carolina mountains, she wanted "more than ever . . . to take some real action." Another student who had served in 1964 and reapplied in 1965 reported that involvement with the North Carolina Fund had marked a turning point in her life. In her second application, she wrote, "The program was one of the most worthwhile things that has ever happened to me. . . . It forced me to look at myself, while I was helping others to look at themselves." A young woman from Stedman, a small town in eastern North Carolina, shared that assessment. "The experience of this summer," she declared, "has begun . . . to break a cycle of my own poverty." While the trajectory of these transformations seems clear, their depth is less easily plumbed. Nevertheless, contemporary and retrospective evidence leaves no doubt that many of the volunteers found themselves caught up in experiences with a potential to shift their loyalties away from the world of their parents' generation and its established principles of power and privilege.[43]

THE VOLUNTEERS PROGRAM AIMED to improve the life chances of poor North Carolinians. But in practice, the students, too, were beneficiaries of their summers of service. Perhaps the program's most significant consequence was that it exposed the limitations of the racial liberalism that animated the Fund and its young foot soldiers. Most of the white volunteers emphasized in their application essays their capacity to "work with any ethnic group" and their commitment to breaking down racial divisions. Putting those principles into practice, however, was often harder than the students had imagined. After all, they came from schools and communities that had undertaken only the most limited forms of desegregation. In 1965–66, most black elementary students in three of the state's largest urban districts — 95.7 percent in Charlotte, 98.5 percent in Raleigh, and 88.7 percent in Winston-Salem — still attended predominately black schools (with 80 to 100 percent black enrollment). The white volunteers' summer experiences forced them to confront the oppressive power of racism — their own and that which permeated society at large.[44]

The challenges came right from the start. The Fund made no mention of interracial living when it recruited volunteers. As a result, students were surprised when they arrived in Durham for orientation and discovered that they might be assigned to an integrated team or, in 1965, that they might work under the supervision of a black director. A few accepted those arrangements without question. Midway through the summer of 1964, a sophomore from Gardner-Webb College, a small Baptist school in the western Piedmont, addressed the issue in her response to an evaluation undertaken by Fund staff. "Now I hadn't been made aware that the program was bi-racial until the program began," she wrote. "[But] I had and have no objection to this and think there is no other possible way for such a program to be handled."

Others found the adjustment more difficult. In some cases, the problem was not so much with the students as with their parents. One volunteer reported that she had developed an excellent relationship with her teammates, "both white and Negro," but early in the program she withdrew because of "the extreme pressure put upon her by her segregation-minded parents." When the volunteers themselves stood by Jim Crow, the effects were even more disruptive. Joan Atkins, a student from East Carolina College, served in 1964 as a member of an all-white team assigned to the WAMY project in the mountains. Her group and several integrated teams traveled together to their assigned locations. Atkins recalled that at one stop along the way, a "[white] lady expressed concern because there were Negroes on the bus. She thought we had brought our maids with us." Reflecting on that encounter, Atkins noted the wisdom of not assigning black students to the western part of the state, where the African American population was quite small. "I feel it was better not to have Negroes in this area," she wrote. "We would not have

A summer of service provided many student volunteers with their first experience of working with peers across the color line. Photograph by Billy E. Barnes, courtesy of the North Carolina Collection, Wilson Library, University of North Carolina at Chapel Hill, Billy Ebert Barnes Collection.

been accepted as well if we had had them." Atkins applied to return to the Volunteers program in 1965 and declared in her letter a willingness to "work with people of different racial, religious, and ethnic backgrounds." But when the Fund assigned her to a team in Durham led by a black couple, she balked. She requested not to have a black roommate — it was "bad enough," she confided to another volunteer, to have been placed in "a Negro community" — and when that request was denied, she refused to speak to the girl who shared her room. Atkins also "stir[red] up friction and animosity" among her teammates concerning "the desirability and capability of Negro leadership." She resisted instruction from the team directors, appealing in every instance to her superior wisdom as a veteran volunteer. "Joan never participates in team discussions," complained the team leaders, "except to indicate 'we didn't do it this way last year' and 'The Fund doesn't want it done this way.'"

With few exceptions, white students had been raised to believe in their own racial superiority; they had learned from an early age to accept white supremacy as a truth that required no explanation. That was the experience even for children who grew up in liberal households. Julie Habich, who volunteered in coastal Dare County, would later recall the "insidiousness" of racism. "Just as the people who are oppressed come to accept it as the norm, everybody else does too. We used to go out for Sunday rides and we always stopped at the Starlight Drive-In for ice cream. Over the door was a big sign that said 'White Only.' I remember one Sunday asking my daddy why it said 'White Only,' and he said, 'Because colored people can't eat here.' And I remember saying, 'Oh, okay.' And that was that, that was my mind-set, that's how it was."[45]

Such habituated ways of thinking and behaving were not easily changed. Indeed, the white volunteers' best intentions were often caught short. A young woman who worked as a teacher's aid in an all-black elementary school titled an entry in her log "My most embarrassing moment as a Volunteer (I forgot my children were Negro)." "Last week I went downtown and bought paint for puppets' faces, and paint for a puppet stage, and yarn to use for puppets' hair," she wrote. "My selections were good, I thought. This morning I went to the room and asked each child to get his puppet. Then I showed them how to put on the hair — paint the face and features. One of the children said, 'where is the brown paint?' You see I had purchased 'flesh colored paint' and yellow hair, and black and brown hair — and the children wanted to make puppets like themselves. I almost died. I said very quickly, 'Children since we are pushed for time we will *not* paint your puppets' skin today. We will just try to get their hair on.'" That delaying tactic gave her time to make another trip to the hardware store for more appropriate paint.

In a similar situation, a group of white volunteers who worked with a black preschool teacher were at a loss to understand the woman's coolness. One of the students wrote that "Mrs. Brown keeps herself very removed from us: She's the boss." The relationship became so strained that the volunteers mentioned the problem to the local school superintendent, who surprised them by suggesting that they had given offense in ways they never understood. "He thought the reason for our cool relationship . . . was due to the fact that we were white," one of the students explained, and the teacher "wanted to show she was perfectly competent and didn't need our help." Through such experiences, the volunteers came face-to-face with the paternalism that too often characterized their labors. They learned slowly — and sometimes painfully — the limitations of patron-client relations.

The fact that the students not only worked but also lived in interracial groups gave white volunteers little reprieve from critical self-examination. That was particularly true for teams that were housed on black college campuses. The Fund made such arrangements for roughly a third of its student corps, not so much out of principle as practical necessity. As the team directors in Charlotte noted, "It [was] easier to handle an integrated group in a Negro society than it [was] in a white society." Placing white students on black campuses gave less affront to Jim Crow than housing black students at white institutions, and black communities were in general more hospitable toward the volunteers. In Winston-Salem, city leaders greeted the students with "an attitude of . . . indifference," but at Winston-Salem State College they were "warmly received." The college president and "the summer school students were very cordial and made [the volunteers feel] welcomed." Even so, residing in a black community put white students off balance. For the first time in their lives, they got a taste of what it was like to live on the margins. Hollis Miller recalled, "I had been taught to love everybody," but the consequences of that principle "took some getting used to. Suddenly, I was the minority. Going to the dining hall to eat — whether I went with my group or just showed up by myself — I might be the only white face in the whole place."[46]

As Miller and other white students interacted with black teammates as peers, they opened themselves to criticism that ordinarily would have remained hidden behind a mask of racial deference and civility. In weekly group meetings, black volunteers spoke frankly about the insensitivities of their coworkers. They demanded to know why, whenever teams moved into new quarters, they were the last to get a roommate; they chastised white volunteers for describing the diet of poor families as "typical Negro food"; and they insisted that their teammates learn to pronounce "the word 'Negro'" and abandon the polite disrespect of "Nigra." White students also found themselves exposed to black anger and an increasingly assertive stance of opposition. A volunteer with Cumberland Community Action in Fayetteville, for instance, accompanied a white teammate to a "folksong concert in the gym" at all-black Fayetteville State College. As his team director explained, "It turned out to be mainly freedom songs." The students "felt out of place because they were the only white people there." With some trepidation, one young man asked the other, "You know what we shall overcome means, don't you? It means overcoming the white race." For perhaps the first time in their lives, these volunteers caught a glimpse of the fact that blacks — and perhaps the poor more generally — saw them not as redeemers but as oppressors. What they and others would make of that revelation was always an open question. For some, the experience was eye-opening; for others, it created such anxiety that they quickly put it out of their minds. In the case of the volunteers assigned to Fayetteville, the team director was not optimistic. The students, he observed, had failed to question "our system of values very deeply. . . . I expect to see them in complacent middle-class kitchens in 6 or 7 years. They conform unquestionably."

White volunteers' sense of dislocation grew as they ventured out in public with their black coworkers. There they confronted head-on taboos prohibiting bodily intimacy between blacks and whites. Early in the summer of 1965, Charlotte team leaders took their group for a swim at Lake Catawba. They asked for directions in a community near the lake and were pointed toward the Shuffletown boat landing, which "appeared to be a public bathing beach." The team leaders recounted for Fund officials the harrowing experience that followed:

> After the girls had changed we all started toward the lake. At this point a middle aged man who had had too much to drink approached me and asked what we were doing there. We had two Negroes in the group, one boy and one girl. I explained who I was and began to tell him about the N.C. Volunteers. He cut me off and said he had no education and didn't understand about that sort of thing. I asked him if he wanted us to leave and tried to find out if he had any authority to remove us. He wouldn't answer but questioned my race, citizenship, and motives in derogatory terms. Several teenage boys had collected around us just after we had arrived, but as soon as this man came up to talk to me they dispersed. Looking back on it now it is obvious that this fellow couldn't have been satisfied merely by our leaving—he was determined to provoke us and get something started. I assured him that we were not there to demonstrate, that if we were out of line in being there, all he had to do was tell us. After he had said his piece to me he turned and began yelling to the boys who began to gather around us again. By the time Bonnie and I had gotten the girls out of the water and headed toward the cars, twenty to thirty boys had gathered and they began yelling and making threatening remarks. We managed to get into the cars, but not before one of the boys in the other car had been hit while trying to roll up the window.

The black female volunteer, who had been taught as a child to avoid confrontation with whites, suggested that "it might be better if [the students] didn't go out in mixed groups" again. The team leaders disagreed, in part because of a sense of security and entitlement they felt as white people, and also because of a conviction that principles of justice and equality could not be championed in one context and compromised in another. They conceded that "the

Fund's [first] concern [was a battle against] poverty" but concluded from their experience at Lake Catawba that "integration and civil rights" must of necessity be "more than silent partners" in that effort.

Eating together, too, could provoke anxiety among the volunteers and hostility from those around them. Sharing a meal was a fundamental taboo of Jim Crow. After all, when people gathered to eat, they acknowledged a universal need for physical sustenance; they affirmed the bonds of caring, shelter, and mutual provision that defined families and communities; and in the Christian tradition in which black and white southerners were deeply rooted, the rituals of the table—a shared meal, communion in the body of Christ—celebrated the fellowship of all believers and a divine love that made no distinctions among the children of God. On her first day in the field, a sophomore from Atlantic Christian College in Wilson responded viscerally to the tension between her religious upbringing and "southern customs." She and several other volunteers had spent the afternoon tutoring a group of black students. As a gesture of gratitude and welcome, the children's parents organized a community dinner. The volunteer recorded the event in her daily log. "Tonight we ate supper in a Negro school," she wrote. "I felt a little nauseated, mainly because I had never before eaten in a Negro school, and I was becoming sick psychologically." That reaction so disturbed the young woman that she resolved to make the examination of her racial phobias one of her chief projects. "By the end of the summer," she consoled herself, "I should feel completely different."

When volunteers carried such convictions into their daily lives, they made themselves into objects of ridicule and disdain. Hollis Miller recalled that in 1964, as his Rocky Mount teammates awaited reassignment to Winston-Salem, they ran afoul of Jim Crow at Harvey's Cafeteria, a popular Durham establishment. The group had tired of the fare at Duke's dining hall and decided to venture downtown for something better. Miller described the scene:

> We were a predominantly white group, but out of the ten to twelve of us I think there were three blacks, so we thought, "Well sure, we'll get served." We went into the restaurant and all sat down together. On our own we pulled up a couple of tables to make sure that we could all sit [as a group]. That may have been a bad move, but we just did it. Time went by; we talked a while, laughed a little, cut up, and didn't think anything of it. But then, we noticed nobody was waiting on us. Nobody. And folks who were sitting at other tables were staring at us, or those just coming in or leaving

the restaurant were looking at us and staring. And we thought, "Well, what gives here?" Our supervisor asked one of the waitresses to wait on us. And the waitress said she wasn't supposed to. So, he demanded to see the manager, and then he came back [to explain]. "Here's the situation. Yes, they are integrated. But it's a half-assed integration. They will let blacks come in the restaurant and eat. But whites sit with whites at their table; blacks sit with blacks at their table."

Miller and his teammates got up, told the manager that "his policies [were] an outrage and shameful," and then marched out of the eatery. Another volunteer recalled that several angry patrons followed the group and subjected them to "outlandish comments" as they made their way to the safety of the North Carolina Fund headquarters, located just a few blocks away. A Fund staff member later visited Harvey's to inquire about the incident. The manager explained, "[We're] integrated but not mixed up."[47]

Such incidents became commonplace for the volunteers. In Morehead City, an eastern coastal town, another integrated team managed to finish a meal together without incident, but as they were standing in line to pay their bill, a white man came up behind Robert Thore and "hit [him] in the back." The man then motioned toward Patricia Andrews, a black volunteer, and said, "Why didn't you kiss her you G–d D— nigger lover." Thore tried to ignore the provocation "as best possible," but acknowledged privately that the encounter made him "graphically aware of just how much prejudice and hate [were] still extant." Andrews had understood that all along. As her team traveled east, she confessed in her log: "To be honest, I think I am really afraid. This is very weak on my part but the fear is there and I cannot ignore it. I keep telling myself you are supposed to be a mature young lady, but it does not work too well." Thore, too, worried throughout the summer. He and Andrews appear to have had a close relationship, which he discussed at some length with their team director. "[We] had a talk . . . about the problem which my friendliness with Pat . . . could cause if displayed publicly," he wrote in his log. "I hope I will be able to keep this in mind but it is very difficult to cut a friendliness toward another person on and off as you would a light." At some point during the summer—whether at the restaurant or another location is unclear—a white man threatened to kill Thore when he put his arm around one of his black teammates, most likely Pat Andrews.[48]

Detractors reminded white volunteers—through stares, taunts, and intimidation—that when they ventured into public places and openly flaunted the conventions of Jim Crow, they in effect surrendered the protections of white privilege. Anne Jones, a student who worked in Craven County in 1965, recalled visiting the white Episcopal church in New Bern, where she had a shocking introduction to the "fragility of privilege": "I went with my room-mate Naomi to talk to them about giving toys to our project, and they were very cold. They didn't even let us come into the church and make our appeal. My first reaction was, I'm an Episcopalian! I'm the daughter of a professor! What are you doing? And then I realized my identity wasn't carrying me anywhere. The only identity I had to them was that I was with a black person asking for things that involved racial change." At that moment, Jones had an important insight: "If you happened to be with a black person doing something that was against protocol, that crossed the boundaries, then your white skin meant nothing; it meant worse than nothing." Venturing into that forbidden territory was humbling and potentially dangerous. Volunteers who paused to reflect on the situation recognized how close to the surface deadly violence lurked. Looking back on his summer of service in 1964, Hollis Miller shuddered: "I could have been shot and killed. I mean, things like that were happening around the United States of America—1964 was the summer of the murders [of civil rights workers James Cheney, Andrew Goodman, and Michael Schwerner] in Mississippi."[49]

As white volunteers breached the color line, they also exposed their own deep-seated conflicts over racial etiquette. They grew indignant when segregationists challenged their moral judgment and sense of justice. Steve Bates, one of the volunteers involved in the incident at Harvey's Cafeteria, was enraged at having been "served poorly, ordered around, talked about, [and] called names." "Personally, I think that someone ought to bomb the place," he confided in his daily log. But a few weeks later, Bates reacted with comparable distress when a white female coworker became "too friendly . . . with some of the [Negro] boys" at the recreation center to which they had been assigned. The facility was located in a neighborhood that the volunteers' team director described as one of "the very worst [in] Winston-Salem—Juke joints, houses of prostitution, shack-row housing." Bates worried that it was all too seductive for his friend, Sharon. "[She] dances to slow music with the boys, kids around with them, and is generally suggestive," he complained. "This afternoon after the center closed, Sharon, [one of the center directors], and a lifeguard from 14th Street pool drank together—only a little, but still it upset me to see Sharon drinking on the job, and most especially with two young Negro men, one of whom is married. She also went swimming with them this afternoon. Sharon and I have been swimming at [the black pool] before, but I do not think that she should go swimming [without] me or one of the [other white] volunteers." Bates agonized over what to do. He felt obligated to offer Sharon the protection that was expected of him as a white man. "I have tried to talk to [her] (and I have been very blunt about it)," he wrote, "but she refuses to listen." He feared that in the end the only way to solve the problem would be to reveal Sharon's indiscretions and have her "sent home."

Sexual temptation was one of the disruptive subtexts of the summers of 1964 and 1965. The volunteers belonged to a generation poised for sexual revolution. The U.S. Food and Drug Administration had approved the birth control pill in 1960, and by 1963 more than two million women were using it as their primary form of contraception. A year later, Lyndon Johnson made access to the Pill a key element of the War on Poverty. A number of volunteers, in fact, spent their summers assisting with the operation of birth control clinics, where they "carr[ied] the gospel of the pill to the unenlightened." The volunteers' task was to educate poor women about their reproductive choices and to help them understand that they no longer had to "trust to luck or to God," or to bend to the will of a husband.[50]

As the students preached this message, they also began to reflect on their own sexuality. The Fund had thrown them into settings that encouraged exploration. Before their summer of service, few had lived outside their family home or a college dormitory, where dating was strictly regulated by parents and housemothers, curfews and visitation policies. Now, in what they described as "group living" situations, they had greater latitude for making their own decisions. The volunteers were pulled between conventional mores and the forbidden. Part of the team directors' job, as one student explained, was "to make sure there wasn't any intergender fraternizing or socializing to an extent unpermissible." But those "chaperones" were only a few years older than the volunteers in their charge, and they were just as likely to be caught up in a new sexual awakening. Members of one team wrote extensively about their leader's wife. "She tells us how disappointed we will be after we get married," a volunteer reported to Fund staff in Durham. "She tells us things our mothers would not even think of telling us . . . things we should learn ourselves on our wedding night. . . . She even thinks that either the boy or girl should have experience before they are married and she does not mind telling us this." Some of the volunteers considered such ideas to be "beyond the pale." Others found them "enlightening." All sensed the attractions and dangers of "brand new" freedom.

The perils of that freedom grew even more acute when intimacy crossed the color line. In 1964, white volunteers who lived at Winston-Salem State College quickly made friends with black summer school students. "We have moved in and seem to have established very good relations on campus," Sarah Gold noted in her daily log. "We mix with the other students a lot, and they invite us to their get-togethers." As the weeks passed, team director John Matthews became concerned that such socializing had gone too far. "Because we [live] in an all negro area," he wrote in one of his weekly reports, "I dislike my white girl volunteers dating negroes and frequenting Negro taverns. . . . Only last weekend [one of the young women] went on a date with 5 Negro college students (men) to Greensboro — and stayed out till 2:30 a.m. — although she informed me that she would be back by 12 a.m. One of the men volunteers has joined her in her outings — and together [they] have made a name for themselves." To make matters worse, the women were nonchalant about such interactions. Sarah Gold, for instance, chaperoned a number of teen dances in the black neighborhood to which she and her coworkers were assigned. After one of those events, she wrote matter-of-factly in her daily log (which Matthews read): "Really good turnout at the teen-age dance. . . . It was at an all Negro school, and they seemed to accept whites. . . . Either for the novelty or for the show, [the boys] asked us for nearly every dance." Matthews was so concerned about that behavior and attitude that he discussed the matter with the president and dean of women students at Winston-Salem State and with Fund officials in Durham.

There is no evidence that Fund staff intervened in this or similar situations, but their response was swift and decisive when the transgressions occurred within a volunteer team. Events in Salisbury during the summer of 1965 are a case in point. Racial tension "was running high in the community," and Klansmen were following volunteers to their dormitories on the Livingstone College campus, "circling in and out of the area all the time." Then the Fund office got word of what appeared to be a sexual relationship between a black volunteer and one of his white teammates. "Two people on the Salisbury team were being too intimate (bi-racial) and upsetting the team," a staffer reported. "The T[eam] D[irectors] tried to hush it up but the two were caught lying on the couch together early in the morning and they deny anything happened." Jack Mansfield, director of the Volunteers program, and Frank Rush, a field supervisor, traveled to Salisbury to investigate. They talked with "the boy," who, rather than admitting guilt, "was openly aggressive and thought he was a gift to the girls." Angered by this breach of racial etiquette and defiance of their authority, Fund officials "fired" the young man and sent him home. They put the girl "on 'probation.'"

In the Fund's record of these events, one can hear echoes — intended or not — of enduring characterizations of black male sexuality. At the turn of the century, the architects of white supremacy had built their political campaign for black disfranchisement and the social order of Jim Crow on appeals for white men to fulfill their masculine obligation to protect the virtue of white womanhood. Similar calls reverberated through white resistance to the civil rights struggle, as defenders of segregation accused young people in the Student Nonviolent Coordinating Committee and other movement organizations of sexual depravity. In North Carolina, Jesse Helms, a key player in the Smith-Graham contest of 1950 and now general manager of Raleigh's WRAL-TV, repeated the charges in his nightly "Viewpoint" editorials.

In early April 1965—as the nation recoiled from scenes of Alabama state troopers attacking marchers on Selma's Edmund Pettis Bridge, and as a second crop of volunteers prepared for a summer among the poor in North Carolina—Helms laid out in explicit terms the link he perceived between social activism and moral decadence. He quoted the testimony of Alabama congressman William L. Dickinson, who claimed that during the march from Selma to Montgomery that followed the attack, "Negroes and whites . . . engaged in sex orgies of the rawest sort, including burlesque shows advertised by handbills in advance. On one occasion, they were even driven out of a Negro church because of their . . . debauchery." Such behavior could also be found close to home, Helms warned. He had learned that student demonstrators in Chapel Hill had been led by a young man who had once "entered a plea of guilty . . . to the charge of sending obscene materials through the U.S. mails," and in Guilford County, the "Sheriff . . . [was] said to have related some incredible details of what reportedly went on when hundreds of white and Negro demonstrators were arrested and confined together in Greensboro a couple of years [earlier]." Such was the "morality," Helms concluded mockingly, that Martin Luther King, Lyndon Johnson, and their accompanying host of civil rights and antipoverty agitators had in mind when they preached freedom and equality at the expense of "personal responsibility."[51]

AS STUDENTS IN THE volunteers program took their idealism and hopefulness into recreation centers, classrooms, and libraries across the state, they became ensnared in the tangle of connections that tied racism and poverty to political power, class interests, and the privileges of whiteness. The volunteers were most surprised by the wariness of poor whites, who were deeply suspicious of the Fund. Few openly embraced the students; many actively rejected them as "communists," "freedom fighters," and "civil rights demonstrators." Poor whites obviously had much to gain from the Fund's programs but, in their estimation, even more to lose from the prospect of racial leveling. For three centuries, race had been the primary organizing principle in southern society. Since the birth of racial slavery in the late seventeenth century, poor whites had defined their own liberty in opposition to black bondage. To them, being free had always meant not being black, not being a slave. The white supremacy campaign of the late nineteenth century affirmed that understanding by tying citizenship rights to skin color. Such ways of thinking about the social order were deeply rooted and difficult to dislodge. For a volunteer in Laurinburg, two encounters revealed the depth of the racial hostility that he and his teammates had tapped. The first, the young man explained in his daily log, was a confrontation involving two representatives of the Peace Corps who had come to inspect the Fund's work. Their taxi driver "asked where they were going, and when he was told that they were 'going to Laurinburg Institute to visit the N.C. Volunteers,' he replied, 'If I had known you were going to see that nigger group, I would have told you I had a fare.'" The second experience was personal. "I was talking to two high school seniors in a local drug store," the student wrote, "and the very moment I mentioned being with the N.C. Volunteers, they, without one further word, got up and left."

The most astute volunteers began to understand that the problem was not simple prejudice, but rather the interests that prejudice served and the unwillingness of most middle-class whites to surrender the prerogatives that racial discrimination helped sustain. Local officials invited the volunteers into their communities to secure needed services and to take advantage of the North Carolina Fund's ties to private philanthropy and the federal Office of Economic Opportunity. Beginning in late 1964, the Fund became a major pipeline for new federal investments in community development and job creation. Yet, even as they sought to benefit from that largesse, local leaders often defended established lines of authority, power, and privilege. Kimberly Harris voiced a complaint from Terry Sanford's hometown of Laurinburg that echoed among volunteers across the state: "Not one white person has gone out of his way to make us welcome. . . . This very obvious 'snubbing' is beginning to tell on group morale. . . . People here seem to be trying desperately to ignore the fact that we are here, as ostriches with their heads in the sands of their own prejudice. It's as if we're the symptoms of some dread disease they don't want to know they have." Torn between outrage and her middle-class manners, Harris fumed, "It makes me so mad at these self-satisfied, self-righteous whites that I could kick them in the wazoo!"

In some communities, the resistance was exercised with a relatively light touch. That was the case in the far western town of Murphy, where trouble sprang up around the volunteers' desire to use the local pool to offer swimming lessons to poor black children. One might have imagined that Murphy and other mountain communities would have been less likely than their neighbors to the east to contest such a small breach of the color line. After all, the black population was tiny and, according to the volunteers' team director, "prefer[red] not to cause an incident." But local elites in Murphy lived by assumptions that differed little from those of their counterparts elsewhere in the state. They understood that even small compromises on race opened to examination other relationships of authority.

Team director Betty Ward explained her interactions with Hobart McKeever, a Murphy lawyer who chaired the committee that had raised funds to build the town pool and that oversaw its operation. When Ward questioned the policy of barring blacks from the facility, McKeever replied, "It's not my rule (defensively) — I have a full-time maid at my house who eats with us and uses our bathroom and even rides in the front seat with me. . . . It's fine with me if Negroes go to the pool, but [the] people of Murphy won't stand for it." The issue for McKeever was not simply one of keeping black children out of the water. In play, too, was his understanding of his own authority as a patron solicitous of black subordinates and duty-bound to discipline the passions of lesser whites. His response echoed the arguments of turn-of-the-century white supremacists, who had justified segregation as an instrument of social order that provided blacks space within which to work out their own destiny, protected poor whites from black competition, and averted otherwise violent conflict between the two groups. When Ward reminded McKeever that her request was not that blacks and whites swim together, but that the pool be opened to blacks during times it was otherwise closed, he answered with more evasion. "We were informed by Mr. McKeever that the pool could *not* be used for instruction to Negro children during hours it is normally closed," Ward reported, "because [it] is cleaned at 8:00 a.m., opens at 10:00 a.m., closes one hour for lunch and dinner and remains open until 7:00 p.m. Thus there is not enough *time* for it to be used." That, Ward lamented, was "an obvious excuse, a pitiful one at that, but there's no way around it without causing more trouble than is probably advisable at this point."

In the rare instances when the volunteers managed to coax poor whites across the color line, the response from local elites was more forceful and direct. The small Harnett County railroad town of Coats was a case in point. There, poor whites and blacks lived close to one another in adjoining but segregated neighborhoods. The volunteers saw this as an opportunity. They split into two groups. One began going door-to-door to survey residents' employment and educational status, while the other started work on reopen-

Children reached across the racial divide more eagerly than their elders. Photograph by Billy E. Barnes, courtesy of the North Carolina Collection, Wilson Library, University of North Carolina at Chapel Hill, Billy Ebert Barnes Collection.

ing a community center and library that had been closed for nearly a year. For one black volunteer, the experience of visiting with poor white families was exhilarating. "As a Negro," she wrote in a series of weekly team reports, "I felt a great feeling when I went out into the white community and sat on porches and talked with the 'folks' and their neighbors. . . . I for the first time . . . communicated with some citizens in a relationship that [I] had never had [before]. . . . What a challenge this has been for me!"

After a week of hard work, "clean[ing] and dust[ing] and clean[ing] some more," the volunteers announced throughout town that the library was ready for visitors. On the appointed day, "Negro and white children and adults . . . came in droves." "Black and white . . . mixed with a noticeable unawareness," the students observed. "Everyone played together and enjoyed every minute." Children gathered outside for games; they huddled in small groups for singing and storytelling; and at the end of the day, they carried home more than one hundred books from the library shelves. To the volunteers, "everything looked promising." They found great "joy . . . at seeing the large integrated group so happily getting to know each other." "Many of us," wrote one student, began to question "the feeling that the southern white was a backward prejudiced soul, for nothing we encountered supported this assumption. . . . It seemed that we had won the town with friendliness and co-operation." "Oh," exclaimed another, "I felt that there was no place I would rather have been at that moment!"

The joy did not last. In the afternoon, a handful of white parents who had not accompanied their children to the library showed up to take them home. Then, at the end of the day, a "'local civic leader' who serve[d] on the board of trustees of the community center came by to protest. She told [the volunteers] that it was never her understanding that the facility would be used for an integrated program and she felt sure that the other members of the board would not want the program conducted in the building." The team leader protested that the students had been clear all along that they wished "to have the building used for an integrated program," but when the visitor refused to back down, he "had no alternative but to close the building until he could get things straightened out."

That night, the team turned to Mrs. Haywood Roberts, "a fairly liberal local citizen" who had given the volunteers a warm welcome. They hoped that she might be able to mobilize the support of friends and neighbors, but Roberts "encountered more antagonism than success." A day of spontaneous race mixing had convinced Coats's leading whites "that the Volunteers were civil rights workers." Throughout the night, "Mrs. Roberts received phone calls greeted by silence on the other end of the line.... A couple of other local people connected with the Volunteers were called and Dixie played into the receiver. Someone also received a threat, supposedly from the Klan, saying that the Community Center would be burned if the program continued." The next day, as the volunteers sought to continue their canvassing of poor households, doors that previously had been open to them were now closed. "People refused to talk with [the students]," a member of the team reported. "People made nasty comments. A local businessman followed them part of the day in his auto yelling things like 'Civil rights workers!'" Local white ministers also called the volunteers "and requested that [they] not attend church even in segregated groups."

All of this transpired on a Thursday and Friday. Over the weekend, influential members of the local committee that had invited the volunteers to Coats made it clear that they no longer approved of the students' presence. The volunteers' chief advocate, Mrs. Roberts, "was upset and surprised that [her neighbors] had reacted with such hostility." She and the team leader "agreed that the only possible solution was to call a meeting of the Coats action committee, redefine the program to them and see if they were willing to provide the support the volunteers needed in order to continue working in Coats." The committee convened for a public hearing on Monday evening, but the gathering "was stacked with . . . 'Klan types'" scattered throughout the audience. White townsfolk expressed vehement objections "to admitting Negroes to programs" and also "to the fact that the Volunteers, themselves, were integrated." In the end, the Coats committee voted twenty to ten to discontinue the volunteers' work, which gave the students "no alternative but to leave." Volunteers noted in their reports to Fund headquarters that a number of committee members voiced private support for them, but only the "mayor and two women" spoke up. "Too many good men remained silent," one student observed. That "two-faced, abandon-sinking-ship, wash-my-hands-of-you attitude . . . sickened" another. On the morning after the vote, Coats town officials sent sheriff's deputies to retrieve the books that black children had checked out of the library.

Several days later the volunteers relocated to a nearby black community called Shawtown, but they could not escape the enmity that they had provoked in Coats. The Harnett County team spent the rest of the summer under a cloud of disapproval and intimidation. Soon after their move, the automobile dealer who had loaned them a used car showed up at the Shawtown School to take it back. When the students inquired about the possibility of extending their work to the town of Angier, local officials replied that they would accept the team only "as long as the programs were not [integrated]." In Lillington, an outing to see a movie as a mixed-race group stirred up rumors of "Negro and white hugging and kissing" in the darkened theater and incited local toughs to assault the black projectionist. Most disturbing was the fact that the volunteers were tailed in their movements around Harnett County and received numerous warnings—from the black community in Shawtown and Raleigh newspapermen—that the Klan intended to attack them with "dynamite throwing" or "a planned accident or shooting on the road."

These events left the Harnett volunteers angry and disillusioned. They felt mostly for the children who had been so excited by the library's opening. "It was frustrating and heartbreaking to see the bright potential of little children stunted by the pigheadedness of adults," wrote one volunteer. "The town's power structure," observed another, had "witnessed the compatibility of their children with the children of their maids," and they were horrified by the scene. These "mommies and daddies . . . could not stand aside, not yet." That boded ill for Coats and North Carolina at large. The students were quick to note, as Terry Sanford had argued in setting up the Fund, that the state would have to abandon "tradition" if it hoped to develop economically and join the

Klan organizations operated with impunity in many North Carolina communities. In Johnston County, half an hour east of Raleigh, the Klan offered prizes and refreshments to attract new recruits to its rallies. Photograph by Billy E. Barnes, courtesy of the North Carolina Collection, Wilson Library, University of North Carolina at Chapel Hill, Billy Ebert Barnes Collection.

national mainstream. That included facing up to the racism that historically had been so critical to producing wealth for the few and poverty for the many. Unfortunately, Coats and too many other communities remained caught in "the grip of a great fear . . . fear of integration, fear of the Negro." "Everything else is subordinated to this fear," noted a member of the Harnett team. "The happiness of the child is subordinated to this fear; the emergence of industry is subordinated to this fear; the enlightenment of ignorance is subordinated to this fear; the advancement of the community is subordinated to this fear; the dignity of man is subordinated to this fear."

The volunteers had put a finger precisely on the problem. The issue they confronted was racial prejudice and its connections to power, political and economic. What local leaders—including many of those who had initially embraced the Fund and its volunteers—feared most was that antipoverty programs would encourage the poor to pursue their interests as equal members of the community. Penn Szittya discovered this when his team was assigned to work with the Parks and Recreation Department in Durham. At first, Szittya felt excited by the job's possibilities. After an introductory meeting with Durham civic leaders, he felt confident that "the upper levels of the Durham bureaucracy are vitally concerned with the problems we have been sent to help out with." But the limits of that concern soon became apparent. Szittya and his teammates grew weary of "keeping order" on ball fields and began organizing parents to build a playground in a poor black neighborhood where the city refused to provide recreational services. That affront prompted a tongue-lashing from the mayor. "The mayor launched a politely-phrased tirade," Szittya reported. "To wit, we, the volunteers, must remember that we were employees (in effect) of the City of Durham, and under the city's thumb. We are here to serve as requested, not to change the requests. In short, we are here to be uncreative, and not to fight poverty, but to play the city's conservative ball game."

Further east, in Greenville, other volunteers learned just how deplorable "playing the game" could be. Soon after their arrival, they took part in a cleanup campaign sponsored by the local Public Works Department. They were surprised when a policeman joined them, and they watched in disbelief as he interacted with residents of the neighborhood they had been sent to help. "He swaggers into a client's yard or house," the students complained, "ignoring all conventions of privacy or good manners (after all, the people he is working with are Negro, so it isn't necessary to observe any conventions of 'privacy,' etc.). He begins shouting something (near-incoherent) about 'house inspection,' then proceeds, 'This has got to go. . . . This old tub is no good to anybody—get it out of here. . . . I want all this junk out beside the street; I'll be back in an hour with a truck to pick it up.' Naturally he has no opposition, and he *does* get results . . . city police uniform, badge, .32 caliber pistol strapped to his hip. . . . *Naturally* he gets results. Of course, the fact that he often scares the Hell out of the people he bullies around is unimportant—he gets results." The volunteers refused to continue under those circumstances. "I don't want to work with a policeman," one wrote to Fund headquarters, "especially a white hate-monger like the one I worked with on Friday. He went into houses w/o knocking . . . and treated the people like animals." In the end, the Greenville volunteers salvaged their summer by disassociating themselves from the cleanup campaign and finding alternative placements on their own.

South of Greenville, in the town of New Bern, a similar conflict with local officials erupted into a full-blown crisis. There, students assigned to Craven County's Operation Progress grappled with the politics of poverty. As they began their work in disadvantaged neighborhoods, they recognized that the chief problem for the poor—black and white alike—was "the absence of any voice in the government activity of New Bern and Craven County." A small group of volunteers set out to correct that situation by launching a project in James City, a black community across the Trent River from New Bern. James City dated to the time of the Civil War, when federal troops confiscated the land of a white planter in order to offer refuge to runaway slaves. The students partnered with ministers, teachers, and other neighborhood leaders to organize and legally charter a community action agency through which James City residents could begin to "press for getting men employed, improving the schools and the learning environment, paving the streets, getting running water and inside bathrooms." The agency, volunteers promised, would be a vital instrument for realizing "a New Day . . . for Negroes."

Another cluster of Craven County volunteers demonstrated the potential of that kind of grassroots organizing. They worked just outside of New Bern in a suburban community of about 150 "middle-low income" black families. These were people with "a rare type of courage," one student wrote. They had moved out of New Bern to escape "the constant gnawing of the slumlord's rent [and] to dare to hope that they too could own a home." County officials paid little attention to residents' aspirations. The community had few paved streets, no water or sewage service, and no trash collection. Refuse piled up on "overgrown vacant lot[s]" and became "harborage for snakes, rats, mosquitoes [and] flies." With help from the volunteers, residents organized "delegations" to attend meetings of the county commissioners. They lobbied loudly—and effectively—for "better roads, drainage and law enforcement," and they incorporated a community improvement association that applied for state and federal grants to do the work that county government ignored.

In the "slums of New Bern," too, volunteers exposed abuse and neglect. They undertook a study of the city's Trent Court public housing project that left them appalled. The students estimated that 35 percent of families living in the project were "charged unfair rent"; they uncovered administrators' illegal use of maintenance personnel to complete work at their own homes; and they discovered serious building code violations. In the winter of 1964, two residents had died of carbon monoxide poisoning "because soot in the chimney had closed the vents which were supposed to permit the gas to escape." A couple of years earlier, two sisters had nearly died under similar circumstances. The volunteers collected affidavits to document these and other irregularities and published their findings for broad circulation. They charged that the housing authority had "exploited" the people at Trent Court "as much as any 'slum lord,' and in some instances maybe worse." In letters to Fund headquarters and to the Office of Economic Opportunity in Washington, they recommended the immediate removal of New Bern's public housing director, who was also president of the city's leading bank, and called for a full-scale investigation of his office. "[The] people [of Trent Court] are angry, and with good reason," the volunteers argued. "[We] hope that you will find it within [your] power . . . to help these oppressed people who strongly wish to help themselves."

The Craven County volunteers also worked closely with a youth employment and job training program administered by David Entin and Audrey Bunce, Fund veterans from 1964. At the end of their summer of service, Entin and Bunce had signed up for a new Fund initiative to train "community action technicians," full-time antipoverty workers assigned to select communities across the state. They took up their post in Craven County in the early fall of 1964, just after passage of the Economic Opportunity Act, and immediately submitted a proposal to the Office of Economic Opportunity to fund a local Neighborhood Youth Corps (NYC) program. The NYC, a key component of President Johnson's war on poverty, helped young people gain work experience and earn part-time income, so that family economic needs would not force them to drop out of school. Entin and Bunce received a federal grant of $1 million for their NYC program, the first in the nation to target a predominantly rural and small-town population. By the summer of 1965, they were employing more than a thousand students, most of them African American, as teacher's aides, library assistants, playground monitors, nurse's aides, and the like. This made the NYC the largest employer in Craven County, which had a total population of only fifty-seven thousand. As Entin remembered, he and Bunce had set in motion what many locals thought of as "social revolution." The NYC paid the federal minimum wage of $1.25 an hour, which was well above the going rate for unskilled labor. Craven County employers bristled at this unwelcome intervention. Many were old enough to remember the New Deal jobs programs of the 1930s, which had similarly threatened a low-wage economy. Like Fund critics elsewhere in the state, they grumbled that Entin and Bunce were not only "civil righters" but equally reprehensible "extension[s] of the Federal Government."[52]

Little wonder, then, that the volunteers in Craven County found themselves "shunned, slandered, gaped at, hated . . . and totally neglected and misunderstood." They suffered taunts when they ate or went out in public together, and they frequently found notes on their cars warning that the "Klan is Watching You." The most frightening incident occurred at the end of the team's second week in Craven County. They had not been able to find a house to rent in New Bern, so they were living in a relatively isolated rural area nine miles outside of town. Early in the morning of July 9, 1965, someone approached their house and fired five shots into the upstairs living area. Several of the volunteers were awake and in the room, but no one was injured. They immediately notified the local sheriff and Fund officials, who in turn brought in FBI investigators. In the days that followed, the New Bern newspaper ran stories that denounced the attack but also turned a spotlight on the volunteers' interracial living arrangements. The paper implied "that the presence of the team at the [house] was for less than moral purposes and that their activities were improper." Law enforcement officials never identified the shooter.[53]

George Esser and the Fund's board of directors at first wanted to reassign the Craven volunteers to another location, but program head Jack Mansfield warned that the young people were devoted to their work and that "any attempt to remove them would bring about a terrible squawk and rebellion on their part. Indeed, I am sure that if we attempted to remove them, they would resign from the Vol[unteers] and remain in the community on their own." Mansfield was right. The students saw themselves as the avant-garde of the nation's "fledgling war on poverty," and they felt duty-bound to stand firm and "Fight!!" After much debate, the Fund conceded to that view and moved the team to "more defensible" housing at New Bern's Governor Tryon Inn.[54]

Like their counterparts in Coats, the Craven County volunteers could never escape the hostility that marked the beginning of their summer's work. "Now we were Communists, beatniks, outsiders, immoral, and dirty," reported Anne Jones in a speech to her Hollins College classmates later in the fall. "When we moved into town we had to eat in restaurants; the waitresses suddenly became clumsy and our food was in our lap." Things were no better at the Governor Tryon Inn. Sandra Johnson, a Craven volunteer who later became an attorney, recalled an incident that particularly shocked her. "There was a person [at the hotel] who later became the chief justice of the North Carolina Supreme Court," she explained. "He and his wife were [staying there] because he was in New Bern trying a case. And when we would go down to dinner at night, it was very obvious when we would come in and they were there that [we were not welcome]. He had actually run for governor—it was Beverly Lake—in a very racist campaign. I actually saw him one night stand at the door as we were leaving the restaurant and hold the door for all of the white women in our group and close the door in the face of one of the black women." More than forty years after the fact, Johnson still struggled to "get over Justice Lake's rude behavior." "I never went before the North Carolina Supreme Court when he was on it that I didn't think of [what he had done]," she said. "That was inconceivable to me. I'd been raised in the rural South, I went to school when schools were segregated, but that a person would do that to another individual person, that was absolutely inconceivable."[55]

When faced with white hostility, volunteer teams across the state adopted a common strategy: they hunkered down in black communities where they were welcomed and felt that they could make a meaningful contribution. George Hall, an engineering student from North Carolina State University, spoke directly to that experience in his daily logs. He had grown up in a white working-class home—his mother worked in a textile mill and his father was a welder—so he felt particularly bruised by the hostility of the sort of folks he had always known as friends and family. The Fund sent Hall and several of his teammates to the Robeson County town of Lumberton, where they staffed a playground in a black riverside community known as "the Bottoms." At first, the assignment was unsettling—he had never before spent so much time among black people—but that changed once he made the effort to befriend members of the community and to make it clear that he had come to serve their needs.

Hall was gratified—and given the novelty of the venture, also a bit surprised—by the outcome. "The first few days that I spent in the community were sheer terror," he wrote near the end of the summer. "Every time that I walked down the streets I was the object of stares. I had expected their stares for a few days but it continued much longer. Well, I decided to stay on the playground. Then I met Sister Ida Floyd, the minister of the largest church in the Bottoms. I asked her what her people [wanted] most and she said that a basic reading course for the adults was urgently needed." Hall and his teammates worried that if they offered instruction, "fear and mistrust" would keep people away. But after the first meeting with older members of the community, "everything began to snowball. The people decided that if they were going to have school they would need a building, so they rented a house . . . and fixed up four rooms to hold the classes in. . . . We have visitors most every night who want to begin in a class, but we have to turn them away with a promise that there will be more classes started when more personnel and money are available." With an obvious sense of pride, Hall concluded his report by noting, "I am no longer feared or mistrusted, but accepted and respected."

Not far away, in a black church in rural Robeson County, Elizabeth Silver, a freshman art major from the University of North Carolina, had a similar experience. "This morning, I integrated a church," she declared in her daily log. "Halfway through the opening hymn, I thought to ask the student I had gone to church with if any whites had ever visited before." Silver's friend answered by contrasting the black congregation's openness with the less hospitable attitude of white churches that had turned away integrated groups of volunteers. "Don't worry," she said, "they won't throw you out." As Silver sat and listened to the black preacher's civil rights sermon, she "felt conspicuous, but welcomed."

Experiences such as these had a clarifying effect for the volunteers, who began to recover their self-confidence and to embrace their role as "charter members of an idea." With renewed certainty, they sought to set "the pace for integration" and to model for others a vision of what "could be." In Laurinburg, for instance, they chose to end a summer of rejection and disappointment by organizing a forum for black and white high school students. Desegregation of the city's schools was scheduled to begin in the fall of 1965, and the volunteers hoped that they might ease the process by sharing their own stories of integrated living. In a similar way, Anne Jones, who had experienced the terrible events in New Bern, continued to give gentle witness to new possibilities for race relations. One day she entered a corner grocery store where she regularly shopped. She had passed by earlier taking a black child to a recreation program. Jones noted in her daily log what happened when she returned to buy a Coke from the white store owner: "As usual, we spoke; he then said 'well, I'd thought I would never see the day when a white girl carries around a Negro baby.' I said, 'well, that day has come, sir, hasn't it?' He replied, 'yeah, guess you're right.' I answered, 'it's a good day too, isn't it?', and he nodded, slowly—and still skeptically."

Emboldened by support from their black hosts, the volunteers also openly defied local government officials and pressed for economic and political changes that would improve the lives of "the people of poverty." After battling with Durham officials over the building of recreation facilities in poor black neighborhoods, Penn Szittya and his teammates wrestled with the question of how they might "satisfy the Durham Committee, including the mayor, but still get at poverty problems, and not spend the summer making 'pot holders'—so to speak!" Their answer was to strike an alliance with the city's director of black playgrounds, who helped quietly and out of sight of his supervisors, and to work through local churches to organize men and teenage boys to clear a vacant lot, lay out a ball field, and arrange a program of recreational activities that the neighborhood would sustain with or without the city's assistance. In other communities, volunteers undertook similar efforts. One team set up a mothers club for poor women, so that "they [might] investigate for playgrounds" and a community center for their children; another helped neighbors in a poor coastal town secure federal dollars for an after-school tutoring program that local officials refused to fund; and, in yet another location, a group of volunteers worked with poor parents to win a grant to make their summer play school part of the Johnson administration's Head Start initiative.

Such organizing efforts could go only so far in the course of ten weeks of summer work, but even so, they reflected a fundamental change in the students' understanding of citizenship. The volunteers had come to embrace activism no less than service as an essential element of democracy. The poor, they began to argue, had not only a responsibility to live as productive, self-reliant citizens, but also a right to demand political representation, higher wages, improved housing, and better schools for their children.

THE VOLUNTEERS' EXPANDED SENSE of rights and obligations—their own and those of the poor—helped steer the North Carolina Fund in new directions. At the end of their summer of service, many of the students complained about the ephemeral nature of their work. What good was it to tutor a child or to provide organized recreation, they asked, if those programs would disappear as soon as the summer ended? Others openly mocked the idea that poverty might be eradicated by rehabilitating the poor rather than addressing issues of political and economic privilege. "Taught one 7 year-old boy to tie his shoes," a volunteer quipped in her log. "Very important for breaking the cycle of poverty: if we're to help them lift themselves by their shoe straps, it helps if their shoes stay on."

Those challenges resonated with new demands rising up from within poor communities. In many places where the volunteers worked, the summer program provided a public stage for indigenous leaders who had their own ideas about how best to fight poverty. In Durham, for instance, the men and women who had worked with Penn Szittya to build a playground moved next to organize a rent strike and to picket city hall. They insisted that the streets in their neighborhood be paved, that garbage be collected more regularly, and that housing laws be enforced against white slumlords. As poor communities began to act on the opportunities that the volunteers had helped create, they sent a message back to the Fund that might have surprised the students: "Residents of poverty neighborhoods are 'tired of seeing North Carolina Volunteers' and would rather do [the work] themselves." As Fund staff observed, the poor were becoming "advocates in their own behalf, seeking representation on community action boards and on neighborhood councils. A new voice was being heard."[56]

By late 1965, Fund officials were ready to shift course. When the summer program ended in August of that year, they disbanded the volunteers. A number of factors contributed to that decision. First, Fund staff had grown increasingly concerned about the safety of the volunteers, the majority of whom were white women, as the civil rights movement heated up and violence directed at interracial groups intensified. Second, federal underwriting for the volunteers had run out by 1965, and Fund leaders had not been able to locate another source of support. To continue the Volunteers program would have required the Fund to draw more heavily on its own resources at precisely the time when many within the organization were raising questions about the efficacy of spending money on middle-class volunteerism instead of developing the capacities of the poor. "It seems to me that the North Carolina Volunteers have done what they intended to do," observed staff member Betty Ward, who had served as a team director in Clay and Cherokee Counties. "That is, they have demonstrated that college students, with their refreshing idealism and enthusiasm, can show us a different way of looking at the poor." It was now time to take the next step. Ward and other Fund leaders had come to the same conclusion as many of the student volunteers: "The real issues . . . were issues of power, and . . . not a whole lot was going to change . . . without changing . . . [the arrangement of] power." For that reason, the Fund began in late 1965 to direct its efforts toward more purposeful community organizing.[57]

AN ARMY OF THE POOR

By 1965, community organizing was also very much on the minds of policy-makers in Washington. The Economic Opportunity Act, which Lyndon John-son signed into law on August 20, 1964, included in Title II a requirement that federally supported community action programs (CAPs) provide for the "maximum feasible participation of the residents of the areas and the mem-bers of the groups" that they sought to serve. That mandate echoed guide-lines that the North Carolina Fund had spelled out a year earlier in its call for CAP proposals from local communities. Initially, such requirements seemed to pose no obvious threat to established power. They simply asked middle-class Americans to consider the concerns and outlook of their less fortunate neighbors. But as federal officials, local activists, and the poor themselves sought to give meaning to "participation" and "understanding," they moved the antipoverty battle onto terrain that was more openly political. That cer-tainly had been the case for members of the North Carolina Volunteers. Their experiences ultimately convinced Fund staff and many of the young people themselves to "chuck" the "volunteer approach" and instead to organize "poor power" so that the "vested interests [of the downtrodden] could be served." That shift laid bare the relationships of power and privilege that structured economic inequality into the very fabric of American life and, in doing so, ignited a firestorm over the objectives and methods of the War on Poverty.[1]

Ironically, the call for maximum feasible participation made its way into the work of the North Carolina Fund and the framing of the Economic Op-portunity Act with little debate or anticipation of its disruptive potential. The idea derived primarily from the Ford Foundation's Gray Areas projects and related urban reform initiatives, particularly the Mobilization for Youth pro-gram, which was designed to battle juvenile delinquency in New York's im-poverished Lower East Side. There, Paul Ylvisaker and others had promoted community mobilization as a means of battling anomie and "awakening self-respect" among young people who felt alienated from mainstream society and powerless to alter their life circumstances. Ford officials and their local allies also viewed community action as a tool for goading rigidified social welfare bureaucracies into adopting more responsive and effective methods for the delivery of services.[2]

The same thinking was critical to the establishment of the North Carolina Fund, which Washington policymakers took as a model for their own national efforts. In late January 1964, shortly after Lyndon Johnson proposed a war on poverty in his State of the Union address, White House aides identified three candidates to lead that effort: Richard Lee, mayor of New Haven, Connecticut, where the Ford Foundation had established one of its early Gray Areas projects; Sargent Shriver, President Kennedy's brother-in-law and director of the Peace Corps; and Terry Sanford, who had "launched a very imaginative program . . . more or less along the lines [that Johnson was] considering." Shriver got the job, but Sanford remained a close adviser to policymakers in Washington. As they drafted the Economic Opportunity Act, legislators and White House staff called on the governor and Fund director George Esser "to lend the value" of their experience. The two North Carolinians placed great emphasis on community action and the involvement of the poor. Sanford told a congressional committee that he "had come to believe that charity and relief [were] not the best answers to human suffering." "Instead of providing for people," he urged, "we ought to attempt to find ways to help them work out of their situations of poverty and become self-respecting and self-supporting."[3]

That conviction resonated with Shriver's team, particularly Richard Boone, who in the Kennedy administration had been deeply involved with the Gray Areas idea and the work of the President's Committee on Juvenile Delinquency and Youth Crime. Adam Yarmolinsky, a lawyer on loan to Shriver from the Department of Defense, recalled that Boone kept repeating the phrase "maximum feasible participation." At one point, he confronted Boone, saying, "You have used that phrase four or five times now." "Yes, I know," Boone replied. "How many more times do I have to use it before it becomes part of the program?" "Oh, a couple of times more," Yarmolinsky joked. Boone spoke up again, and the idea was soon "incorporated into the language of the bill." There was humor in the exchange, Yarmolinsky explained, because at the time, "the possibility of major conflict between the organized poor and the politicians in city hall was simply not one that anybody worried about."[4]

Lyndon Johnson's political advisers embraced maximum feasible participation for reasons of their own. Anxious to establish himself as a worthy successor to John Kennedy and eager to maintain the Democratic Party's lock on black votes in the urban North, the new president sought early on to signal his responsiveness to the civil rights movement. That concern quickly became part of the planning for the War on Poverty. Daniel Patrick Moynihan, then assistant secretary of labor, recalled that aides close to the president started to ask, "What about Negroes in the South?" "Inasmuch as the local white power structure would control" federal funds allocated for community action, "how could it be ensured that impoverished Negroes would get something like a proportionate share?" The answer was to write such a provision into law, and here the call for poor people's participation served a practical political purpose. It would guarantee "that persons excluded from the political process in the South . . . would nonetheless participate in the *benefits* of the community action programs of the new legislation." At the time, Moynihan added, no one involved in drafting the Economic Opportunity Act viewed it as an instrument for remaking southern politics. Indeed, "it was taken as a matter beneath notice that [community action] programs would be dominated by the local political structure."[5]

Members of North Carolina's congressional delegation took a less sanguine view of the legislation. On August 8, 1964, they called Shriver to a meeting in the office of the Speaker of the House of Representatives and demanded "as a price of their support" that Adam Yarmolinsky not be appointed deputy director of the Office of Economic Opportunity (OEO). The lawmakers' opposition derived from the fact that as assistant to the secretary of defense, Yarmolinsky had argued vigorously for the constitutional rights of black military personnel stationed in the South. Knowing that passage of the Economic Opportunity Act depended on support from southern Democrats, Shriver and Johnson sacrificed the man whom many observers regarded as the brightest of Secretary of Defense Robert McNamara's "wiz kids." The North Carolina legislators walked away from the showdown confident that they had limited the War on Poverty's potential to become yet another instrument for federal involvement in southern race relations. But, in fact, they had opened the door to an antipoverty warrior who embodied their worst fears. With Yarmolinsky off the short list, Shriver offered the position of deputy director of the OEO to Jack T. Conway, a United Auto Workers (UAW) union official and a chief architect of efforts to forge a political alliance between organized labor and the civil rights movement.[6]

Scholars have largely overlooked Conway's role in shaping the work of the OEO and for that reason have missed connections that tied the War on Poverty to a larger tradition of progressive social action. Conway grew up in Detroit in a working-class family. As a student at the University of Chicago during the late 1930s, he became active in Socialist Party politics, and in 1942 he took a part-time job at the General Motors plant in Melrose Park, Illinois, and joined Local 6 of the UAW. Less than a decade earlier, the United Auto Workers had bolted from the American Federation of Labor (AFL) and had joined other dissidents in establishing the Congress of Industrial Organizations (CIO). The CIO committed itself to organizing workers according to industry rather than craft tradition, and to that end it recruited aggressively within the ranks of semi- and unskilled laborers, including women, blacks, and other minorities who, with few exceptions, had been excluded from the AFL. The UAW and other CIO unions undertook that campaign against the backdrop of Franklin Roosevelt's New Deal, which dramatically enlarged the role of the federal government as a guarantor of the public welfare. The New Deal stretched a social safety net beneath the nation's most vulnerable citizens, provided a basic measure of economic security for the aged and un-employed, and, through the Wagner Act of 1935 and establishment of the National Labor Relations Board, affirmed working people's right to organize and bargain collectively with their employers. Conway and like-minded labor activists of his generation embraced those policies as instruments for fash-ioning a new national consensus around broadened notions of political and economic citizenship. They rallied to the project of "peaceful revolution" that Roosevelt outlined in 1941 in his famous "Four Freedoms" State of the Union address. "There is nothing mysterious about the foundations of a healthy and strong democracy," the president declared. "The basic things expected by our people of their political and economic systems are simple. They are equality of opportunity. . . . Jobs for those who can work. Security for those who need it. The ending of special privilege for the few. The preservation of civil liber-ties for all."[7]

From the end of World War II through the early 1960s, Conway served as chief aide to UAW president Walter Reuther, a labor statesman known to his detractors as "the most dangerous man in Detroit." Reuther led the UAW from 1946 to 1970, and during that long tenure he distinguished himself by insisting that the union could be a force not only for bettering conditions in the workplace but also for improving the welfare of all Americans. Through-out the better part of two decades, he and Conway devoted their considerable political talents to forging a cross-class, biracial alliance of organized labor, white middle-class liberals, and blacks. Such a coalition, they believed, could bridge the historic fault lines of American politics and work a thoroughgoing reconstruction of the nation's economic life. In its broadest terms, theirs was an old dream, one that echoed the social democratic aspirations of ardent New Dealers and would have rung true with the black and white Fusionists who, in the late nineteenth century, sought to create a similar moment of democratic possibility.[8]

The UAW was often at odds with itself on matters of race. Union leaders lacked the ability—and oftentimes the will—to eradicate deeply held prejudices and structural inequalities on the shop floor and within their locals. Nevertheless, they threw the UAW's institutional weight behind the civil rights movement. The union supported the National Association for the Advancement of Colored People (NAACP) by filing an amicus curiae brief in *Brown v. Board of Education*, and in 1954, when the Supreme Court struck down the doctrine of separate but equal, Reuther welcomed the judgment as a "heart-warming affirmation of . . . American democratic principles." The UAW also provided financial backing for the Montgomery bus boycott, and in 1963 it organized a bail fund for demonstrators arrested in the Southern Christian Leadership Conference's assault on racial discrimination in Birmingham, Alabama. When police chief Eugene "Bull" Connor insisted that the protesters' bond be paid in cash, UAW emissaries traveled to Birmingham with the money hidden beneath their clothes.[9]

In the summer of that same year, Reuther and Conway joined forces with black labor and civil rights activists A. Philip Randolph and Bayard Rustin to stage the March on Washington for Jobs and Freedom. The UAW leaders rallied support from white religious and civil liberties organizations in what Reuther called a "coalition of conscience." Departing from the "neutrality" of most other unions, the UAW also paid for the sound system that was installed at the foot of the Lincoln Memorial, provided transportation for five thousand of its members (the largest delegation representing any single organization), and distributed thousands of placards that proclaimed the inseverable relationship between civil rights and economic opportunity. "We March for Jobs for All at Decent Pay Now," the signs shouted. "Freedom is a Lie for America's Not So Invisible Poor." "Civil Rights Plus Full Employment Equals Freedom."[10]

On August 28, more than a quarter of a million Americans—black and white, from all walks of life—gathered in the nation's capital to demand passage of the civil rights bill then pending in Congress, adoption of a $2-an-hour federal minimum wage, and amendment of the Fair Labor Standards Act so that agricultural and domestic workers—the vast majority of them black—would be included in the law's wage and workplace protections. Today, most Americans remember the August rally as simply the March on Washington. Few recall its more expansive name and purpose, and with that forgetting has come diminished understanding of the event's significance in joining two of the twentieth century's most dynamic social movements. The march reflected civil rights advocates' concern for economic justice as well as social equality and their awareness, in Reuther's words, that "without a job and a paycheck," triumph over Jim Crow would be "a largely abstract and empty victory." It also represented the UAW's conviction that the black freedom struggle could provide the kind of mass mobilization required to forge an enduring realignment in American politics. The civil rights movement promised to deliver black votes that could break the hold of white supremacy in the Solid South and, in so doing, undermine the alliance of conservative Republicans and segregationist southern Democrats that had frustrated efforts at reorganizing the nation's economy and redistributing its abundance.[11]

During the years immediately after World War II, that alliance steered American politics sharply to the right and halted—in some cases, even rolled back—the advances of the New Deal. In 1946, Republicans, campaigning on the slogan "Had Enough?" won control of both houses of Congress in landslide victories. Together with hard-line southern Democrats, they rejected President Harry Truman's call for strengthened civil rights protection; defeated legislative plans for full employment, universal heath care, and expanded Social Security coverage; and in 1947, over the president's veto, passed the antiunion Taft-Hartley Act, which outlawed the closed shop and authorized individual states to adopt right-to-work laws.[12]

Walter Reuther and Jack Conway saw in the War on Poverty an opportunity to institutionalize a labor–civil rights coalition capable of reversing that tide and reinvigorating a social democratic agenda. At the request of White House aides, they provided language for the State of the Union address in which Lyndon Johnson announced his campaign against poverty, and months later, Reuther wrote to the president pledging the UAW's support as "loyal soldiers in the unconditional war" against deprivation and want. From the beginning, however, Reuther and Conway had a more expansive conception of the battle than did Johnson and most liberals. Daniel Patrick Moynihan incisively characterized the difference. "Where the President hoped to help the poor," he wrote, UAW leaders "wished to arouse them." Reuther made that point clear in a resolution set before the UAW's March 1964 convention and in testimony before Congress. "The fight against poverty must not develop along the lines of a well-intentioned social welfare program of the rich doing favors for the poor," he cautioned. It should seek instead "to organize the poor so that they are not only visible but have a voice."[13]

That idea became the leitmotif of Conway's work as deputy director of the OEO. He made his mark on the agency early and indelibly as cochair of the

committee that prepared grant guidelines for local community action programs seeking federal financial assistance. Key parts of the OEO's *Community
Action Program Guide* read like a union-organizing manual. From the outset,
it placed a premium on grassroots participation. "A vital feature of every community action program," the *Guide* explained, was to be "the involvement of
the poor themselves—the residents of the areas and members of the groups
to be served—in planning, policy-making, and operation of the program."
That was common sense for Conway and UAW colleagues who understood
that it was not organizers from the outside but workers on the shop floor who
had built their union. Walter Reuther observed that John L. Lewis, head of
the United Mine Workers and the CIO's fiery first president, "didn't go into
a single General Motors plant. . . . The guys in the plants did the job and that
is what has got to be done with the poverty neighborhoods." The OEO *Guide*
insisted accordingly that poor people's participation in the War on Poverty
should be organized from the bottom up: "It should be brought about by
'traditional democratic approaches and techniques such as group forums and
discussions, nominations, and balloting.' It should be stimulated by 'grassroots involvement' committees; by 'block elections, petitions, and referen-
dums'; by 'promotional techniques, including use of films, literature, and
mobile units operating from information centers.' Further, residents should
be given 'meaningful opportunities . . . either as individuals or as groups, to
protest or to propose additions to or changes in the ways in which a community action program is being planned or undertaken." The ultimate objective
of these activities was to identify and train leaders from within impoverished
neighborhoods, to articulate shared problems and concerns, and to provide
the poor with the human and institutional resources necessary to bargain
with local political leaders, their employers, and social welfare agencies.[14]

Daniel Moynihan argued that "the Conway group" gave to community
action "a structure that neither those who [proposed the War on Poverty],
those who sponsored it, nor those who enacted it ever in any way intended."
That assessment is misleading—the architects of the War on Poverty were
a diverse lot who often disagreed about the capacity of the poor to solve
their own problems—but Moynihan did put his finger on something important about Conway's influence. The UAW official came to the OEO when the
agency was still a blank slate. For his own political reasons, President Johnson
had pressured Congress to act swiftly, and as a result, the War on Poverty was
launched with minimal planning and little more than a general mandate to
"eliminate the paradox of [want] in the midst of plenty." Conway brought to
an as yet uncharted battlefield more than three decades of personal and insti-

tutional experience in securing a middle-class standard of living and a political voice for blue-collar autoworkers. That knowledge gave practical meaning to the otherwise vague notion of the maximum feasible participation of the poor. To Conway's ear, the idea echoed the CIO's call in the 1930s to "organize the unorganized." Such thinking saturated the work of the early OEO. In explaining his agency and the law that created it, Sargent Shriver often drew explicit links between the activism of the 1960s and that of the 1930s. The Economic Opportunity Act, he said, was "for the poor what the National Labor Relations Act [of 1935] was for unions. . . . It recognizes the principle of representation, full participation, of fair bargaining. It establishes a new relationship, a new grievance procedure between the poor and the rest of society."[15]

For fiscal year 1965 (beginning October 1, 1964), Congress approved an initial budget of $800 million for the Office of Economic Opportunity. As soon as the new antipoverty agency was open for business, the North Carolina Fund insisted that the eleven CAPs it had approved and financed a year earlier apply for federal support. The reasons were obvious. The CAPs were precisely the type of agency through which Congress intended to funnel public funds; securing grants from Washington would heavily leverage the Fund's investment of private capital; and partnership with the OEO promised to integrate the Fund's work into the national effort for which it served as an important model. The initial response from the local CAPs was enthusiastic, and by year's end all had begun negotiations for federal funding. Before long, however, the process of preparing grant proposals brought to the surface old concerns about the consequences of linking local initiatives to federal largesse.[16]

Throughout the first half of the twentieth century, the South had managed to sup at the federal trough while maintaining a rigid system of Jim Crow. Under the New Deal, the region benefited from millions of dollars invested in agricultural subsidies, and in the 1940s southern congressmen lobbied aggressively to lure billions more in the form of defense contracts and new military bases. After World War II, however, preservation of the "southern way of life" became more difficult, first as President Truman ordered the desegregation of the armed forces in 1948, and then with passage of federal civil rights legislation in 1957 and 1964. With that history in mind, many of the more conservative members of the CAP boards perceived the federal War on Poverty, with its insistence on nondiscrimination and participation of the poor, as little more than a "way of forcing integration by dangling funds." The North Carolina Fund reported that "in every community at least one Board member resigned as a direct result of the switch to Federal funding. Virtually all protested that this was *not* what they had anticipated." One local official stated his objections bluntly. "If . . . we must concede to any given segment of the population, [the Negroes]," he declared, "we will not have it."[17]

The work of crafting proposals for the OEO also exposed opposition to key objectives of the War on Poverty. The founders of the local CAPs appreciated the need for economic development in their communities. They welcomed federal dollars that would help them train the unemployed in new job skills and provide opportunity as a reward for ambition and industriousness. They understood that better housing, nutrition, and health care not only would improve the lives of the poor but also would lighten the welfare burden on local taxpayers. But few were prepared for the truly radical implications of a seemingly simple and compelling idea: the eradication of poverty. Local leaders worried about the consequences for an economy built on cheap labor and for their own economic security and position of privilege. "We just about can't get any colored people to work anymore," complained one mayor. "I guess in 4 or 5 years we won't even be able to get maids. I just don't know what we'll do." In other locations, CAP board members hesitated to enlarge their "work training programs" too quickly. The "economic stability of [their communities] depended upon the availability of a large pool of unskilled workers," they explained, and "many industries . . . would move if they were no longer able to hire at the current low wage rates."[18]

And so the objections mounted, piling high one upon another as local leaders hedged their commitment to an "all-out war on poverty." Over time, the Fund compiled a catalog of equivocation and outright obstructionism: "In one rural area an association of farmers sought to force the [local CAP] not to hire anyone or support any jobs during the harvesting seasons since they claimed they were unable to get workers to pick their crops. . . . In another county public welfare programs including the food stamp programs are regularly curtailed during the summer months to 'make sure we have a labor supply that is willing to work.' In this county the local welfare agency officials sought to get the [CAP] to take similar action. In this same county it is the practice of the welfare board to give food stamps, during those months that it issues them, to the owners of the land on which . . . tenants live. This enables the landowner to regulate the tenants more closely." North Carolina Fund staff observed that evidence of this sort "could be continued at length. The point is, however, that there [was] considerable opposition to the anti-poverty program, by elected officials and [CAP] board members alike, because of the changes that would occur if incomes were raised and jobs provided for the marginally employed." As that opposition revealed, the persistence of poverty amid plenty—despite the proclamations of politicians and pundits—was not truly a paradox. Poverty was instead intimately bound to relationships of power—political and economic—and for many CAP board members, rearranging those relationships was not the fight for which they had volunteered.[19]

The story of each CAP is, in and of itself, a fascinating tale of the interplay of race, class, and politics. But despite the particularities of place and personality, the experience in every community demonstrated just how difficult it was for the poor to mobilize themselves and to effect substantive social change. As Fund staff explained, the advantage always belonged to the "power structure": "In our political system those who would block action, who would exercise veto power, who would delay change have every structural advantage. Positive changes can be made only if the action is approved on numerous occasions and before numerous legislative, executive and judicial bodies. You must be a winner at every decision point (and there are many in a pluralistic system). But to defeat change one must be victorious at only one place in the network of decision-making situations. Objectors, if they can muster support in only one arena, can be victorious. So in many ways the specific structural characteristics of our governmental system give a distinct advantage to those unwilling, for example, to grant true equality to the Negro." That reality, one Fund report observed, was "what Paul Ylvisaker referred to when he complained that [the establishment] had 'nay saying power' but [those advocating change] had no power"—or, at best, limited power—"to say yes."[20]

In the end, this disparity meant that CAP officials who were wary of federal intrusion into local affairs had considerable leeway to play for time and to bend new initiatives to their will, even as they complied nominally with OEO guidelines. They put "representatives" of the poor and of black communities on their boards, but never in proportionate numbers. They also chose individuals whose capacity for independent expression was compromised—for instance, a black school principal who served alongside his white superintendent. In similar fashion, CAP boards curtailed or declined federal support for programs they deemed too controversial. Summer youth employment programs, for instance, were welcomed, but only if they limited the number of participants so as to minimize the impact on local wage rates. That same ambivalence greeted Head Start, the OEO's flagship school-readiness program. Although CAP boards and local politicians appreciated its benefits for young children, they were prepared to reject the initiative outright rather than let it become a Trojan horse for "forced integration" or an alternative source of employment for poor mothers that bid up the price of labor. In short, CAP leaders were constantly on the lookout for programs that threatened to make too much change too quickly.

In North Carolina, the mobilization of the poor—what one antipoverty warrior described as the building of "an army of dissenters"—gained its strongest foothold in two locations: the tobacco and textile manufacturing city of Durham and the rural Choanoke region in the northeastern corner of the state. At first glance, those places could not have been more different. Durham, with its "Black Wall Street," had a vibrant black business community, while outsiders often referred to the Choanoke as "North Carolina's 'little Mississippi.'" Beneath those differences, however, lay two crucial similarities. The black community in both places had a long tradition of independent political activity that dated back to the late nineteenth century, while the white establishment lacked cohesion and was only loosely organized as a political force. Durham's industries were operated by absentee corporate owners, and as a result, day-to-day governance fell to a loose-knit group of merchants, realtors, and lawyers. In the Choanoke, white landlords exercised extraordinary authority over their tenants, but they seldom acted in concert as an organized bloc. The region resembled a collection of small fiefdoms more than a tightly integrated political and economic system. Those circumstances left open opportunities for the poor—particularly the black poor—to organize their own institutions and to test the War on Poverty's capacity to make meaningful change.[21]

DURHAM, PERHAPS MORE THAN ANY other city, symbolized North Carolina's aspirations as a "progressive" New South state. The city did not show up on the census of 1870, but by the early twentieth century, it had developed into a booming center of tobacco and textile manufacturing. Tobacco was one of the few industries in the segregated South that offered factory employment to blacks, and for that reason, Durham, along with Winston-Salem, became a magnet for African American migration off the land. The city's large black population, in turn, helped support a thriving black business sector and a small but prosperous black middle class. Hillside High School and North Carolina College—the first publicly funded African American liberal arts institution in the United States—offered educational opportunities that were rarely available elsewhere in the state or region, and two of the city's financial institutions, the North Carolina Mutual Life Insurance Company and Mechanics and Farmers Bank, ranked among the largest black-owned enterprises in the nation. Blacks across the South saw in Durham a testament to the potential of self-help and the power of "the almighty dollar [to knock] the bottom out of race prejudice and all the humbugs that fatten it." White supremacists, looking at the same city, found evidence that Jim Crow might yet endure on the pretense of separate but equal.[22]

In the 1960s, Durham was poised for another great transformation. Duke University, along with North Carolina State University in Raleigh and the University of North Carolina's flagship campus in Chapel Hill, anchored the Research Triangle Park, a high-tech industrial campus carved out of the pine forests of southern Durham County. With the arrival of IBM and the National Institutes of Environmental Health Sciences in 1966, the project began its steady growth toward becoming the largest facility of its kind in the world. Duke University's Medical Center worked similar changes in the field of health care. By the mid-1960s, Duke had become the largest employer in Durham County, and the city, once known around the globe for its tobacco products, was on its way to becoming a self-styled "City of Medicine."[23]

When compared to North Carolina at large, Durham appeared to be thriving. The county ranked seventh in the state for median family income and twelfth for average years of schooling among persons over twenty-five years of age. But, as one student of the city has observed, "the law of averages obscured the vast gulf between the rich and poor in Durham." Twenty-eight percent of families lived below the Fund-designated poverty line of $3,000 a year, and roughly an equal share of the city's housing stock was classified as "unsound and/or lacking adequate plumbing facilities." An official of the Southern Christian Leadership Conference who visited in 1966 wrote, "Never before have I seen a Southern city that looked so much like a depressed backward country." In Durham's most impoverished black neighborhoods, "the streets [were] narrow, unpaved, and unlighted, the houses uniformly dilapidated, the plumbing nonexistent . . . and the rats and the cockroaches abundant."[24]

John Wheeler, president of Mechanics and Farmers Bank, had lobbied hard to have the North Carolina Fund headquartered in Durham, and he urged local civic leaders to embrace the new agency as a means of addressing the problems of the city's poor. That appeal struck a chord with the merchants, bankers, and real estate developers who ran city hall. In the midst of the civil rights unrest of 1963, they were eager to calm black protest. From their offices atop the city's tallest buildings, they could also see the scars that poverty left on the urban landscape. Such scenes were incompatible with their vision of a "Greater Durham" reaching for the fruits of an emerging high-tech economy.

Wheeler found a willing partner in Durham mayor R. Wensell Grabarek, who had actively campaigned for black votes and had run on a platform of moderation in race relations. Grabarek won election on May 18, 1963 — one day after the ninth anniversary of *Brown* and on the same day that Durham's black youth, organized by the Congress on Racial Equality (CORE) and the NAACP, began an "all-out drive for desegregation." The city's jail quickly filled with protesters, and each day ever-larger crowds of angry whites gathered to jeer the civil rights demonstrations. Grabarek attempted to avert a crisis on the order of Birmingham by pressuring a handful of white restaurant owners to serve blacks on an equal basis. With that concession in hand, he appeared at a large gathering at one of Durham's leading black churches and pledged his support for efforts to "resolve and reconcile" the city's racial troubles. Grabarek left with an agreement from black leaders to "suspend mass demonstrations 'for the time being,'" and a day later he appointed an interracial committee to work toward voluntary desegregation. The truce, however, did not last. Defiant to the end, Durham's white restaurant owners association voted "to continue its practice of segregation."[25]

Grabarek viewed antipoverty work as a key component of his effort to manage social change through negotiation rather than public confrontation. As the standoff between civil rights protesters and segregationists continued, he convened a small working group of Durham civic leaders to consider how the city might benefit from a partnership with the North Carolina Fund. In addition to Grabarek, the committee included the Durham County manager, the president of the city's chamber of commerce, and Robert Foust, a social worker who headed the Durham Community Planning Council, a United Fund agency responsible for coordinating the work of public and private welfare services. The group held a series of public hearings during the summer and early autumn in which they presented the benefits of an antipoverty campaign in terms calculated to appeal to fellow business owners. They promised that raising the income of Durham's poorest citizens above the poverty line would increase tax revenues by $2.4 million a year, would decrease welfare payments by $3.6 million, and, as those funds circulated through the economy, would produce a total stimulus of $68.7 million. That was a compelling message. With the support of Durham's white business community, Grabarek appointed a forty-seven-person ad hoc committee called Action for Durham Development (ADD). Its charge was to plan a local community action program and to submit a proposal to the North Carolina Fund. Victor Bryant, a prominent local attorney, chaired the group, and J. A. McLean, vice president of Central Carolina Bank and Trust Company, served as vice-chair. Remarkably, the committee included only three representatives of Durham's black community.[26]

Everett Hopkins, professor of psychology and vice president for planning and institutional studies at Duke University, led the work on ADD's proposal. In keeping with the military tone of the War on Poverty, he dubbed the Durham plan "Operation Breakthrough." Hopkins sketched a conventional, top-down approach to poverty reduction that focused on the rehabilitation of poor families and individual self-improvement. The program was to proceed in two stages. In the preparatory phase, teams of social welfare professionals would work with target families to diagnose their problems and develop "breakthrough plans" for escaping poverty. Then, in the action phase, the families would implement the plans by seeking out a variety of social services, such as after-school tutoring, vocational training, and job placement. To support the poor in that effort, a group of up to one thousand community volunteers would work to "bridge the gap between community resources" and participating families, thus ensuring the efficient and effective delivery of welfare assistance.[27]

The North Carolina Fund awarded ADD a grant of $11,000 in early July 1964. In August, the committee incorporated Durham's new community action program under the Operation Breakthrough banner, and in October, it named Robert Foust to serve as the agency's executive director. Foust's first challenge was to square Operation Breakthrough with the OEO's emphasis on maximum feasible participation. That proved to be an arduous task. Operation Breakthrough's founders had embraced antipoverty programs, at least in part, as a means of "pre-empting Durham's scrappy civil rights organizers" and quelling dissent. The OEO's policy of maximum feasible participation, however, pointed in the opposite direction. Federal officials aimed to develop indigenous leaders among the poor who could provoke and sustain vigorous, open debate. To that end, the OEO demanded that one-third of Operation Breakthrough's board come from Durham's low-income communities and that the board be thoroughly integrated. After several failed drafts, Operation Breakthrough finally satisfied the OEO by adding to its funding proposal a plan to organize neighborhood councils in the areas targeted for intervention. Foust and his associates conceived of the councils in strictly practical terms: they were a means "to get some representatives of the poor elected by the poor on [Operation Breakthrough's] Board of Directors." Little did Breakthrough's founders imagine that those councils would soon challenge them for control of the local assault on poverty.[28]

The OEO awarded Operation Breakthrough a grant of $181,000 in late December 1964. Five months later — in May 1965 — Foust hired a young black activist named Howard Fuller to coordinate the program's community organizing efforts. Fuller had been born in Louisiana and at age six moved with his family to Milwaukee. He grew up in public housing and learned to play basketball in neighborhood pickup games. An athletic scholarship took him to Carroll College, a Presbyterian liberal arts institution in Waukesha, Wisconsin, where for three years he was the only black student on campus. After graduating, Fuller moved to Western Reserve University in Cleveland, where he earned a master's degree in social work, joined CORE, and participated in voter registration drives, school boycotts, and other civil rights protests. Fuller worked briefly for the Urban League in Chicago but found the position frustrating. As an employment counselor, he operated in an environment that compromised his principles. Too often, his task was to find "a Negro who was just the right color brown to fill a job slot." Eager for a change, Fuller welcomed news from his friends James McDonald and Morris Cohen, both Fund employees, that Operation Breakthrough was "looking for a black man with a master's degree in social work to head [its] community organizing component." He had known Cohen, a Chicago native and former director of a South Side settlement house in that city, when they were in graduate school together at Western Reserve. McDonald grew up in Milwaukee, studied law at the University of Wisconsin, and returned home to direct an Urban League youth program that Fuller participated in as a teenager. When Fuller arrived in Durham, he was struck immediately by the Janus-like character of white North Carolina politics. He had been drawn to the state by Governor Sanford's progressive reputation and the "innovative idea" of the North Carolina Fund, but soon after arriving in Durham he tuned in to Raleigh's WRAL-TV and heard Jesse Helms disparage the work of Martin Luther King Jr. "That's when I understood that I was in the South," Fuller recalled, "and that this was going to be an interesting experience."[29]

By his own account, Fuller moved to Durham with a head full of theory and limited practical experience as a community organizer. But his personality and approach to people made him highly effective in the job. He focused initially on a section of Durham identified in the original Operation Breakthrough plan as Target Area A. It was one of the city's most deprived districts, consisting of six geographically distinct neighborhoods: Hayti, Pickett Street, St. Teresa, Hillside Park, Morehead, and a public housing project called Mc-

Howard Fuller on the porch of a Durham home. Photograph by Billy E. Barnes, courtesy of the North Carolina Collection, Wilson Library, University of North Carolina at Chapel Hill, Billy Ebert Barnes Collection.

Dougald Terrace. Fuller took seriously the idea of identifying and developing indigenous leadership, so to organize these communities he and his field superviser, Charlie Hedgepeth, assembled a staff recruited from among the poor. Hedgepeth was a Durham native and graduate of North Carolina College. She had become involved with the North Carolina Fund during the summer of 1964 and had received through the agency some training in community organizing. To work under her direction, Fuller selected five North Carolina College students, all of them from poor families. During the summer of 1965, Hedgepeth and the students introduced themselves to residents of Target Area A by inviting neighborhood children to attend a day camp run by the North Carolina Volunteers. With that entrée into individual households, Fuller's team then undertook a round of regular visits to build personal relationships with parents. The process was time-consuming. "Workers spent from eight to ten hours a day in their various neighborhoods . . . ask[ing] questions about the community" and acquiring "some notion of the problems that were facing the residents."[30]

Fuller sought not to impose organizational structures on the target communities, but to facilitate a more organic process of self-organization. "I can't say that there was any big theoretical construct that drove me," he recalled. "You go talk to people, you identify [what] they see as problems, and then you bring them together to try to go do something about it. It's not like rocket science or anything. It's like, here's a street that ought to be paved. How come this street's not paved? Well, what do you do to get the street paved? And you go from there. Or people got rats in their house. People shouldn't have rats in their house. Who's responsible for this house? If it's an absentee landlord, what are we going do to make him or her do something that they're supposed to do? What is the city supposed to do about this? And what do you mean they can't do anything about it because you're black?"[31]

To Fuller, this process seemed "logical," but for Durham's black poor, it required conquering the apprehension instilled by decades of Jim Crow's rule. "What's going to happen to us?" they wanted to know. "Would life really be better? It hadn't changed in all these years, why would it change now?" "We saw all of that," Fuller recalled, "people not understanding their own power, not believing in their capacity to exercise leadership." By forging personal relationships with the poor, by winning their trust and encouraging neighbors to talk to one another, Fuller and his coworkers sought to break through that wariness and sense of vulnerability. We "aimed at strengthening people's resolve and getting them not to be fearful, and not to be intimidated by people who had power," he explained. "Our view was to get people to see that [they had] dignity, [that they didn't] have to be intimidated by anyone. That wasn't always easy; it's easy to say, but it was harder to get people to the point that they had that kind of confidence in themselves."[32]

Ann Atwater, a resident of Hayti, turned out to be one of Fuller's most important neighborhood allies. Atwater had grown up in Hallsboro, a small lumber town in the southeastern corner of the state. She and her husband, French Wilson, moved to Durham in 1950, hoping to find work in the tobacco factories and to escape deteriorating economic circumstances in the countryside. The struggle to make ends meet soon took its toll. French turned to drink, and when he became abusive, Ann had him arrested. After several failed attempts at reconciliation, French abandoned Ann and their two daughters. In 1965, when Howard Fuller first met her, Atwater was surviving on a welfare check for $57 a month and occasional earnings from domestic work in white homes. She remembered that at the time she took little interest in politics and "didn't participate in anything"; she was too busy "concentrating on taking care of [her] children." The family lived on a diet of fried fatback, rice with gravy, and cabbage. Atwater used flour and rice bags to make slips and dresses for her daughters. "The bags had little designs on them," she explained, "and I thought they were right pretty. I thought the children were right cute, clean—I wanted them to be clean."[33]

Atwater's life changed one August evening when Howard Fuller and Charsie Hedgepeth knocked on her door. Earlier that week, she had visited the welfare office looking for $100 to pay her overdue rent and avoid eviction. When Fuller and Hedgepeth asked about the things that concerned her, she showed them around her house. The front porch leaned precariously toward the street, the roof was so full of holes that Atwater had to put out buckets during storms, and her bathtub had fallen through the floor. "The house was [also] so poorly wired," she said, "that when the man cut off my lights for nonpayment, I could stomp on the floor and the lights would come on, and I'd stomp on the floor [again] and they'd go off. So I kept the lights like that for about a year. They came back out to try to see where I was getting the electricity from, but they never could find out—it was one little wire that they were always missing to cut off." Atwater thought of the faulty wiring as a blessing from the Lord.[34]

Fuller asked if Atwater wanted help getting her house repaired; she answered skeptically, "Yes, [but] how are you going to get the landlord to fix my house?" "Well," he said, "if you come to the meeting tonight, we'll talk about that." So Atwater went, and she shared her story with neighbors who told of living in equally deplorable conditions. The next morning, Fuller and Hedgepeth accompanied her to a face-off with her landlord. Fuller told the man that he had the $100 in back rent that Atwater owed, but he would pay only after necessary repairs had been made. The landlord relented—at least partially. He sent a carpenter to lift Atwater's tub up through her bathroom floor and to secure it with fresh timber. The repair fell far short of all that the house needed, but it was more than Atwater had ever been able to extract on her own. She was impressed by Fuller's ability to carry through on his promises. Later that week, she joined him, going "door to door telling people how they could get their house repaired." As Atwater went on those visits, she began to believe that she had found her calling. "I had it at the heart," she remembered, "and I really wanted to help not only myself but other people. God had given me the gift of reaching out, touching, and I wanted to fulfill the obligation that God gave me to do. I just didn't know how to go about doing it until the North Carolina Fund and Howard taught us. [They] taught me that whatever I believed in, stand on that, don't let nobody change me from it. If I knowed

Ann Atwater canvassing for Operation Breakthrough. Photograph by Billy E. Barnes, courtesy of the North Carolina Collection, Wilson Library, University of North Carolina at Chapel Hill, Billy Ebert Barnes Collection.

it was right and I believed it, then stand on it, and I've been doing that ever since."[35]

Fuller and Atwater were soon canvassing Target Area A as comrades in arms. Together, they worked out the tactics of successful community organizing, each teaching and learning from the other. Fuller impressed upon Atwater and her neighbors the importance of working the process of petition and complaint, so that when public confrontation became necessary, it could be framed as a reasonable act of last resort. "You learn the process," he explained, "because you don't want [the bureaucrats] to jam you [by saying], 'Oh, you didn't fill out the right form.' That's one thing I learned as an organizer. You have to first understand how the system is supposed to work, so that when you follow all of those steps and it doesn't work, you can't get jammed on. If it gets to the point where you've got to demonstrate in front of city hall to get the building inspector to come out and do an inspection, you're able to say, publicly, 'We filled out the form, we talked to this man, he still didn't come, this is why we're out here.'"[36]

Atwater proved to be a masterful practitioner of that strategy. As an on-again, off-again recipient of welfare services, she understood firsthand the condescending and paternalistic treatment that poor people often had to endure. Caseworkers used information as a mechanism of control and dependency. "They wouldn't tell the poor folks anything," and when clients applied for assistance, "they'd swear they was out of money." Atwater set out to help her neighbors get what was rightfully theirs by beating the welfare office at its own game. "One day we were working with a welfare problem," she recalled. "People weren't getting the type help that they were supposed to get. So, I took one of the ladies and went down to the Department of Social Services. Right out front was the [program] manual. I had my coat on, and I took the big book off the desk and put it under my coat while she was fussing about coming there and not getting any help. While they were fussing, I went back down the street to [Operation Breakthrough], and we xeroxed the part that told the welfare recipients their rights." Afterward, when she and her neighbors sought public assistance, they were prepared to cite chapter and verse from the welfare department's own rules and regulations. "When we found out what the rights was, we stood on it, and got some changes made."[37]

Atwater also insisted that black welfare clients be treated with common decency and respect. "You would go in the [welfare] building and it was just open space," she remembered. "They'd call the white people up to the desk and ask them, 'Your name, address? And what are you here for?' And they would whisper like, talking to them. But I could be sitting there and they would holler, 'What you here for? What's your name?' And then if you're fat like I am, they wanted to know if you was pregnant." It was all terribly humiliating. When Atwater decided to take action on this issue, she employed a tactic that soon became her trademark. She leveraged the strength of numbers by organizing small groups of women who visited the welfare office regularly and pressed for reform. The women argued that if caseworkers could not— or would not—change their prejudiced attitudes, they should at least give their clients "a little bit of privacy." Eventually, the welfare office conceded, at first constructing small booths and then remodeling the building so that each caseworker had a semiprivate office. "That's one of the changes that we made," Atwater noted with pride, "and it's still like that now today."[38]

Howard Fuller's concern for encouraging the poor to become their own best advocates struck a chord in Target Area A. By fall 1965, he had organized five neighborhood councils. Out of those groups, he hired additional field

Howard Fuller and Ben Ruffin (standing in the truck) help community residents clear broken-down furniture from porches and yards. Photograph by Billy E. Barnes, courtesy of the North Carolina Collection, Wilson Library, University of North Carolina at Chapel Hill, Billy Ebert Barnes Collection.

staff, and by early 1966, the number of councils had grown to seventeen. One of the new community organizers was a student from North Carolina College named Ben Ruffin. Ruffin had grown up in Durham and had learned about social activism from his mother, a tobacco and domestic worker who had led an earlier effort to build a community center in their neighborhood. He attributed Operation Breakthrough's success to the fact that the agency did not immediately push big issues such as housing and voter registration, but began instead by helping communities discover their own untapped capacity. "I remember one of the first activities we involved ourselves in was a cleanup campaign," he said. "We would drive through these neighborhoods and there were old refrigerators and just a whole bunch of junk outside the houses, not because the people didn't want to move it, [but because] they didn't have money to rent a truck to move it. So we got the city to let us have garbage trucks on a Saturday. People brought all the stuff out to the front, and the men went around picking it up. And the ladies fixed the food, and after we finished working, we went over and had a great big repast. Everybody was involved and there was a lot of pride. The communities were clean. Folk came together and they could see it, everybody could see it. They said, 'Dag gum, this is the first time this has ever happened. Our numbers really count.'"[39]

As the neighborhood councils began "putting their issues on the table," public officials grew wary that even the most innocuous demands had the potential to upset settled structures of authority. Perhaps no case better illustrated that point than the troubles of Joyce Thorpe. Thorpe had grown up in Roxboro, a tobacco town thirty miles north of Durham, in a middle-class black family. Her father was a carpenter and her mother, a schoolteacher. Thorpe married in the mid-1950s, and for several years, life seemed promising. Her husband had a good job as an auto mechanic and she was working toward her degree at North Carolina College. Then her marriage fell apart and she found herself alone and vulnerable. She dropped out of school and in late 1964 traded the home that she and her husband had bought for an apartment in the McDougald Terrace housing project. "[It] was devastating," Thorpe remembered. "Here I am coming from a middle-class neighborhood to public housing. . . . I'm bringing my children from a house with a yard to an apartment." Concern for the children drew Thorpe into efforts by Operation Breakthrough to organize a neighborhood council at McDougald Terrace. In a community meeting in 1965, tenants agreed that their most pressing need was for a day care center, which would have made it easier for the mothers of young children to seek employment. When housing authority officials refused even to discuss the issue, residents organized a mothers club and elected Thorpe president. Howard Fuller remembered that he and his staff gave careful thought to the question of how best to characterize the organization. "We came up with that name [thinking], 'Who's going to mess with mothers?' Well, the housing authority [did]." On August 11, the day after her election, Thorpe received notice that her lease was to be terminated on August 31.[40]

Thorpe and her neighborhood organizer, Joan Alston, immediately contacted Fuller, who was traveling at the time. He took up Thorpe's case with federal Housing and Urban Development officials in Washington and Atlanta, but in both instances was told that the conflict was a local matter in which they had no authority to intervene. Fuller realized that this was the first critical challenge to the neighborhood organizations that he and his coworkers had so carefully built during the summer. A loss at this stage would undermine the entire effort at developing indigenous leaders among the poor. Fuller fought back by orchestrating protests outside the Durham Housing Authority's main office. He relied heavily on students from North Carolina College, because most McDougald Terrace residents were frightened of retribution—but the Durham newspapers could not tell the difference. They announced with alarm that sixty tenants were involved. The local justice of the peace court refused Thorpe's appeal and on September 17 ordered her eviction. Three days later, a Durham County sheriff's deputy arrived to remove Thorpe and her children from their apartment. Thorpe remembered that at that point, she panicked. She locked the door and shouted to the deputy on the other side, "Step through . . . and I'll blow your brains out!" Thorpe was unarmed, but the deputy took no chances. While he called for reinforcements, Thorpe got in touch with Howard Fuller and Joan Alston. For the next few hours, the three of them held the sheriff's men at bay while Durham attorney Floyd McKissick obtained a stay from the North Carolina Supreme Court.[41]

While her case was on appeal, Thorpe remained in her apartment and paid her rent into a special trust fund rather than to the housing authority. In 1966, both the Durham County Superior Court and the North Carolina Supreme Court upheld Thorpe's eviction. In December of that year, the U.S. Supreme Court agreed to hear her appeal, and in the following April remanded it to the state court with instruction to abide by new regulations from the federal Department of Housing and Urban Development, which required public housing agencies to give explicit reasons for evicting tenants. The North Carolina Supreme Court ruled that those guidelines did not have the force of law and reaffirmed its original judgment that the grounds for Thorpe's eviction were immaterial to her case. Finally, in January 1969, the U.S. Supreme Court settled the matter by ruling in Thorpe's favor and, in doing so, established landmark protection of due process for residents of public housing.[42]

As Joyce Thorpe was beginning her long battle with housing officials, members of other neighborhood councils were engaging in similar, though less highly publicized, skirmishes with local authorities. In the early summer of 1965, the Durham city schools fired a handful of black cafeteria workers with only a vague reference to "problems in the kitchen." Officials were in fact troubled by the women's participation in the newly formed School Employees Benevolent Society, which just weeks before had appealed to the school board and the state legislature to raise hourly wages from $.57 to the federal minimum of $1.25. The employees modeled their efforts on those of food workers and housekeepers at Duke University, who had organized their own benevolent association in the spring of 1965 and in August of that year affiliated with the American Federation of State, County and Municipal Employees as Local 77. Both groups demanded higher wages, better working conditions, and the use of courtesy titles (Mr. and Mrs.) by white supervisors. Duke administrators responded with small pay raises but otherwise dug in their heels for a protracted struggle that would continue until final recognition of the union in 1972. The Durham city school board took an even harsher line. It refused to negotiate and forced a strike by more than two hundred cafeteria and maintenance workers in the fall of 1965. The workers had strong support from Operation Breakthrough's neighborhood councils; even so, their protest collapsed. Their benevolent association lacked the financial resources to sustain a prolonged walkout, and in a Jim Crow labor market they had limited opportunities for alternative employment.[43]

The neighborhood councils' agitation around economic issues provoked the ire of employers and public officials and at the same time opened a rift within Operation Breakthrough's board of directors. From the beginning, there had been differences of perspective among the directors, but few had imagined that their antipoverty program would breathe new fire into the civil rights and labor struggles. Now, instead of calming unrest, Operation Breakthrough was mobilizing a stratum of the black community that had been largely on the sidelines of the youth- and church-led protests of the early 1960s. An army of the "organized and articulate poor" was in the making. As described by one North Carolina Fund staffer, its recruits were "creative, tough, and militant." They were "people long kicked down" who were now determined to steer the War on Poverty along a radically democratic course that at the outset its generals had "only dimly perceived."[44]

By the late fall of 1965, meetings of Operation Breakthrough's board of directors were becoming contentious. Several of the board's more conservative members insisted that Operation Breakthrough's purpose was to coordinate the delivery of social services, not to fan the flames of public controversy. Board chairman Julius Corpening, the white minister who led Durham's Temple Baptist Church, saw things differently. "Many people on the Board of Directors seem to think that [Operation Breakthrough] has changed its philosophy," he explained to North Carolina Fund officials, "but they are wrong. It is simply that now they are beginning to realize what Breakthrough stands for. When many of the Board members were selected . . . they thought Breakthrough would be a nice small experiment, a welfare program that would be a salve for their conscience. One which would not shake up their community too much. It is only recently that many of them are realizing what Breakthrough really stands for. That it really means to have social change here in Durham."[45]

Regardless of which view was more accurate, the division within Breakthrough's board posed a serious challenge. Executive director Robert Foust defended Howard Fuller's work with the neighborhood councils, but he also recognized the importance of putting some distance between Breakthrough and grassroots militancy. "We can't work with the school superintendent," city council, and welfare agencies on "vital complex programs," he explained, "when part of [our] staff is outside . . . picketing." At the same time, Fuller and the neighborhood councils were anxious "to consolidate their growing strength in an organization separate and independent of [Operation Breakthrough], and safely outside the control of [Breakthrough's] board." Only in that way could they continue their campaign of direct action. By early 1966, Foust, Fuller, and their liberal allies at Breakthrough had worked out a new plan for waging Durham's war on poverty. They pulled the neighborhood councils together in a confederation called United Organizations for Community Improvement (UOCI), which had its own board and officers elected from the ranks of the poor. Their aim was to give neighborhood activists the freedom "to engage in . . . controversial activities such as 'marches to city hall,' picketing, and so forth, all without undermining Operation Breakthrough." As Fuller explained, Foust could now answer critics of poor people's protests by saying, "Well, that's not a part of OB. [That's] UOCI."[46]

The new alliance of neighborhood councils first flexed its muscles during the spring of 1966. In March, Durham school officials rejected federal funds for summer Head Start and teen employment programs because they objected to the nondiscrimination guidelines attached to the money. UOCI responded immediately with a series of "mass rallies and marches" outside the city school system's administrative offices. The local press largely ignored the black protests for "fear that publicity would help consolidate Negro power and damage Durham's reputation as a modern Southern city." That conspiracy of silence, however, failed in its desired effect. As UOCI applied pressure in the streets, representatives of Operation Breakthrough and Durham's middle-class black leadership carried on private negotiations. Together, the three groups choreographed a skillful assault. Operation Breakthrough and the black leaders kept "a mild punch going inside," while UOCI delivered the "knockout punch outside." In late May, the Durham school board surrendered with a vote to reverse itself on the federal preschool and employment programs.[47]

With this victory behind them, UOCI moved forward simultaneously on several fronts to advance the concerns of the black poor. Given the determination of public officials to make change in only the smallest increments, electoral politics was an obvious point of engagement. Since the 1930s, blacks in Durham had made considerable inroads against disfranchisement. The city's sizeable black middle class and black-owned businesses provided a measure of protection from the intimidation and economic retaliation commonly visited upon blacks elsewhere in the state who aspired to the basic rights of citizenship. As a result, blacks in Durham registered and voted in significant numbers. In 1928, there had been only fifty black voters in the city, but by 1939 that number had increased to three thousand. This plunge into politics was the handiwork of the national NAACP and the Durham Committee on Negro Affairs, organized by Charles C. Spaulding, president of the North Carolina Mutual Life Insurance Company; Louis Austin, editor of Durham's black newspaper, the *Carolina Times*; and other black leaders. These men recognized a clear connection between political participation and any constituency's capacity "to command a decent share of the services and benefits of government." They championed black voter registration in order to capitalize on the democratic thrust of the New Deal, to improve black access to federal relief programs, and, within Durham proper, to convert their own economic power into political influence. By 1960, more than two-thirds of eligible blacks were registered to vote in Durham. But even that increase was inadequate to dislodge white privilege. In 1949, as the number of black voters grew, Durham shifted from a ward to a modified at-large system for electing members of the city council. That arrangement made black voters an electoral minority even in those parts of the city where they made up an overwhelming majority of the population. By 1966, when 85 percent of eligible blacks were registered to vote, they managed to elect only one representative to the city council.[48]

This history of black political agitation in Durham taught UOCI that change required not only an assault on the ballot box but also an incursion into the inner workings of party politics. In May 1966, as the confrontation with the Durham school board over Head Start and youth employment programs was still ongoing, UOCI offered its members an object lesson in the making of political power. Across the city, Democratic Party faithful were convening precinct meetings to elect county officers and delegates to the state convention. In neighborhoods with a significant black population, UOCI leaders loaded community activists into Operation Breakthrough vehicles and transported them to the gatherings. There, representatives of the neighborhood councils raised questions from the floor and spoke about the issues that concerned them. In one precinct, where they constituted a majority, they sidelined several of Durham's most influential white power brokers, including Victor Bryant, who served on Operation Breakthrough's board of directors. As UOCI executive director Ben Ruffin remembered, Democratic Party bosses reacted with stunned disbelief. "What are you doing at a precinct meeting, and why are you organizing to do this?" they asked. "You're bringing people here . . . trying to tell us what to do! We're not going to stomach that!" For Ruffin and his compatriots, that anger underscored the significance of their undertaking. The experience showed "people the process," Ruffin said, and taught them "what their strength could be if they got involved." UOCI's rank and file took the lesson to heart. They continued to push their way into precinct-level politics and to attend the meetings of county commissioners and the city council, seizing every opportunity "to get right up in [the] face" of those who wielded power. By 1968, the organized poor, in league with white liberal and labor allies, had grown influential enough to elect Ann Atwater as vice-chair of the Durham County Democratic Party.[49]

UOCI also fought to give the poor greater autonomy in their economic lives. Demands for higher wages and expanded job opportunities were an important part of that effort. So, too, was a campaign to address consumer issues. As UOCI explained, "Credit, or more to the point, the lack of credit at reasonable rates plays a key role in the perpetuation of the cycle of poverty." The "charge account and credit card" were "part and parcel of middle-class and upper-class life styles," but the poor had no access to those financial tools. They relied instead on "credit from corner merchants and loan companies" that "stifle[d] selective buying, timing of purchases, and a program of saving." The end result was a downward spiral of debt much like that experienced by an earlier generation who had worked the land as sharecroppers.[50]

In one of its proposals to the North Carolina Fund, UOCI offered a practical example of poor people's predicament: "Mrs. A is now paying for a washing machine on the installment plan. The washing machine had a sale price of $199.95. After the service and carrying charges were added, the cost of the washing machine was $213.41. This $213.41 was added to an old bill of $125.00. She was given 18 months to pay the total $338.41 in $25.00 monthly payments. At the end of these monthly payments, she will have paid $450.00. This is a true interest rate of 41.5%." In an effort to help the poor escape such financial entrapment, UOCI organized a federal credit union through which members of its neighborhood councils pooled their meager savings and made low-interest loans to one another. UOCI also established a number of community buying clubs that offered groceries and other essentials at costs below the predatory prices charged by many corner stores. Over the long term, neither the credit union nor the buying clubs could be sustained; Durham's poor simply lacked the necessary capital resources. Even so, both experiments served an important purpose. As Rubye Gattis, UOCI's first president, remembered, they provided "a learning experience on how to negotiate to get things that you want, and [they were] helpful in teaching people how to save, or [to] take a look at how they shop[ped] in the stores." "I was proud that we were able to [do] that," she said. "Some good came out of it."[51]

By far, the largest item in poor people's budgets was the monthly rent they paid to keep a roof over their heads. Concerns about housing conditions had sparked the creation of UOCI, and they remained at the top of the organization's agenda. Since the early twentieth century, Durham's black working class had been confined to overcrowded Jim Crow neighborhoods, where they had few options but to rent at exorbitant rates from absentee landlords (most of them white, a few black). During the 1930s, the New Deal made federal funds available to replace dilapidated housing in urban areas across the country, but Durham declined to apply. As the *Durham Herald* noted in 1937, "Several members of both the city council and the board of county commissioners [were] known to be heavily invested in 'shanty property,'" and they evinced no interest in "support[ing] a movement [that] might seriously destroy or curtail their earnings."[52]

Durham did not establish a public housing authority until 1949, when a postwar surge in migration off the land created an acute shortage of rental property. With federal assistance, the city built two public housing projects, Few Gardens in 1953 and McDougald Terrace in 1954. Carvie Oldham, a former cotton mill executive, served as director of the Durham Housing Authority, a post he retained until the late 1960s. Oldham was notorious among project residents for his heavy-handed management style. As Joyce Thorpe's case demonstrated in 1965, the housing authority's standard lease offered no protection for tenants' rights and allowed Oldham to evict residents at will and without cause. Oldham also had close ties to the Ku Klux Klan in Durham and often conferred with local grand dragon C. P. Ellis. When UOCI challenged the housing director, Klan members provided visible public support by attending meetings of the housing authority, city council, and county commissioners.[53]

In the late 1950s, as whites abandoned inner cities for the suburbs, the federal government made billions in new funding available for the revitalization of the nation's urban centers. Government programs encouraged the clearance of blighted slums, the construction of new public housing, and the building of expressways to move people and goods efficiently into and out of central business districts. In Durham, a broad coalition of power brokers, including real estate developers and the Durham Committee on Negro Affairs, embraced the federal initiatives as tools for growing the city's economy and addressing long-standing housing shortages. The city established a redevel-

A defiant tenant challenges Carvie Oldham and staff of the Durham Housing Authority.
Photograph by and courtesy of Bill Boyarsky, Hillsborough, North Carolina.

opment commission in 1958 and approved a plan to tear down and rebuild
a 200-acre section of the all-black Hayti district. During the early 1960s, the
redevelopment commission began buying up and demolishing homes in the
area. Local residents were promised new and better accommodations in as
yet unbuilt public housing. But in Durham, as in cities across the nation, such
pledges were only partially fulfilled. Urban renewal, as Hayti residents (and
their counterparts elsewhere in the country) joked with bitterness, became in
the end a process of "Negro removal." In 1965, Durham began construction
of a new east–west expressway through the heart of Hayti to connect Duke
University and the downtown business district to the rapidly expanding Research Triangle Park.[54]

The destruction of low-income housing and Durham's failure to build adequate replacements tightened the rental market for the poor and gave slumlords free rein to exploit the situation. The most notorious case was that of
Abe Greenberg. In the fall of 1965, Greenberg purchased twenty-one rental
properties in the Edgemont community, a transitional neighborhood with a
roughly equal mix of black and white residents. He immediately raised the
rent on those houses and the twenty-two others he already owned in the area.
When Greenberg refused to make needed repairs, Edgemont residents, sup-

ported by Operation Breakthrough, complained directly to the Durham City Council. They demanded that the council enforce the city's housing code and require Greenberg to bring his properties up to standard. Durham's housing inspector visited Edgemont and sent Greenberg a letter detailing code violations, but when Greenberg took no action, neither the inspector nor the council followed up.[55]

In March 1966, Howard Fuller assigned two neighborhood organizers to work in Edgemont and bring new pressure to bear on Greenberg. The organizers found that black residents were eager to form a neighborhood council. Whites, however, were much less enthusiastic. They had more opportunities than blacks to find cheaper housing elsewhere in the city, and many were making plans to relocate. Most white residents also refused to participate in any organization that was interracial. Only blacks joined the Edgemont Community Council, which Fuller's team and UOCI established in early April. Through the end of May, council members made repeated efforts to convince the city housing inspector to force a response to their grievances, but the inspector replied that he was powerless to do so. Durham's housing code provided no instrument of enforcement other than the issuing of notices like the one Greenberg had already received, or the boarding up of substandard housing. Neither promised much relief to black Edgemont residents, who had nowhere else to go.[56]

By early June, the Edgemont Community Council had decided on more direct action. On the sixteenth, council members began picketing outside Greenberg's downtown office and that of the realty company that managed his properties. "High Rent for Fire Traps," their signs exclaimed. "Greenberg, Fix Our Houses." For the first five days, Durham's newspapers chose to ignore the demonstrations, which relieved some of the pressure on Greenberg and threatened to put the protest effort "in danger of failing." On June 21, Edgemont residents raised the stakes. They traveled in Operation Breakthrough vehicles to the street on which Greenberg lived and marched in front of his house. "Your Neighbor is a Slumlord," their placards informed nearby residents. "My Children Sleep with Rats," they explained to "Mrs. Greenberg." A few days later, the *Durham Herald* chastised Operation Breakthrough for involving itself in such "questionable practices." The paper insisted that the agency would "be more effective in relieving poverty if it disregard[ed] the spectacular and follow[ed] regular procedures."[57]

That advice was misplaced. On June 27, Greenberg seemed to offer the protesters an olive branch. In an agreement brokered by Operation Breakthrough, he promised to complete repairs to his houses within ninety days.

Protesters marched daily to demand that the Durham City Council enforce the local housing code against slumlord Abe Greenberg. Photograph by Billy E. Barnes, courtesy of the North Carolina Collection, Wilson Library, University of North Carolina at Chapel Hill, Billy Ebert Barnes Collection.

But by mid-August, no work of any consequence had been undertaken. A month later, Greenberg's attorney requested additional time to bring the properties up to code. The city council granted the extension over strong objections from Edgemont residents and the Durham Committee on Negro Affairs. In December, when the clock had once again run out on Greenberg's promises, UOCI made a final plea to Washington. President Rubye Gattis wrote to Robert Weaver, secretary of the Department of Housing and Urban Development and the first black to serve in a cabinet-level post, asking that the agency mount an investigation and withhold urban renewal funds from Durham until the city developed a "workable plan" for housing code enforcement. "We are indeed poor, but we are trying to move out of our condition," she explained. "We need *your help*." This appeal, too, went unheeded.[58]

The months-long struggle with Greenberg and the Durham City Council left many in UOCI deeply frustrated. As one contemporary observer noted, Durham was a city that "wanted a progressive image on race relations, but really did not want to give up its regressive ways." That tension produced deepening divisions within Operation Breakthrough's board of directors. The community action program, Howard Fuller observed, was "ready to split right down the middle." Conservatives on Breakthrough's board, particularly attorney Victor Bryant and downtown merchant A. C. Sorrell, objected vigorously to the agency's support of protests outside Greenberg's home and use of the term *slumlords* to characterize "men of property and position in the community." They and like-minded members of the board warned that such "activity was arousing public opinion to an extent that could well be fatal to the entire [Breakthrough] program." Agency director Robert Foust answered with equal firmness that UOCI's picketing was "in line with Operation Breakthrough policy" and should continue to enjoy agency backing so long as it was "beneficial to the protesting group." His allies on the board argued that Breakthrough's "primary commitment was to the poor and held that to 'desert' them now — to 'throw a rock and then run' — would seriously damage [the organization's] standing with neighborhood residents." Determined to "save the poverty program from itself," conservative board members kept up the pressure on Foust, who resigned on June 25, 1966. For UOCI, Foust's departure raised serious questions about Breakthrough's commitment to an effective assault on poverty. At a meeting on July 25, a UOCI spokesperson read a prepared statement that challenged the board of directors. "We feel strongly that [public demonstrations] should continue and that this is the proper role for Operation Breakthrough," he declared. "How can we put our faith and trust in an organization that will support us only if we remain complacent . . .? How can we support Operation Breakthrough if you will not support us?"[59]

As the showdown over housing made clear, the North Carolina Fund had spawned in Durham a mobilization of the poor that was "tough, massive, and black." That accomplishment forced the agency to confront a "crucial question," for itself and for the larger War on Poverty. What, in practical terms, satisfied the mandate for maximum feasible participation of the poor? "Did [the term] mean simply the creation of advisory committees of the poor or, to go one step further, the inclusion of representatives of the poor or even the poor themselves" on CAP boards? Activists in UOCI insisted that neither arrangement was sufficient. In fact, they rejected any limitation on their participation in efforts to end poverty. After all, no one spoke in such terms when "men of property and position" organized to pursue their self-interests through the Jaycees, civic clubs, or chambers of commerce. Some of the North Carolina Fund's advisers urged caution in associating the agency with such radical claims to equality and autonomy, lest it deviate from its founding purpose.

"I can imagine situations where the Fund's right hand may be supporting a [CAP] which its left hand is attempting to destroy," warned one CAP director. "I submit that this is a paradoxical situation which rational men would attempt to avoid." Many within the Fund's staff argued just the opposite. "The North Carolina Fund," they contended, "should be[come] a 'counterweight to traditionalism' in the state, it should provide a loyal opposition to the status quo, and play the role of constructive critic, not afraid of conflict." That line of reasoning crystallized changes in the Fund's orientation that had been taking shape incrementally—and sometimes inadvertently—since the summer of 1964. The tension between these two points of view was not easily resolved. It would vex the Fund not only in Durham, but also a hundred miles to the northeast, in the rural region known as the Choanoke, "one of the most deprived areas in the state, and, indeed, in the country."[60]

THE CHOANOKE SPREADS ACROSS broad flatlands that form the basins of the Chowan and Roanoke Rivers. The area encompasses four counties: Northampton, Hertford, Halifax, and Bertie. Although twice the size of Rhode Island, the Choanoke was in 1960 thinly populated by fewer than 150,000 inhabitants. Only the textile town of Roanoke Rapids in Halifax County had more than 5,000 residents; the remainder of the Choanoke's population was scattered across the countryside in small farming communities. The local economy depended on the production of cotton, corn, peanuts, and tobacco, augmented by small-scale industry, most of it locally owned and centered on the lumber trade.[61]

Before the Civil War, the Choanoke had been home to some of North Carolina's largest plantations and wealthiest slaveholders. A century later, it still bore the marks of that past. The region was predominantly black, and most of its citizens were desperately poor. The vast majority of rural families—black and white—worked the land as sharecroppers and tenants, much as their forebears had done since the end of the nineteenth century. On average, more than a quarter of the Choanoke's adult population aged twenty-five and older had less than five years of formal schooling. As a result, the region offered little to potential investors and nonagricultural job opportunities remained limited. Black women found employment as domestics in the Choanoke's small towns; men of both races labored in sawmills and lumberyards; and whites in Roanoke Rapids worked in the J. P. Stevens cotton mill. Like farming, these jobs provided a meager living. Thirty-five percent of the Choanoke's white families and more than 80 percent of blacks lived below the Fund-designated poverty line. The human consequences of such deprivation were obvious at every turn. Two-thirds of all Choanoke families lived in "unsound housing" that was either dilapidated or lacked indoor plumbing. Tuberculosis infection rates in the region were among the highest in the state, and for blacks, the infant mortality rate, ranging from 38 to 52 deaths per 1,000 live births, was twice that for whites.[62]

The immediate future held few prospects for improvement. Since the end of World War II, conditions had in fact steadily worsened as white landowners chased new efficiencies and a competitive edge through the rapid mechanization of farming. By the early 1960s, machines had replaced human labor in more than 85 percent of the Choanoke's peanut harvest and 50 percent of its cotton production. Hundreds of sharecropping families were turned off the land, and young people began to leave the region at an alarming rate. Between 1950 and 1959, the Choanoke lost nearly a quarter of its black population and 40 percent of its young adults under the age of twenty-five. These developments put new strains on meager family resources, increased the burden on already inadequate public welfare services, and pushed those who stayed behind even deeper into poverty.[63]

Electoral politics and local government offered limited options for addressing this suffering. The continued disfranchisement of black voters muffled dissent. It closed the polls to a majority of citizens and, along with the practices of Jim Crow, blinded poor whites to shared interests across the color line. As a North Carolina Fund staff report noted, "The leadership pattern in each of the four [Choanoke] counties was, true to tradition, predominantly white. Despite the fact that a majority of each county was black, there were no Negroes holding public office [and] the development of leaders among the indigenous poor"—white or black—"was strongly resisted by the white 'power structure.'" A "poverty-segregation complex remained . . . intact," retarded economic growth, and set the Choanoke apart from the general prosperity of the post–World War II era. One simple fact captured the extremity of the Choanoke's plight: Bertie, its largest county, and neighboring Northampton ranked among the one hundred poorest counties in the nation, a status they shared with the most destitute areas of the Deep South.[64]

That was not the kind of distinction that Governor Terry Sanford wanted for his state. It underscored the need for decisive change, which he had championed on the campaign trail and in his call for a "New Day" in North Carolina. Sanford took that challenge directly to the Choanoke and other poverty-stricken areas. He pressured and cajoled local leaders to form multicounty, regional alliances to spur economic development. In November 1961, a group of the Choanoke's most influential landowners, business leaders, and politicians gathered at the Rebel Restaurant in Roanoke Rapids to make plans for such an organization. Archie Davis, chairman of Wachovia Bank and president of the Research Triangle Foundation, offered remarks about efforts elsewhere in the state to modernize North Carolina's economy. Because the Rebel was segregated, no blacks—not even the black county extension agent who had participated in earlier discussions—were invited to attend the meeting. Five months later, in April 1962, a group of wealthy landowners, business leaders, and county agricultural agents chartered the Choanoke Area Development Association (CADA), which they imagined would operate as a regional "Chamber of Commerce, proclaiming the area's positive aspects and great potential."[65]

CADA's founders recognized the need for economic growth, but at the beginning they gave no specific attention to poverty. That changed in 1963 with the establishment of the North Carolina Fund. In November, Michael Brooks, the Fund's director of research, and board member Thomas Pearsall visited CADA officials to brief them on the new agency and the financial resources that it might make available for local programs. Pearsall, himself the owner of extensive sharecropping operations in Nash, Edgecombe, Halifax, and Martin Counties, was an effective envoy. His presence put to rest—at least for the moment—any concerns that CADA leaders might have had about the match between the Fund's objectives and their own. By the end of January 1964, CADA's board had prepared a proposal for Fund support as a community action program and had amended the organization's bylaws so that it might officially take up the antipoverty banner.[66]

From the beginning, CADA was a source of trouble for the North Carolina Fund. The association's proposal was surprisingly disorganized and demonstrated little understanding of the Fund's concern to coordinate the activities of government agencies responsible for aiding the poor. The document took note of the disruptive effects of farm mechanization and recommended compulsory "rehabilitation training" for the unemployed, but it said nothing about the kinds of jobs for which those thrown off the land would be prepared. Nor did the proposal link job training to the support requested for "industry hunting." CADA also trumpeted tourism as a potential cure for the Choanoke's economic ills—the area, after all, was home to dozens of plantations and historical sites that dated back to the colonial era—but the only substantive discussion of benefits to the poor focused on teaching black women to make baskets for sale to visitors at roadside stands. For these reasons, the Fund "passed by" CADA in April 1964 when it announced the first seven community action programs to receive financial support. The Fund finally provided a start-up grant in October, after extensive negotiations with CADA leaders and Governor Sanford's insistence that no meaningful state-wide poverty program could go forward without including the Choanoke, one of North Carolina's poorest sections. "If it hadn't been for Sanford," one local official later remembered, "CADA would never have gotten funded by the North Carolina Fund."[67]

Money and persuasion, however, were insufficient to shake loose the grip of white paternalism. The enduring influence of that worldview became star-tlingly apparent in CADA's first application to the Office of Economic Oppor-tunity, which it submitted in June 1965. The language and analysis that CADA leaders chose to describe the Choanoke's situation echoed arguments that white supremacists had used since the turn of the century to deny any com-monality of experience between the white and black poor. What mattered most for the poor white farmer, they insisted, was not the economic difficulty of the moment but the advantages associated with the "color of his skin." "His children have attended schools with the children of the landed aristocracy," the CADA proposal explained. "His daughters have sometimes 'married well.' His sons have been exposed sufficiently to culture, art, crafts, the humanities, athletics and wealthy 'cousin Jonathan' that he has been and is beginning to break out of his state of economic depravity." Even as mechanization caused an upheaval in southern agriculture, the poor white farmer managed to adapt. "He is being forced from the farms to a lesser degree than is widely believed," CADA insisted. "He stays, sometimes now as an employee drawing wages. He stays because he is mechanically inclined, and can both operate and repair the giant tobacco or grain harvester. But he stays. Perhaps he opens a small business or takes a part-time job 'in town.' Some, of course, do leave the farm completely. But when they do, they have some place to go."[68]

CADA officials acknowledged that rural blacks enjoyed few of those op-portunities to escape poverty. But rather than explaining that fact as the flip side of white privilege, they attributed it to racial inadequacies that, if not inherent, had at least been made hereditary by generations of destitution. A majority of the Choanoke's black inhabitants lived "in a state of poverty," the CADA proposal explained, because they lacked ambition and had no "desire for anything better." That attitude, in turn, was to "be blamed on ignorance and the lack of exposure to anything outside the imprisonment that is the 'Cycle of Poverty.'" CADA's leaders viewed themselves, and were thought of by their white contemporaries, as racial moderates. They conceded the need for change in southern race relations and willingly acknowledged the injuries of "inhumane slavery" and discrimination. But they could never quite escape the shadow of an old idea — a mainstay of academic as well as popular historical understanding throughout the first half of the twentieth century — that slavery and Jim Crow had been schools of civilization, instilling in a backward race the virtues and habits of modern economic life. In their view, the way to win the battle against poverty was to accelerate that process of education and uplift, not to unleash a precipitous transformation of the political and economic order. As every white school child learned, rashness had been the "mistake" of the first reconstruction; it was, in like manner, the peril to be avoided in the second.[69]

The Choanoke's black citizens thought otherwise. They, too, had been organizing, and to quite different ends than CADA. Schoolteacher Willa Cofield recalled that the "social revolution of the '60s" came to the region in the spring of 1963, when her husband, Reed Johnson, director of one of the Cofield family's funeral homes, ran for a seat on the town council in the small Halifax County community of Enfield. Inspired by his example — and by the mass demonstrations across the South led by the Southern Christian Leadership Conference (SCLC), the Student Nonviolent Coordinating Committee (SNCC), and CORE — local high school students affiliated with the youth branch of the NAACP organized a "demonstration summer" of protests against segregation at the town's theater, swimming pool, and library. In August, the students traveled north with busloads of Halifax County residents to join the March on Washington for Jobs and Freedom. "They returned fired up to break the back of segregation," Cofield recalled. "The mass demonstration in Washington gave them new spirit, and their conversations with youth from other communities gave them new ideas." Taking a lesson from the SCLC's Children's Crusade in Birmingham, Alabama, young people — some of them elementary school students — picketed Enfield's business district and provoked an "all-out battle" with police. When they marched on city hall, the fire department "wheeled a truck into action" and turned hoses on the crowd. Police chief F. C. Sykes told newspaper reporters that the protesters "acted like a damn bunch of heathens. . . . If it becomes necessary . . . we'll use anything we've got to stop them." By year's end, however, Enfield's black community had prevailed. They responded to white intransigence by organizing an economic boycott that eventually persuaded merchants to employ black clerks and forced the town to hire a black police officer and desegregate public facilities.[70]

Emboldened by that success, local activists incorporated a countywide political organization they called the Halifax Voters Movement and reached out to civil rights groups that were active elsewhere in the state. They made contact first with John Salter, a field organizer for the Southern Conference Educational Fund (SCEF), the successor organization to the Southern Conference for Human Welfare, which University of North Carolina president Frank Porter Graham had led during the late 1930s. Salter joined the civil rights movement while employed as a professor of sociology at Tougaloo College in Jackson, Mississippi. He took a job with SCEF in 1963 and moved to North Carolina to assist with CORE's campaign to desegregate Chapel Hill. As that effort stalled, Salter turned his attention to the Choanoke region. He helped the Halifax Voters Movement field a slate of eleven black candidates for local and state offices, organize a voter registration drive, and win a federal court order "directing expeditious registration of Negroes on equal basis with whites." With that injunction in hand, the Voters Movement added more than two thousand black voters to the Halifax County rolls.[71]

Over the next year, Salter and local activists spread that upsurge throughout the Choanoke region. They called in Septima Clark and Dorothy Cotton from the SCLC to conduct citizenship schools that "taught unlettered people to read" and "gave . . . students and adults basic political education." Volunteers from SNCC assisted in that work and the League of Women Voters and the AFL-CIO's Committee on Political Education provided financial support. The Halifax leaders also called home Ella Baker, veteran community organizer and founding mother of SNCC who had spent her childhood in the Choanoke. In March 1965, she addressed a conference of over a thousand area residents who gathered to prepare for "concerted and intensive civil rights activity throughout the entire North Carolina Black Belt." Baker, a champion of participatory democracy, called for "militant organized grass-roots action" to upend political power in a region where the black majority were poor and the white minority ran local government. The conference ended with the organization of new voters movements in Bertie and Northampton counties and with unanimous resolve to eliminate "all vestiges of discrimination."[72]

That militancy stood in stark contrast to CADA's wariness of "meaningful social change." The agency's loyalty to the status quo became particularly obvious during the summer of 1965, when it received its first OEO grant: $347,000 to fund a Head Start school-readiness program for nearly twenty-three hundred low-income students in the Choanoke counties. OEO guidelines required that the program be run on a strict nondiscriminatory basis, but CADA officials and local school boards construed those regulations narrowly. They assigned mixed-race teams of teachers to some, but not all, of the Head Start centers. Beyond that, they were careful neither to reject racial

Ella Baker visits with SNCC organizers Ginny and Buddy Tieger at the civil rights conference sponsored by the Choanoke's black voters movements. Photograph by J. V. Henry, courtesy of Hunter Gray (John Salter), Pocatello, Idaho.

integration nor to confront the rule of Jim Crow. In Halifax County, for instance, school administrators declined to provide transportation that would have allowed children to attend centers outside their own segregated school districts. The school board excused that decision by citing not racial concerns, but rather the need to service county-owned buses in preparation for the fall term. A parent from Northampton County expressed the anger that such duplicity provoked among black families throughout the Choanoke. "As the program was conducted in our county," she snapped sarcastically, "our children were 'helped' by experiencing a three-month 'headstart' in segregated education." For her and others, CADA's management of the summer program amounted to nothing less than "a negation of the expected changes and equal opportunities" promised by the War on Poverty.[73]

When officials in Washington discovered what was happening in the Choanoke, they held back the final $138,000 of the region's Head Start grant. CADA leaders protested that they were "shocked and disappointed" by the federal bureaucrats' high-handed tactics; the local Head Start program, they insisted, had followed OEO "guidelines to the letter and in the spirit of the law." Throughout the month of August, OEO and CADA officials traded bitter recriminations, each accusing the other of acting in bad faith. The standoff ended when two senior members of North Carolina's congressional delegation, Representative L. H. Fountain and Senator Sam J. Ervin Jr., interceded on CADA's behalf. OEO director Sargent Shriver was in no position to refuse their appeals. His agency's very existence required that he act cautiously and avoid giving offense to southern Democrats. But in notifying CADA of his decision to release the remaining Head Start funds, Shriver ceded no ground. To withhold the money any longer, he explained, would only injure hard-working teachers, not punish the officials who had flaunted federal policy. Shriver chided CADA's board of directors. "Among the most gratifying aspects of the summer Head Start program just completed," he wrote, "was the high level of compliance with the local requirement that there be no racial discrimination. . . . Only a very small minority of the 2,300 programs [funded nationwide] proved disappointing in this respect. Regrettably, your agency's program was among the small minority." Shriver put CADA on notice: "Your failure to comply with the nondiscrimination requirement this past summer, despite your written word of honor accepting clear instructions to do so, will be considered strong evidence of your intention not to comply with this requirement in the future." For that reason, any subsequent requests to the OEO would "be given special scrutiny."[74]

In mid-September 1965, soon after the Head Start crisis had passed, CADA director Roger Jackson—a former state legislator from Hertford County—took a delegation of board members to Washington, where they met with OEO officials. Jackson's intent was to demonstrate biracial support for CADA's programs, but the visit did not go as planned. The delegation included Doris Cochran, an officer of the Halifax Voters Movement, wife of a local physician, and one of the small contingent of blacks who served on the CADA board. Over the summer, she had grown increasingly critical of CADA, worrying aloud to fellow board members about a lack of trust between the agency and the people who needed its help. When OEO regional administrator Harold Bailin invited Cochran to share her assessment of CADA, she answered forthrightly: there was "not enough Negro representation on the [agency's] board, no poor people [served] on the board, [and] Negroes [were] not represented in policy-making positions." Bailin probed further, asking Cochran for an appraisal of CADA's director. With Jackson sitting across from her, she again gave a frank reply. "There was definitely a gap," she said, "between the kind of leadership he *is* providing and that which he *should be* providing." The conversation continued in that vein for two and a half hours. Finally, "Bailin made it very clear" that if CADA hoped to receive additional federal grants, it would have to follow OEO guidelines on nondiscrimination and maximum feasible participation. He reminded his guests that the Choanoke included some of the nation's poorest counties and suggested that the people there "should not be made to suffer" because of CADA's intransigence.[75]

A week after the Washington meeting, members of the Northampton Voters Movement followed up with a letter of their own to Sargent Shriver. They complained that in the Choanoke "the whole anti-poverty program has been conducted very effectively to exclude both the Negro and the poor." While it was true that CADA had added black representatives to its board, it had done so by selecting individuals who owed their livelihood to white power brokers. Two board members, for example, were principals of black schools who served alongside their county superintendents. "As such," the letter writers explained, "they are not free from pressure from the school board. Nor are they poor. In fact, in this poverty-stricken county, they are among the wealthiest Negroes." Shriver's petitioners warned that such paternalistic arrangements made "a farce . . . of the War on Poverty," and they urged the OEO director to join them in demanding that the Choanoke campaign be "completely reorganized." "We are tired of having our spokesmen hand-picked by the white power structure," they declared. "We are tired of the way we have been represented by the black power structure. When representatives must be chosen, we will choose them. We are ready now to speak for ourselves."[76]

CADA director Jackson and whites on his board of directors did not know what to make of such declarations. When challenged, they refused to engage their critics, closed ranks, and sought, "whenever possible," to "avoid [further] contact with the Negro organizations." The problem was that despite their moderate stance on race, they were nonetheless products of a Jim Crow world. They had been taught since childhood that blacks were incapable of self-direction and political responsibility. Jim Crow's purpose, after all, had been to shore up the ideology of white supremacy by overwriting memory of a more complex past and, as W. E. B. Du Bois argued in his classic study of Reconstruction, "to treat the Negro's part" in the story of American democracy "with silence and contempt." But behind the veil of racial discrimination, black men and women preserved and passed from one generation to the next a different understanding of historical "Truth, on which Right in the future [might one day] be built." When the Choanoke voters movements declared that they intended to take leadership of the War on Poverty, they drew on a legacy of self-organization and political engagement that reached from the end of the Civil War into their own time. The struggle had been long, but the weight of history, they believed, was on their side.[77]

THE CHOANOKE COUNTIES OF Halifax, Northampton, and Bertie were part of North Carolina's Second Congressional District, which had been created in 1872 by conservative Democrats in the state legislature who were eager to remove the majority-black area from the adjoining First and Third Districts. The Black Second, as it came to be known, soon developed into an important center of Republican political power. Over the next quarter century the district sent more than fifty black representatives to the general assembly in Raleigh and elected four black candidates to Congress. The last of those congressmen was George H. White, who first won his seat in 1896, when the state's Fusion alliance of white Populists and black Republicans was at its zenith. White had been born in 1852 to free parents in rural southeastern North Carolina. He later graduated from Howard University, served two terms in the state legislature, and, before moving to the Black Second, practiced law as a federal solicitor.[78]

When White ran for reelection in 1898, conservative Democrats pointed to his presence in the House of Representatives as evidence of the threatening reach of "Negro domination." For Democratic Party leader Furnifold Simmons, the attacks on White and the larger campaign for white supremacy were, in part, about settling old scores. In 1888, after serving only one term in Washington, he had lost the Second District's congressional seat to White's brother-in-law and predecessor, Henry P. Cheatham. Simmons's chief aide, Bertie County native Francis D. Winston, had also forged his political career amid shifting racial alliances. He had joined the Republican Party as a young man, and as late as 1890 declared himself to be "a friend of the Negro," but by mid-decade he had switched sides and become a fierce champion of white rule. Winston came up with the idea of organizing White Government Unions to intimidate black voters and their white allies, and in 1899, he introduced in the state legislature the disfranchisement amendment to North Carolina's constitution, which won approval a year later in a popular referendum.[79]

George White won reelection in 1898, but he was powerless to hold back the tide of white supremacy. He decided in 1900 not to stand for a third term; with black men having lost the right to vote, his defeat was all but assured. But in his final speech on the floor of the House of Representatives, White made clear that he and his people would not surrender their claim to equal citizenship. "This," he said, "is perhaps the negroes' temporary farewell to the American Congress. . . . Phoenix-like [they] will rise up some day and come again. These parting words are in behalf of an outraged, heart-broken, bruised, and bleeding, but God-fearing people, faithful, industrious, loyal people — rising people, full of potential force."[80] White was the last black southerner to serve in Congress until the election of Georgia civil rights veteran Andrew Young in 1972, and the last black North Carolinian to hold congressional office until the election of Mel Watt and Eva Clayton in 1992. Clayton represented North Carolina's First Congressional District, which was redrawn in 1990 under pressure from the U.S. Justice Department to include most of the counties that historically had been part of the Black Second.

Once forced from politics at the turn of the century, black North Carolinians focused inward on their own communities. They devoted themselves to building institutions — churches, newspapers, fraternal lodges, and women's clubs — that strengthened the bonds of mutual aid and provided a measure of security in an otherwise hostile and uncertain world. They also seized every opportunity to forge alliances — whether with northern philanthropists, Franklin Roosevelt's New Deal, or national civil rights organizations — to restore in everyday life the ideals of American democracy.

Like their counterparts elsewhere in the South, the Choanoke's black citizens gave particular attention to education, which was the resource they could most effectively leverage for self-help and racial advancement. They took special pride in the Brick School, located on the outskirts of Enfield, a small Halifax County town. The school dated to 1895, when local residents founded it with a donation of land from Brooklyn philanthropist Julia E. Brewster Brick and financial support from the American Missionary Association, which from the time of the Civil War had invested heavily in black education across the South. Throughout the early twentieth century, Brick operated as an industrial school on the model of Tuskegee and Hampton Institutes. It prepared young women to work as classroom teachers and offered young men training in skilled trades and farming.[81]

During the Great Depression, the Brick School (now reorganized as the Brick Rural Life School) also helped black sharecroppers acquire farms of their own and establish some measure of economic independence on the land. In 1934, the Roosevelt administration sought to address the problem of rural poverty with a resettlement program that offered displaced tenants an opportunity to start anew in government-built communities in which they received forty acres of land, a house and outbuildings, and access to education and health services. One of the nation's largest projects was located in Halifax County, where the federal government purchased several thousand acres of prime farmland along the Roanoke River and created a new town called Tillery. From the outset, federal officials ran the project in close collaboration with the Brick School. Tillery residents took classes that mixed the study of great books with lessons on farm management and scientific agriculture. The objective was to educate participants to become active citizens and to prepare them to purchase and operate their own farms. By 1943, when Congress cut off funding for the resettlement program, ninety-three Tillery families had acquired homesteads and reclaimed a dream of independence that reached back to emancipation. A decade later, Tillery residents led in founding Halifax County's first chapter of the NAACP.[82]

This was the history, the collective memory that the Choanoke's civil rights and antipoverty activists invoked when they declared their independence from CADA. They understood the War on Poverty as an opportunity to assert anew their claims to citizenship, to chart for their state and nation a future that was more just and equitable, and to redeem their "faith in American democracy." The Reverend James A. Felton, a leader of the Hertford County NAACP, laid out that vision in a play he wrote in 1957 and then published in 1965 as a novel titled *Fruits of Enduring Faith*. Felton was born in 1919 in Perquimans County, just east of the Choanoke, and served in World War II as a member of the Marine Corps' first black company, which trained at Montford Point, North Carolina. After the war, he attended Elizabeth City State Teachers College and pursued a dual career as a schoolteacher and pastor. Felton drew on those experiences to craft a story of racial reconciliation. The tale turns on the efforts of a fictional white Marine Corps veteran, Ed Tuso, to convince his wife, Betty, and young son, Bobby, that "racial prejudice, inequality, segregation, and discrimination" no longer have a place in America. Tuso makes the point by telling his family of Jack Wynn, a black Marine who had saved his life in the battle for the South Pacific. He insists that in an America now threatened by Cold War with the Soviet Union, what matters most is the human bond between true patriots. "Betty!" Ed exclaims. "Can't you understand? All this stuff about color and this man is better than another because of his race is nothing but ignorance. This stuff will sink our country. Listen! . . . The enemy! . . . They want to destroy America and rob all of us of our freedom. . . . Can't you understand, Betty? Can't you hear? . . . The Russians are trying to take this country, and all you care about is race and color." To those who argued that the civil rights movement and the War on Poverty were divisive forces in American life, Felton answered that they offered instead an opportunity for "racial unity . . . peace, understanding, and prosperity within." These would be the "fruits" of black citizens' "enduring" — and long-suffering — "faith in God and true American democracy."[83]

For Roger Jackson and many other whites on CADA's board, such pleas were too unsettling to comprehend. They did not know the history that Felton invoked, they were unprepared to surrender their own privilege, and, like

The Reverend James Felton in his Marine dress uniform. Courtesy of the Southern Historical Collection, Wilson Library, University of North Carolina at Chapel Hill, James A. Felton and Annie Vaughan Felton Papers.

Betty and Bobby Tuso, they were deaf and could not hear. As relations with his black critics worsened, Jackson chose to resign from CADA. Board chair and president Fred Cooper, a retired insurance executive and former secretary of the Roanoke Rapids Chamber of Commerce, moved in immediately to fill the office of director and took two quick steps aimed at appeasing black activists. Neither was entirely satisfactory.[84]

Cooper first convinced the CADA board to add new black members, but the board insisted that it retain the authority to appoint those individuals and rejected the idea that representatives might be elected directly by the poor. Cooper next responded to a request made nearly a year earlier that CADA employ a black assistant director. He created such a position and promoted CADA staffer John Taylor to fill it. Taylor was a graduate of Hampton Institute and an Army veteran who had worked briefly as a plasterer in Norfolk, Virginia. The job paid well, but it required that he commute and left him with only the weekends to spend with his family. Working for CADA allowed Taylor to stay close to home and offered him an opportunity to use his college education. During Roger Jackson's tenure, Taylor had been an outspoken critic of the director's failure to consult the poor, but, as a North Carolina Fund field-worker observed, his attitude changed after his elevation to a management position. Taylor felt "exceedingly grateful toward Cooper for having promoted him" and for "granting [him] real authority and responsibility" over CADA's day-to-day operations. The two men got along well, and Taylor quickly adopted Cooper's strategy of avoiding conflict, whether with conservative members of CADA's board or black community organizations.[85]

Cooper believed that conflict, particularly in matters connected to race relations, only "led to bad feelings with nothing to show in the end." "Why," he asked, "should there be conflict in administering an anti-poverty program?" Cooper and Taylor insisted that the wiser approach was to provide the CADA board and community groups "with as little information as possible." They figured that the less either party "[knew] about a proposal, the fewer questions they [could] ask and the greater the possibility of avoiding" disagreements that would "solidify the Whites and Negroes into 'two opposing camps.'" Cooper argued that "if the Fund would only let him do it his way—keep down conflict—he could prove his theory and they would have 'the best CAP in the country!'"[86]

In the spring of 1966, the CADA administrators pursued that strategy to disastrous effect. In May, Cooper and Taylor submitted to the OEO a $500,000 proposal to establish in the Choanoke a network of facilities they described as "multi-service centers." Their idea was to bring a variety of social welfare providers—adult education programs, job referral bureaus, public health clinics, and the like—under one roof, so that existing agencies might deliver their services to the poor more effectively and efficiently. Taylor wrote the proposal single-handedly; he and Cooper violated CADA's bylaws by not sharing drafts for review by county subcommittees; and when they finally brought the document to the full CADA board, they did so nearly two weeks after submitting it to the OEO. Faced with that fait accompli, the board had little choice but to suspend its rules and endorse the proposal.[87]

Cooper's high-handed tactics angered conservative whites on the CADA board, who feared that the multiservice centers would become staging points for civil rights protests, as well as black community representatives, who felt marginalized yet again. The proposal and its handling also caused alarm at North Carolina Fund headquarters in Durham. A year earlier, the Fund might have embraced the idea of welfare service centers, but by early 1966, its thinking about effective strategies for an assault on poverty had changed. Fund staff characterized CADA's proposal as "paternalistic." It engaged the poor as clients rather than partners in shaping an antipoverty program. It promised services to the poor but did nothing to engage them in building the institutions and skills that might make a long-term difference in their condition. Those shortcomings seemed so severe that some Fund staff recommended intervention with the OEO to scuttle the project. CADA and the North Carolina Fund had never been in total agreement about such matters; now they seemed at loggerheads over the core "purposes and objectives of the war on poverty."[88]

The situation alarmed George Esser, who asked field-workers in the Fund's community support office to figure out how to mend the rift. Jim McDonald and his staff construed that request more broadly than Esser intended. They were inspired by the grassroots activists in the Choanoke whom they had come to know as friends and allies, and—unlike Fred Cooper, who sought to avoid conflict at all cost—they had concluded that effective change could be accomplished only through direct action and confrontation. In June, Mc-Donald's field-workers organized a round of consultations with leaders of the county voters movements in the Choanoke, and by early July they had settled on the idea of convening "a people's conference on poverty." The Fund staff took their cues from prior experiences with UOCI in Durham and the Choanoke conference a year before that had seeded voters movement organizations across the region. Their aim was to give the poor a public venue for claiming their rightful role as leaders in the War on Poverty and assuming responsibility for the welfare of their communities.

George Esser did not learn of these plans until mid-July, and he initially "raised a 'caution flag.'" He questioned the wisdom of putting the Fund at odds with itself by encouraging a challenge to one of its own community action programs. McDonald answered by arranging to have forty Choanoke activists stage a sit-in at Fund headquarters. Nathan Garrett, the Fund's director of finance, complained to others in the office that McDonald had "gone off at the 'deep end'" and was "acting like a 'damned fool,'" but he also agreed that supporting direct action by the poor was the right thing to do. After all, he asked, how could "the poverty program" justify "turn[ing] its back on several thousand people in a community?" On July 18, Esser approved funds for the proposed conference. Choanoke activists announced their plans in black churches on the following Sunday, and during the next week and a half they mobilized precinct-level recruiting committees to spread the word door-to-door.[89]

On July 30, 1966, a standing-room-only crowd of roughly one thousand people gathered at the National Guard Armory in the Northampton County community of Woodland. Sharecroppers, domestic workers, schoolteachers, preachers, and students assembled to think and plan together for "their own future and destiny." The organizers opened the event with the singing of the "Battle Hymn of the Republic." That was a bold gesture in the heart of the Carolina Black Belt; it reached back in time and made connections to the Civil War, emancipation, and promises of freedom as yet unfulfilled. Abolitionist Julia Ward Howe had written the words to the anthem in 1861, and it quickly became the marching song of Union troops. Its fifth verse, in particular, spoke to ideals of sacrifice and redemption that linked the conflict of the 1860s to the struggles that followed a century later:

> In the beauty of the lilies Christ was born across the sea,
> With a glory in his bosom that transfigures you and me: .
> As he died to make men holy, let us live [originally, "let us *die*"] to make
>   men free,
>   While God is marching on.

The Reverend A. I. Dunlap, a leader of the Halifax Voters Movement, echoed similar themes as he led the assembly in prayer. He invoked the suffering of a subjugated people and implored God to give them strength that they might overcome obstacles and redeem the nation. It was a "magnificent" prayer, wrote one observer. "The memory of it still moves me."[90]

Fred Cooper's performance was less inspiring. In fact, Fund staff who attended the Woodland rally described his speech as "the most inept" they had ever heard. "I felt sorry for Fred Cooper," one of them said, "and for the white race in general." Cooper "just didn't know how to communicate with the people he was dealing with." He had decided to attend the conference in hopes of demonstrating that CADA—after two years of delay and conflict with local communities and the OEO—was finally prepared to deliver on its promise to uplift the poor. With great fanfare, he announced that he had "just heard that afternoon that OEO would come through" with half a million dollars to fund CADA's controversial multiservice centers. Immediately, Golden Frinks, the Southern Christian Leadership Conference's field director for eastern North Carolina, began to challenge Cooper: "Why didn't any poor people help you write this proposal?" "How can you pretend to know what the poor people want unless you ask them?" Cooper, realizing that "he was in bad shape with the audience," tried to deflect the questions. A Fund staffer reported what followed: "'I think I just gave you some good news about the multi-purpose centers being funded,' [Fred reminded the crowd.] 'I think we should make some noise over this fact, so I'll tell you what I'm going to

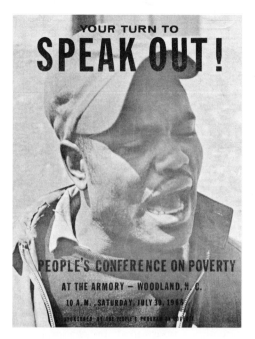

YOUR TURN TO
SPEAK OUT !

PEOPLE'S CONFERENCE ON POVERTY
AT THE ARMORY — WOODLAND, N. C.
10 A. M. , SATURDAY, JULY 30, 1966

The People's Conference on Poverty, convened in July 1966, marked a turning point in the North Carolina Fund's strategy for battling poverty. Courtesy of the Southern Historical Collection, Wilson Library, University of North Carolina at Chapel Hill, North Carolina Fund Records.

do, I'm going to take my handkerchief and throw it up into the air and when it goes up into the air, I want everybody here to holler. And when it comes down and I catch it, I want you to stop.' Well, Fred took his handkerchief and threw it up into the air and everybody screamed, and he caught it and everybody stopped, and then he took and threw it up into the air again, and everybody screamed and hollered, and when he caught it they stopped." Pleased with his performance and "smiling to himself," Cooper then sat down.[91]

Howard Fuller, the Fund's chief community organizer, rushed to the podium, and he scolded both Cooper and the audience. "I'm sitting here in a meeting in the year 1966," he exclaimed, "and see a white man take a handkerchief and throw it up in the air and tell us to yell when it comes down . . . and what I don't understand about it is the fact that you yelled when he threw it up. . . . I think it's time . . . that we had a little soul talk." Were black folk still so captive to white paternalism, Fuller wondered, that they believed that "as long as you keep saying 'yes suh,' 'no suh,' . . . everything's going to be alright"? "You got white people running you, white people determining if you're going to breathe or not," he reminded the crowd. Wasn't that the case with CADA? The community action program promised better access to public welfare services, but what black people needed more than another caseworker was a job that paid "enough money to survive." CADA offered job training, but vocational programs would do little to alleviate poverty unless there was also an end to discrimination and whites stopped relegating blacks to "dead-end" employment. Likewise, community improvement programs would make little difference in black living conditions until the Choanoke region had enforceable housing codes and open housing markets, "so that the white man knows no matter where [he] move[s], a brother can move next door."[92]

Fuller explained to his audience that in order to make social welfare policy responsive to the poor, they needed to encourage militant leadership and to believe in their own capacity to effect change. In a thinly veiled reference to John Taylor, who was also sitting on the stage, Fuller complained that a false sense of pride and accomplishment often took hold of black leaders when powerful whites appointed them to agency boards. "I just get amazed," Fuller mocked, "at how unmilitant Negroes get when . . . elected to one of those boards. We're so glad to be sitting with the white folks." In a region that was majority black, there was no reason for such accommodation; black people should be running the boards and setting the agendas. But, Fuller warned, that day would come only when the black poor repudiated the inferiority and inadequacies ascribed to them by Jim Crow and theories of a culture of poverty. He pointed to himself and others assembled on the stage—none of them, he said, could solve the problems of the poor. Only the poor could accomplish that task, by organizing, finding the courage to speak, and taking up the responsibilities of citizenship. Fuller urged his listeners to begin then and there. The time had come for asking tough questions and demanding honest answers. "I want to hear some nitty-gritty questions," Fuller insisted, "and don't tell me nothing about I can't talk so well—I don't care how it sounds. Ain't nobody gon' care how your English sounds. I don't care, as long as you get that point across. And you are as capable as anybody up here or anywhere around here to talk about it, and you oughta talk about it, because can't nobody talk about it better than you."[93]

Fuller's "soul talk" pricked deep-seated white anxiety over control of the public agenda in a region of black majorities. News staff from WITN, northeastern North Carolina's only local television station, ran a three-part series on the Woodland meeting. The mood of the gathering had been "friendly, positive and constructive," the station reported, until Fuller delivered his "ten minute tirade of heaped up, packed down and running over hatred for the white race. . . . When he finished he was given a standing ovation by the crowd and . . . any spirit of mutual cooperation was . . . gone with the wind of his remarks." Essie Mattison, a California resident who attended the rally while visiting relatives in Northampton County, heard things differently. She wrote to Jim McDonald and Nathan Garrett to share her outrage at the television news coverage. "I heard nothing at all wrong," she explained. In fact, Fuller's remarks were just what whites needed to hear. "The reason they were upset," Mattison wrote, "was because every word he said was true. They do not want anyone to come here and tell these contented colored people anything that would arouse them and start them thinking deeply of their plight and doing something about it." Years later, Fuller recalled that Jim Crow had such a grip on the white imagination that his critics could hear his call for black citizenship only as a "racist outpouring": "'Oh, my god,' [they thought], 'he's got an Afro and he's talking about power, black people having power,' which meant that we're supposed to hate white people."[94]

IN THE MONTHS SURROUNDING the Woodland rally, poor people's protests in the Choanoke and Durham converged. Taking their cue from UOCI, Choanoke activists chartered a new organization that they called the People's Program on Poverty (PPOP), and by autumn 1966, both UOCI and PPOP had requested grants from the North Carolina Fund that would enable them to operate as freestanding enterprises financially and administratively independent of Operation Breakthrough and CADA. That move effectively cornered the Fund and demanded that it declare itself politically. Over the next six months, Fund staff produced a flood of internal reports in which they took stock of the agency's "shifting priorities" and effectiveness in advancing its campaign against poverty. They concluded that CAPs such as Operation Breakthrough and CADA could not represent the community at large and at the same time serve as "insistent [advocates] for the poor." Those functions were, in some fundamental measure, at odds. Howard Fuller identified the predicament with plainspoken clarity: "If this is a war on poverty," he asked, "how can you have people who are helping cause the problem be on the board to plan the strategy?"[95]

This problem was not unique to North Carolina or the South; it was a challenge faced by combatants in the War on Poverty across the nation. From the beginning, big-city mayors had made clear that they expected to control the purse strings of new antipoverty programs. They welcomed the federal government's largesse so long as they were able to direct it through established agencies and networks of political patronage. At congressional hearings on the Economic Opportunity Act in 1964, New York mayor Robert F. Wagner Jr. had argued "that the sovereign government of each locality in which . . . community action is proposed should have the power of approval over the makeup of the planning group, the structure of the planning group, and over the plan." Chicago mayor Richard J. Daley echoed that sentiment, insisting that the proposed assault on poverty would succeed only if "administered by . . . elected officials." The mayor of Syracuse added pointedly, "If we [cannot] have direct control of the program, we [do] not want it."[96]

As the War on Poverty took shape, that insistence on top-down control ran afoul of the insurgencies that maximum feasible participation had ignited in poor neighborhoods. The poor — particularly the black poor — seized upon the War on Poverty as a means of redistributing economic and political power. They sought to extend the struggle of the civil rights movement by claiming a "voice in the political community," pursuing "security in their material existence," and exercising "control over their destiny." In 1966, OEO director Sargent Shriver ardently defended that conception of the War on Poverty's purpose. "The Office of Economic Opportunity funds, delegates, administers, or coordinates a vast array of programs," he said. "Every one of those programs can be perverted into a form of dole — paternalistic, unilateral, and degrading." It was imperative, therefore, that "the poverty program . . . stake its existence on the same ideal upon which [the American nation had] gambled from the outset: Democracy." To big-city mayors, such notions seemed threatening and outlandish. In San Francisco, John F. Shelley complained that the local antipoverty program was headed "in a direction we don't want. . . . It has the potential for setting up a great political organization." Mayor Daley of Chicago scoffed at the idea of maximum feasible participation, suggesting that it was akin to "telling the fellow who cleans up to be the city editor of a newspaper."[97]

Staff at the North Carolina Fund kept close watch on these battles elsewhere in the nation. Several, including John Strange from Duke University's Department of Political Science and Morris Cohen from the University of North Carolina's School of Social Work, were, in fact, heavily engaged in national policy debates about the appropriate role of the poor in community action. From those exchanges and their own firsthand observations, Fund staff drew one critically important lesson: winning the War on Poverty required that the poor be fully outfitted for battle. Above all else, that meant providing the poor with the resources to support their own, independent institutions, within which they would develop leadership skills; merge experiential knowledge with broader understandings of policy, politics, and economics; and build their capacity to engage public life as citizens and constituents rather than as clients. Morris Cohen conceded to his colleagues the difficulties inherent in that course of action. It denied state and national policymakers the comfort of channeling assistance through "'the same old crowd,' the politicians, the professionals, and the familiar community leadership structure." It also demanded that welfare workers "be prepared to relinquish—or at least to share—their role of 'running things' . . . [and] entertain the possibility that the poor can make a contribution to society's plans in their own way."[98]

As politically charged as that course of action might be, Cohen concluded that there was no viable alternative. He warned that too many "middle-class laymen and professionals [wanted] the 'name without the game' or the 'flower without the fruit' in the War on Poverty. They [wanted] the *appearance* of a benevolent assault on poverty as a social problem, without in any way disturbing any of the underlying relationships that contribute to it." That was a dangerous inclination. It risked widening the rift between the two Americas, one affluent and the other chained in the "prison of poverty." Cohen insisted that commanders in the War on Poverty faced a critical decision. Having mobilized a vast army of the poor, would they institutionalize its "full participation" in civic life, or leave it to struggle on its own without a plan or direction? One path pointed to the possibility that the poor might contribute as a disciplined, "constructive force" in social change. Down the other lay the making of what a later generation of social scientists would describe as a permanent underclass, in Cohen words, "cynical, skeptical, and pessimistic," lacking any instrument other than violence for pressing its grievances.[99]

The question that arose most immediately from that line of reasoning was how best to move from protest to the building of institutions that could effect long-lasting change. One option was for the Fund to acknowledge that it "had been backing the wrong horses," to sever its relationship with the current CAPs, and to turn the table on whites by shifting "all support" to new community action programs run exclusively by the poor. That strategy, despite its appeal to some at the Fund, was politically impractical, primarily because it risked alienating white moderates and surrendering control of the existing CAPs' considerable resources and influence to their more conservative board members. An alternative was for the Fund to maintain its ties to established programs and at the same time to invest in "counter CAPs" that would mold poor people's activism into a significant political force. That approach, a Fund staff report explained, acknowledged another important tactical consideration: "organized Negro groups" had become "a force which must be dealt with by politicians and other opinion leaders." In fact, "the rate of progress in North Carolina depend[ed] . . . upon the speed with which [such] groups" were treated as "public realities."[100]

From that perspective, Fund staff concluded that conflict of the sort that had erupted in Durham and the Choanoke was more an asset than a liability. If properly managed, it could be used to cut through the rhetoric of "cooperation" that conceded the authority of powerful whites to "make the decisions" and obscured the inequalities and injustices from which poverty arose. In proposing such a strategy, Fund staff drew directly on the analysis of social change that Martin Luther King Jr. had articulated in his "Letter from Birmingham Jail." "I must confess," King had written, "that I am not afraid of the word 'tension.' I have earnestly opposed violent tension, but there is a type of constructive, nonviolent tension which is necessary for growth. Just as Socrates felt that it was necessary to create a tension in the mind so that individuals could rise from the bondage of myths and half truths to the unfettered realm of creative analysis and objective appraisal, so must we see the need for nonviolent gadflies to create the kind of tension in society that will help men rise from the dark depths of prejudice and racism to the majestic heights of understanding and brotherhood."[101]

Fund director George Esser agreed with such arguments, but he was wary of asking his board of directors to give UOCI and PPOP direct financial support. He knew that they would be squeamish about endorsing "independent organizations of the poor." He also worried about violating a Fund policy that required channeling all grants through existing CAPs. In UOCI's case, Operation Breakthrough eventually removed the barrier by approving the organization's proposal. That move reflected the influence of UOCI representatives such as Ann Atwater on Breakthrough's board and the realities of black political power in Durham. The situation in the Choanoke, however, was different. There, CADA director Fred Cooper firmly opposed separate funding for PPOP. He insisted that his program could succeed in the battle against poverty only by "keep[ing] things peaceful" and not "anger[ing] the power structure, because after all, they [were] the ones who [made] the decisions."[102]

The internal debate over the future of UOCI and PPOP reached a crisis point in the spring of 1967. On March 21, four of Esser's "top black staff members"—including James McDonald and Nathan Garrett—threatened to resign if the Fund's board of directors refused grants to the two organizations. "I decided that the Fund, without this additional step, had outlived its usefulness," Garrett explained. "Once you had poor people banded together and ready to do something they ought to be funded." On the evening of March 22, in a dramatic "break with precedent," Esser invited representatives of PPOP and UOCI to make their case directly to the board. The next morning, McDonald and Garrett followed up with a report titled "Staff Analysis of the

Community Corporation Concept," in which they summarized the conclusions drawn from months of self-study. The report argued that the establishment of counter-CAPs such as UOCI and PPOP was the logical next step in a "spiral of participation" that the Fund had set in motion with its first call for community action proposals. "As in other areas of the anti-poverty effort," the staff analysis reminded board members, "the Fund [had] been a pioneer in advocating the necessity for poor people to develop the capacity and the leadership to help themselves." It had affirmed that objective in its 1963 manual for prospective community action agencies, and again in its "1965 statement of goals." A year later, the Fund went even further by "encouraging the independence of organized neighborhood groups." In the staff's view, UOCI and PPOP were exemplary products of that process. They had marshaled the poor as a political force, and then, by working the system and marching in the streets, they had focused public attention on issues that poor people identified as critically important. Now, the time had come to provide UOCI and PPOP with the resources required to transform themselves from "crisis-oriented" organizations into permanently established agencies capable of "deal[ing] with . . . problems on a long-term basis [and] in greater depth." In an effort to clinch the argument, staff suggested to the board that by taking that step, the Fund would remain on the cutting edge. "Poor people's corporations have been tried primarily in large metropolitan areas," they noted. "There have been no poor people's corporations similar to Durham's UOCI in small Southern urban settings, and there have been no local poor people's corporations in large isolated rural tenant farming areas similar to PPOP." Board members were persuaded. With "several abstentions but only one or two opposing votes," they approved direct support for PPOP and UOCI.[103]

George Esser had gone to the Choanoke a few days earlier to prepare CADA leaders for the shift in policy. While he acknowledged their reluctance to go along, he also urged them to understand that the poor needed organizations of their own: "You will, and have, said many things in rebuttal—'Our program is just getting started and hasn't had a chance.' 'We want to solve our problems cooperatively, and we are taking steps to do this.' . . . '[PPOP's] proposal will lead to conflict and trouble, instead of cooperation.' '[It] will kill CADA.' 'We can't go this fast up here.'" Esser did not question "the sincerity of any of these statements," but he did ask CADA leaders to consider an alternative view. "Let me tell you what I see in [PPOP]," he said. "I see people with a dream who have not lost hope despite many frustrations. I see concerned people who want to be constructive in seeking solutions to the problems of both poverty and race. I see people with ideas and independence, people . . .

who may have something to say to the State, the South, the entire country in terms of how to give people—frustrated people—both motivation and opportunity." The poor, Esser added, now embraced a "new concept of possibilities, new expectations." CADA leaders would do well to recognize that fact. In doing so, they might also gain fresh perspective on themselves. Esser urged them to remember the words of Scottish poet Robert Burns: "Oh wad some power the giftie gie us, / To see ourselves as others see us."[104]

For PPOP organizers, the Fund's endorsement opened a window onto possibilities once only dimly imagined. PPOP promised to shift the balance of power in the Choanoke. It offered the poor a forum in which they could "operate without fear of retaliation from the 'white power structure'" and could define their own priorities for the War on Poverty. Alice Ballance, one of PPOP's founders, wept when the grant announcement was made. "[It] was the happiest day of my life," she said in a letter to Fund headquarters. "I am writing this personally but I am sure all the poor people of the [Choanoke] area feel like I do. I have a feeling of honor and dignity that I've never had before and I am sure many people will be made to feel richer and dignified because of your . . . concern."[105]

On May 1, 1967, PPOP opened an office in Rich Square, a predominantly black town in Northampton County. Following the model set by UOCI, its first priority was "to organize the people of the Choanoke Area." PPOP worked through existing church and voters movement networks to establish more than fifty neighborhood councils in towns and rural communities throughout the region. Isolation and the tenacious sovereignty of Jim Crow at times made that work difficult. Eleanor Chavis, one of PPOP's founding directors, remembered that in Northampton County "there were places [where] the blacks were way up in the woods, or on the plantation. And they were actually afraid to talk with us, so we had to talk with them in the fields, if we saw a group in a field chopping. You couldn't [reach] large groups like that, but you could talk to at least some people." By the spring of 1968, such efforts to engage even the most marginalized inhabitants of the Choanoke had brought PPOP nearly three thousand members.[106]

PPOP focused much of its effort on gaining access to existing public services and resources, which white elites had historically controlled for their own benefit. The story of roads in the Northampton community of Cumbo symbolized a pattern of exclusion that persisted throughout the Choanoke. There, the county "fixed and paved" a primary road up to the last house occupied by whites and then abruptly stopped the work. In the Choanoke's towns, black residents not only did without paved streets but also lacked access to basic sanitation services. Even in Roanoke Rapids—the area's largest municipality—most black residents relied on outdoor privies and some had no sanitary provision of any sort. PPOP's neighborhood councils appeared regularly at town meetings and berated officials for the neglect that their communities suffered. One activist noted, "We have been able to get the people to speak out for their rights like never before. They don't mind telling the white man like it is. . . . And thanks to the North Carolina Fund we don't have to stick our heads out to be cracked for helping poor people help themselves."[107]

As in Durham, nothing in the Choanoke spoke more directly to the deprivations of poverty than the lack of safe and habitable housing. Sharecropping families often lived in broken-down cabins that had seen little modification since they were originally constructed as slave quarters. Banks systematically denied black families access to credit; city and county governments refused to enforce—or often even to enact—housing codes; and while the federal government had offered various forms of housing assistance since the New Deal, local administrators rarely helped blacks learn about or benefit from those programs. The Reverend James Felton, a PPOP founder, made these problems his special concern. He developed an expert knowledge of federal housing policy, traveled to Washington to visit with officials, and organized workshops to "interpret and explain [government] programs to needy persons." As a result of his efforts, more than one hundred families applied directly to the Farmers Home Administration for low-interest mortgages and home-improvement loans. Fourteen rural communities also secured grants from the agency to build community water systems that replaced the shallow, often polluted wells on which residents had long relied. A sharecropper who wrote to Felton in the spring of 1967 was typical of the people who sought PPOP's aid. "I will be glad for you to consider me [for housing assistance]," he said. "I have been a farmer and laborer for 75 years and haven't lived in nothing but old leaking houses all my life. I will be so glad to live in a good house what time I have [left] to live." Felton replied with the good news that the poor had allies in Washington. "Thanks for your letter . . . saying that you would like to have a decent house to live in," he wrote. "I am happy to inform you that the United States Government wants to see people like you and many, many others in a decent house. My trip to Washington, D.C. Wednesday of last week convinced me that you will be able to get a house."[108]

PPOP also sought to create economic opportunity for the hundreds of Choanoke families turned off the land by the mechanization of agriculture. One obvious option was to create industrial jobs that paid a living wage. The Choanoke's rich landowners historically had used their political clout to keep industry out of the region, thus maintaining a captive pool of cheap labor. Like their counterparts elsewhere in the South, they also lobbied their congressional representatives to continue the exclusion of household and agricultural workers from federal minimum wage laws. As a result, there was little manufacturing in the Choanoke; the few factories that operated in the region paid meager wages, even by the standards of North Carolina, a state whose industrial workers claimed some of the lowest average earnings in the nation; and factory employment, with few exceptions, was restricted to whites only.

Acting individually, black residents—even those who owned a small farm or business—were powerless to alter those circumstances. But the ongoing civil rights and antipoverty struggles in the Choanoke suggested new ways of thinking about the economic clout that they might exercise collectively. In the spring of 1966, the Bertie Voters Movement became embroiled in a fierce battle with the county board of education, which, rather than accept federal desegregation requirements, turned back funds that would have financed a second summer of Head Start programming. That refusal cost the black community not only opportunities for its children but also employment for women otherwise limited to domestic labor. In response, the Voters Movement immediately announced an economic boycott of white businesses in Windsor, the county seat, and organized a delegation to visit OEO officials in Washington. Out of that protest emerged the idea of establishing a black, community-owned business. A group of Voters Movement veterans and PPOP founders soon incorporated a company they called Bertie Industries, which the North Carolina Fund assisted with grants for employee and management training. The founders capitalized the firm by selling $21,000 worth of stock at $25 a share; two-thirds of purchasers had earnings below the poverty line, and more than half of the company's employees had at some point in their lives been on welfare. Bertie Industries was a "cut and sew operation." It cashed in on its proximity to large military bases in eastern North Carolina by securing contracts to manufacture uniforms for the growing number of soldiers being mobilized for war in Vietnam. Bertie Industries' workforce eventually numbered 120, making it the sixth largest employer in the county. The company struggled during its early years, largely as a result of its undercapitalization and its managers' limited business experience, but by the mid-1970s, it was reporting annual profits in excess of $100,000 and the value of its stock had quadrupled.[109]

Turning to the land from which its members' slave ancestors had extracted great wealth for the benefit of Choanoke planters, PPOP also conjured a vision of independence that dated back to emancipation and that since the time of the early republic had defined the way that Americans conceived of liberty and citizenship. At the end of the Civil War, former slaves urged Union lawmakers to confiscate and redistribute some portion of Confederate lands. They argued that they had a moral right to the soil on which they had labored and that landownership was essential to giving their freedom substance in day-to-day life. "Give us our land," they insisted, "and we can take care of ourselves, but without land the old masters can hire us or starve us as they please." A century later, those words still rang true. As activists battling the Choanoke's "poverty-segregation complex" declared, "Power comes from the land, control of the land, use of the land."[110]

The PPOP neighborhood council in the Bertie hamlet of Woodard put those ideas into practice. A small group of local and absentee white landlords had a lock on the community's agricultural resources. They owned 90 percent of the land and an equal portion of farm machinery and storage facilities. Those white families also controlled access to credit and to the services of state and federal farm agencies. With four acres of land donated by local civil rights organizer Tim Bazemore, Woodard's black residents sought to crack open that system by establishing a community farming cooperative that they incorporated under the name Woodard Enterprises.[111]

Bazemore had first distinguished himself in the struggle to integrate the Bertie County schools. In 1964, he and other parents successfully pressured the board of education to approve the transfer of sixty-three black students, one of whom was Bazemore's son, to a formerly all-white elementary school. Powerful whites retaliated. A local lumber company stopped buying pulp wood from Bazemore, and the bank in Windsor called in a loan on his land. At that point, North Carolina Fund officials, familiar with Bazemore's civil rights efforts, stepped in to save him from economic ruin. The Fund employed him as a recruiter for an adult vocational education program that prepared displaced farmworkers for industrial employment elsewhere in the state. Bazemore recalled the freedom and self-confidence that the job gave him. On one occasion, he happened upon a Klan cross-burning and felt emboldened enough to confront the gathering. "I came along by myself and walked right out there in the middle of all those white folks," he said. "They knew who I was, but I didn't know who they were because they had hoods on. I know they had to have thought that I had some protection, because that was unheard of."[112]

Support from the North Carolina Fund offered Bazemore's neighbors and Woodard Enterprises a similar measure of autonomy. With assistance from the Fund's community support staff and Student Nonviolent Coordinating Committee veterans Ginny and Buddy Tieger, Woodard's fifty-one black families applied through PPOP for a $22,000 grant. They used those funds to furnish their cooperative with seeds, tools, fertilizer, livestock, and feed. Their short-term goal was to a help local families grow and preserve more of their own food, so that they could devote a greater portion of their cash income to other essential needs: clothing, health care, and children's school supplies. "The great importance of this step is evident," the Woodard petitioners explained, "as soon as one enters the community and sees children without shoes and households — surrounded by fields — who subsist on a substandard, largely store-purchased diet." The cooperative, like the Brick School and the New Deal resettlement project at Tillery, was also a teaching institution. As one member of the Woodard cooperative remembered, she and her neighbors had learned from sharecropping few of the skills required for success as independent producers. Since childhood, local residents had been "brought up to just dig peanuts, [chop] cotton — work for somebody else, not for themselves." Woodard Enterprises aimed to set its members on a different path by providing practical experience in farm planning, budgeting, and saving. Through such self-directed effort, the families who established the cooperative sought to accumulate sufficient skills and resources to operate their own farms and thus to "[win] a foothold in the cash economy" and lift themselves out of poverty.[113]

In all of these ways, the People's Program on Poverty continued a quest for democracy that, for generations, had been punctuated by "ragged bursts" of struggle, setback, and rebirth. PPOP argued that the strength of its projects lay in the "utilization of cooperative work and thinking by members of the community. Each component was worked out in community discussions . . . [and] coordinated by [boards] chosen by and from the families involved." Such communal decision-making taught basic lessons in democracy and cultivated leadership skills that were essential to participation in civic life and to advancing the larger antipoverty agenda. PPOP acknowledged that its projects would "not wipe out the problems of poverty" in the Choanoke, but they did have the capacity to produce "practical, observable effects" in participants' day-to-day lives: indoor plumbing installed for families who had once relied on shallow wells and outdoor privies, a pantry stocked with canned produce that made people less dependent on credit at the country store, a tenant shack replaced by a modest home financed with a federal loan, or a steady job for men and women made redundant by agricultural mechanization. Just as important as these material improvements, PPOP's ventures affirmed to the poor that they were not simply a "dispossessed people who [had] no say in what happen[ed] to them." They had ideas, they had abilities, and they were entitled to the same chances in life that more well-to-do Americans viewed as a birthright: the opportunity to pursue their interests in the public arena, to realize their individual potential, and to determine their own fate.[114]

IN DURHAM, THAT SAME DESIRE for self-determination thrust members of UOCI deeper into local politics and an escalating confrontation over public housing. By the early summer of 1967, work on Durham's new east–west expressway was continuing apace, the city's redevelopment commission was purchasing and demolishing more low-income housing in Hayti to make way for the project, and an increasing number of the black poor were left with nowhere to turn. Segregation remained as rigid as ever in Durham's housing market, and the public housing authority had made only limited additions to its rental stock. More than eighteen hundred families had their names on the agency's waiting list. White power brokers responded with callous disregard. One official dismissed the poor families of Hayti as drunkards and prostitutes, and a local real estate developer answered critics of the redevelopment commission with assurances that the displaced poor "would house themselves as they always [had] in the past . . . without any strain on the rest of the community."[115]

The situation reached a flash point in mid-July with news of two projects under consideration by the Durham Housing Authority. The first involved an option to purchase the Damar Court Apartments, a relatively new complex located across the street from Duke University's married student housing, and transform it into the first public housing development outside the city's segregated black neighborhoods. On July 14, Duke officials — concerned that the university's property was about to become "less useful . . . less marketable, and less valuable" — made a counteroffer on Damar Court. At about the same time, the housing authority filed a formal request for the city to annex and rezone an industrial area on Bacon Street, near the eastern edge of Hayti, where it planned to build a high-rise public housing complex. UOCI and others in the black community perceived these twin events as expressions of deep-seated racism. Duke University had made clear its unwillingness to accept poor neighbors — particularly if they were black — and, along with the housing authority, appeared determined to pack the black poor ever more tightly into a "Negro ghetto" in the segregated southeastern corner of town.[116]

On July 17, more than 150 black citizens, most of them members of UOCI, appeared before the city council to demand that the housing authority drop its plans for Bacon Street and actively promote residential desegregation by following through on the Damar Court project. They also used the occasion to rehearse a long list of ongoing grievances against slumlords and to insist once more that the city enforce its housing code. Late in the evening, Howard Fuller rose to make a plea for understanding and constructive action. "I didn't come to beg, and I didn't come . . . with my hat in my hand," he told city leaders, "because we've come up here too many times with hat in hand. . . . We're tired of you white folks turning down everything that will benefit Negroes. . . . You all better wake up, you all better lean back on those chairs and listen to what these folks are talking about. And you all better start doing something to benefit these black people. 'Cause they're tired, and they're frustrated, and people who get tired and frustrated do things they wouldn't ordinarily do." Fuller made his demands as the nation was rocked by six days of urban unrest in Newark, New Jersey, which *Life* magazine characterized as a "predictable insurrection" fueled by police brutality, unemployment, poverty, and the inequities of urban renewal. The violence left twenty-six people dead and more than a thousand injured. With that news ringing in their ears, Durham's city leaders heard Fuller's call as a threat to unleash a black mob to loot and burn. The next morning, an oversized headline on the front page of the *Durham Herald* screamed, "'ANOTHER NEWARK' THREATENED HERE."[117]

Two days after its showdown with the city council, UOCI convened a meeting at St. Joseph's African Methodist Episcopal Zion Church in Hayti. The main speaker took the stage to recite a list of complaints compiled by the organization's neighborhood councils, but when the church's sound system failed, she called on Ann Atwater, who had a deeper, more powerful voice. North Carolina Fund finance director Nathan Garrett recalled that in "reading the grievances, Mrs. Atwater amplified on them considerably and before long there were shouts of anger and defiance from the group." At that point, Atwater exclaimed, "You've heard enough. You want to march. Let's go." The crowd, nearly two hundred strong, then marched from St. Joseph's to city hall. On the way back, several youths began to throw rocks, breaking windows and slightly injuring one policeman.[118]

The rock-throwing hardly constituted a riot — the worst the *Durham Sun* could say was to call it a "ruckus" — but Mayor Wensell Grabarek responded as if the city were under siege. Without consulting the city council or informing Durham's mainstream black leaders, he asked Governor Dan Moore to call out the National Guard and the state Highway Patrol to join local police and sheriff's deputies in securing downtown streets. Incensed by what they felt was an unnecessary display of force, UOCI leaders called for a march of defiance on the evening of July 20. "We must show that we are unafraid," they

Howard Fuller walked a barricade to enforce discipline among UOCI protesters and to keep them apart from the National Guardsmen called out by Mayor Grabarek and Governor Moore. Photograph by Jim Thornton, courtesy of the *Durham Herald-Sun*.

explained, "and that the city must do more than show how fast the police forces of the state and the National Guard can be mobilized."

Once again, hundreds gathered at St. Joseph's. This night, the talk was not so much of demands and grievances, but of the discipline that would be required to prevent whites from starting a full-scale riot. As the demonstrators gathered, Howard Fuller and Ben Ruffin "pointed out that there was a good deal of danger because the Klan was gathering downtown. Everyone was told to empty his/her pockets of rocks and any other objects which they might be tempted to throw and told not to pick up a rock or anything during the course of the march." The group then gathered outside in a carefully planned formation. Adults were placed among the children to ensure their protection and "several people were asked to out-station themselves so that they could keep the marchers in single file and could deal with persons who either got nervous or rowdy. Care was also taken to place certain individuals at points in the line where it appeared that potential troublemakers were grouped." As the demonstrators approached city hall, they encountered a phalanx of guardsmen and police officers and, standing nearby, a crowd of jeering whites and armed Klansmen. The group paused to sing freedom songs and to hear brief remarks by Ben Ruffin. At that point, a white man pitched a bottle and struck one of the protesters in the head. A small group of young black men surged from the line "as though to go after the whites," but they were "restrained

Young middle-class white men found amusement in heckling poor blacks who marched for better housing and respect as equal citizens. Photograph by Harold Moore, courtesy of the *Durham Herald-Sun*.

two or three times by Howard Fuller" and his lieutenants. Concerned by the "apparent ferociousness of the whites lining the streets," the demonstrators decided to march back to St. Joseph's as a group rather than, as originally planned, disbanding and returning home individually. Along the way they continued to be heckled and taunted by whites who trailed close behind. The evening ended without further incident, but only because of the leadership of Howard Fuller and the discipline of the UOCI marchers, who refused to compromise either their commitment to nonviolence or their determination to seek redress of their grievances.[119]

The Durham City Council responded to the July protests by appointing an ad hoc committee "to coordinate meetings between UOCI and the various governmental, civic, and agency officials with whom they wished to lodge complaints." Over the next several months, negotiations produced a number of concessions. Duke University agreed to withdraw its offer to purchase Damar Court and — still for largely self-interested reasons — offered to sell its married student apartments for conversion to public housing. The city council refused the rezoning request for the proposed housing project on Bacon Street, and the Durham Merchants Association agreed in general terms to

In a statement to the Durham City Council and the press, Rubye Gattis argued that dignity and economic opportunity were essential elements of social order. Photograph by Billy E. Barnes, courtesy of the North Carolina Collection, Wilson Library, University of North Carolina at Chapel Hill, Billy Ebert Barnes Collection.

employ more blacks in jobs once reserved for whites. The behavior of the chairman of the association's equal opportunity committee suggested, however, just how much work remained to be done. After being reprimanded for using the word *nigger* in a public meeting, he agreed to make changes in his own business. "I'll hire one," he said. "I need a salesman."[120]

In the fall of 1967, it was still not clear how those concessions should be read. Did they represent a turning point, the beginning of a new era in which "the voices of the poor" would be acknowledged in the halls of power? Or had Durham's white leadership merely surrendered what was necessary — and no more — to maintain order and protect the city's reputation? In testimony before the city council earlier that summer, UOCI president Rubye Gattis had urged white officials to think carefully about what was at stake. "Our organization is designed to be a voice for peaceful protest," Gattis assured the council. "We do not believe that Newark [is] the answer." But, she added, peace should not be construed as simply the absence of conflict and physical violence. "A peaceful community," Gattis explained, "is one that works to give everybody a chance to live in dignity and health and prosperity."[121]

The North Carolina Fund experienced considerable success in organizing the black poor in Durham and the Choanoke region. But the fact remained that a majority of the poor — in North Carolina and the nation — were white. From the outset, the architects of the War on Poverty had wanted desperately to include that constituency. One reason was practical: the sheer number of poor whites meant that their participation in a campaign against poverty would yield the greatest returns in the form of economic development and value added to human capital. Another reason was decidedly tactical: Lyndon Johnson and allies such as Terry Sanford knew that the War on Poverty would fail if it became too closely identified with the black freedom struggle. In hopes of holding on to conservative southern Democrats, Johnson distanced himself from the agenda of civil rights and characterized his assault on poverty as a means of creating "opportunity for all."[1]

When Americans thought of white poverty, most turned almost instinctively to the people of Appalachia. The area's inhabitants seemed to epitomize the plight of the poor as depicted in Michael Harrington's *Other America*. They were, in one essayist's words, "yesterday's people," left behind by modernity. Beginning in the late nineteenth century, timber and coal barons had come to the region and carted off much of its vast natural wealth. In the post–World War II era, automation took away jobs as well, and tens of thousands of mountaineers moved north and west to cities in America's industrial heartland. The political and economic roots of Appalachia's misery were easy to identify. Even so, most observers placed a large portion of the burden and blame on the shoulders of the people most affected. "Who stayed behind?" they asked. "The poorly trained and poorly educated . . . the unambitious, who could tolerate a subsistence living at home . . . the aged, the sickly, and the retarded; and the psychologically immobile, who could not move away from the familiar, protective mountain culture." In such circumstances, friends of Appalachia argued, a "culture of poverty [was becoming] all the more entrenched [and] a whole segment of the region's people [was] on the way to being destroyed by forces too great and problems too long standing for them to cope with."[2]

In North Carolina, some of the worst mountain poverty was concentrated in four contiguous counties in the northwestern corner of the state — Watauga, Avery, Mitchell, and Yancey (the WAMY region) — and from there the North Carolina Fund received one of its most ambitious community action proposals. The four counties occupy a narrow corridor of land between the Tennessee border and the Blue Ridge Parkway. The area is "studded with massive mountain peaks" — including Mount Mitchell, the tallest summit east of the Mississippi — and during the early twentieth century it had become a retreat for the industrial barons and the growing middle class of the urban Piedmont. Resort towns — Banner Elk, Linville, Burnsville, Boone, and Blowing Rock — dotted the countryside, and two expansive parks recorded the influence of wealthy outsiders, textile magnate Moses H. Cone and insurance executive Julian Price, both of Greensboro. During the late 1890s, Cone had acquired thirty-six hundred acres of woodland just outside Blowing Rock, where he developed miles of carriage trails and built Flat Top Manor, a twenty-three-room Georgian summer home. Nearby, Price purchased forty-six hundred acres, which he intended to develop as a retreat for senior managers from his Jefferson Standard Life Insurance Company. Both properties were later given to the federal government to create adjoining recreational areas along the Blue Ridge Parkway. Begun as a New Deal work relief project during the 1930s, the parkway had become a major tourist attraction. It beckoned suburban families, who piled into their station wagons and drove back in time to what they imagined had been a simpler way of life.[3]

Set against that backdrop of natural beauty, wealth, and leisure, the region's poverty statistics were startling. In 1960, 58 percent of all families lived on incomes below the Fund-designated poverty line of $3,000 per year, and a nearly equal share of housing was classified as "dilapidated or deteriorating." The local poor found few opportunities to improve their lot. The natural resources that had once supported jobs in mining and the timber industry had been depleted; much of the most accessible and fertile land had been taken out of production by absentee owners in the scramble to exploit Appalachia's forest and mineral wealth; and mountain families, pushed into remote coves and hollows by those economic forces, had exhausted the fertility of the marginal land that was left for farming. To make matters worse, the federal government owned vast tracts of national forest, on which it paid no taxes that might have supported public services. Instead, profits from those reserves went to the national treasury and to the private firms that leased the land for

A majority of people in the WAMY counties lived in substandard housing. Photograph by Billy E. Barnes, courtesy of the North Carolina Collection, Wilson Library, University of North Carolina at Chapel Hill, Billy Ebert Barnes Collection.

logging. Those conditions set in motion an exodus that began in the 1920s and accelerated dramatically after World War II. Between 1950 and 1959, the four counties lost on average a quarter of their population.[4]

Work on a proposal to the Fund began with a small group of local leaders who participated in the statewide fact-finding tour that Terry Sanford and his aides organized for Ford Foundation officials in the winter of 1963. The Ford entourage stopped for a full day's visit at the Nu Wray Inn, a historic hotel in Burnsville, the Yancey County seat. There, they met with more than a dozen representatives from mountain communities, including four from the WAMY region: William Plemmons, president of Appalachian State Teachers College (now Appalachian State University) in Boone; Robert K. Helmle, the reform-minded mayor of Burnsville; C. Ray Braswell, a lawyer and president of the Avery County Chamber of Commerce; and Benjamin V. Mast, a journalist and native of Watauga County who had produced a documentary film on the "problems of the mountain people." Governor Sanford led a frank discussion of poverty conditions in western North Carolina and prodded the group to think creatively about solutions.[5]

The Ford representatives and the local leaders liked what they heard from one another. The foundation had commissioned a major study of Appalachia, published in 1962, and was eager to identify local partners who would commit themselves to substantive, pragmatic action. For their part, the local group saw an opportunity to leverage outside support for regional development. They returned home and quickly organized working groups of school and social welfare officials, politicians, and business leaders who surveyed the status of the poor in each county and drafted plans for "experimental action." A steering committee chaired by William Plemmons then integrated the results of those efforts into a formal proposal submitted to the North Carolina Fund in January 1964.[6]

Members of the steering committee acknowledged up front that they faced a crisis that they could not resolve on their own. Solutions to the region's problems were "simply beyond the capacity of local resources." Education offered a sobering case in point. The four counties spent up to 47 percent of their tax revenues on schools, but the value of taxable property in the region was so low that even such strenuous effort was insufficient. Of the counties' fourteen secondary schools, only two were accredited. The quality of instruction fell far below state and national norms, and for many students education seemed to have little practical relevance. The consequences were predictable: a third of all students dropped out before earning a high school diploma, and the median level of schooling among adults twenty-five years of age and older hovered around eight years. With such an inadequately educated workforce, the counties had little chance of attracting high-wage industries. Local boosters complained that "the 'big ones' continue[d] to get away, being caught downstream, below the mountains," by communities with more to offer. Taxable wealth remained limited, and the WAMY region found itself "caught in a self-perpetuating cycle of poverty."[7]

Money for education was but one of a litany of needs. "We need many other things," the petitioners confessed. "We need re-training for new kinds of jobs. We need additional sources of information and advice for farmers on kinds of crops to grow and better marketing procedures. . . . We need to . . . to make our area more appealing to [tourists] who . . . will spend money in large amounts . . . helping everyone who is in business here and creating new jobs." Despite "local reluctance to ask for . . . help," the magnitude of those challenges made it clear that they could not be addressed "on a sufficiently large scale" without outside assistance. The local leaders were quick to explain that they did not need "help in terms of doing the job for us, but help in the form of *catalysts*" that would revitalize the region.[8]

The Fund selected the mountain alliance as one of its initial grantees, and in July 1964 local organizers incorporated WAMY Community Action (or WAMY). The agency's original bylaws called for the appointment of a board of directors with seventy-two members. On one hand, that number reflected wide-ranging support among regional power brokers. The board included thirty-eight representatives of public and private social service agencies, eighteen representatives of county government, and an assortment of ministers and businessmen. On the other hand, such a large board revealed the difficulty of overcoming "diverse interests, inter-county jealousies, and pride in local independence." As money began to flow, that challenge would bedevil WAMY Community Action at every turn.[9]

THE FIRST ORDER OF BUSINESS for WAMY's founders was to hire a program director. They settled quickly on a young man named Ernest Eppley, who came to their attention through the North Carolina Fund office in Durham. Eppley had grown up in Cramerton, a Piedmont cotton mill town, and began his professional career as a teacher, first in two Greensboro-area high schools and then at Brevard Junior College, located in the mountains south of Asheville. In the years immediately preceding his involvement with the North Carolina Fund, he and his wife, Anita, had served as missionary teachers at the American Institute in La Paz, Bolivia. The school ministered to poor migrants from rural indigenous communities who traveled to the capital in search of employment. There, the Eppleys worked on a variety of community development projects that included adult and elementary education, the delivery of health services, and practical instruction in commercial agriculture.[10]

Once back in the United States, Ernest enrolled as a graduate student at Duke University, where he began study for a doctorate in education. He heard about the North Carolina Fund and the job at WAMY from a friend whose daughter was working in Yancey County as one of the "First One Hundred" summer volunteers. He followed up with an interview with Fund staff in Durham, who recommended him to the WAMY organizers. They, too, were impressed. In October, Eppley moved his family to Boone and took up his new responsibilities as WAMY's first executive director. The assignment paid a comfortable salary—the first that Eppley had earned in many years—and,

WAMY director Ernest
Eppley. Photograph by
Billy E. Barnes, courtesy
of the North Carolina
Collection, Wilson
Library, University of
North Carolina at Chapel
Hill, Billy Ebert Barnes
Collection.

most important, it "was the right kind of work for him . . . the sort of thing
into which he could put his whole heart."[11]

Eppley arrived fired up with idealism and an ambitious sense of possibility,
both of which had been nurtured by his missionary work in Bolivia. He and
his wife had labored among some of South America's poorest citizens, and
he was determined to bring that experience to the battle against poverty in
the highlands of North Carolina. In November 1964 — a little more than a
month into his new job — Eppley made plain for WAMY's founders the full
ramifications of the campaign that they had launched. "We are trying to bring
about a social and economic revolution," he explained, "and it means that
many of our own attitudes will have to change." Perhaps that was true, but for
the time being the board embraced a more modest view. Its members "envi-
sioned [WAMY as] primarily a coordinating [body] which would bring [social
welfare] agencies closer together and help them" achieve greater efficiency
and effectiveness in the delivery of services to the poor.[12]

WAMY Community Action was an exemplar of the cautious reformism
that characterized the first skirmishes in the War on Poverty. When WAMY
applied for federal funds from the Office of Economic Opportunity (OEO)
in early 1965, the directors presented the organization as primarily a pass-
through agency that would subcontract most of its work to existing providers
of social welfare and educational services. In June, WAMY received a twelve-
month grant of $653,000, and by the fall it had seventy-five employees on
its payroll, more than two-thirds of whom worked under the direction and
supervision of various county agencies. Early-childhood educators and reading specialists, lodged in the public school systems, ran Head Start and summer remedial programs. An expanded staff of guidance counselors worked

to bring dropouts back into school and designed programs to prevent other students from leaving. In the public health departments, nurses, health educators, and part-time subprofessionals staffed clinics and visited in local communities to promote routine screenings and immunizations. Similarly, new staff in the county agricultural extension bureaus, managed by North Carolina State University in Raleigh, offered small farmers advice on profitable crops and effective marketing strategies.[13]

WAMY opted for this decentralized approach for several reasons. In its early days, the board of directors was "'loaded' with agency people" who were eager to steer new resources to their own coffers. In some measure, that attitude was understandable because paltry tax revenues left the WAMY region's schools, health departments, and welfare offices starved for funds. Political concerns also demanded the routing of money through established channels. The four-county region was predominantly Republican, a holdover from Union sympathies and resentment of an eastern slaveholding elite during the Civil War. Nevertheless, mountain Republicans shared with their Democratic cousins a visceral aversion to what they perceived as federal meddling in local affairs. Commissioners in Avery County, for instance, rejected federal surplus food for school lunches, even though many children went hungry every day. As one observer explained, if WAMY had not worked through existing agencies, those commissioners and others "probably would have refused the [antipoverty] program, even if [Washington] did offer funds."[14]

Early on, the WAMY staff took responsibility for only one antipoverty project, a handicrafts program designed to cash in on Appalachia's purported isolation from the mainstream of American life. The authors of WAMY's original proposal to the North Carolina Fund adopted the language of outsiders and, in a curious way, separated themselves from their neighbors. They explained that "historically, the fact that [the WAMY] counties lie at such high altitudes and their land areas are broken by few mountain passes has been very important in their development, from a cultural as well as economic standpoint. . . . The pioneer settlers were compelled to become almost self-supporting. . . . All items of wearing apparel, many of the medicines, dye-stuffs, foods, furniture, and most of the other necessities of life had to be produced in the homes. This condition promoted in the people the development of exceptional skills in various crafts," many of which survived "well into the twentieth century." WAMY's crafts project sought to make those skills a source of hard cash. The agency employed a number of crafts specialists — most but not all of whom were college-educated outsiders — who scoured the countryside for local artisans. The culture workers also arranged crafts instruction for

A western North Carolina woodwright who participated in the WAMY crafts program. Photograph by Billy E. Barnes, courtesy of the North Carolina Collection, Wilson Library, University of North Carolina at Chapel Hill, Billy Ebert Barnes Collection.

local people who were eager to supplement their incomes but had no experience with weaving, whittling, or the making of corn-shuck dolls. In this way, WAMY sought as much to create as preserve mountain traditions.[15]

This strategy of cultural revival and economic uplift had a long pedigree. Its origins in the southern highlands can be traced to the church workers and educators who settled in the region during the 1910s and 1920s to build schools, to serve the needs of the mountain poor, and to rescue a dying craft tradition. The production of handicrafts, the reformers insisted, not only held practical value for mountaineers, but also offered a balm for the disaffections of modern industrial life. In a Faustian bargain, Americans had acquired an abundance of material possessions at the expense of "individual initiative, ownership of tools, and use of [their] hands." The crafts revival promised to ameliorate those losses for producers and consumers alike. The manufacture and marketing of handicrafts, promoters believed, could reestablish a human relationship between an object's maker and its user, and from that exchange both parties might extract a measure of joy and aesthetic pleasure unmatched by goods "cheaply bought, not lovingly made." There was, of course, bitter irony in this nostalgic view of the mountains as a reservoir of authenticity. In the early decades of the twentieth century, thousands of families from western North Carolina had abandoned the poverty of self-sufficiency in search of a better life in Piedmont textile factories and mill towns.[16]

The WAMY region was home to two of the southern highlands' most celebrated crafts revival projects. In 1913, Eustace and Mary Martin Sloop launched the first of the pair in the Avery County town of Crossnore. Mary Martin had grown up in Davidson, a foothills community one hundred miles southeast of Crossnore, where her father was a professor of natural sciences at Davidson College. She received the equivalent of a high school education at a private female academy, and in 1902 traveled to Philadelphia, where she studied at the Woman's Medical College and earned her credentials as a physician. Six years later, she married Eustace Sloop, also a physician. Mary had aspired to serve the Presbyterian Church as a medical missionary in Africa, but at age thirty-three she was too old to secure such an assignment. Eustace shared her interest in mission work, and together they decided that they could best pursue their ideals in the North Carolina mountains. "If we could not be foreign missionaries," she explained in her autobiography, "we could serve at home."[17]

In Crossnore, the Sloops opened a medical clinic and Mary established a small school for orphans and for boarding students who did not have a school close to home. By the end of the 1930s, the Crossnore project had grown to occupy more than twenty buildings and three hundred acres of land. Students supported the enterprise by working on a school farm and in a weaving program, to which Mary attached particular significance. She saw weaving instruction as a way to revitalize a native mountain craft and as a means by which mountain girls could earn an independent income and forestall the hardships of early marriage and childbearing.[18]

A decade after the Sloops' arrival in Crossnore, Lucy Calista Morgan took up a similar project in the Mitchell County town of Penland. Morgan grew up in Cherokee County, located in the far southwestern corner of North Carolina. Her family was comfortably middle class; her father owned a printing business and her mother was active in the Episcopal Church. Morgan attended a private high school run by her aunt and then traveled north to prepare for a career in teaching. In 1920, she returned to North Carolina to work at the Appalachian School, a church boarding and country day school for children in the elementary grades founded by her brother Rufus, an Episcopal priest. Morgan added a weaving department to the school during the mid-1920s and began traveling the surrounding countryside to encourage local women to provide handicrafts for sale through an enterprise she called Fireside Industries. In 1929, she founded an independent Penland School of Handicrafts on thirty acres of her own land and opened the institution to students from outside the immediate region. Morgan connected Penland to a national circle of weaving revivalists by inviting Edward F. Worst, director of handwork for the Chicago public schools and a leading champion of Arts and Crafts design, to run regular summer workshops. She also evidenced fierce determination in marketing Penland "homespuns." She displayed her students' wares in local tourist hotels and in 1933 transported a log cabin to Chicago, where she set it up as a sales booth at the World's Fair. In all of those efforts, Morgan shared Mary Martin Sloop's sense of purpose. "There were two things I wanted very much to do," she wrote. "The first was to help bring about a revival of hand-weaving. . . . The other thing I wanted to do was provide [Penland's] neighbor mothers with a means of adding to their generally meager incomes."[19]

Thirty years later, during the early 1960s, Appalachia and its folk schools stood again at the center of national attention. John F. Kennedy's campaign for West Virginia votes in the 1960 Democratic presidential primary brought into the nation's living rooms disturbing television images of grinding, seemingly pathological poverty. Within months of taking office, the new president pushed through Congress the Area Redevelopment Act, which promised federal aid to "stranded" communities, particularly those of the southern mountains. At the same moment, a postwar folk revival began celebrating Appalachia and its people as "protectors of the nation's past," keepers of the virtues of "an earlier and nobler time." The revival found expression in the Newport Folk Festival, established in 1959, and the campus hootenannies where a generation of middle-class youth sang along with Bob Dylan, Pete Seeger, Joan Baez, and Peter, Paul, and Mary, seeking in the music of marginal folk the "real and human values" that seemed to have been lost in a "thoroughly rationalized, regimented . . . bureaucratized" and militarized Cold War America.[20]

This fascination with mountain culture found its way even into commercial television. In 1962, CBS first aired *The Beverly Hillbillies*, one of the most successful situation comedies in the history of American broadcasting. It was modeled on Al Capp's satirical comic strip *Li'l Abner*, which became popular during the 1930s when mountaineers first streamed north. The show told the story of Jed Clampett, "a poor mountaineer"; his mother-in-law, known simply as Granny; a beautiful and far-too-innocent daughter, Elly Mae; and Jethro Bodine, a half-witted nephew—all of whom had moved to Beverly Hills after Jed struck oil while hunting on his east Tennessee farm. The premise was more or less the same from week to week: the Clampett clan risked humiliation—or worse, loss of their fortune—as they confronted greed, cynicism, and smug sophistication in America's glamour capital. But in the end, they always prevailed, thanks to their rustic integrity and country wisdom. *The Beverly Hillbillies* ran for nine years and throughout that period ranked among the nation's top ten television shows.[21]

For WAMY's founders, the idea of creating a handicrafts program to tap into this cultural phenomenon held an obvious attraction. After all, the folk revival had roots in their own local history; in 1962, the Ford Foundation had singled out crafts-making as an economic development strategy in its survey of the southern Appalachian region; and the ever-increasing numbers of tourists who vacationed in the North Carolina mountains offered a ready market for the consumption of homespun goods. The idea looked compelling on paper, but in practice it was fraught with difficulties. To begin with, there were few true artisans in the WAMY area; launching a crafts program required an all-out effort to teach local people skills—weaving and basket-, broom-, and doll-making—that their families had long ago abandoned in exchange for the convenience of store-bought goods. Most of those who picked up such skills were realistic in their expectations. They saw handicrafts as a way to earn a bit of pocket cash but realized the difficulty of turning such work into a full-time job. Few had the financial resources to purchase raw materials year-round and to make objects that they would place on consignment and not sell until the busy Christmas and summer tourist seasons.[22]

The formation of a cooperative called Blue Ridge Hearthside Crafts, which WAMY incorporated in 1966, solved the issue of producers' access to credit and won national attention for local goods. WAMY crafts were sold in New York art galleries and put on display at the Smithsonian Institution in Washington. Even so, WAMY director Ernest Eppley felt deeply ambivalent about the enterprise. At best, it promised to provide a livable income to only a few of the most talented producers. Of the 204 people who participated in the program in 1966, 10 earned an average of $100 a month, 2 earned more than $200 a month, and the remaining 192 averaged only $3.16. At worst, the crafts enterprise threatened to propagate a nostalgic view of highlanders that obscured the realities of mountain poverty. "The tendency . . . has always been to glamorize the mountaineer," Eppley explained, "especially among the middle class people—you hear them talking all the time about how wonderful the mountains are and how wonderful mountaineers are and how independent they are and how much they like the way their life is and how much they don't want to be changed. . . . I had a very literate person who worked on the *Watauga Democrat* [say] to me . . . that she certainly would be happy to have the kind of life that a poor mountaineer has out in a shack . . . and [that] this would be a wonderful life for anyone." That exchange annoyed Eppley, who quipped, "I don't know if she's tried it or not."[23]

On the whole, WAMY's crafts project, like its policy of subcontracting programs to existing agencies, looked backward to well-worn solutions to mountain poverty. The community action agency moved haltingly toward the kind of experimentation the North Carolina Fund had called for, and at the outset it did so only in small free spaces that afforded the poor an opportunity to speak and to contribute their own knowledge to the antipoverty campaign. The most notable place where such exchanges occurred was in the work of the Friendly Home Visitors, a group of women subprofessionals, seven in each WAMY county, who were assigned to local health departments. The group's title, now part of the common parlance of social welfare organizations, was first used during the nineteenth century to describe women volunteers who did charity work among the poor. WAMY employed a visitor from each school district in the four-county region and instructed the women to call on every family in their territories. "They told us . . . 'don't skip any houses,'" remembered Yancey native Betty Whitson. "If people live in a shack, you go and tell them what you're starting to try to do [and if] they live in a nice brick home you go and tell them the same thing," educate them about the War on Poverty.[24]

Betty Whitson was typical of the women who signed on as Friendly Home Visitors. She was in her late thirties, the eldest child in a family of nine, and had grown up on a small mountain farm. While she did not characterize herself as poor, her family needed whatever income she could earn by taking a "public job." Her husband was disabled, and they had four children, two of them under the age of five. Betty heard about the home visitor jobs from a friend who worked for the town of Burnsville. Shortly after WAMY received its OEO money, the woman called and suggested that she pick up an application. Betty's husband liked the idea. "Why don't you fill it out and think about it?" he urged. "We really, really need the extra income." Six weeks later, "two strange people"—WAMY staffers—appeared at the Whitsons' door. They chatted with Betty and asked why she was interested in working as a home visitor. She explained that she had always been the one in her neighborhood

A Friendly Home Visitor calls on Mrs. Warren, a Watauga County resident. Photograph by Billy E. Barnes, courtesy of the North Carolina Collection, Wilson Library, University of North Carolina at Chapel Hill, Billy Ebert Barnes Collection.

to care for the sick and to take on odd chores as "a community taxi, the barber, you name it." "God gave me these two hands, and he expected me to use them," she said. "And I plan to use them as long as I live, doing what I can for people." The strangers left, promising to give her an answer within a week. A few minutes later, they returned—Betty had the job.[25]

The home visitors' initial assignment was to conduct a health census of the WAMY counties. As they went from house to house, they recorded in their notebooks details about each family. "Every member . . . had to be listed," explained True Elliott, "the age of each child . . . the name and address of the father, directions to the house, and the conditions they were living in." Beyond that, the visitors' charge was vague: they were to "be a friend to the poor, to listen, to share, to understand . . . [to] help poor persons discover resources for solving their problems [and] get needed services they [were] entitled to from the social [welfare] agencies." The work was physically demanding and the days long. Home visitors drove up and down mountain roads that often were little more than rutted lanes; they forded rivers and creeks; and in places where there were no roads, they walked for miles to reach houses tucked away in mountain hollows. The women got an early start, transporting neighbors to medical appointments or children and their mothers to Head Start programs, and they returned home late after completing the route in reverse. On clinic days, home visitors assisted county public health nurses. They took case histories, weighed and measured babies, and helped "hold children for 'shots' . . . when the parents 'chicken[ed] out.'"[26]

As the home visitors made their rounds, they confronted conditions of deprivation and social isolation that, even as mountain natives, they "did not know existed." Deep in a mountain hollow, True Elliott walked into a scene that was Dickensian in it pathos:

> At the end of this road, I found a family of twelve children, man and a woman, living in a four-room boxed house, wood floor with cracks in it, a tin heater. I don't know how they survived. They had very little furniture, they had one child that was crippled, his feet were turned backwards and he was laying on a pallet in the floor. He could crawl just a little bit, couldn't walk. . . . I worked with that family for a long time, took the little boy to rehab, and his feet later in life was corrected and he could walk normal. But the family lived there a long time and they did a little farming for our wealthiest man in Burnsville. I think they were paying $15 a month rent, which I'm sure was hard to do. A lot of the other houses I visited was in the same situation and a lot of them were drying moss and digging ginseng, and that was the things that they sold to make money to buy what they had to have at the store.

A tangle of disadvantages — inadequate education, a scarcity of jobs, ill health, and limited access to social services — locked such families into poverty and sapped their capacity to alter their circumstances. The home visitors' case reports also made plain the psychological wounds that poverty inflicted on families. Sporadic employment left men with a sense of shame that they could not provide for their families. They grew weary from the endless struggle to put food on the table, to clothe their children, and to pay for medicine and doctor visits. Many relieved the pain with alcohol and, in doing so, compounded their families' misery.[27]

The home visitors took particular interest in the mothers and wives of poverty, many of whom were doubly disadvantaged by economic hardship and the authority of no-good men. That concern grew in part from the visitors' own life experiences. They were active, resourceful women — their neighbors recognized them as community leaders, as people one could call on in times of need. As a matter of pride and practical necessity, they had taken control of their lives. By signing on with WAMY, they stepped outside the home and demonstrated their capacity to assume responsibility for themselves, their families, and their neighbors. True Elliott recalled that most poor women were denied that opportunity. She and her coworkers "found that a lot of [wives] were so cowed [that] they'd talk to you if their husband wasn't around, but if he's around they wouldn't talk. It was like they had total control." It "was hard for me to accept that," Elliott said, "because I just couldn't imagine . . . not having freedom of speech, and they didn't even have that." Then she quipped to Betty Whitson, her longtime friend and fellow visitor, "It didn't take us long to train them, did it?"[28]

As the two women went from house to house, they shared the strength that had gotten them through their own life struggles. Whitson's earnings as a visitor replaced the wages that her disabled husband no longer brought home, and Elliott had been supporting herself since the early death of a husband given to drink. They said to the poor women they called on, "Hey, get out of here. C'mon let's go." "We got them out of [the house]," Whitson recalled, "and maybe they had a fight with their husband later, I don't know, but they'd go the next time we went after them. They [got] some willpower and some freedom to get in and out [of the house] and maybe to go to a store or to take a child to a doctor." Together, Whitson and Elliott were "teaching people to come out of the conditions they was in."[29]

The home visitors quickly realized that one of the things poor women needed most was a place to gather, where they could break out of their "social isolation," learn about available social welfare services, and "share for the first time their interests [and] talents." To that end, the visitors spearheaded the creation of community centers in the districts they served. Their immediate challenge was to address the dearth of public space, especially in rural areas. By the 1960s, mountain school systems, like their counterparts across the state, had undertaken an aggressive program of consolidation. As a result, individual schools were located miles away from most of the families they served, and travel times by way of narrow, winding mountain roads were long. That meant that in most communities churches were the only buildings available for meetings. But country congregations were small, they could afford only a sanctuary for worship, and frequently, ministers and congregants resisted the use of sacred space for secular purposes. That situation left the home visitors to scrounge for whatever alternatives they could find.[30]

Betty Whitson was fortunate. "My husband and I had a little house on our property that was empty," she explained. "And I told the women that they could use it. I said, 'It won't cost you any rent or anything.'" In Burnsville, True Elliott had to be more resourceful. Along with a circle of women pulled together by her weekly visits, she laid claim to an abandoned jailhouse. Town leaders "were thinking about tearing it down," Elliott said, "and we stopped them from doing that and we opened it up as a community center." Across the WAMY region, other home visitors exhibited similar determination and ingenuity. They recruited young men from the Neighborhood Youth Corps to clean, paint, and repair old barns and other outbuildings for use as meeting halls, and they mobilized local residents, who put on "ham supper[s]" to raise money for furnishings — tables and chairs, projectors and screens for showing films, and recreational equipment for children. By early 1967, the Friendly Home Visitors had established twenty-three community centers, where neighbors "could get together . . . to discuss their needs."[31]

The centers offered poor women "something [to] belong to outside of the home and outside of themselves." The home visitors sought to develop bonds of friendship among neighbors, to teach homemaking skills, and ultimately to help each woman discover "her abilities as a leader among her peers." That work could not be forced; instead, it had to grow incrementally out of group activity. Home visitors often began their efforts by inviting women to join sewing and quilting circles. Those were familiar activities, and they had an immediate practical payoff for poor families. Even so, attendance was spotty at first, and the women who showed up often "sat with their eyes fixed on the floor" and hesitated to speak. To counter that reticence, the home visitors shared stories of what other groups were doing and asked participants around the circle to talk about their families, the things that made them happy in life, and how they wanted to use their time together.[32]

As women sat and sewed, they became "more confident, self-sufficient individuals." In a variety of ways — at first glance, seemingly mundane — they acquired a measure of control over "life as it was lived day-to-day — sometimes chaotic and unpredictable, always difficult." The quilting circles addressed the simple fact that "most of the women [were] cold, [had] many children, and not enough bed clothes to go around." They also turned out hand goods that women could sell for ready cash through WAMY's crafts project. Putting meals on the table was another of the unyielding challenges of daily life. Poor families were eligible to receive surplus food from the U.S. Department of Agriculture, but many did not know about the program, and often those who did failed to sign up. The home visitors registered women at the community centers, brought food from county warehouses and distributed it themselves, and, perhaps most important, offered cooking classes that taught women how

Quilters participate in one of the sewing circles organized by WAMY's Friendly Home Visitors. Photograph by Billy E. Barnes, courtesy of the North Carolina Collection, Wilson Library, University of North Carolina at Chapel Hill, Billy Ebert Barnes Collection.

to use the food. While women were involved in these activities, Volunteers in Service to America (VISTA) members and work-study students from Appalachian State watched their children. They engaged the youngsters in "planned work and play with the aid of educational toys, puzzles, blocks, clay, paint, stories (read aloud and told), and records." Middle-class women would have called the occasion a mother's morning out. For poor women, the meaning was much the same. The children's program offered them something they rarely experienced: the luxury of time to themselves, time for "laughter [and] self-reflection."[33]

Arguably, the most important service the home visitors supplied to poor women was providing information about family planning and access to birth control. Overpopulation in Appalachia had long been a concern for policymakers and social scientists. They argued that a leading cause of poverty in the region was the imbalance between large family size on one side of the ledger and, on the other, limited economic resources and employment opportunities. Poverty would be brought under control only when those elements were in equilibrium. In the 1962 Ford Foundation report on Appalachia, University of North Carolina sociologist Rupert Vance coolly dissected the problem. "If people should no longer rear their children to go into subsistence farming," he wrote, "if large contingents of mountain youth must migrate to strange cities to engage in new trades and crafts; if . . . the rate at which the regional labor force replaces itself . . . exceeds the rate at which its members are [employed] or migrate outward; if the Region's problem is thus self-renewing—a certain drastic conclusion is inevitable. It may be that the people of [Appalachia] can no longer allow themselves the luxury that the American people are now enjoying in the midst of the new prosperity—that is the enjoyment of the 'baby boom.'"[34]

Mountain women hardly viewed large families as a luxury; they were instead one of the hard facts of life. Most women experienced serial pregnancies throughout their childbearing years. In a region where poverty limited access to health care, this exposed them constantly to the risk of maternal death and the personal anguish associated with high rates of infant mortality. The luxury they desired was one that middle-class families could more easily afford—the ability to space their children and limit family size. Fund staff noted that "contrary to public beliefs, [the poor did not] want large families any more than the . . . affluent." Indeed, research revealed that "poor parents actually want[ed] fewer children than those of high income." Why, then, did they fail to control the size of their families? "There were many reasons for this," but most significant was "the fact that in most communities, poor people d[id] not have available to them comprehensive health services which include[d] competent medical guidance in modern family planning procedures." Across the state, "Public Health Departments—the main providers of health care for the [poor]—ha[d] been slow or derelict in making family planning services available." The poor thus faced an old and familiar problem: "Having less to buy health with, the poor ha[d] less health."[35]

For a brief time during the late 1930s and early 1940s, North Carolina had stood at the forefront of a national family planning movement. In 1937, it became the first state to launch a government-supported birth control program. That effort was largely the handiwork of George M. Cooper, director of the State Board of Health's Division of Preventive Medicine. Cooper had been a country doctor for more than two decades before entering government service. In his practice, he had gotten to know "many a girl wife living in a two-room mountain shack with six children and a tubercular husband. He had heard women tearfully beg, 'Isn't there something we can do?' He had seen a

Negro couple married seventeen years who had produced twenty children—twelve of them to die in infancy. Good, hard-working people, desperately poor—bewildered." When Cooper moved to Raleigh to work for the State Board of Health, he began to preach "that North Carolina could not climb far toward better health and happiness without birth control for the poor." He shared that view with Clarence J. Gamble, a fellow physician and "heir of the Procter and Gamble soap fortune." At the time, Gamble was conducting research on contraceptive powders, and he provided Cooper with funds to extend the experiment to communities across North Carolina. By late 1938, the state had established fifty-four public birth control clinics, more than half the number of such clinics in the nation as a whole.[36]

Watauga County had one of the early clinics, and for a time the county employed a public health nurse who offered condoms and Gamble's contraceptive powder to all interested women, rich and poor. But despite that auspicious start, the campaign was not sustained. Cooper had to be careful not to provoke private physicians, most of whom disapproved of public health agencies providing direct patient services and were even less tolerant when those services included birth control. For that reason, Cooper never sought large-scale publicity for the statewide program. His cautiousness frustrated Gamble, who in the early 1940s cut off his funding of Cooper's work. Across the state, many public birth control clinics closed. The program in Watauga remained in operation but severely limited its outreach efforts. The clinic provided care only for women who managed on their own to learn about its services and had the means to travel to the health department's offices.[37]

The situation was even worse in neighboring Avery, Mitchell, and Yancey Counties. They had no public health officer and had never offered family planning services. To fill that void, WAMY applied to the North Carolina Fund for a starter grant, which it used to purchase contraceptives, to reimburse physicians for accepting referrals, and to deploy the home visitors as family planning counselors. During the summer of 1967, WAMY also sent a number of its home visitors to Chapel Hill, where they participated in a family planning conference organized by university faculty at the Carolina Population Center. The center and the conference received significant support from the Ford Foundation, which during the early 1960s had begun to make major investments in social science and medical research on population growth in the developing nations of the postcolonial Third World. The foundation's objectives were to spur economic growth and promote social order and economic stability through the development of effective strategies for population control. While in Chapel Hill, the women from WAMY attended seminars with family planning educators from India, Brazil, Iran, Egypt, and other points around the globe. The delegates bridged vast cultural differences with common concern for issues of population, poverty, and economic opportunity. The stories they told had a familiar ring; at some level, the hollows of Mitchell County were not all that far removed from the highland villages of Iran.[38]

Back in the mountains, the home visitors eagerly put their training to work. In Yancey County, for instance, they developed a pamphlet that provided basic sex education, complete with hand-drawn anatomical diagrams. The pamphlet also cataloged the benefits of effective birth control: fewer "money problems," a more comfortable life, and a happier marriage and better "sex relations" free from the "fear of unwanted pregnancies." True Elliott recalled that the case for family planning was relatively easy—although at times awkward—to make: "You know what you had to do? You had to take the father behind the house and explain to him about the birds and the bees, because the mother wouldn't talk to you. . . . [We'd tell] the father about the [family planning] clinic, and, 'Oh,' he'd say, 'that's just what we need.' So then we could get the mom stopped from having those babies. I [worked with] two sisters, one lived in Mitchell County, right on the line, the other lived in my area, and each of them had twelve kids, and they were still having babies. But we got them fitted with IUDs, which they were supposed to take out after so many years, but I think most of the mothers didn't take them out, they didn't want to get rid of them." Elliott took pride in such results. They demonstrated her success in teaching women to take control of their lives.[39]

As Elliott and other home visitors made their daily rounds—sharing their knowledge of birth control, organizing community centers, and ferrying poor children to and from doctor visits—they proved themselves to be "movers of mountains, as well as movers of tables, chairs, people and food." They and Fund staff often struggled for words to explain the value of their efforts. The visitors went about their work with "no textbooks, no printed outline or great philosophies, no formalized teaching." Theirs was a "do-it-yourself . . . approach." That made tangible results difficult to measure. Indeed, a WAMY newsletter explained that the full significance of the visitors' accomplishments could not "be grasped and put on paper or felt without knowing the women [they served] and being involved in the whole continuum of change and learning." A Fund staffer turned to a familiar metaphor to describe the ineffable "something" that emerged from the women's work. The home visitors, she said, had created a "secular church"—a community of individuals bound together by common hardships, shared aspirations, and a commitment to mutual aid and support.[40]

FAMILY
PLANNING

YANCEY COUNTY PUBLIC HEALTH DEPT.

BURNSVILLE, N.C.

(Printed as an educational service
    by W.A.M.Y. Community Action)

DATE: _____   TIME _____

Friendly Home Visitors used a simple mimeographed pamphlet to promote family
planning and reproductive health. Courtesy of the Southern Historical Collection, Wilson
Library, University of North Carolina at Chapel Hill, North Carolina Fund Records.

AS WAMY BEGAN SPENDING its OEO funds during the summer of 1965, it
faced a challenge shared with all of North Carolina's community action programs: how best to comply with the federal mandate for maximum feasible
participation by the poor. The home visitor and crafts programs were steps in
the right direction, but they were only two of more than a dozen initiatives,
most of which focused on providing service *to* the poor rather than working
collaboratively *with* the poor. WAMY's board of directors took an important
step toward redressing that imbalance in September 1965. It increased the
number of directors from seventy-two to ninety-six and enlarged its executive committee from thirteen to seventeen members. Both moves were meant
to make room for "a broader cross section of people in the area, especially
those . . . whom [WAMY's] programs were designed to help." But that begged
two obvious questions: Where were representatives of the poor to be found?
and How would they be identified and recruited?[41]

Answers to such questions had been close to hand in the poor black communities of the Piedmont and the eastern coastal plain. There, the War on
Poverty overlaid a civil rights movement that had roots stretching back for

more than a century and that had reached new heights of mobilization during the early 1960s. Nothing similar existed in the WAMY region. Blacks comprised only 1 percent of the population, and civil rights protests were limited and sporadic. Similarly, the Carolina mountains stood far removed from the tradition of labor organizing and bitter class conflict that characterized the history of the United Mine Workers and the coal towns of West Virginia and Kentucky. The WAMY counties also had no substantial connection to the struggles in the textile mills of the North Carolina Piedmont, despite the fact that thousands of families had left the mountains to work in those factories. During the late 1920s and early 1930s, mountaineers-turned-millhands participated in a great labor uprising that included violent clashes in Marion and Gastonia in 1929 and the General Textile Strike of 1934, which, at the time, ranked as the largest labor protest in American history. These events captured national—even international—attention, but in the absence of significant return migration to the mountains, their memory did not become a part of local culture.[42]

The poor in the WAMY region were disadvantaged in other ways as well. In rural areas, individual settlements were small—in many cases, populated by no more than a dozen families—and separated from one another by some of the tallest peaks and ridges of the Appalachian chain. Residents had to drive for miles along steep, winding roads to reach neighbors who, as the crow flew, lived just over the hill. Outside of town, institutions of civic life were sparse. Courthouse cliques of merchants and large landholders kept tight control of politics, and in the countryside there were few of the clubs and associations one found in town or even in impoverished black communities down east, where fraternal organizations and burial societies were commonplace. Poor mountain folk lived in significant geographic and social isolation. Their identities were rooted in relationships of family and faith; they spoke of themselves as Baptists or Methodists, Campbells or Fraziers—but seldom did they think of themselves as "the poor."[43]

Before it could act on the principle of maximum feasible participation, WAMY would have to cultivate new forms of group consciousness and action among the mountain poor. To accomplish that task, Ernest Eppley had recruited an idealistic young staff of community organizers. The team included John Morgan Freas, a native of nearby Yadkin County and a graduate of the University of North Carolina who had served during the previous summer as one of the first members of the North Carolina Volunteers; Hugh Brinley Wire, a Californian, a graduate of Yale University's Divinity School, and an ordained minister in the United Presbyterian Church in the USA; Bobby

Wagoner, also from Yadkin County; Kenneth Sanchagrin, a midwesterner who had studied theology at the University of Notre Dame and the Glenmary Seminary in Cincinnati, Ohio; and Eugene Burris, a graduate of Wake Forest University and Southeastern Theological Seminary. Religious faith and the moral example of the black civil rights struggle steered each of these men toward the War on Poverty. Hugh Wire, for instance, had traveled to Albany, Georgia, in 1962 to join the sit-in campaign directed by the Student Nonviolent Coordinating Committee and the Southern Christian Leadership Conference. He was one of more than a thousand demonstrators arrested and jailed during eight months of sustained protest. Wire later moved to Atlanta, where the deacons at Martin Luther King Sr.'s Ebenezer Baptist Church offered him employment as a minister of Christian education. But, as he explained to Eppley, he wanted more than anything else an opportunity to live and work among poor whites, to lighten their burden, and to help them "become reconciled to the 'new' Negro."[44]

Bobby Wagoner found his "keen sense of justice" working in the tobacco fields on his family's farm. "On priming day," he recalled, "we hired blacks for extra hands, because back then it was all hand labor, there was no automation to it. It was backbreaking hand labor, and it was not something my mother and daddy wanted to do." Wagoner defended his parents. They "were not racist," but they did abide by "the customs that they had grown up with." "Whenever you worked for a farmer," he explained, "the lady of the household provided lunch, and Mother always put on a spread. But the blacks would never come into the dining room. They would eat on the porch or out in the yard somewhere. I remember that it bothered me so much, I wouldn't do it. I went out and ate with them. You just knew, this is not right." In telling that story, Wagoner underscored moral principles that were never to be compromised: all people, he insisted, deserve "validation as to their own worth" and, by extension, "a sense of empowerment that they [can] do something that [will] affect their own destiny." Those were the convictions that drove Eppley's young lieutenants. As Hugh Wire explained, they were committed to working among the people at the "very bottom" of the social hierarchy, "the ones not yet mobilized, not yet touched by any sense of . . . 'opportunity' being for them."[45]

That commitment found its clearest expression in WAMY's incentive grants program, which the agency launched on an experimental basis in 1966. The program made small awards of $1,000 or less directly to the residents of poor neighborhoods to pursue improvement projects of their own design. The idea grew out of an encounter with families in Wildcat Hollow, a small settlement in northern Yancey County. In the early summer of 1965, William Koch, the Fund's director of community development, met there with WAMY director Ernest Eppley and assistant director Jeff McArthur. Residents told them of a dire need for basic sanitation facilities. Eppley quickly offered to assign students in the Neighborhood Youth Corps to do the work of digging privies and installing septic systems, provided that the people of Wildcat Hollow put up the money for supplies. The locals thanked him for his concern, but suggested that he had things backward. They explained that they could not afford to buy materials and that "it would be better to have a project which would provide money if the local people would contribute labor." As similar meetings were held in other communities, Eppley and his coworkers "observed that this feeling was rather typical. Many [people] talked about projects they would like to carry out if they had some financial assistance." WAMY staff took that lesson to heart. In December 1965, they won approval from the North Carolina Fund to redirect $38,875 to a small grants program that would take the unorthodox step of putting money directly into the hands of poor people. Over the next eighteen months, WAMY made twenty-four such awards to community groups throughout the four-county region.[46]

The chief objective of the incentive grants program was to help the poor develop the social capital necessary to advance their claim to a fair share of America's wealth, resources, and opportunities. No one used the term *social capital* in the 1960s, but WAMY staff and other antipoverty warriors spoke in ways that theorists today would easily recognize. Political scientist Robert Putnam is widely credited with bringing the term into mainstream thinking about economic development and the alleviation of poverty. He has defined *social capital* as the "features of social organization such as networks, norms, and social trust that facilitate coordination and cooperation for mutual benefit." Such resources, Putnam and others have maintained, play a critical role in a community's capacity to sustain a democratic culture and achieve economic prosperity.[47]

WAMY staff understood that deficits of social capital were a primary cause and characteristic of poverty. "Members of the middle and upper classes," one community organizer observed, "have a substantially higher rate of participation in political, social, and of course economic life than do the poor. [A] lack of participation effectively isolates the poor from the democratic decision-making process. Although ideally all have a voice in American political and economic life, actually those who influence decisions are those with some bases of power — money, class and status, or natural or social resources. The poor, having none of these, have no lever to move the decision makers" or to demand of them a "just distribution of rewards."[48]

That insight marked a critical turning point for WAMY. It sprang from the freedom to experiment that the North Carolina Fund and private philanthropy made possible in the WAMY region and elsewhere across the state. Out in the field, poverty workers escaped the constraints of bureaucratic accountability and prepackaged ideas. They had leeway to enter into dynamic relationships with the poor, to learn from their own mistakes and misconceptions, and to adopt tactics that emerged from within local communities. In the process they came to understand that victory in the War on Poverty would depend on their ability to mobilize the poor as "participating citizens," to make them a "viable, constructive, competitive" force.[49]

Community organizer Marguerite Kiely prepared a series of essays and memoranda in 1966 that explained WAMY's incentive grants program as a strategy for achieving that goal. The consequences of poor people's exclusion from civic life were deadening, she argued. Few among the poor expected their lives to improve or for any of their self-styled betters to extend a helping hand. The challenge for poverty warriors was to crack that "hard shell" of frustration and disengagement. Kiely and her coworkers began to do so by traveling extensively through the four-county area. They called on as many people as possible for personal, face-to-face meetings, often making use of contacts already established by the Friendly Home Visitors or by the North Carolina Volunteers who spent the summers of 1964 and 1965 in the WAMY region. The point of this work was to build expanding circles of trust—trust between the organizers and local residents and trust among community members themselves.[50]

Once they had established an adequate foundation, WAMY staff scheduled public gatherings in dozens of individual communities. They encouraged residents to bring their neighbors and family members, aiming for as large a turnout as possible. Folks met in private homes, in the community centers the home visitors had helped establish, and at crossroads country stores. In each instance, the floor was open to a freewheeling discussion of projects that might improve community life. To the extent that WAMY staff sought to steer the conversations, it was only to ensure that each community identified a project that was "important *to it*," rather than mandated from the outside, and that the projects were feasible—small and focused enough to succeed. The process could be "slow and arduous." People might deliberate for months before making a decision, and as a result, there was always a danger that participation would wane. But that risk was more than offset by what many at WAMY saw as "the ultimate goal of . . . community action—education of the poor in the *process* of democracy." The aim was to develop neighborhood "organizations in which all have the courage to speak, all are equal in voice, and *consensus* is the result of discussion."[51]

The structure set up for evaluating incentive grant proposals reflected the same concerns. WAMY established "community development advisory councils" in each of the four counties it served. The neighborhood organizations first set up by the Friendly Home Visitors elected representatives to the councils, and the councils, in turn, chose four people from within their ranks to fill the seats set aside for the poor on WAMY's board of directors and to serve on county-level incentive grant screening committees. WAMY director Ernest Eppley, the federal Farmers Home Administration agents for each of the four counties, and a representative from another public agency also served on the screening committees in an ex officio capacity. Giving the poor majority membership on the committees was a calculated choice. It inverted the way that public policy was ordinarily made; in this instance, the poor, not their "status-superiors," were in control. That arrangement also stimulated interest in the incentive grants program. The screening committees were "prejudiced towards the poor," and knowledge of that fact encouraged more communities to apply for grants.[52]

The county screening committees judged proposals according to three criteria. First, they looked for evidence of broad participation in the planning of each project. WAMY sought to ensure that proposals had emerged from genuinely democratic conversations and that as many participants as possible had learned the value of cooperation. Second, the committees evaluated individual communities' commitment to self-improvement, as evidenced by their participation in programs such as adult education and home management classes, workshops on small farm marketing, and clinics for childhood health and immunization. "The more a community utilizes these resources to meet its needs," WAMY guidelines made clear, "the more favorable its chances for a grant." Third, and most important, communities had to agree to cover 15 to 50 percent of their project costs with matching contributions. Often, this was done with in-kind donations of labor or materials. The payoff from this process, WAMY argued, reached far beyond the projects immediately at hand. As neighbors worked together, they began to recognize their strengths as well as their needs and discovered within themselves a new capacity to make change.[53]

The tiny Yancey County settlement of Colberts Creek offered an example of how effectively communities could be mobilized for self-improvement. At first glance, it seemed an unlikely place for a success story. Fourteen families lived in Colberts Creek. "There were no bathrooms, no privies, and no running water in the community," WAMY staff reported. "Housing was cold and crowded and some homes had no electricity. The primary sources of income were welfare and the picking and selling of a wild leaf called galax." Incomes were in "the lower-lower category," and the illiteracy rate was high. Only limited social activity took place outside the orbit of individual families. There was a church, but it met only twice a month and was poorly attended. Civic participation fared no better. Most residents did not vote. They often complained about laws they did not like but had little knowledge of how to act on their grievances.[54]

WAMY began its organizing efforts in Colberts Creek with two VISTA volunteers, a retired couple named Floyd and Gretchen Basinger who took up residence in a rented house trailer. The Basingers came from Florida, where Floyd had worked as a carpenter. The couple struck first at the deplorable lack of basic sanitation in Colberts Creek. They called in the Neighborhood Youth Corps, which had a crew of ninety high school dropouts attacking the same issue throughout the WAMY region. The young men participated in six to eight hours of remedial education classes and counseling sessions each week. Then, for another thirty-two hours, they and community residents built privies, installed septic tanks, assembled spring houses, and laid water lines. The change wrought by this partnership was startling. Streams that had once been polluted now ran clear, and for the first time in their lives residents enjoyed comforts that most Americans took for granted.[55]

The Basingers also spearheaded a cleanup campaign in Colberts Creek. The scene in the community affirmed every stereotype of the rural poor. Rusting trucks and cars littered front yards, and garbage was scattered behind the houses and along the roadsides. The problem, though, was not that residents were apathetic hillbillies or carriers of a culture of poverty. The community was "trashy" because county government made no provision for garbage collection and operated no rural landfills. That left residents of places like Colberts Creek to create their own solutions. With direction from the Basingers, local families negotiated access to a nearby federal dump, probably one operated by the National Forest Service, which managed vast tracts of land in the WAMY region. They then organized a cleanup day. Men and boys hauled off truckloads of trash, and women cooked for a dinner when the work was done. The effort did not stop there. To keep the neighborhood clean, residents bought used oil drums for individual households to use as garbage cans, and they set up a small business for one of the local men, who collected trash each week and carted it away.[56]

That work resembled, in many respects, the community improvement efforts that people like Howard Fuller and Ann Atwater had organized in Durham and other Fund-supported communities across the state. The strategic objective was to achieve success in small tasks, to produce highly visible results that gave poor people "confidence that change [could] take place," and to instill in participants "courage enough to try something bigger." In Colberts Creek, the sanitation and cleanup projects led to the scheduling of regular biweekly neighborhood meetings. When residents learned of WAMY's incentive grants program, they decided unanimously that their most pressing unmet need was to improve the roads in their part of Yancey County. The paved state highway ran up to the edge of the Colberts Creek community, and from there "four undrained and never maintained dirt trails fanned out." "When it got bad weather," one resident reported, "we couldn't get in and out to get [things] we needed—wood, groceries, feed nor nothing—it was awfully hard. It was just a mud hole—that is all." The busiest of the byways—known locally as "the road to Connie Fender's house"—was traveled by more than fifty vehicles a day and thus qualified for state maintenance. The families of Colberts Creek mounted a successful letter-writing campaign to convince the state highway department to accept that responsibility, but other roads did not pass the department's use test and would have to be improved with local labor. Residents applied for and received $1,000 from WAMY to cover the cost of gravel and a bulldozer operator to complete the work. What followed was a model of the democratic give-and-take that poverty warriors often idealized.[57]

The first challenge came when highway workers began staking off the right-of-way along Connie Fender's road. They ran head-on into Mrs. Earley's "pig pen and out house," which she refused to move. Careful negotiations resolved that standoff, but then a dispute erupted over Max Presnell's road, which required an easement across land belonging to Merrit Strickland. Strickland and the Basingers suggested that incentive grant money not be used for that work, because Presnell had seldom attended community meetings. But other neighbors argued persuasively that "Max had as much right to a road as anybody else." Then, yet another problem presented itself: the incentive grant did not provide enough money to pay for the installation of culverts at the places where the roads crossed small streams and other lines of drainage. Floyd Basinger prevailed on Max Presnell to take an active role in the neighborhood effort, and together with another man, they laid the necessary piping. After nearly a year's effort, the families of Colberts Creek took pride in the work they had done — despite the fact that the state had yet to finish the road to Connie Fender's house. "It was a mighty good job done there," a resident bragged. "It helped out everybody real good."[58]

A water project in the Avery County community of Blevins Creek became a national showcase for the same kind of neighborhood initiative and co-operation. The settlement was home to thirty-two families scattered along a narrow road. Living conditions were deplorable. On average, adult residents had no more than a sixth-grade education, earned only $600 to $1,000 a year, and lived in houses with no indoor plumbing. The water in the creek from which the community drew its name was too polluted to drink, so residents had to rely on small springs located on higher ground up to a half hour's walk away. "It has been hard on us all . . . getting water," a woman told visitors. Every few days, she and her mother "carr[ied] as much as six wash tubs for laundry, besides the water for dishes and drinking. . . . [We] just go and get it when we [need] it, snow and all. I have gone when it was so slick that you could hardly stand up."[59]

The area was first reached by the North Carolina Volunteers during the summer of 1965. The students ran a youth recreational program at a local church and noted immediately the desperate conditions in which many of the children lived. They alerted WAMY staff to the need for a clean and reliable water supply in Blevins Creek. WAMY assistant director Jeff McArthur followed up by convening a series of community meetings to discuss the problem and to prepare residents to seek advice from Avery County's sanitarian and the local agent of the federal Farmers Home Administration. The various parties worked together, and by summer's end the people of Blevins Creek had a verbal commitment for a government loan of $12,000 to cover the cost of drilling a community well, installing a pump, and laying a network of water mains. But before money could be awarded, residents had to hire a lawyer, incorporate a local water authority that would hold title to the well site, and recruit from their own ranks a board of directors to manage the new entity. That they did with assistance from WAMY staff. The heads of household, all of whom became members of the new utility, also agreed to a monthly fee of $4 per family, which would pay off the federal loan over a forty-year term. Once those arrangements were in place, the Farmers Home Administration made the promised money available and construction began. There was, however, one final task to be completed: the connection of individual households to the new water mains. The Blevins Creek community applied for and received a WAMY incentive grant to purchase the necessary materials and, as in Col-

Student workers from the Neighborhood Youth Corps lay a water line in Blevins Creek.
Photograph by Billy E. Barnes, courtesy of the North Carolina Collection, Wilson Library,
University of North Carolina at Chapel Hill, Billy Ebert Barnes Collection.

berts Creek, called on the Neighborhood Youth Corps to join local men and
boys in digging trenches and laying water pipe.[60]

In May 1967 Sargent Shriver, director of the Office of Economic Opportunity, and evangelist Billy Graham, a native of the North Carolina mountains,
visited Blevins Creek for the dedication of the water system. They traveled
to the area by helicopter, took a short car ride to the community, and then
walked a quarter mile to the well site. As he joined Graham in switching on
the pumps, Shriver underscored the larger political significance of the work
at Blevins Creek. "This is your day," he said to residents. "You have created
this water system with your own hands. We congratulate you." Shriver and
WAMY field staff saw the Blevins Creek project as validation of the guiding
principles of the War on Poverty. It stood as an exemplar of what could be accomplished through a coordinated approach to the problems of the poor: one
that worked through agencies like WAMY to build cross-community interest
in antipoverty efforts among business leaders, religious groups, and private
charities; one that facilitated collaboration among local, state, and federal

Billy Graham, Bible in hand, and Sargent Shriver drink the first cups of water from the Blevins Creek project. Still image from *Beyond These Hills*, courtesy of the National Archives and Records Administration, Records of the Community Services Administration.

social service agencies; and, most important, one that promoted the maximum feasible participation of poor people themselves. Projects like the one at Blevins Creek, argued WAMY field-worker Marguerite Kiely, represented "the first revolution in a spiral of participation aimed at destroying the 'cycle of poverty.' . . . The more [that poor] communities participate in the larger society, the greater will be the proportion of society's resources brought to bear on [their] problems."[61]

In a news conference at the end of the Blevins Creek celebration, Sargent Shriver suggested how disruptive of the status quo such ideas could be. When asked by a reporter to respond to congressional critics who proposed that the Office of Economic Opportunity be disbanded and its duties reassigned to other agencies, Shriver rejected the idea. He insisted that poor citizens had a right to be treated as a political constituency on par with other major players in American economic life. "After all," Shriver observed, "businessmen have a voice through the Commerce Department, labor has a voice through the Labor Department, and bankers have a voice through the Treasury Department, so why shouldn't the poor have a voice in government through a department staffed and equipped to handle their needs?" That, of course, was the fundamental point of contention around which the War on Poverty was being fought.[62]

IN THE LATE SUMMER OF 1966, as the first of WAMY's incentive grants projects began to show results, the North Carolina Fund undertook a review of all eleven of the community action programs it supported. The Fund sent a team of eight evaluators to the WAMY region. They included members of the Fund staff and board of directors, representatives from other community action programs around the state, and antipoverty policy experts from elsewhere in the nation. The visitors spent five days in the WAMY counties, conducting extensive interviews with the program's staff and board, directors of social service agencies, newspaper editors and politicians, and some of the new leaders who had emerged from among the ranks of the poor. When the team filed their report in early December, they spoke with piercing clarity. They were highly critical of WAMY's practice of funneling most of its antipoverty money directly to county social welfare agencies. The reviewers acknowledged the political expediency of that arrangement, which mollified county commissioners—mostly Republicans—who felt that the War on Poverty was "an LBJ program crammed down their throats." Even so, the team noted a number of serious problems. To begin with, WAMY had no supervisory authority over the agency personnel whose salaries it paid and on whom it relied to do the work of battling poverty. Those employees continued to report to administrators who were strongly committed to business as usual in dealing with the poor, and that, in turn, put WAMY in the position of "delegating the 'guts'" of its program to the very people whose attitudes it sought to reform. Worse yet, relying on others to do the work of battling poverty exposed WAMY to the cronyism that infected much of county government. The reviewers spoke cautiously of this problem and offered few details, but they left no doubt that agency personnel employed with WAMY funds too often got their jobs on the basis of political connections rather than credentials or commitment to the poor. They blamed political patronage for the "lack of vitality" in many public agencies and worried that its effects had "spilled over into the WAMY program."[63]

As a counter to those concerns, the review team embraced the incentive grants program and encouraged WAMY to make it the centerpiece of the agency's fight against poverty. In part, that advice reflected the Fund's own reorientation. As it pushed WAMY in new directions, it was also deeply involved in the formation of the People's Program on Poverty (PPOP) in the Choanoke region and United Organizations for Community Improvement in Durham. Two and a half years of experience with efforts to work from "local agencies down to the people" had exposed the limitations of that approach, and the Fund was attempting to chart an alternative way forward, one that would "go down to the people and work up through the people to the agencies."[64]

Fund director George Esser hammered this point when he conveyed the review team's final report to the WAMY board. The incentive grants program sought "to stimulate and cultivate individual initiative and a high sense of self-confidence and self-worth" in poor communities. It aimed to "help rural citizens discover how to make the democratic process work, so that they [might acquire] a real voice in their own government and [realize their capacity to] influence the outside world." Esser championed those objectives and urged WAMY to build upon them with a vigorous program of citizen education. He offered three broad recommendations:

> Involve the poor more extensively in the initiation and development of programs, so that the priorities . . . which they set can be reflected in the priorities of WAMY.
>
> [Develop] a voter education program [to] provide the poor with information and skills which will enable them to have access to, and participate fully in, the institutions of their communities.
>
> Continue to support indigenous leaders . . . in order that groups of the poor will be able to come to grips independently with significant issues which affect their lives.

Esser and the review team also reminded the WAMY board of the need to re-educate themselves and the larger public. To wage an effective campaign for opportunity, they would have to surrender the idea that the "poor are the way they are, because they like it that way, or just don't know any better."[65]

Such frank talk alarmed some members of WAMY's board. Burnsville mayor Robert Helmle, who had been a key proponent of the community action program at the time of its founding, was particularly outspoken. When the board met in late January 1967 to discuss the review, he complained about the Fund's change of direction. It was clear that the Fund now wanted WAMY "to educate poor people about govt institutions [and] to get poor people to bring pressure to bear on institutions & change them." This was a radical move, Helmle complained, and had not been a part of WAMY's original proposal. The mayor invoked the memory of John F. Kennedy to illustrate just how far off course the Fund was straying. The martyred president had urged Americans, "Ask not what your country can do for you. Ask what you can do for your country." Now, in what Helmle viewed as a perverse inversion of Kennedy's patriotic appeal, the "poverty program [was] trying to get the poor *to ask their government to do things for them.*" Robert Walker, a field agent for the Fund who was sitting in on the WAMY meeting, answered the mayor angrily. He pointed out the hypocrisy of people such as Helmle who used the government to their advantage every day, through mortgage deductions on their income taxes, small business loans, and cheap tuition for their children at public universities. "You know quite well what [I'm] talking about," Walker exclaimed. "The rich have been using the system for quite a while." There is no record of how Helmle answered Walker's rebuke. In fact, the exchange was not a part of the official board minutes. We know about it only from notes made by another participant in the meeting, most likely WAMY director Ernest Eppley.[66]

Eppley managed, at least for the moment, to contain the dissent within his board. Colleagues described him as a strong leader who worked diplomatically to direct an attack on the structural causes of poverty. In an interview conducted in June 1968—nine months after he resigned his post as WAMY director—Eppley explained his approach to the job. "We didn't begin with a radical kind of program," he acknowledged. "We were in the process originally of trying to work with [the social welfare] agencies and sub-contracting our projects to them, and trying . . . to convince them that their agencies and our projects needed to be focused on those who needed the services most." But "as time went by"—and as the limitations of subcontracting became apparent—Eppley shifted his tactics. "My [new objective] was . . . to push for change," he remembered. "To state clearly and concisely at every opportunity what community action was all about, what was meant by involvement of the poor, what was meant by participation of the poor. . . . These kinds of things had to be stated . . . without any equivocation . . . over, and over, and over again." The key to success in such maneuvering "was to push for as much progress, as much change as possible without being so offensive that the whole thing would go down the drain." Eppley's plan of attack was to press for change, to "consolidate" whatever ground he could capture, and then "to push forward again."[67]

The tactic worked—at least through the spring of 1967—because Eppley had a number of stalwart allies on the WAMY board. William Plemmons, board chair and president of Appalachian State Teachers College, used his personal stature to provide political cover and affirm Eppley's authority. Eppley also counted on Lawson Tate, a respected local surgeon who commented often on how direct experience with the poor had changed his thinking, and Dorothy Thomas, a regional librarian from Spruce Pine who "could generate new ideas, could think of new ways to do things, could see the principles involved and the reasons behind so many things [that WAMY staff] proposed."[68]

Plemmons, Thomas, and Tate played important roles in helping Eppley shift the balance of power on the WAMY board. In September 1966, as the Fund review was under way, they pushed through a resolution that made two significant changes to board membership. First, the resolution reduced the number of directors from ninety-six to sixty, twenty of whom were to be representatives of the poor. Eppley argued for the change on the grounds that it would make the board more manageable and effective — ninety-six was, on the face of it, an unwieldy number — but there was no hiding the fact that the reform also increased the proportion of seats reserved for the poor from a quarter to a third of the total board membership. Second, the resolution mandated that all representatives of the poor be elected directly by residents of the "lowest-income communities in each county." Prior to this point, a third of that group had been appointed by the executive committee of the board, which in effect gave the WAMY board power to police its membership.[69]

Newly elected representatives of the poor did not take their seats until January 1967, but Eppley and his staff wasted no time in taking advantage of the tilt in the balance of power. Soon after elections were completed in the fall, they began orienting these new members of the board, who had little or no experience with such an assignment. They needed training in the use of parliamentary procedure to advance their interests; they needed coaching in the art of debate, so that they could speak out effectively about the concerns of their constituents; and they needed encouragement in standing up for their interests. With support from Eppley and sympathetic board members such as Lawson Tate and Dorothy Thomas, the newcomers found their voice — and, in doing so, helped make the WAMY board a more inclusive institution. Their arrival marked a moment of possibility, a time when it appeared conceivable that the poor had "the knowledge and insights and imagination to contribute to the war on poverty — a war in which they [were] presumably the ones to be liberated."[70]

A controversy over a community organizing meeting in the Yancey County town of Micaville offered a case in point. Board member and county school superintendent Hubert Justice was incensed by what he witnessed there. He complained that the meeting, held at a local school, "had been publicized as a talent show but had actually been an effort" to "get a bunch of rabble rousing poor people involved in a revolution." Robert Helmle rushed to Justice's side, and other board members suggested "that some of the people attending the meeting at the Micaville School were unworthy of the attention of community action staff." Eppley answered the charges not by arguing with Justice, but by turning to one of the new board members, Beatrice Young. Young was a black woman from Burnsville, a widow who taught Sunday school in her church and made a living as a domestic laborer. Eppley informed the board that Young had been at the meeting and had a different point of view. Young welcomed the invitation to speak up, and in doing so challenged all that her fellow board members had been so quick to assume. She reported that it had been "a very good meeting . . . and that many of the poor people were given an opportunity to express their problems and needs openly." "We had a good time," she said. "We'd like to do more of it. It's a good thing." For the moment, Justice and Helmle sat silent.[71]

Eppley and his staff also benefited from the fact that doubters on the WAMY board did not have recourse to the language of race in quite the same way as their counterparts in Durham or the Choanoke region. In his critique of efforts to mobilize the poor as a political force, Burnsville's Robert Helmle suggested that the War on Poverty had fallen under the spell of "Civil Rights and integration." Such charges could—and did—do great damage to anti-poverty work in the eastern part of the state, but in the mountains they gained limited traction. After all, blacks made up only 1 percent of the population in the WAMY counties. "Civil rights groups—there are none," a Fund staffer reported, and "in spite of small pockets of Negroes in Boone, Burnsville, etc. [there has been] little action here."[72]

But there were also ideological forces at play. Moderate and conservative whites in the industrial towns of the Piedmont and the farmlands of the east could turn easily to a racialized language of inferiority and separation that resonated with a broad audience of fellow whites. That language could be used to deny black access to civic participation—forever, as segregationists would have had it, or until the time was right, as gradualists so often argued. It also could be used to mobilize poor whites in opposition to class-based biracial alliances, as had been the case many times in North Carolina's past. But things were different in the high country, where the population was over-whelmingly white. Political leaders and middle-class townspeople could talk about the mountain poor as "sorry folk," they could "hold their noses while dishing out [meals] at Christmas," they could lament the "apathy" of the poor—but what they could not do was stand up at a church picnic or a down-town political rally and suggest that, in principle, their less fortunate neigh-bors deserved anything other than a full claim to the rights of democratic citizenship. That, after all, was what Jim Crow had promised poor whites in exchange for their complicity in segregation.[73]

Using this maneuvering room, Eppley and his staff moved aggressively on the recommendations of the Fund's review committee. The staff quickly began work on a plan to cancel key subcontracting relationships with social welfare agencies. They were particularly keen to remove the Friendly Home Visitors from the supervision of county health departments. Over time, that relationship had become increasingly problematic. As the visitors took the lead in identifying health needs and providing health education, they treaded on carefully guarded turf. Doctors and nurses in the health departments generally believed that "there [was] a place for professionals and a place for the untrained, and that everyone should stay in this place." The visitors complained that such attitudes demeaned their contributions, and that if the health directors prevailed, they would be reduced to doing little more than providing taxi service to and from county clinics. Canceling the subcontracts for the visitors was a way of resolving that tension and assuming direct responsibility for WAMY's most effective organizers—the women Eppley described as the agency's "fingertips" in local communities.[74]

In January, Eppley and his staff launched a "citizen education" campaign that focused WAMY's resources with new intensity on the "objective of motivating and equipping the poor to conduct their own war on poverty." Eppley's first step was to bring in a consultant named Ed Adkins to provide training for his staff and leaders of WAMY's community development advisory councils. Adkins was a native of Breathitt County, Kentucky, located in the heart of the state's eastern coalfields. He studied briefly at Bible Standard College (now Eugene Bible College) in Eugene, Oregon, and subsequently earned a degree in theology from the city's Northwest Christian College (now Northwest Christian University). By the time he arrived in North Carolina, Adkins had accumulated broad experience in community organizing. He had worked from coast to coast for the Teamsters union; he had directed a youth program in Jackson, Ohio; and, most recently, he had served on the staff of the Cumberland Valley Area Economic Opportunity Council, an OEO-funded community action project in Kentucky's eastern coalfield region. The last of those jobs immersed Adkins in some of the most dynamic antipoverty organizing in the nation. The Cumberland Valley includes Harlan County, the site of bitter battles between miners and coal companies throughout much of the twentieth century. During the mid- to late 1960s, the Appalachian Volunteers, a project that grew out of nearby Berea College, focused much of its efforts on combating the valley's endemic poverty and corrupt politics. In particular, it targeted the destructive effects of strip-mining and the collusion between coal companies and local government officials.[75]

Activists in the Cumberland Valley knew of the North Carolina Fund and recognized in its programs a shared conviction that "the poverty-stricken would work toward their own betterment." In eastern Kentucky, reported the *Louisville Courier-Journal and Times*, "the poor want[ed] more voice in decisions having to do with their promised escape from want and misery.

Mostly, they want[ed] to take the spending of anti-poverty money—'our money'—away from 'political bosses and big-shot businessmen.'" Such common concerns suggested the possibility of building a coalition of anti-poverty forces. Toward the end of 1966, in fact, members of the WAMY staff and Robert Walker, one of the Fund's field agents for community development, attended meetings to discuss the idea of convening a regionwide "Appalachian People's Congress" or a series of linked, state-based gatherings of the poor. The meetings were sponsored by the Appalachian Volunteers; the Council of the Southern Mountains, a reform organization based at Berea that dated back to the early years of the twentieth century; and the Congress for Appalachian Development, a short-lived alliance of regional advocates for public ownership of mountain communities' mineral and water resources. These individuals and organizations shared a desire to promote coordination in the development and implementation of antipoverty programs, "to build up a regional consciousness," and "to assist poor people [in] attain[ing] the power to participate in civic life."[76]

Adkins had particularly strong ties to a grassroots movement of self-described "common people" and their advocates, who in late 1966 chartered an organization called United Appalachian Communities (UAC). UAC began as an insurgent movement within the Cumberland Valley Area Economic Opportunity Council. In that way, it resembled the People's Program on Poverty in North Carolina's Choanoke region and United Organizations for Community Improvement in Durham. UAC was particularly concerned to ensure continued funding for the Work Experience and Training Program, established by the Economic Opportunity Act in 1964. Known locally as the "Happy Pappy" program, it made the federal government the "employer of last resort" in a region where rates of male joblessness ranged as high as 50 percent. The program provided work on public projects and income support for unemployed coal miners—young men who had been displaced by the rapid mechanization of mining, and older men whose bodies had been ruined by years of laboring underground.[77]

United Appalachian Communities also demanded that the poor have a greater role in the administration of Work Experience and Training funds. Members complained that for decades local government officials had used public welfare dollars as a weapon for silencing dissent over issues of workers' rights, environmental destruction, and the absentee ownership of the coal region's mineral resources. "Everybody knows," one local activist explained, that recipients of public aid were "afraid to speak up, for fear they would be cut off." In a series of meetings during the late winter of 1967, UAC members confronted the directors of the Cumberland Valley Area Economic Opportunity Council on these and related issues. They demanded that the agency abide by OEO guidelines that required that a third of the seats on its board be reserved for representatives of the poor, and that those representatives be elected directly from poor communities rather than appointed by the existing board. Such demands provoked the council's ire. When scores of UAC members showed up at a regularly scheduled meeting to make their grievances known, the organization's chairman shouted them down, exclaiming, "Communist-paid hecklers are with us tonight."[78]

Such were the sensibilities that Ed Adkins brought to WAMY. He made the move in January 1967, not entirely by choice. Robert Walker informed North Carolina Fund finance director Nathan Garrett that the authorities in Clay County, Kentucky, had threatened Adkins with a grand jury indictment "aimed at running [him] out." "Since he is no longer there," Walker reported, "they have what they want and will not press it." Ernest Eppley employed Adkins on an open-ended contract financed by a direct grant from the Fund. Adkins's approach was to teach by example. He set out to spend a week or more in each of the WAMY counties. He held conferences with WAMY staff, particularly the Friendly Home Visitors, and then had them accompany him as he called on people they had found difficult to recruit for community clubs and improvement projects. In this "'apprenticeship' fashion," Adkins demonstrated how to communicate more effectively and how to draw the poor out as leaders more quickly than the WAMY workers "had ever thought possible." His charismatic personality made those lessons all the more persuasive.[79]

Adkins ended each week of travel with a "Poor People's Mass Meeting" and "a talent show or gospel sing" held at county courthouses or in school auditoriums. The gatherings drew 250 to 300 people, making them by far some of the largest public events in the WAMY region. Only high school sporting matches and tent revivals attracted comparable crowds. These poor people's meetings were brilliant in their conception. They tapped into core traditions of rural Appalachian culture — music and religious faith. Adkins invited the poor — so often characterized as apathetic and inert — to take the stage and to share their talents and abilities. After an hour or so of performance, he then gave the altar call. At one gathering, according to the *Watauga Democrat*, "[Adkins] said the 'poor people themselves are not speaking out — are not championing their own cause. You're the only ones who can help yourselves,' he told his audience.... 'If you can get up here and perform, you can certainly go before [county commissioners,] Congressmen, Legislators and agencies.'" At that point, Adkins invited the assembled to come forward and give witness

Be heard! Talent on stage!

A chance for the poor to speak!

COMMUNITY MEETING

💲 And 🎁🎁

Talent Show

Plan for the future

7:00 p.m. Tuesday February 21st.

Watauga County Court House

VALUABLE PRIZES!

All low-income people are invited to attend community meeting and be in talent show!

A hand-lettered broadside announces one of the talent shows and "Poor People's Mass Meetings" organized by WAMY worker Ed Adkins. Courtesy of the Southern Historical Collection, Wilson Library, University of North Carolina at Chapel Hill, North Carolina Fund Records.

to their troubles. And witness they did. A young mother spoke up, saying that she and her family lived on less than $15 a week. She had been unable to get on the welfare roll and was surviving only with the help of friends. Another woman told about a community of twenty-two households, only three of which had bathtubs and many of which lacked even outdoor privies. And finally, "a mother of nine told the crowd of her children going to school without lunch, the family living on $7 a week for groceries."[80]

The mass meetings were electrifying, for WAMY staff no less than for the community folk who had gathered. "The staff saw that poor people were ready to identify themselves as poor, ready to speak up about their problems, and [ready] to do something about them," wrote Hugh Wire, WAMY's coordinator for Watauga County. "The knowledge that WAMY is here to help the poor and that we can work together for the good of all is *spreading*." As she left the stage, the mother of nine who had lamented her children's hunger at lunchtime affirmed that appraisal. "We've got this started," she rejoiced. "We're going to fight, we're going to win."[81]

As a follow-up to the community "speak out[s]," Adkins encouraged the poor to form citizens committees to work on issues of shared concern. High on the list was a demand for transparency in the administration of welfare benefits. Poor people across the WAMY region complained that they had no access to the rules and regulations that governed welfare services and that agency staff often seemed capricious in the way that they doled out relief. A Mitchell County resident, for example, told of a time when her family moved to Yancey County and their "welfare check was reduced from $128 a month to $72." After "their only additional resource—a bean patch—was devoured by insects," they had no choice but to return to Mitchell County, where the welfare office was more generous. As people told—and heard—multiple variations of stories such as this one, personal experiences of indignity co-alesced into collective grievances. That new consciousness motivated a group of welfare recipients, all volunteers, who in February 1967 asked for Adkins's assistance in organizing a trip to Raleigh to visit with the state commissioner of public welfare, Clifton M. Craig. Their purpose, a WAMY staffer reported, was to talk with Craig about the arbitrary enforcement of welfare policies and to encourage the state's participation in an experimental OEO program that provided funds to employ the poor as welfare caseworkers—enabling them in a substantive way to lend support and encouragement to one another.[82]

The WAMY delegation delivered a forceful message to Commissioner Craig: they desired an active role in combating poverty. They complained that local officials' refusal to share information about welfare policies denied them full understanding of their rights and entitlements as citizens. That ignorance deprived poor people of the tools required to access social services; it per-petuated the notion that they were blighted by a culture of poverty and were incapable of changing their circumstances. Commissioner Craig seemed not to comprehend this claim to citizenship and self-determination. Through-out the meeting, he directed his remarks to Adkins as "spokesman for [the WAMY] group," even though Adkins "kept bringing [the commissioner] back to the people" and insisting that they, not he, had come to speak and be heard. At every turn in the exchange, a WAMY staffer reported, Craig repeated his constant refrain: "The poor we always have with us." The commissioner would not—perhaps could not—embrace the idea that welfare, once imag-ined as something more than poor relief, might be used as an instrument of constructive social change.[83]

The confrontation in Raleigh touched off a tempest of the sort that was becoming all too familiar to Fund officials in Durham. George Esser, who had been unaware of WAMY's employment of Adkins, requested an immediate briefing on the affair. Field agent Robert Walker offered assurance that WAMY director Ernest Eppley was "highly enthusiastic about Adkins' work and support[ed] him totally." Adkins had "great talent, [was] a natural organizer, and [was] great with the poor," Walker advised. "So long as [Eppley] is happy with the results, I hardly see how the Fund is in a position to be unhappy." One of Eppley's staff added — with some emphasis — that the mountain poor who had called on Commissioner Craig believed that they had done nothing more than exercise their rights. "Any public official," they reasoned, "should be ready to appear before a group of citizens to discuss his particular office and work." But as private complaints to Esser and dissent within the WAMY board made clear, that was not an opinion shared by many state and local power brokers. In an earlier board meeting, Robert Helmle and Hubert Justice had openly denounced Adkins's campaign "to arouse the poor people to demand their rights."[84]

When he first employed Adkins, Ernest Eppley had vowed to stand down "any conflict that [might] result from an honest effort to organize the people to solve their problems." By late February, however, the pressure to be rid of Adkins had grown too intense to resist. As a matter of political expediency, Eppley terminated his contract on March 2. Adkins's confrontational style conflicted with Eppley's strategy of making change in step-by-step fashion, pausing after each advance to consolidate gains and to build new alliances before taking on the next challenge. Even so, Eppley confided to his staff that he had learned important lessons from Adkins's "radical approach to the involvement of the poor." He could no longer entertain the idea that "the poor do not consider themselves poor," that they "could not talk about their situation with others," and that they lacked the capacity and initiative to help themselves. Adkins had "exploded [those] myths" forever.[85]

Adkins's departure did nothing to dampen his coworkers' enthusiasm for mobilizing the poor as a political force. During the spring and summer of 1967, WAMY staff produced and distributed two pamphlets that make clear how purposely the agency had left behind a simple social-service approach to battling poverty. The first pamphlet, *What WAMY Can Do*, illustrates in comic-book fashion the power of collective action. It details the history of WAMY's accomplishments — among others, better roads in Colberts Creek, the distribution of family planning advice door-to-door by Friendly Home Visitors, the water system in Blevins Creek, Head Start programs that prepared poor children for school, and the Neighborhood Youth Corps projects that helped older students stay there. The lesson was clear and direct: "One man can't do much by himself," but "a community working together can do anything it wants to do." The pamphlet's opening page conveys that message in pictures as well as words. A man, his arms flung wide in frustration, exclaims, "I've tried but I can't get nowhere." In the next panel, a group of men

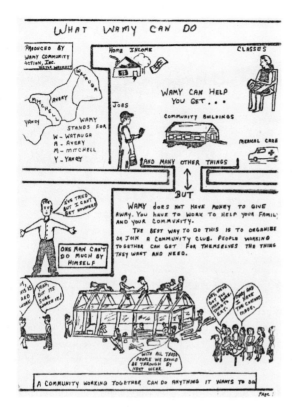

A hand-drawn picture book explains WAMY's role in building community partnerships in the battle against poverty. Courtesy of the Southern Historical Collection, Wilson Library, University of North Carolina at Chapel Hill, North Carolina Fund Records.

swarm around the frame of a community center under construction. "Boy, this is hard work," one complains. But, answers another, "with all these people we should be through by next week." Off to the side, a group of women announce, "We've got you men something to eat," and "Mary and I have the curtains made."[86]

The other pamphlet, titled *County Government: The Commissioners and Their Job*, offers a basic lesson on the operation of local government and explains how poor people who band together can bring pressure to bear on critical public policy decisions. "The commissioners control" the public purse, the pamphlet observes, and "decide how county money is going to be spent." They had the power to create new programs and reform old ones. They could "build new libraries, hospitals and schools"; budget matching funds to "help to get Food Stamps in the county"; employ "men to collect trash," so that people would have an alternative to dumping "their garbage into the creeks"; and hire "building inspectors . . . to insure that everyone [had] a safe place to live." Of course, the fact that county commissioners had the authority to

Students dressed in their Sunday best to celebrate Head Start's arrival in the WAMY region. Photograph by Billy E. Barnes, courtesy of the North Carolina Collection, Wilson Library, University of North Carolina at Chapel Hill, Billy Ebert Barnes Collection.

undertake such projects offered no assurance that they would do so. Setting a progressive agenda that met the needs of the poor required advocacy on the part of those who stood to benefit. "It's up to you," the pamphlet urges its readers. To make change, poor people would have to lobby local officials for more money and better services, and if those officials failed to respond, the poor had a right and a responsibility to elect people who would. Citizen participation and electoral accountability were the foundation stones of democracy. "It's your job to ask questions," the pamphlet instructs the poor, and county commissioners' job to get things done.[87]

By early 1967, WAMY's efforts at mobilizing the poor had grown from the Friendly Home Visitors' door-to-door canvassing to the countywide mass meetings organized by Ed Adkins. Thousands of people participated in one or more of WAMY's programs. But such activism still did not constitute a full-scale social movement that could galvanize the poor as a political force and create for them an equal voice in public affairs. For the most part, WAMY's successes were contained within the boundaries of individual communities and projects. The task now was to unite those strongholds around a greater awareness of common "predicaments, problems, hopes, and aspirations."

The WAMY staff found inspiration in the precedents of the twentieth-century labor movement and the ongoing civil rights struggle. Both had built bonds of solidarity that united people across differences of geography, race, ethnicity, gender, and class—and through those bonds, people "were able to demonstrate to the nation their plight and their strength, to appeal to the moral commitments of large sectors of the population, and to make some far-reaching changes . . . in the distribution of rewards."[88]

Building that kind of collective force was a challenge in Appalachia, where history and geography isolated the poor from one another and where stereotypes of backwardness distanced them from their town-dwelling neighbors and other Americans. In the face of such circumstances, WAMY staff worried about the limitations of traditional methods of organizing. The "only means we have of communicating with [the poor] is either through the use of postal services, posters placed in strategic locations throughout the area, [or] personal visits," WAMY staff complained. That required constant driving along narrow, winding roads and consumed "a great deal of *time.*" Getting poor people's story out to the general public was even more daunting. The poor had no direct access to local newspapers, most of which were weeklies with neither the staff nor the inclination to open their pages to people whose voices mattered little in town affairs of politics and business. Avery County had no radio stations, and viewers throughout the WAMY region received their television news from broadcasters in Asheville, Charlotte, and Winston-Salem, who of necessity pitched their coverage to the interests of urban audiences and paid scant attention to the circumstances of rural mountain life. Ineffective communication was WAMY's greatest weakness. What the agency desperately needed, a staffer wrote, was a "new technique," a "creative thrust."[89]

The answer had been sitting on Billy Barnes's desk since 1965. In his role as director of public information for the North Carolina Fund, Barnes was charged with communicating the story of antipoverty efforts to audiences across the state. He supervised the production of documentary films and radio spots, wrote hundreds of press releases, organized speaking tours for the Fund's senior staff, and traveled widely with his camera to record Fund projects in action. A leading newspaper described Barnes as "an idealistic young man . . . blessed with a particularly inventive turn of mind." He "bubbl[ed] with ideas for helping the poor communicate with the non-poor and with each other." Barnes's most creative scheme involved giving poor communities direct access to print and broadcast news reporting. He proposed setting up neighborhood newspapers and low-power radio stations operated by local residents. The idea was to turn conventional reporting on its head. The poor, so often written about by others, would be the interpreters of their own lives.[90]

A key feature of the newspapers, Barnes explained, would be letter-to-the-editor sections that highlighted readers' "suggestions, gripes and opinions." The radio stations would operate in much the same way: "We could have man-in-the-street opinion programs, with the poor telling what they think their problems are. We could let the poor call in questions about how [to] register to vote, how [to] qualify for welfare, how [to] go about getting a road paved." In all of these ways, Barnes's proposal aimed to pull the poor "out of their anonymity," to nurture "feelings of self-significance and importance," and to create the sense of shared "identity necessary to concerted effort for improvement." Barnes also hoped to increase middle-class understanding of poor people's problems. That would be achieved, he predicted, "through the middle-class's exposure to the radio broadcasts and occasional reading of the weekly newspaper[s]."[91]

The media project won enthusiastic support from the Fund's board of directors but immediately ran into "a flurry of negative reaction" at the local level. Barnes planned to pilot his ideas in the Choanoke region during the summer of 1966. His timing could not have been worse. The Fund was caught up in the power struggle between the Choanoke Area Development Association (CADA) and the newly formed People's Program on Poverty. In the minds of many "members of the non-poor, white community," the black PPOP insurgency and the media project "were connected": both seemed subversive and unwelcome. Barnes's proposal also faced challenges in the African American community. Leaders from the CADA counties and the various civil rights groups in the region were "eager to see the [newspaper and radio] program adopted," but they quarreled over control. In light of that difficulty, and the "increasing conflicts relating to all of the anti-poverty programs" across the state, Fund director George Esser decided in November to abandon Barnes's scheme entirely.[92]

That might have been the end of the media project had the OEO not shown an interest in its resurrection in early 1967. Congress had recently earmarked money for "anti-poverty programs dealing with the problems of communication within rural areas." A former researcher for the Fund had taken a copy of Barnes's proposal with him when he joined the OEO's Washington staff, and he circulated it widely among his new colleagues. The OEO administrators liked what they read. Eager to identify a demonstration project for the new resources set aside by Congress, they jumped at the opportunity to partner once more with the Fund. After a brief round of negotiations, Barnes and OEO staff agreed that the WAMY area "would be a good location for the project." Given "the fact that funding seemed assured," Ernest Eppley and WAMY board chair William Plemmons were keen to submit a proposal.[93]

WAMY requested $179,000 from the OEO to run the media demonstration project for one year, May 1, 1967, to April 30, 1968. The plan called for employing three professional staff—a newspaper editor and two radio producers—plus more than two dozen low-income people who would work as clerks, technical assistants, and reporters. The poor people's newspaper was to be published as a weekly and distributed through the mail to more than eight thousand recipients. It would report matters of local interest—"births, deaths, marriages, [and] hospital notes"—from small communities otherwise neglected in the region's mainline press. The paper would also carry "'how-to' columns on home management," discussions of legal issues affecting the poor, and a "citizen's advice column" through which readers could "directly request services from agencies" and acquire "information on voter registration and the organization of all local political parties."[94]

The radio portion of the project was more experimental. The plan was to conduct much of the work in the field rather than the studio, an approach that, at the time, was rare in broadcasting. WAMY would use two mobile recording vans that would travel to different community centers each day. Reporters drawn from the target neighborhoods then would conduct interviews with beneficiaries of WAMY programs and collect questions for a "citizens' advice bureau," which would subsequently call on government leaders and agency heads to answer poor people's queries. The recorded sessions were to be broadcast daily in five- to fifteen-minute spots purchased on two commercial AM stations.[95]

WAMY's proposal emphasized that this entire enterprise "would be run by and for the poor people of the mountains." The media project was to "have its policies determined not by WAMY but by its own board of directors—one member from the local press, one representative from local radio, one from the WAMY staff, one from the WAMY board, one from Appalachian State Teachers College, and eight poor people selected by the poor themselves."[96]

At the outset, all involved in the media project acknowledged that it entailed political risks, but they concluded "that careful explanation of the program to community leaders . . . would forestall the development of any strong opposition." They were wrong. The first signs of trouble came at the April 1967 meeting of WAMY's board. When the media project came up for discussion, Burnsville mayor Robert Helmle and four other board members raised forceful objections. Helmle warned that the proposed newspaper would become "a class paper" and nothing more than "an organ by which the poor people could just ask for more." The Reverend Woodward Finley from Yancey County pressed the point, asking if the media project "would provide a place for the low-income people to go against the middle-class people." When the vote was called, five board members stood to register their opposition, another fourteen rose up in support, and the remaining eleven in attendance remained seated and abstained.[97]

Disagreement within the WAMY board soon erupted into a political firestorm. The trouble began on May 3, when the Associated Press (AP) picked up a story about the media project in the *Herald Courier*, published in nearby Bristol, Virginia. The AP "put the copy on the wire and within seconds the Teleprinters at all of North Carolina's big dailies were tapping out a story that started off calling WAMY Community Action, Inc. a 'regional branch of the Office of Economic Opportunity.'" The North Carolina Press Association and an overwhelming majority of editors across the state complained of potential competition from a publicly funded paper that would carry no paid advertising and might, in that way, threaten the financial interests of commercial news outlets. Editors also denounced OEO backing of the media project as an inappropriate intrusion of federal authority in local affairs. This, of course, was an ancient battle cry in the South—it had been sounded in the nation's nineteenth-century debate over slavery and had reverberated through Reconstruction and the white supremacy campaign for black disfranchisement. It rang on with every significant advance in social welfare during the twentieth century—child labor reform, Social Security, protection of workers' rights to organize, and the minimum wage—and had been heard most recently in congressional filibusters around the Civil Rights Act of 1964 and the Voting Rights Act of 1965.[98]

The *Statesville Record and Landmark* denounced the WAMY media project as yet another liberal concession to undeserving claims on rights and entitlements. "They want to organize another pressure bloc," the paper exclaimed, "teach all the techniques of palms up, and then point it in the direction of the public till." "Why not label [the newspaper] for what it is, wrote the *Sanford Herald*, "a propaganda arm? It prostitutes the very name 'newspaper.'" With an ear to Cold War anxieties, the *Asheville Citizen-Times* riffed on that theme. "If the OEO can publish a weekly newspaper in Northwest North Carolina," the editors cautioned, "Washington [might] eventually spread its newspaper network to cover the [entire] United States" and "develop—gradually, insidiously—a federal press, financed by taxpayers' money and telling the American people only what it wants them to hear." "What is about to happen in North-west North Carolina—unless YOU stop it," the *Citizen-Times* continued, "is a limited experiment in printed brainwash—a disguised attempt to insinuate the federal voice as a weekly Bible." WAMY and the OEO, the paper charged, were attempting to establish "America's Pravda," a homegrown counterpart to the official news outlet for the Soviet Union's Communist Party.[99]

The controversy over the newspaper and radio project quickly spread to the state legislature and to Congress. In Raleigh, state senator R. T. Dent, Republican from Mitchell County, introduced a resolution that criticized the WAMY demonstration project as a "thinly veiled effort to control public opinion." In Washington, Representative Basil L. Whitener, Democrat from the WAMY region, read the media project's OEO funding proposal into the *Congressional Record*. He and a conservative chorus—including Representative Roy A. Taylor, also from the WAMY area, North Carolina senators Sam J. Ervin Jr. and B. Everett Jordan, South Carolina senator Strom Thurmond, and Virginia senator Harry Byrd—lambasted the media scheme as "unrealistic, unwise, and un-American."[100]

Roy Parker Jr., Washington bureau chief for the *Raleigh News and Observer*—by any measure the most liberal paper in the state—watched the ruckus with amusement. He dismissed the attack on WAMY as much ado about nothing. The "gale force" of criticism suggested not that the War on Poverty was in jeopardy, but that it had in fact "seated itself rather firmly in the galaxy of government programs in [North Carolina]." "Despite their grumbling," Parker wrote, "those who would find an excuse to denounce the [antipoverty] program have found little to grab onto in the past few months. The newspaper idea provided a rare opportunity and its very audacity . . . provoked what could only be described as an overkill reaction. The lawmakers went hunting a rabbit with elephant gun oratory." The "thunderstorm of criticism" notwithstanding, WAMY and other antipoverty efforts were "not likely to be blown out of the water." In fact, Parker predicted, "by the time the 1968 election campaign rolls around, poverty programs will be hailed as positive achievements rather than as political albatrosses."[101]

Parker's assessment was gravely mistaken. The WAMY media project had touched a raw political nerve, not only among elected officeholders but also for a broad swath of white, middle-class citizens. Those men and women held to a fiercely individualistic ethic and faith in free enterprise. In the world as they understood it, poverty had little or nothing to do with structures of power or institutionalized inequities; it sprang instead from personal failures of ambition, initiative, and responsibility. There was obvious comfort to be found in that outlook on life. It assured the winners in the affluent society that their privilege was justly earned and well deserved, and that they had no culpability for the suffering of those left behind.

WAMY's news demonstration project threatened to pull back the veil on that worldview by revealing the structures of class that determined differences of comfort and want, opportunity and hopelessness. The newspaper and radio broadcasts were to be instruments of the poor, created by and for the benefit of the people of poverty. They would enable poor people to speak publicly of broken promises, shattered dreams, and the injuries inflicted by their station in life. That collectivization of grievance and desire posed a direct challenge to the individualism that was so deeply ingrained in American social and economic thought; it advanced group demands for redress in the distribution of life's opportunities and rewards; and it insisted that suffering in the world was no simple fact of life, but rather an injustice imposed by some to be endured by others.

To such assertions, WAMY's detractors had a ready reply: "This country recognizes no classes. Middle income and low income, yes" — but no classes. Claims to the contrary were, by definition, un-American and could have only one source: they were imposed from the outside. In a Senate speech, Sam Ervin, ignoring the two-year evolution of the news demonstration project, assured fellow lawmakers, the press, and his constituents that the "plan did not originate with North Carolinians, but was in a very real way imposed upon them by OEO." Back home, others looked farther afield for the wellspring of dangerous ideas. In a letter published in the *Yancey Record*, a local Democratic Party stalwart denounced Ernest Eppley and his staff as "present-day disciples of Lenin . . . starry-eyed fools whose chief aim in life seem[s] to be to recreate this country in the image of Karl Marx." "Until now," he declared, "I have suffered in silence, but this asinine scheme by Ernest Eppley is the last straw. When the United States Government goes into the field of broadcasting and the publication of newspapers we can kiss freedom and democracy goodbye. It would only be the first step to the establishment of an iron-clad dictatorship."[102]

Eppley and his allies were not entirely blameless for this crisis. They had come a long way in their appreciation of the capacities of the poor to help fight the War on Poverty, but even so, they could not escape entirely popular stereotypes of mountaineers. The newspaper and radio proposal had gone to some length to explain the mountain poor's underdeveloped sense of "group feeling." It attributed much of the blame to organized religion. Poor people's "only significant tradition of group participation, passive at that, is in their church congregations," the proposal argued, "but these congregations are many and small, many led by lay preachers who continue to promote a tradition of bigoted [denominational] separatism. Their 'communities' are in many cases not communities at all, but merely clusters of interrelated families, fractured by generations-old feuds stemming from personal hurts and differences of religious belief." That characterization of religious life outraged ministers and many of the middle-class people whom WAMY hoped to woo to its cause. "Since those of us in the ministry seem to be the principle cause of [poverty] conditions, with our lay brethren assuming the remainder of the responsibility," one pastor complained, "I am wondering if [the poor people's newspaper] would not seek to undermine the effectiveness of our churches. At any rate, it will contribute nothing to the general welfare of this region." Worse yet, attacks on the insularity of mountain churches provided WAMY's detractors an easy way to sidestep debates over the political and economic causes of poverty and to dismiss antipoverty activists as outsiders who understood nothing of mountain life. This was precisely the frame that Congressman Basil Whitener put around the media proposal when he attacked it in the House of Representatives. "I am astonished at some of the language used by WAMY, Inc.," he exclaimed. "The gratuitous assault which this application makes upon ministers of the gospel and upon their followers . . . is shocking."[103]

This wide-ranging attack—from the halls of Congress to local pulpits and editorial pages statewide—knocked Eppley and the WAMY staff back on their heels. On May 11, William Plemmons called a meeting of the board of directors to consider the future of the newspaper and radio project. After two hours of "lively discussion, both pro and con, on this much-condemned subject," Yancey County commissioner Dean Chrisawn made a motion to withdraw the proposal from the OEO. Burnsville mayor Robert Helmle seconded the resolution, which the board approved by a lopsided vote of twenty-one to six. The *Asheville Citizen* found satisfaction in that outcome. "A case of acute bad judgment has now been reversed," its editors crowed.[104]

TWO DAYS AFTER THE VOTE, Sargent Shriver and Billy Graham made their tour of Blevins Creek. For a brief moment, WAMY basked in press coverage that praised it as an exemplar of all that was good about the War on Poverty. The truth of the matter, however, was that the window of opportunity for building a social movement among the mountain poor was closing. Ernest Eppley—who had exhausted himself and his influence with the WAMY board—resigned in August 1967 and moved to Durham to work as a special assistant to George Esser. Key staff, including Hugh Wire, also left the agency. Before stepping down, Eppley confronted his critics. In June, the Boone Rotary Club invited him to discuss lessons learned from the ill-fated "Community Action News Proposal." "Frankly, I would prefer to talk about other WAMY programs," he told his audience. But if they insisted on hearing his opinions, he would pull no punches. "We felt, and we still feel [that the media project was] a good idea [and] a good way to motivate and educate low-income people," Eppley declared. "[The poor] need information about government, about available services, about the duties and responsibilities of citizens in a democracy. They need to communicate with each other about their successes, their problems, their needs. They need to see their picture in newspapers and hear their voices on the radio."[105]

Eppley warned his audience against taking comfort in the project's defeat. The problem that the initiative was meant to solve had not gone away, and he and his listeners still bore an obligation to correct it. The "strength and stability" of the nation depended on the inclusiveness of civic life, he insisted. "This is as true today as it was in the time of Thomas Jefferson, or in the time of Abraham Lincoln. . . . All of our great presidents were involved in expanding the depth and scope of citizen participation in our democratic processes" — and, like WAMY, they "were vilified for their efforts." Eppley pressed on, lecturing the Rotarians just as sternly about the duties of their religious faith: "Our Christian tradition requires that we be our brother's keeper, that we concern ourselves with the problems of the poor. The fact that the Federal government, private foundations, and the intellectuals in our universities are now telling us *that what we have been doing in the past has in fact kept the poor in poverty* is offensive to us. But, even though we are offended and our consciences bother us, we must admit that they are right. Today it is as obvious as it can ever be that the Christian's responsibility goes much deeper than the distribution of castoff clothing or Christmas baskets to the poor. We can no longer in good conscience be 'keepers of the poor.' This is a bitter pill to take, but as Christians we cannot avoid taking it." Eppley closed with a call to courage and commitment: "If we play the role of catalyst and point out community problems, we will be unpopular, yet that is one of our responsibilities." "I hope," he implored, "that this Rotary Club will consider [favorably] the opportunity we now have to improve our community by helping low-income citizens become more active, intelligent, and productive."[106]

That appeal had little effect on local civic leaders. Six months later, Boone's Junior Chamber of Commerce (Jaycees) joined their counterparts across the country and Republican congressional leaders in a campaign "to help bring the 'War on Poverty' closer to the private sector" and to roll back efforts at organizing the poor as a political force. The Jaycees undertook an independent review of WAMY programs. Their report—issued in December 1967—recommended turning the antipoverty agency back toward traditional forms of poor relief and charity. The Jaycees urged that "more use be made of existing agencies"; that "more local people" be employed as senior administrators; that authority over day-to-day operations be shifted from field staff to the board of directors; that WAMY salaries "be scaled down to be more in line with local [wages]"; and that antipoverty "personnel 'better adhere to local custom[s].'" Regional newspapers gave extensive coverage to the Jaycees' report. As one joked in its headlines, the "whammy [had been] put on WAMY."[107]

The Jaycees based their recommendations on surveys completed by six hundred residents of Boone and Watauga County. A majority of the respondents believed that there was "no poverty in Watauga County that [could] be effectively eliminated by WAMY," that much of the $3.5 million the agency received had been squandered, and that the problems WAMY set out to solve "could be handled as effectively by existing agencies or private enterprise." Those results were not particularly surprising, given the demographic profile of the survey participants. By the Jaycees' own account, "the typical person interviewed" was a male between twenty-two and fifty years of age who had graduated from high school and owned his home. That was hardly a representative sample of public opinion—not in an area where nearly 60 percent of residents lived in poverty, half of all houses were run-down and barely habitable, and the majority of adults never made it past the eighth grade. The Boone Jaycees had taken a snapshot of themselves, and they used the results to challenge WAMY with their own countermobilization of the middle class.[108]

Just days after the Jaycees issued their report, television station WBT in Charlotte—the state's largest city, located one hundred miles south of Boone—aired a half-hour exposé on WAMY's efforts to alleviate mountain poverty. The station called the program *Retreat from the Hills*, a broad hint that the story to follow would not be uplifting. Reporter Dave Larson ignored WAMY's local beginnings and the work of people like the Friendly Home Visitors. He took aim instead at outsiders—the North Carolina Volunteers, VISTA workers, and members of Ernest Eppley's staff—who, as he read the situation, had tried to introduce alien ideas into highland communities. "In 1964, the OEO warriors drove into the mountains from Chicago, Milwaukee, Washington, and even from Haight-Ashbury," Larson declared. "They were dedicated to the proposition that to do battle with poverty they must organize the poor" and foment "revolution against . . . county politicians, health departments, and even the Welfare Department itself." The young activists sported "mod clothes and hippie haircuts"—and wherever they went, "talk of immorality," "wild parties," and "radical teachings" followed close behind.[109]

To demonstrate the danger posed by the poverty "fighters," Larson referred to a letter that East Yancey High School principal Woodrow Anglin had written to North Carolina congressman Basil Whitener. Anglin reported on a training camp, "sponsored by Mr. Eppley's office," where several of his former students had gone to prepare for "work with the poor." "They were encouraged to organize the poor people to march on local governments, to appeal to their emotions, to encourage them to make certain demands by refusing to work, or sit ins and mob violence," the principal explained. "One speaker even encouraged burning a school bus [and] said that they would not be prosecuted as long as they operated as a mob." Howard Fuller, whom Anglin described as a "colored man from Chicago," made an appearance to tell of his success in organizing poor blacks in Durham, and "a Mr. Myles Horton," a cofounder of the Highlander Folk School and a longtime champion of labor and civil rights who had interacted with Ed Adkins in eastern Kentucky, spoke openly of "organiz[ing] a rebellion." Anglin's students thought that much of what they heard was "ridiculous," but, the principal warned, "recent insurrections in our cities"—the summertime riots in Newark and Detroit and the poor people's marches that Fuller had led in Durham—demonstrated just how dangerous the situation might become. Something had to be done before the contagion of civil rights spread from northern cities and Piedmont towns to infect Appalachia's mountain coves.[110]

On that point, Larson found cause for encouragement. WAMY's misadventures had provoked the ire of "the conservative highland middle class," who "rebelled—they wouldn't join the fight and believe in the new ideas." These were Woodrow Anglin's neighbors: "patriotic citizens" fortified by "respect for their country." They stood up to WAMY's "radical element," and now "the revolutionaries," their "uniforms tattered" and torn, were in full "retreat." Ernest Eppley had resigned, Larson told WBT's viewers, and many of his coworkers had gone back north, where they found employment with other "poverty agencies in big city slums." Larson gave the vanquished no quarter. He charged that Eppley and his associates had indulged their radical fantasies at the expense of the very people they claimed to serve. Now it seemed that "the mountain man" was once again "to be forgotten." "WAMY came to fight, but, so far, it has failed," Larson concluded in solemn, sarcastic tones.

"The original warriors are gone, but the mountaineers and their problems remain." Much of what Larson conjured was pure fantasy. Most of the young people who came to the WAMY counties as volunteers or staffers were serious and straight-laced, and rather than provoking intergenerational conflict, they built meaningful relationships with the people they set out to serve. It was that very success that called forth the stereotyping that Larson promulgated and the effort to link WAMY with the unsettling images that people saw on the evening news. Larson was right about the poverty workers' radical intent, and his effort to dismiss it as a symptom of immorality rather than democratic purpose was as old as the hills.[111]

The controversy generated by the critical reports from the Boone Jaycees and WBT weighed heavily on the search for Eppley's successor. Shortly after his departure, the WAMY board appointed H. C. Moretz Jr. as interim director. Moretz had grown up in Watauga County and had attended the local public schools. He graduated from Appalachian State Teachers College in 1950 and spent most of his career in education. In 1966, Eppley had hired Moretz to run WAMY's Neighborhood Youth Corps program. That background made Moretz particularly attractive to the agency's board. He seemed to be the perfect response to the Jaycees' complaint that antipoverty efforts were being led by outsiders rather than locals.[112]

At Fund headquarters, George Esser, Robert Walker, and Ernest Eppley worried over the prospect that Moretz might be appointed executive director on a permanent basis. They admired his work with young people in the Neighborhood Youth Corps, but they also doubted his ability to stand up to local politicians and business leaders who were leading the attack on WAMY. The selection process dragged on for a number of months, ending in March 1968 when the board awarded Moretz a permanent appointment. That action disappointed, but did not surprise Robert Walker. Eppley's determination to mobilize the poor, he noted, had "aroused fears in people that made them want a man that would cool it, would run a nice tight ship, and would not arouse controversy." "To some of the powerful people," Moretz seemed "to be such a man."[113]

As Ernest Eppley watched WAMY's retreat from controversy, he worried about a crisis of faith among fellow antipoverty workers. He acknowledged that when they took up the struggle they had been "too idealistic and too hopeful." In their innocence they had miscalculated how difficult it would be to change "negative attitudes" toward the poor and to reform political and economic structures that stood "in the way of poor people [and kept] them ... subjugated and unable to move forward." Eppley saw in poverty activists the same impatience and weariness of the soul that he had observed among missionaries in Bolivia. Both were "so committed to overturning things and making things right very rapidly" that they suffered great "emotional strain." Under such circumstances the temptation to compromise — to give up and "be absorbed in the milieu of middle-class lethargy" — grew ever more powerful. In the closing weeks of his work in the mountains, Eppley advised his staff to steel themselves against surrender. He rejected the argument that the War on Poverty could be won only by making itself more "respectable." To the contrary, it was all right for poverty warriors to be "angry," and it was essential that they be "fearless." To strike any other pose would be to "retreat before the battle begins — before we have even mobilized our troops."[114]

COUNTERASSAULT

In the months leading up to the WAMY Community Action (or WAMY) media project controversy and the housing demonstrations in Durham, the North Carolina Fund was riding high. George Esser and his staff looked to the future with confidence and a deep sense of satisfaction. When representatives of the Ford Foundation reviewed the Fund in late 1966, they heaped praise on the agency's efforts. In less than three years, it had "helped initiate and finance innovative, experimental projects . . . to better educate the young and give job skills to unemployed adults, to improve health and sanitation in backward communities . . . to initiate farm coops, and to begin imaginative projects organizing domestic workers, establishing day care centers . . . training and developing indigenous leaders, and a host of other activities, indispensable to ending poverty." Even so, the Ford team noted, there was much work yet to be done. Scores of communities across North Carolina remained captive to "the inertia and the irresponsibility of conservative local power coalitions." In those places, "where intense social problems [had] long festered" and "progress had been quiescent for 100 years," poor people still needed allies "to foster institutional, political, economic, and social change" that would "bring about a functioning, democratic society." Mindful of that need and the Fund's record of achievement, Ford urged Esser and his colleagues to give serious thought to ways that their work, particularly at the community level, might be continued beyond the organization's planned termination in September 1968.[1]

The obvious response to that encouragement would have been to ask the Ford Foundation for another five-year grant, which Ford leaders had indicated they would happily provide. Quickly, however, Esser and his staff decided to follow a different course. In May 1967, they convinced the Fund's board of directors to honor Terry Sanford's pledge to close shop at the end of five years. The staff laid out their argument carefully, insisting at every turn that the board pay heed to the Fund's founding principles. They reminded board members of the value of a flexible, experimental approach to solving social problems, warned against the dangers of bureaucratization, and pointed out opportunities to take the Fund's battle onto new terrain.[2]

The issues that had called the Fund into being were not limited to North Carolina; they reached across the South, and indeed, the nation. As Esser and his colleagues looked outside the state, they identified the same "multitude of problems" that they had first confronted in 1963. The deprivations of the South looked most familiar and, in many respects, most daunting. The entire region continued to underinvest in the education and welfare of its people; the "stifling status-quoism" of state and local politics silenced debate on important issues of public policy; racial animosity still blighted individual lives and hindered economic development; and, worst of all, the South had too few civic leaders with the "imagination and intelligence and commitment and skills" to tackle these problems. The region—like the nation—stood at a crossroads. The civil rights movement and the War on Poverty had harnessed the energy and idealism of millions and had made great strides in loosening the grip of Jim Crow and fulfilling the nation's democratic promise. But the work was hardly complete. Those gains were fragile and tenuous; the challenge was to institutionalize hard-won victories and move forward on new fronts or to risk losing ground to a newly reorganized conservative opposition. In George Esser's judgment, that state of affairs demanded that the Fund's leaders lift their sites, refocus their energies, and broaden their campaign for democracy "to include the entire South."[3]

One of Esser's greatest strengths was his ability to "think boldly, not timidly." In a series of letters and memoranda written between early 1967 and 1969, he and his assistant Lucy Rodgers Wadkins developed a proposal for a Fund-like agency to take up the work of the South's revitalization. They imagined a "private corporation, independently financed" by a $100 million endowment comprised of a major gift from Ford and "matching [contributions] from Southern foundations," such as Z. Smith Reynolds and Mary Reynolds Babcock in North Carolina. That war chest would guarantee the new agency's "freedom and independence to speak out" on controversial issues and to operate as "a catalytic agent, a mobilizer of resources, a demonstrator of ideas, a 'countervailing force'" opposed to entrenched power. A board of directors representing southerners from all races and walks of life would oversee the new agency, and an integrated staff would offer living witness to the type of "racial, economic, social and political change" that the region so desperately needed. In Esser's model, those employees would coordinate the activities of nonprofit antipoverty organizations across the South and help them maximize their access to federal resources. They would promote "the *study and analysis* of public policy"; they would use film, radio, television, and print journalism for "the *transmission of this information* to the general public"; and in each of these ways, they would work to cultivate forward-looking leaders.[4]

The new, South-wide antipoverty agency would also replicate the Fund's commitment to grassroots mobilization. It would make hundreds of small grants at the community level to build on the oppositional culture of the civil rights movement and to seed the region with stable poor people's organizations similar to United Organizations for Community Improvement (UOCI) in Durham and the People's Program on Poverty (PPOP) in the Choanoke. Esser's staff, who were often less politic than he, drove straight to the point when describing such community councils: they were to act as "harassers" who would disrupt the status quo and, by so doing, create space for progressive change. "This recognizes the central [role] of compromise [in] the whole political scheme," the Fund veterans explained. "There isn't such a thing as total victory, but there can be a process by which a change can be brought about faster if the compromise positions can be moved forward by the presence of a harassment element." This was the most important lesson the poverty warriors took from the black freedom struggle, which relied on direct action and civil disobedience to provoke a crisis and, in Martin Luther King's words, "open the door to negotiation." On that point, if not the choice of language used to describe it, Esser and his younger colleagues agreed. "One of the several naïve hopes with which we entered the Fund experience," he wrote in his plan, "was the idea that a spirit of community dedication and cooperation, backed by some grant monies, might bring about a willingness to admit the poor, especially the Negro poor, to the community decision-making process. Now, of course, we know that it is not in the nature of human beings . . . to share power willingly. Representation on school boards, welfare boards, city councils and housing authority boards is not likely to be welcomed simply because it is right or because it is fair. Representation of the poor commensurate with their numbers will come only through use of the ballot box, through a vigorous show of interest in community affairs, and through enlightened democratic action by an informed and motivated low-income population."[5]

Esser and his colleagues felt exhilarated as they prepared to take their campaign against poverty onto new ground. To be sure, they had encountered opposition all along the way, some of it anticipated, much of it a surprise. Few among them, for example, had imagined the power of playgrounds and garbage collection to provoke the ire of local elites. But rather than stalling the Fund's efforts, those skirmishes moved the organization forward, sharpened its political sophistication, and underscored the critical importance of mobilizing the poor as engaged citizens. In early 1967, Fund leaders had every confidence that they could continue to outmaneuver their detractors. They held fast to Lyndon Johnson's hope that the War on Poverty would unite the nation around a shared vision of the common good. In hindsight, that was a terrible miscalculation. Rather than bring Americans together, the campaign against poverty, along with the epic civil rights legislation of 1964 and 1965, became the social irritant around which a powerful conservative movement coalesced.

SIGNS OF THE STORM AHEAD were first apparent in 1964, when Richardson Preyer, Terry Sanford's designated heir, lost the Democratic gubernatorial primary to conservative judge Dan Moore. That contest was, in effect, a referendum on Sanford's progressive policies and vision for a "New Day" in North Carolina. In the same year, activists on the right took control of the national Republican Party and leveraged Arizona senator Barry Goldwater onto the national ticket as its presidential candidate. Leaders of this conservative movement defiantly challenged the party's ruling "eastern establishment," many of whom held liberal views on social issues and had voted with Democrats on civil rights legislation. Goldwater himself was blunt and to the point: "You might not like us, but you're stuck with us, and we're Republicans." In November, Lyndon Johnson defeated Goldwater in a landslide victory—at the time, the largest in American history—and pundits were quick to declare that he had "broke[n] the back" of postwar conservatism. But in point of fact, the state-level results foretold a seismic shift in political alignments. Goldwater bested Lyndon Johnson in the Deep South (South Carolina, Georgia, Alabama, Mississippi, and Louisiana) and garnered a majority of white votes in Virginia, North Carolina, Tennessee, and Arkansas.[6]

Two years later, in the 1966 midterm elections, the voters whom Goldwater had inspired—many of them once-loyal Democrats—helped the Republican Party win forty-seven new seats in the House of Representatives and three in the Senate. Democrats still held a majority in Congress and controlled statehouses across the South, but many felt a closer affinity for the social attitudes of the Republican new guard than for those of their president. In Mississippi, archsegregationist James O. Eastland, one of the pillars of Democratic strength in the United States Senate, boasted, "The sentiment of the entire country now stands with the Southern people"—by which, of course, he meant those whites who felt threatened by the civil rights revolution and Johnson's Great Society.[7]

In North Carolina, no single figure better represented this emerging realignment than a newly elected Republican congressman named James C. Gardner. On June 14, 1967 — only five months into his term — he took the floor to attack the North Carolina Fund and speak against "irregularities" in the Office of Economic Opportunity (OEO). He reported that in Durham's recent municipal election, antipoverty workers, "employees of Operation Breakthrough," had "spent taxpayers' dollars to create and organize a political machine." They "devoted months of their time, during working hours, researching registration and voter lists"; they "used Government automobiles" to transport poor residents to voter registration sites; and then, on election day, they leafleted poor communities with sample ballots and drove residents to the polls. "I severely condemn such activity on the part of Federal employees," Gardner exclaimed, "and charge that it is completely outside of the limits and purpose of the poverty program." He then read into the *Congressional Record* a lengthy letter of complaint addressed to OEO director Sargent Shriver. "Unless you render a decision now as to the propriety of these activities," Gardner warned, "this action could set a national precedent."[8]

Shriver had heard this before. From the outset, those who felt challenged by poor citizens' involvement in shaping antipoverty programs had complained bitterly. Within the Democratic Party, big-city majors were openly covetous of "anti-poverty money — and the votes it [could] influence." They resisted any suggestion that the poor should "determine public policy and spend public money." Syracuse mayor William Walsh spoke for his colleagues when he declared, "If we cannot have control of the [poverty] program, we do not want it." In 1965, the Johnson White House sent Vice President Hubert Humphrey to the annual meeting of the National League of Cities to assure municipal leaders that the OEO's purpose was not to usurp their authority. Sargent Shriver had also sought to soothe local concerns by issuing a series of policy statements that prohibited poverty workers paid with federal funds from participating in "*partisan* political activity intended to further the election or defeat of any candidate for public office" (emphasis added). But the directives left open a large loophole, which Shriver exploited in his reply to Gardner. He reminded the congressman that employees of community agencies were free to take part in voter registration drives and "activities in connection with campaigns for office which are run on a *non-partisan* basis and are of a strictly local character — that is, completely unrelated to issues

Congressman Jim Gardner made criticism of the North Carolina Fund the hallmark of his political career. Courtesy of the *Raleigh News & Observer* and the North Carolina State Archives.

and candidates identified with national and state political parties" (emphasis added). Durham's municipal elections, in which candidates ran without party affiliation, fell clearly within the bounds of that exemption. "I'm sure you know," Shriver wrote sarcastically, that "numerous civic organizations including the League of Women Voters long have been engaged in insuring that all eligible Americans are registered so that they may exercise their choice on election day." Operation Breakthrough employees had done nothing more.[9]

Gardner was not to be dismissed so easily, for he had more on his mind than simply disciplining violations of OEO policies. He was the "golden boy" of a youthful uprising that had taken control of the state's Republican Party in 1964 and had steered it hard to the right. Born in Nash County in 1933, Gardner grew up on a large dairy farm outside of Rocky Mount, where, by his account, he learned that "with plenty of hard work you can accomplish your goals." He studied for two years at North Carolina State University in Raleigh and served in the army from 1953 to 1955. During the early 1960s, Gardner and a business partner bought the franchise rights for a hamburger stand in Greenville and quickly built the enterprise into Hardee's, one of the nation's leading fast-food chains. That success gave Gardner entrée into

Rocky Mount's civic elite. He joined the Jaycees and moved easily among a close network of the city's bankers, lawyers, doctors, and business owners. Their conversations often turned to politics and concern over the impending "end to a way of life" in the South. The men and women within Gardner's circle differed in their views on what was to be done. Some remained loyal to the Democratic Party and sought to hold the line against Lyndon Johnson's Great Society from within, while others—the ultraconservatives—established a local chapter of the John Birch Society, a fiercely anticommunist and libertarian organization founded by North Carolina native and University of North Carolina alumnus Robert W. Welch Jr. Gardner cast his lot with a third group, friends who had bolted from the Democratic Party and formed a small but vibrant Republican county committee. In the summer of 1963, he officially changed his party affiliation from Democratic to Republican.[10]

Gardner approached politics with an entrepreneur's eye. He recognized that there was a vast untapped political market of white North Carolinians like himself who felt abandoned by the Democratic Party and did not know where to turn. He also saw promise in the fact that the Republican Party—anchored in the western part of the state, where it fed on deep-seated regional grievances more than ideological antipathies—had no effective organizational structure in the east. Here was an opportunity to tap into white, middle-class discontent and to build a conservative movement capable of wresting power from the Democratic Party. Gardner wasted no time. Within two months of changing his registration, he assumed the chairmanship of the Nash County Republican Party, and in the fall of 1963 he organized a rally in Rocky Mount to draft Charles Jonas, a Republican congressman from Lincolnton and the dean of the state's GOP, as a candidate in the upcoming 1964 gubernatorial contest. The effort failed—not least of all because Jonas had no interest in the job—and political pundits sniffed at the naïveté of launching such an effort in the Democratic heartland. But Gardner had accomplished his goal. He had challenged the Republican establishment to make its party into a statewide contender, and he had demonstrated to disaffected eastern Democrats that there was a home for them outside the party of their forebears.[11]

In the early summer of 1964, Gardner pressed on in his effort to build a new Republican movement in North Carolina: he announced his intent to challenge Democratic congressman Harold D. Cooley, who had first been elected in 1934 and whose fourth congressional district stretched from Nash and Johnston Counties in the east to Randolph and Davidson Counties in the Piedmont. Gardner found inspiration in Republican Barry Goldwater,

Republican presidential candidate Barry Goldwater campaigning in downtown
Raleigh, September 1964. Courtesy of the *Raleigh News & Observer* and the North
Carolina State Archives.

who was campaigning for the presidency on a platform of individual liberty,
free enterprise, small government, and states' rights. He met Goldwater on
several of the candidate's North Carolina visits, including at a Jaycees luncheon in Kinston, an eastern tobacco town. "I came out and was fired up,"
Gardner recalled. "This is what I believe in. . . . This is where I belong." In a
calculated effort to win support from restless white Democrats, he posted
billboards throughout the district that made no mention of his party affiliation but loudly announced his ideological disposition. "Goldwater-Gardner:
Conservatives," they declared. Like Goldwater, Gardner lost the 1964 election, but his ability to convince otherwise loyal Democrats to cross over and
cast their ballots for him was impressive. He won 48 percent of the vote.[12]

Republican elders in North Carolina recognized the promise of Gardner's
leadership and the shrewdness of his strategy for loosening the Democrats'
hold on power. In August 1965, they named him state party chairman. The following month, Sim A. DeLapp, who had recently served as the party's general
counsel and was himself a former chairman, wrote to congratulate Gardner
and to urge him on. "From the standpoint of voter sentiment," he advised,
"we are in the best shape that we have ever been [in] during my lifetime.
People are permanently angry at the so-called Democratic Party. . . . They
are mad because Johnson has become the President of the negro race and of

all the left wingers. If properly led, people are ready to go to town in North Carolina for the Republican Party."[13]

DeLapp encouraged Gardner to avoid what he described as the extremes within their party: John Birchers on the right, who frightened many voters, and moderates on the left, who compromised the conservative message. He had no use for establishment Republicans such as the New York triumvirate of Representative John Lindsay (later mayor of New York), Senator Jacob Javits, and Governor Nelson Rockefeller. Nor did he care much for Michigan's Republican governor George Romney, who supported civil rights legislation and had helped draft an amendment to the state's constitution that established a permanent civil rights commission. When Romney endorsed the Civil Rights Act of 1964, DeLapp wrote an angry letter. "I don't think you or any other candidate should believe that any country or party can force social equality," he told Romney. "When the present civil rights bill goes so far as to say that all public accommodation places must serve all persons regardless of race, which in the South means that they must serve the smelly, filthy, diseased Negro, along with the clean, intelligent white man, then I cease to go along with such a bill." A year later, when Romney and other Republican moderates threw their support to the Voting Rights Act, DeLapp was incensed. "You may be misled into thinking that the more intelligent people of the South will go along with the mistaken philosophy of the North with reference to the race question," he warned. "They will never do so, and all that you are doing to the Republican Party . . . is helping to destroy and keep it from growing." For DeLapp, there was only one way forward: "Our political possibilities lie with the white race, who in the North and in the South and in the East and in the West are growing tired of seeing the Negro raised above his natural and normal level."[14]

DeLapp worried that his party might yet squander a historic moment of opportunity. He drew on his understanding of the past to make the case. During Reconstruction and again in the Fusion era of the late 1890s, he would later observe, white Republicans had made common cause with blacks newly freed from slavery. That alliance cost them dearly. A "skillful Democratic state leadership used the race issue . . . in order to regain power" and to roll back efforts at establishing "decent election laws" and "local self-government." Three-quarters of a century later, the table had been turned. Blacks were "now strongly and steadfastly allied with the Democratic Party," and their presence had become a source of "great discontent" among the white rank and file. Those restive Democrats believed in "individual freedom and free enterprise, in work and thrift, in necessary public welfare, but not in a foolish give-away program," DeLapp explained. "They became accustomed to law and order many years ago. Now it is gone. The streets are filled with violence and discontent and crime. They want to be safe again."[15]

DeLapp believed that with the right leadership, Republicans could tap that discontent and build a new conservative majority. At home, he looked to Jim Gardner, and at the national level he put his trust in Ronald Reagan, who had delivered a passionate speech, "A Time for Choosing," in support of Barry Goldwater's nomination at the 1964 Republican national convention. Reagan drew a sharp contrast between "the freedoms that were intended for us by the Founding Fathers" and Johnson's Great Society, which pointed in only one direction: "down to the ant heap of totalitarianism." Days after the speech was broadcast on television, DeLapp wrote to Reagan and encouraged him to devote himself to politics. DeLapp admired Goldwater's principles but realized that the Arizona senator was too strident to win the upcoming election. By contrast, Reagan was a man of great potential. "The principles for which Goldwater and all the rest of us are fighting cannot be allowed to die," DeLapp insisted. "Sometimes a personality helps to put over the program. . . . You owe it to the country and to freedom everywhere to project yourself into the political life of our country. . . . You can become a spokesman for free enterprise. You have the individual capacity and attractiveness of personality to lead men and women."[16]

Back in North Carolina, Jim Gardner's youthful energy held a similar appeal for would-be Republicans. He was a "political messiah" who "had more charisma in his little finger" than even the best of campaigners, one admirer observed. Gardner also had a sharp tactical mind. One of his first acts as party chairman was to move the state Republican headquarters from Charlotte, located near traditional GOP strongholds in the western counties, to Raleigh, the state capital. His elders howled in disapproval, but Gardner made no apology. Having an office in Raleigh put him closer to eastern North Carolina, where he and his staff threw themselves into "retail politics." They toured local farms and factories, gathered housewives for coffee hours, made stump speeches too numerous to count, and canvassed door-to-door—all with an eye to building a Republican movement in places where the party previously had little or no organizational presence. They appealed to doubting Democrats with the slogan "Sometimes Party Loyalty Demands Too Much." In 1966, when Gardner ran again for congressional office, he handily defeated incumbent Democrat Harold Cooley, despite the fact that only 17 percent of the voters in his district were registered Republicans. On election night, Gardner told cheering supporters, "This was not a campaign. This was a movement of people who want to be heard." He celebrated the success of his political strategy: "We couldn't have won without the thousands of good Democrats who voted for us."[17]

Gardner had attacked the North Carolina Fund on the campaign trail in both 1964 and 1966, and he made relentless pursuit of the agency his trademark in the House of Representatives. He sought to establish for himself an identity as a national watchdog over the excesses of Lyndon Johnson's Great Society. In late June 1967, shortly after reading his initial attack on Operation Breakthrough into the *Congressional Record*, Gardner again stepped forward, this time to challenge Sargent Shriver's dismissal of his complaints and to report warning signs of a revolution in the making. He read into the record an extensive body of correspondence generated by Robert Monte, former director of Operation Progress, the Fund-supported community action program in New Bern and Craven County. Monte had resigned his position in the fall of 1966 to protest the Fund's embrace of maximum feasible participation and efforts that he believed were intended to turn the War on Poverty into "a third political force." He stepped down when he "could no longer stomach the verbal directive[s] from . . . the Office of Economic Opportunity and the rantings" of George Esser's staff. For Monte and Gardner, the Fund's activist rhetoric and political agitation of the poor raised the age-old specter of "Negro rule." They denounced the Fund for "actively supporting the civil rights groups in a so called 'drive for a change in [the] local power structure' which is in essence a shield for the so called 'black power' struggle." This "dangerous situation," Gardner advised his congressional colleagues, not only threatened North Carolina but was also smoldering in communities across the nation.[18]

CONGRESSMAN GARDNER MUST HAVE thought himself prescient when, in mid-July, the cities of Newark, New Jersey, and Detroit, Michigan, erupted in violence. In both places, episodes of police brutality unleashed torrents of rage among black residents who had been bottled up in squalid ghettoes and were all too familiar with harassment that went by the name of law enforcement. Newark burned for six days, from July 12 to 17. By the time the National Guard had restored order, much of the central city was in ruins and twenty-six residents — almost all of them black — had been killed. Less than a week later, even deadlier conflict broke out in Detroit, much of it carried live on national television. Looters and arsonists fought running street battles with police and guardsmen. More than two thousand buildings went up in flame, and forty-three residents died. To this day, neither city has fully recovered from the destruction it suffered during the "long, hot summer" of 1967.[19]

At the end of July, Lyndon Johnson appointed a presidential advisory commission to investigate the civil disorders in Newark, Detroit, and another eighteen cities that had been rocked by racial unrest. The president advised "deeply disturbed" Americans that the nation needed answers to three basic questions about the riots: "What happened? Why did it happen? What can be done to prevent it from happening again and again?" Over the next seven months, the commission—led by Otto Kerner, Democratic governor of Illinois, and John Lindsay, liberal Republican mayor of New York—searched for answers by visiting violence-torn communities and talking with hundreds of people, including politicians, chiefs of police, neighborhood activists, and ordinary citizens. The report it issued in March 1968 spoke sobering truths to white Americans who felt that recent civil rights legislation had gone far enough in redressing racial inequality. In point of fact, the Kerner Commission insisted, the nation was "moving toward two societies, one black, one white—separate and unequal."[20]

A litany of evidence bore out that assertion: black citizens were trapped in crumbling inner-city ghettoes, abandoned by whites who had moved their families and their tax dollars to the suburbs; black children attended school in facilities that were severely understaffed and underfunded; black inner-city residents were twice as likely to be unemployed as whites and twice as likely to live in poverty; and even as black urban populations grew, whites retained a lock on municipal government, so that of the twenty cities studied by the Kerner Commission, none had a black mayor or city manager. Those circumstances stood in stark contrast to the national affluence that "television and other media . . . flaunted before the eyes of the Negro poor and the jobless ghetto youth." They also exacerbated the "unfulfilled expectations aroused by the great judicial and legislative victories of the Civil Rights Movement." All told, this was a recipe for disorder. For many among the urban poor, the "frustrations of powerlessness" led to the "conviction that there is no other alternative to violence as a means of achieving redress of grievances, and of 'moving the system.'"[21]

The Kerner Commission prescribed strong medicine to cure the nation's ills. It demanded that the nation face the fact that "white racism" was "responsible for the explosive mixture which has been accumulating in our cities since the end of World War II." "What white Americans have never fully understood—but what the Negro can never forget—is that white society is deeply implicated in the ghetto," it explained. "White institutions created it, white institutions maintain it, and white society condones it." Correcting injustice and inequality, the commission advised, would require "national action on an unprecedented scale." It recommended massive new federal investments in education, public housing, and job training; vigorous enforcement of antidiscrimination laws; and a concerted effort to open government and political life to participation by all citizens. That work would require "from every American . . . new attitudes, new understanding, and, above all, new will." There was no other choice. "To pursue our present course," the commissioners warned, would "involve the continuing polarization of the American community and, ultimately, the destruction of basic democratic values."[22]

Conservatives diagnosed the problems differently. They charged that organized subversion was the primary force at work in Newark and Detroit. In his ongoing attack on the OEO, Jim Gardner accused poverty workers of being the chief instigators of the urban uprisings. He explained to fellow members of Congress that during the months leading up to the Newark riot, employees of the local community action program had helped organize protests against plans by city and state leaders to bulldoze 150 acres of the predominantly black Central Ward to make room for a new medical college and hospital. Residents complained that the plan, which did not include sufficient replacement housing, constituted the worst case of turning urban renewal into "Negro removal." But Gardner took a different view. The protests, he argued, had been planned by militants who intended to whip the community into a frenzy. To substantiate those claims, Gardner read into the *Congressional Record* a lengthy article from *Barron's* magazine entitled "Poverty Warriors — The Riots Are Subsidized as Well as Organized." *Barron's* reminded its readers that, "like the poor, slums and rats have always been with us." What was new was the presence of "professional agitators who prepare the tinder, await the spark, and fan the flames." With financial support from the OEO, the magazine charged, an army of revolutionaries had infiltrated antipoverty programs. They included "Red-Chinese-inspired" labor organizers, "members of the Communist Party," Black Panthers and Black Muslims, and Student Nonviolent Coordinating Committee (SNCC) workers. As "'liberals' of both parties" looked aside, *Barron's* argued, "the U.S. taxpayer" had been duped into "financ[ing] his own destruction." In its view, the lesson from "Newark, Detroit and scores of other smouldering cities" was clear: "The Great Society . . . cannot coexist with the American way of life. . . . Law and order are the stuff of civilization; they are also the first duty of government. . . . What this country needs is a political and philosophical call to arms."[23]

Congressman Gardner was ready for battle. He made a hurried trip to

Newark to survey the damage and quickly gained national recognition for his dogged pursuit of Sargent Shriver and the OEO. The *New York Times* reported that "the attack on the poverty program was bipartisan, but the vanguard was Southern: Representative James C. Gardner, of North Carolina, and Senators James Eastland, of Mississippi, and John L. McClellan, of Arkansas, [both] Democrats." Eastland, the powerful chairman of the Senate Judiciary Committee and its Internal Security Subcommittee, had been particularly outraged by OEO funding for the Child Development Group of Mississippi, a Head Start program that became an important staging ground for black political and economic organizing, and McClellan, who had made his reputation as a hard-liner on organized crime and political subversion, worried aloud that the OEO had made rioters into "a privileged class in this country." Moving in such company put Gardner in good stead with white supporters back home, both those in his district and others across the state. They wrote scores of letters lauding his campaign to expose the wrongdoings of the OEO and the community action agencies it funded. "KEEP UP THE GOOD WORK," they urged. "You have a large, strong backing."[24]

Most of the letter writers had never before corresponded with a congressman and were unaccustomed to speaking out on public affairs. But the upheavals of 1967 and Gardner's calls for law and order prompted them to voice their racial fears. A woman from Raleigh echoed ancient worries that had haunted plantation mistresses in times of slave rebellion. "The American people are very upset" by the urban rioting, she explained, "and our main concern is when will it strike our homes. . . . Are we to trust our maids and take a chance of returning home some evening and finding our homes burned down, or should we discharge 'innocent' people and give the Government more mouths to feed? . . . Most of the news media attribute the rioting to poor Negroes seeing all of the luxuries advertised on TV, believing all white Americans own these things. The maids working in the homes have built up resentment against their employers for years, because they see some of these things in the homes in which they are employed. Therefore, it would not take much to touch off a catastrophe all over America."[25]

Other correspondents worried about unbridled black sexuality. What black men wanted above all else, they insisted, was "to be on a social level with the whites — to be able to date white girls." And for their part, black women were content to indulge their passions at taxpayers' expense. "These people *don't* want to work," a young woman shouted with indignation. "Why should they, when they receive their welfare checks each month or other 'hand-outs'! . . . And if they want a larger welfare check — all they have to do is have another kid! We are even paying for their sex life!" Gardner's petitioners charged that such promiscuity not only wasted public funds but also bred social disorder. They denounced immorality that produced generations of children "who hate[d] . . . law and order, and civilization, and every semblance of right."[26]

Falling back on ugly stereotypes about black hygiene and accompanying fears of disease and contagion, the letter writers told Gardner that they were tired of hearing complaints about the squalor of slum life. "When my yard needs cleaning up, I clean it up!" one woman exclaimed. "I don't have rats because I take [my garbage] out and put it in a can where it belongs!" A man from a small town near Raleigh agreed, and to underscore the point, he sent along a print copy of one of Jesse Helms's editorials on WRAL-TV. "If you have not read this," he scrawled in red pencil, "please do so now." Helms had explained to viewers that poverty was more a matter of morals and behavior than politics and economic opportunity. "*People* cause slums," the newsman insisted, "people who are too shiftless and lazy to keep themselves and their surroundings clean, people who are too disinterested to carry their refuse to a garbage can 30 feet away, people who would rather fuss about rats rather than put out a dime's worth of rat poison—which they can get free at the nearest welfare office or public health department. . . . The bleeding hearts raise their fists in fury at the nation's landlords, but they point nary a finger at the real cause of slums and squalor—and rats." In Helms's view, antipoverty programs that failed to acknowledge this truth were "a literal manifestation of pouring money down rat holes." No amount of federal largesse was "likely to purchase higher personal standards for people . . . who [chose] to live like pigs."[27]

Gardner dictated lengthy replies that affirmed his petitioners' grievances and assured them that he would fight on their behalf. "I think the time has come for Congress to stop passing major Civil Rights legislation," he said. "No amount of legislation can speed the process of integration. Time is the best and only course left for the negro to achieve equality in our society." Those words were a balm for constituents who wrote poignantly of their own triumphs over hardship and wondered why the same was not demanded of others. "I was born during the depression," one woman explained, "and my Dad worked for 50¢ a day and there were five of us children at the time! But did we riot? No, we did the best we could and prayed to God and with his help—we made it!" Another advised that "the poverty programs should be discontinued and everyone's standard of living should be earned by work and drive." Gardner agreed, and he argued that liberal civil rights and anti-poverty policies had gotten things backward. "I believe that it is the citizen such as yourself who has been hurt by these Great Society programs," he wrote. "Americans who have had individual responsibility and have worked to advance themselves in life are now finding that Government taxes and Government programs are taking a large portion of their salary." Such circumstances undercut "individual initiative" and threatened the "very fibre" of the nation. Gardner promised to set things straight. He assured his constituents that "people simply must be taught" a lesson: "personal and social problems" could be solved only through the exercise of individual responsibility, not the indulgence of protests and collective demands. "We cannot accept individuals or groups of individuals who do not abide by our laws or who are not willing to work and earn their share in our society."[28]

Gardner composed his letters with confidence and resolve. The exchanges confirmed that he and Republican Party elder Sim DeLapp were right about the changing political landscape and the prospects for establishing a new conservative majority. Like the white supremacists of an earlier era, his supporters equated the struggle for civil rights with "Negro domination." "What has happened to the rights of the white people of this nation?" they asked. "People who go to work every day, pay their taxes and obey the laws of this nation. Are we the forgotten people?" And to what end would civil rights and antipoverty agitation lead? "It is not inconceivable," one of Gardner's constituents replied, "that those very Negroes marching will one day encircle our great Capitol building, demanding [that lawmakers] give them control of our nation, or face a 'non-violent' riot which will topple our government." The men and women who penned such prophecies found no comfort in the Democratic Party that had once dominated the Solid South. "I am a Democrat," one woman confessed, "but have voted Republican lately, as I am fed up with the Democrats. The people are going to show their disapproval with the way things are come the next election. . . . Pretty soon you are going to hear about the white uprising." This letter writer spoke for the thousands of white voters who would rally to George Wallace's independent presidential campaign in 1968, and to whom Richard Nixon appealed as aggrieved members of the "silent majority." I. Beverly Lake, who had lost to Terry Sanford in the 1960 Democratic gubernatorial primary and was now a justice on the North Carolina Supreme Court, expressed the depth of their anger. "Keep up your good work," he advised Congressman Gardner. "The apostles of appeasement of rioting and looting . . . must be removed from positions of public trust. . . . We must clean up the whole foul mess and fumigate the premises."[29]

In mid-July, when Ann Atwater and Rubye Gattis led members of Durham's United Organizations for Community Improvement into the streets to protest that city's program of urban renewal, Congressman Gardner seized the opportunity to link local demonstrations to the outbreak of violence elsewhere in the nation. On July 25, less than a week after the Durham march and in the midst of the unrest in Detroit, he held a news conference in which he charged that the North Carolina Fund had become a "political action machine" and called for investigation of its "meddling in the affairs of local communities." Gardner objected to the way that the Fund had become entangled in the civil rights movement and took particular exception to the role of Howard Fuller, who had been giving "inflammatory speech[es] in which he advocated the use of Black Power." As he laid out that indictment, Gardner also revealed a larger fear of biracial politics, the bugbear that had always lurked behind racial epithets and charges of "Negro rule." He shared reports from the eastern part of the state that Fund staff were speaking openly of the need for a "coalition . . . between poor whites and Negroes to give political power to the disadvantaged." Gardner expressed amazement that George Esser and the North Carolina Fund's board of directors countenanced such "revolutionary . . . attitudes." Their complicity in social unrest, the congressman insisted, left him no alternative but to appeal directly to the Fund's backers. "I am sending a complete report . . . to the Ford Foundation, the Reynolds Foundation, the Mary Reynolds Babcock Foundation, and the OEO," he announced, "asking that they suspend funds or exert some corrective pressure such as suspending Mr. Esser or Mr. Fuller. I am also sending [a report] to the Attorney General and the Secretary of State requesting a ruling on the status of the North Carolina Fund as a tax-free corporation in view of its complete political involvement."[30]

Esser and his board defied those attempts at intimidation. Within hours of Gardner's news conference, the board's executive committee approved a statement in which it rejected the congressman's accusations as "untrue, demagogic, and grossly distorted." The directors and other Fund supporters insisted that in Durham, Howard Fuller and the rank-and-file leadership of UOCI had worked to contain, not unleash, the threat of public disorder. When protesters took to the streets, Fuller organized a cadre of young marshals to ensure that the demonstrations remained nonviolent, even when angry whites threw bottles and hurled racial epithets. H. M. Michaux Jr., a prominent black attorney, and Charles D. Watts, a physician and medical director at the North Carolina Mutual Life Insurance Company, joined the effort to counter Gardner's accusations. In letters to Sargent Shriver, they insisted that "Howard Fuller must be given credit for having staved off any chance of a major riot. He should be commended for encouraging civic pride

A weary George Esser appears at a press conference to fend off attacks from Congressman Jim Gardner. Courtesy of the *Raleigh News & Observer* and the North Carolina State Archives.

in that group of people who have not had the opportunity. He should be commended for showing them that they had a voice in the formation of our government." As Michaux and Watts saw things, the "real agitators" — those who posed the greatest danger to public order — were politicians like Gardner, who had "seized upon" the urban unrest in Durham and across the country as "good campaign material."[31]

Watts Hill Jr. — one of Durham's leading business and civic leaders, a former member of the state legislature, chairman of the North Carolina Board of Higher Education, former chairman of the Durham Housing Authority, and, by his own admission, a member of the "white power structure" — added his voice to the chorus. "Howard Fuller," he advised Sargent Shriver, "the center of so much controversy, is a man whose assets far outweigh his liabilities. . . . [He] is the single person most responsible for there not being riots in Durham. Had he been withdrawn from the picture, there would have been a leaderless mob. I believe [he deserves] a commendation rather than a condemnation." Sounding like an rabble-rouser himself, Hill acknowledged the value of protest. "This community needs shaking at the very roots," he argued, "as does every community that I know of no matter where it is located. It is only out of tension, out of conflict . . . that change does take place. . . . Durham is immensely blessed to have an opportunity to listen to its people and to act. . . . We have a unique opportunity . . . to show what can be done. And we can't afford to lose this opportunity because we may never again have so great a one."[32]

The North Carolina Fund survived Gardner's assault. Its financial backers reaffirmed their support, the state attorney general found no cause for revoking the Fund's charter, and federal authorities exonerated Fuller and other antipoverty workers of violating prohibitions against partisan political activity. Nevertheless, Congressman Gardner had accomplished his purpose. He had gained for himself national recognition as a leading critic of Lyndon Johnson's Great Society; he had made antipoverty programs and their connection to black political participation into a wedge issue that would draw disaffected southern Democrats into a resurgent Republican movement; and he had driven forward an expanding bipartisan effort to rein in the War on Poverty.[33]

Gardner launched his attacks in the midst of protracted hearings on the budgetary reauthorization of the OEO held by the House Education and Labor Committee, on which he served as a junior minority member. The hearings began in June and dragged on through August, during which time 138 witnesses gave more than forty-five hundred pages of testimony. Walter Reuther, president of the United Auto Workers and a staunch champion of the Great Society, lent his support to the OEO, as did Billy Graham, fresh from his trip to inspect the Blevins Creek water project with Sargent Shriver. At a luncheon for lawmakers and business leaders, Graham insisted that the War on Poverty was "morally motivated. . . . I tell you today that I have never before testified for anything like I do for this poverty program. I was critical of it when it started. Now I'm a convert. It's not a giveaway program." Republicans in the House and Senate countered with calls to dismantle the OEO and replace it with an "Opportunity Crusade." They proposed that the agency's budget be parceled out among "more established Government departments, such as Health, and Welfare," and from there, that the money be directed to state and local welfare agencies — in effect, rolling the War on Poverty back to where it began. Shriver and the OEO held their own in this contest, until the nation's inner cities caught fire with civil unrest. From that point forward, the *New York Times* reported, "outside events began to shape the destiny of the poverty agency." Multiple committees in both houses of Congress launched investigations of the urban unrest. They called in mayors and chiefs of police, who gave credence to the charge that federally backed community action programs had run amok, that they were doing little more than "organizing people for the sake of organizing them . . . for attacks, rational and irrational, on what they perceived as the evil establishment."[34]

When the reauthorization legislation came up for debate in the fall of 1967, the Johnson administration feared that it lacked enough votes for passage. In the 1966 midterm elections, Democrats had lost forty-seven House seats to Republicans "from the South and the suburbs," most of whom—like Jim Gardner—identified the OEO "with aid to Negroes and [felt] that the summer riots proved that the aid [had] been counterproductive." "These newcomers," explained *New York Times* columnist Tom Wicker (himself a North Carolinian), found allies among old-line southern Democrats, who had been wary of the War on Poverty from the outset, and representatives of big-city political machines, "who wanted poverty projects brought under local political control." As a floor vote neared, OEO supporters had no choice but to "buy" back the votes of those disgruntled Democrats. They accomplished this by supporting a series of "bosses and boll weevil" amendments sponsored by Representative Edith Green of Oregon. The amendments stripped maximum feasible participation from OEO guidelines; required that community action programs operate as public rather than private, nonprofit organizations; "barred the use of funds or personnel in voter-registration drives"; and prohibited "community-action personnel from assisting or participating in any protest, demonstration, picketing, or 'similar group activities.'"[35]

When the final vote was taken in December, the OEO survived and was funded for another two years at levels close to those originally requested by the White House. But the War on Poverty had been "reduced to a helpless invalid," wrote Tom Wicker. The Green amendments had "deliver[ed] political control of community action programs to state and local public officials, a drastic change from the concept of encouraging the poor to take the lead in solving their own problems." The poor would continue to serve on community action boards, but they would now do so as clients "excluded from participation in the determination of policy." Congress, lamented Representative James H. Scheuer of New York City, had effectively "remove[d] the poor from power and decision making over programs designed to liberate them from the shackles of poverty."[36]

GEORGE ESSER AND HIS COWORKERS at the North Carolina Fund watched these developments with deepening concern. Like their conservative adversaries, they believed that the future of American democracy was on the line, but their understanding of the dangers that threatened the republic could not have been more different. Esser kept in his files a clipping from the *Vista*

Volunteer in which Richard Goodwin, an aide and speechwriter for Lyndon Johnson and for brothers John and Robert Kennedy, laid out the choices before the nation. "Most of us are for law and order," he said. "But we are also for justice. . . . We are not well served by those who tell us the answer to civil unrest is simply more and better police, harsher laws and swifter punishment, while refusing to confront the more profound and resistant horrors of poverty and racial hatred. They only offer a prescription for continuing and mounting unrest. If they seek only to protect the many against the few, they will inevitably diminish the well-being and liberty of every citizen."[37]

In speeches delivered across the state and nation and in articles written for policymakers and the general public, Esser threw himself into convincing others to acknowledge the wisdom of Goodwin's warning. He drew on lessons from the Fund and pleaded for rational judgment in the place of demagoguery. Esser urged Americans to listen to the dispossessed, and in listening to remember that theirs was "the language of frustrated people who live with the rats and open sewers and muddy streets and dilapidated housing; rats, sewers, streets, and housing that to *us* are statistics or lines on a map." In this instance, Esser displayed none of the naïveté to which he earlier had confessed. "I do not underestimate the difficulties," he said. "I understand, and have dealt with face to face, the unpleasant realities of prejudice and backlash and self-interest. I know that the 'haves' will not willingly share what they have labored to achieve with the 'have nots.' I know that many who *have* do not recognize that they have been given a push upward by the same systems that slammed doors in the faces of those who have not. Our task is demanding, difficult, challenging. We must move quickly and we must succeed. . . . We have no choice but to move decisively to recreate American democracy. If we should fail, an appropriate epitaph would be the words spoken by John F. Kennedy in March of 1962: 'Those who make peaceful revolutions impossible, make violent revolution inevitable.'"[38]

Esser's sense of urgency reflected not only his anxiety over national events, but also the influence of James McDonald, Nathan Garrett, and other members of his staff who had become increasingly frustrated with the intransigence of local leaders who were determined to protect their political and economic interests at all costs. They insisted that the agency cede the bulk of its financial resources and decision-making authority to the poor, particularly the black poor. Otherwise, the Fund risked watching from the sidelines as opponents rolled back its successes in building new community institutions and making room for the poor to participate in civic life. Persuaded by that argument, Esser and the board of directors accelerated the creation of a spin-off agency that they had originally planned to establish in 1968, at the time of the Fund's closing. In October 1967, they incorporated the Foundation for Community Development (FCD) and, over the next two years, provided it with grants that totaled more than $739,000 and consumed the bulk of the Fund's remaining private assets. That move harkened back to the Fund's beginnings, when Terry Sanford had turned to private philanthropy to finance an end run around entrenched power. The board reasoned that "'free' money"—politically unencumbered and "available for use in areas where public funds cannot be used"—would give FCD the latitude to continue mobilizing the poor and developing their "organizational and political strength."[39]

In establishing the Foundation for Community Development, the Fund's directors revealed how far they had traveled in their understanding of poverty and the means necessary to defeat it. They no longer spoke of individual pathologies and cultural deficiencies; instead, they cut straight to matters of political economy and moral accountability. "The wealth and resources of our nation are allocated as a result of the decisions of those who already possess wealth . . . and power," argued FCD's founding manifesto. "This group . . . does not include the poor. Consequently, the decisions made explicitly or implicitly mitigate against the poor. The poor are not poor because of their decisions but because of the decisions of others." This diagnosis freed the have-nots from the stigma of personal failure. It demanded not so much compassion or charity as inclusion in a genuinely democratic political and economic order.[40]

The Fund affirmed its support of those principles by ceding decision-making authority to an organization that represented—in membership and in action—the aspirations of people in poverty. FCD's leadership was black, battle-tested, and militant. At the outset, a majority of its board of directors came from antipoverty groups across the state. They included Rubye Gattis from UOCI, who served first as board treasurer and later as chair, and Alice Ballance, a founding member of PPOP. Nathan Garrett, the young CPA who had served as the Fund's director of finance, guided FCD as its top executive. Colleagues knew Garrett "as an extraordinarily intelligent, sensitive, candid and pragmatic leader." His calm demeanor complemented the more charismatic and oftentimes confrontational style of Howard Fuller, who worked as FCD's chief organizer. Together, the two men brought most of the Fund's community development staff to FCD and in early 1968 launched an aggressive campaign of grassroots mobilization. Fuller and his team traveled extensively to build alliances with and among civil rights and poor people's orga-

Nathan Garrett, executive director of the Foundation for Community Development. This picture was taken in the summer of 1964, shortly after Garrett joined the North Carolina Fund as its director of finance. Photograph by Billy E. Barnes, courtesy of the North Carolina Collection, Wilson Library, University of North Carolina at Chapel Hill, Billy Ebert Barnes Collection.

nizations—some of them well established, others still in the making. They offered incentive grants to support economic development initiatives that arose from within poor communities, sponsored workshops on leadership, and operated a program of citizenship education that acquainted participants with the inner workings of local government.[41]

At its height, FCD employed thirty office and field staff, along with dozens of summer interns recruited primarily from the state's black colleges and universities. Those young people revived the spirit of the original North Carolina Volunteers. After a crash course in the basics of community organizing, they joined FCD field-workers in small towns and cities down east and across the Piedmont, where they lived with local families and devoted their efforts to mobilizing the poor as a political force. The organizers followed a formula that Howard Fuller had perfected in Durham. They began by calling neighbors together to talk about common problems. It was then the organizer's job to help the group decide which issue to attack first and to develop an incremental protest strategy that, at each step, ratcheted up the confrontation. "If the priority area is housing," an FCD report advised, "the list might run as follows":

Step 1. A letter from the group to the *landlord* . . . asking for a meeting in one of the houses. . . .

Step 2. A delegation to the *landlord's place of business* or his *residence* . . . and a demand that repairs be made by a specific date.

Step 3. A delegation to the *housing inspector* [and delivery of] a written demand . . . to have houses inspected . . . for possible code violations.

Step 4. A delegation to the *mayor*.

Step 5. A large delegation to the *town council* [to] air the grievances publicly.

Step 6. Call a *public meeting* and announce a rent strike if all else fails.

"Throughout this process," community residents "develop[ed] their own cadre of leaders" and learned "that group action [could] bring results where individual efforts" failed.[42]

In community after community, these strategies upset arrangements of privilege and authority. In Fayetteville, a newly organized poor people's association signed up more than four thousand members, convened a countywide black unity conference, secured water service for residents of a run-down neighborhood who "had been pleading for such service for two years," and squeezed out of Governor Robert Scott "an invitation . . . to meet on welfare problems." In Wilson, the local Community Improvement Association "assumed the role of strategy-maker and negotiator" in a wildcat strike by sanitation workers, helping the men secure "sick leave benefits," overtime pay, and the establishment of a grievance committee. Further west, the Greensboro Association of Poor People (GAPP) assisted tenants in bringing suit against slumlords and organized a voter registration drive that "resulted in Greensboro's having the highest percentage of registered eligible Black voters in the state." And in the PPOP counties—where FCD leaders had learned some of their most important lessons—interns and foundation staff helped local activists register 6,585 new voters. That gave black residents of Hertford County the political muscle to defeat a $2.5 million hospital bond referendum and to demand accountability from county commissioners who had rejected both equitable representation on the hospital's planning board and a request "to make the hospital's services available to poor people at rates within their reach." Next door in Northampton County, this growing strength and group consciousness emboldened black citizens to demand an end to white violence and intimidation. In an act that would have been unthinkable even a few years earlier, they "took out an arrest warrant" for the sheriff after he slapped a defenseless black woman who was "a welfare recipient and epileptic."[43]

In short order, FCD proved its ability to create what one Fund official described as "healthy turmoil," but its successes also cast in sharp relief a fundamental weakness that from the beginning had confounded the North Carolina Fund and the larger War on Poverty. With the exception of WAMY's Blue Ridge Hearthside Crafts cooperative, which FCD helped fund, the agency had no presence in poor white communities. Nathan Garrett conceded that "no effective means has yet been found to organize the white poor in areas where there exists a sizeable" black population. That failure raised a question of critical importance: could blacks on their own exercise sufficient political power to secure an equitable redistribution of economic resources? If history and arithmetic offered any guidance, the answer was no. Blacks constituted less than 25 percent of North Carolina's total population, and in the past, divisions between blacks and poor whites had been the mechanism by which a system of racial capitalism immiserated both groups.[44]

That reality was not lost on Fund and FCD staff, who by late 1967 were calling urgently for the promotion of biracial politics as a means — arguably the only means — of winning the War on Poverty and the struggle for racial and economic justice. Whites, who comprised 61 percent of the state's poor, had the numbers necessary to mount a successful assault on entrenched privilege, and blacks, mobilized by the civil rights movement, had developed the organizational skills, institutions, and leadership to wage an effective campaign for economic and political reform. For John Salter, a veteran of civil rights and antipoverty battles in Mississippi and the PPOP counties, those circumstances evoked the lost promise of an earlier moment of struggle. "The interracial Populist vision" of the 1890s, he declared, "is as valid . . . now as it was almost eighty years ago." If the champions of the dispossessed were to break the back of Jim Crow as a system of racial and class subordination, they would have to surmount the challenge that had vexed progressive politics since the time of emancipation. They needed to find some means of establishing a sustainable alliance between the black and white poor, "chained [together] at the bottom of the economic ladder," and they needed to do so quickly.[45]

No one spoke more eloquently to the urgency of the moment than Martin Luther King Jr., who in December 1967 announced plans for his Poor People's Campaign, a march on Washington that would employ "massive civil disobedience . . . to force Congress and the Administration to provide 'jobs or income for all.'" He described the campaign as "a 'last chance' project to arouse the American conscience toward constructive democratic change." With passage of the Civil Rights Act of 1964 and the Voting Rights Act of 1965, the country had seemed to be on the verge of what King described on numerous occasions as a "true revolution of values," but the urban rebellions of the mid-1960s revealed the tenacity of racism and economic inequality. President Johnson had intended his Great Society initiatives as a means of rallying the nation in battle against those twin evils, until another war thousands of miles away in Southeast Asia diverted the nation's energies. "A few years ago," King observed in early 1967, "it seemed as if there was a real promise of hope for the poor — both black and white — through the poverty program. There were experiments, hopes, new beginnings. Then came the buildup in Vietnam, and I watched this program broken and eviscerated, as if it were some idle political plaything of a society gone mad on war." The war abroad siphoned off the nation's treasure "like some demonic destructive suction tube"; with "cruel irony," it sent poor "Negro and white boys . . . [to] kill and die together for a nation that [had] been unable to seat them together in the same schools." Tragically, the strains of an intractable conflict, a mounting body count, and the polarization of public opinion discredited Lyndon Johnson's presidency and fractured the liberal political alliances that undergirded his progressive social agenda. In hindsight, Johnson acknowledged the consequences of escalation in Vietnam: "[When] I left the woman I really loved — the Great Society — in order to get involved with that bitch of a war on the other side of the world, [then I risked losing] everything at home. All of my programs. All my hopes to feed the hungry and shelter the homeless. All my dreams to provide education and medical care to the browns and the blacks and the lame and the poor."[46]

King offered up his Poor People's Campaign as a cure for this "malady within the American spirit." He promised to field an army of the poor of all races that would fight for justice and redeem America's defining values at home and abroad. "Our only hope today," King declared, "lies in our ability to recapture [democracy's] revolutionary spirit and go out into a sometimes hostile world declaring eternal hostility to poverty, racism, and militarism." Friends and critics alike questioned King's opposition to the war in Vietnam and his embrace of the poor as guardians of the nation's fate. Writing in *Reader's Digest*, black journalist Carl Rowan described King as "utterly irresponsible"; *Life* magazine denounced him for preaching "demagogic slander that sounded like a script for Radio Hanoi"; the *Washington Post* charged that he had "diminished his usefulness to his cause, his country, his people"; and the *New York Times* warned that linking civil rights and antipoverty efforts to "the Vietnam issue" would be "both wasteful and self-defeating." Even allies within the black freedom movement questioned King's judgment. Didn't his call for an interracial attack on poverty risk diluting attention to the particular hardships of black Americans? "Aren't you a civil rights leader," others asked, and didn't endorsement of the peace movement jeopardize that position? King answered the naysayers by explaining that he remained true to his original principles. "In 1957 when a group of us formed the Southern Christian Leadership Conference," he noted, "we chose as our motto: 'To save the soul of America.' We were convinced that we could not limit our vision to certain rights for black people," but should promote as well "human rights" and the belief that "every man is an heir to a legacy of dignity and worth." For that reason, King insisted a decade later that the struggle for justice embrace people abroad who were "revolting against old systems of exploitation and oppression," and include at home all of the dispossessed. "It must not be just [for] black people," King insisted. "It must be [for] all poor people. We must include American Indians, Puerto Ricans, Mexicans, and even poor whites."[47]

With the same goal in mind, the North Carolina Fund commissioned John Salter to assess the challenges of interracial organizing and to provide tactical recommendations for mobilizing poor whites. As he prepared his report, Salter drew not only on his extensive organizing experiences, but also on the lessons of history. He began by describing the way that slavery and the white supremacy campaigns of the late nineteenth century had naturalized the "myth of Negro inferiority and white superiority," so that it was "believed as social fact by wide segments of the white population." Racism, he argued, was something more than "patterns of prejudice and discrimination." It was instead a system of authority and subordination that southern elites had used "to keep human beings, black and white, apart and to keep themselves in power."[48]

Through the civil rights movement, black southerners had begun to break down racist mythology and to awaken the nation's conscience. But poor whites remained afflicted with the "social sickness of racism," which blinded them to the realities of power and "caused them to operate against their own interests." As the structures of Jim Crow started to crumble, they asserted ever more forcefully their claim to racial superiority. They clung "to [their] white skin" and vented their "frustration on the Negro." Such behavior revealed white supremacy's capacity to pit those it oppressed against one another. "Never a holder of property or slaves, tenants or commercial power," Salter explained, "the poor white has, not unnaturally, aspired to this station and he and his descendants, right from the beginning, took the racist mythology of the same economic and political elite to which they, themselves, were subordinated. And in the context of all of his rarely fulfilled hopes and aspirations on the one hand and, on the other, his rank poverty and bitter

John Salter drew on his training as a sociologist and experience as a civil rights activist to make the case for an interracial campaign against poverty. Photograph by J. V. Henry, courtesy of Hunter Gray (John Salter), Pocatello, Idaho.

frustrations, the poor white became . . . the deadliest threat faced by his fellow victim — the black man."[49]

Salter pointed to the revival of the Ku Klux Klan as evidence of that tragic, self-defeating worldview. During the mid-1960s, North Carolina became "the most active Klan state in the nation." By 1965 the United Klans of America, the largest of several white supremacist organizations, had over twelve thousand dues-paying members in the state — more than in Mississippi and Alabama combined. Salter and other Fund staffers described that insurgency as "one of the most effective organizing efforts ever conducted among poor whites." The Klan, they argued, was one of the few places where poor whites could find a public voice. Since the turn of the century, one-party government — created and sustained by black disfranchisement — had muzzled debate around fundamental issues of social welfare and economic justice. Poor whites were, for all practical purposes, excluded from the political and civic life of local communities and the state at large. Similarly, fierce antiunionism, enforced by law and the police power of the state, had denied white workers the collective power that elsewhere in the country propelled blue-collar laborers into the lower middle class. By the mid-1960s, when organized labor was at its peak nationally, North Carolina remained one of the least unionized states in the nation and ranked near the bottom for manufacturing wages.[50]

Under those circumstances, the Klan became an outlet for broad-based grievances, directed at blacks but produced primarily by the forms of class subordination that left the white poor ill fed, ill clad, and ill housed. Salter, educated as a sociologist, described the resurgent Klan as a refuge for poor whites who were "angered by the knowledge that the world is passing [them] by, that [they are] sinking lower and lower in the social order. The Negro is [their] scapegoat, for [they know] that so long as the Negro can be kept in his place, there will be somebody on the social and economic scale who is lower than [they]. In the klavern, in [their] robes . . . [they find] the status that is denied [them] outside."[51]

Even as he took the measure of the Klan's resurgence, Salter remained optimistic that the Fund might find ways to tap into poor whites' frustration and channel it in a more constructive direction. He was no romantic or naive idealist. In Mississippi and in the Choanoke region he had confronted the Klan's tactics of "open terror," "intimidation and violence." "I traveled with a .38 Special S[mith] & W[esson] revolver," he recalled. "The Gandhian thing left me cold." But Salter did see, even in the Klan, the flickering possibility that poor whites might look across the color line and recognize the common source of black and white poverty. He pointed with guarded optimism to "minor miracles" in Durham. There, "poor people, ex-convicts, and students" had organized a group they called the North Carolina Justice Committee (NCJC), which picketed for prison reform. Lloyd Jacobs, King Kleagle of the Confederate Knights of the Ku Klux Klan, had set the protests in motion. He was a self-described "Working Man for the Working Man" and "friend to the Alcoholic" who ran for mayor on a promise to "Clean-Up . . . Clean-Out . . . [and] BEAT THE RING" of bankers, real estate developers, and industrialists who controlled Durham's city government. After a riot at the state's Central Prison in Raleigh, in which six inmates died and seventy were injured, Jacobs called on the National Association for the Advancement of Colored People (NAACP), Durham's Operation Breakthrough, and student civil rights activists from Duke University and the University of North Carolina to join him in a vigil outside the prison. "One of the main themes of the NCJC," explained the *Charlotte Observer*, was "the joining together of poor people of both races to fight their common problems." To that end, the NCJC provided advice and support to prisoners seeking parole and "worked for the establishment of a half-way house in Durham." When asked about the odd coalition that he led, Jacobs, who had served a short prison sentence of his own, told reporters that better treatment of inmates was "all that counted this round. 'The color of a man's skin doesn't matter.'" Jacobs did not put away his Klan robe, but he

Vote For	*A Working Man*
LLOYD JACOBS	*for the*
	Working Man.
For	
MAYOR	
We need a Clean-Up!	
. . . A Clean-Out . . .	
BEAT THE RING	A friend to the Alcoholic

did acknowledge, at least on this intensely personal issue, the need to make alliances with people he otherwise vilified.[52]

C. P. (Claiborne Paul) Ellis, Jacobs's Klan rival and compatriot, experienced an even more dramatic transformation. As Exalted Grand Cyclops of Durham's cell of the United Klans of America, he became intensely involved in local politics as an opponent of civil rights demonstrations and the North Carolina Fund's advocacy on behalf of the black poor. Ellis was not satisfied to hide behind the Klansman's mask; instead, he steered the organization into the public sphere. He regularly attended meetings of the city council, county commissioners, school board, and housing authority, where he argued bitterly with Howard Fuller, Ann Atwater, and Rubye Gattis. The experience was exhilarating, especially when Durham's power brokers seemed to acknowledge Ellis as a man of substance and stature. "We would go to the [city council meetings] and the blacks would be there and we'd be there," he recalled. "It was a confrontation every time. . . . We began to make some inroads with the city councilmen and county commissioners. . . . They didn't want integration either. . . . It wasn't long before councilmen would call me up: The blacks are coming up tonight and making outrageous demands. How about some of you people showing up and have a little balance?" Ellis and his Klan associates reveled in the attention and affirmation. "We'd load up our cars and we'd fill up half the council chambers, and the blacks the other half," he recalled. "During these times, I carried weapons to the meetings, outside my belt. We'd go there armed. We would wind up just hollering and fussing at each other."[53]

Ellis, however, had misread the situation. He thought that "because Durham's white elite despised blacks, they did not also despise him." A chance encounter on the street suggested how wrong he had been. "One day I was walking downtown," Ellis explained, "and a certain city council member saw me coming. I expected him to shake my hand because he was talking to me at night on the telephone. I had been in his home and visited with him. [But he] crossed the street [to avoid me]. Oh shit, I began to think, something's wrong here. Most of them are merchants or maybe an attorney, an insurance agent, people like that. As long as they kept low-income whites and low-income blacks fighting, they're gonna maintain control." "They didn't want to give up control to the blacks nor the Klan," Ellis said. "They were using us." That, the once swaggering Klansman reported, was "when I began to do some real serious thinking."[54]

Over time, Ellis came to comprehend the empty promise of white supremacy. In 1971, Durham's civic leaders invited him to join a community council charged with making recommendations for the peaceful desegregation of the city's schools. Ellis accepted the appointment as a proud representative of the Klan. At the council's first meeting, he again encountered Ann Atwater, a representative of Operation Breakthrough, and was dumbfounded when others in the group quickly elected the two of them to serve as cochairs. "A Klansman and a militant black woman," Ellis recalled, "co-chairmen of the school committee. It was impossible. How could I work with her? But . . . it was in our hands. We had to make it a success. This gave me another sense of belonging, a sense of pride. This helped the inferiority feeling I had. A man who has stood up publicly and said he despised black people, all of a sudden he was willing to work with them. Here's a chance for a low-income white man to be something. In spite of all my hatred for blacks and Jews and liberals, I accepted the job."[55]

Ellis wrestled with the conflict between his new sense of purpose and loyalty to his Klan brethren. "My old friends would call me at night: 'C. P., what the hell is wrong with you? You're selling out the white race.' This [began] to make me have guilt feelings. Am I doing right? Am I doing wrong? Here I am all of a sudden making an about-face and trying to deal with my feelings, my heart. My mind was beginning to open up. I was beginning to see what was right and what was wrong." Ellis and Atwater found opportunities "to talk and just reflect." Slowly, they came "to see, here we are, two people from the far ends of the fence, having identical problems, except hers being black and me being white. . . . The amazing thing about it, her and I, up to that point, [had] cussed each other, bawled each other, we hated each other. Up to that point, we didn't know each other. We didn't know we had things in common. . . . The whole world was opening up. . . . I was learning new truths that I had never learned before."⁵⁶

First among those truths was awareness of white supremacy's capacity to mystify relations of power. Like many poor whites, Ellis had labored without reward in a string of dead-end jobs. "I worked my butt off and just never seemed to break even," he recalled. "They say to abide by the law, go to church, do right and live for the Lord, and everything will work out. But it didn't work out. It just kept getting worse and worse." Ellis grew desperate for a way to make sense of his circumstances and to reclaim his dignity. "I really began to get bitter," he remembered. "I didn't know who to blame. . . . The natural person for me to hate would be black people. . . . So I began to admire the Klan. . . . The first night I went with the fellas . . . I was led into a large meeting room, and this was the time of my life! It was thrilling. Here's a guy who's worked all his life and struggled all his life to be something, and here's the moment to be something. I will never forget it. Four robed Klansmen led me into the hall. The lights were dim and the only thing you could see was an illuminated cross. . . . After I had taken my oath, there was loud applause going throughout the building, must of been at least 400 people. For this one little ol' person. It was a thrilling moment." Such experiences forged a bond of solidarity among Ellis's brethren. "The majority of [the Klansmen] are low-income whites," he observed, "people who really don't have a part in something. They have been shut out as well as blacks. . . . Deep down inside, we want to be part of this great society. Nobody listens, so we join these groups."⁵⁷

ELLIS'S STORY FOLLOWED CLOSELY the personal and collective transformation that Salter imagined for the South's white poor. "Only an interracial movement of the poor," he argued, "can dig deeply into the root causes of poverty and exert the pressure necessary to alleviate and cure these causes — and develop a genuinely democratic society." To realize that goal, activists would need to build on small victories like those that occurred in Durham and that surely changed individual lives in other places. Salter warned against writing off poor whites who had been blinded by racism. Their freedoms, he insisted, were "just as much at stake as the Negroes' [in] this system in which we live," and neither group would enjoy the fullness of American citizenship without "working together" for "common cause." Poverty warriors therefore had a moral obligation to take the tactics and objectives of the black freedom struggle into poor white communities and in that way create "a truly integrated Movement for the rights of all people." Echoing Martin Luther King and the religious faith of black allies in the Choanoke, Salter called for radical social change. He spoke expectantly of a new order built on love and justice, redemption and reconciliation. "The Ku Klux Klan and kindred groups notwithstanding," Salter insisted, "the vision of a New South—interracial, well-fed, free and democratic—and a nation functioning along those lines, is far from dead."[58]

That optimism—along with fear that a moment of historical possibility might yet be squandered—was widely shared among North Carolina Fund staff and leaders of the Foundation for Community Development. Howard Fuller, whom the conservative press characterized as a particularly threatening black agitator, argued forcefully for organizing across the color line. He insisted that "race-based solutions," while essential to battling poverty, were not sufficient to win the war, because, as he said, "fundamentally the problem is class." Fuller confounded his critics by supporting a campaign to bring poor whites into Durham's Operation Breakthrough. On the basis of his recommendation, the agency hired Harry Boyte, a young Duke graduate, and Richard Landerman, a "tall good-looking middle class Jewish Yankee with a hip SNCC organizing background," to work among residents of a white working-class neighborhood on the west side of Hayti, the large black district in which Ann Atwater lived. Their efforts mirrored Fuller's earlier interactions with Atwater's neighbors. Boyte and Landerman visited door-to-door and built relationships of trust by making themselves "useful raking lawns, running errands, and doing other such favors for people." In the process, they discovered "a sharp neighborhood woman" named Pattie Harrington, "who liked the idea of organizing people." She helped Boyte and Landerman pull together a group of parents "who wanted a park for their children" and recruited Cuba Matlock, a middle-aged carpenter, to supervise the project. During the early summer of 1967, residents cleared an undeveloped lot donated by Duke University. They "cut down the trees . . . created [a] baseball diamond," and built a "clubhouse out of lumber" scavenged from a vacant and condemned house. Patlock Park—named after the two residents who spearheaded the effort—quickly became a hub for self-help initiatives. More than 150 neighborhood children—black and white—bought membership cards to the park, which offset much of the expense of upkeep, and parents started a tutoring program staffed by local residents and college students. The clubhouse also served as a meeting place for adults who petitioned to be the first white neighborhood council represented on Operation Breakthrough's board of directors.[59]

Boyte and Landerman struggled to build on this initial success. In 1968, they secured a $90,000 grant from the OEO to fund ACT, an initiative that sought to reproduce in poor white communities the success of Operation Breakthrough and its spin-off, United Organizations for Community Improvement. By the summer of 1969, ACT employed thirty community organizers, published its own newspaper, supervised the activities of eleven neighborhood councils, operated a day care center, and joined with black activists from UOCI to establish a racially integrated health clinic staffed by student volunteers from Duke University's School of Medicine. But despite these successes, the organization had a difficult time establishing a lasting institutional presence in Durham's white working-class neighborhoods or stimulating similar initiatives in other North Carolina cities. ACT was effective in mobilizing its constituents around single issues and immediate community needs, but as Harry Boyte later observed, it was unable to bring neighborhoods together and to define an effective citywide political agenda. By the early 1970s, all but two of the "neighborhood councils [had] faded away."[60]

Efforts to integrate the white poor into a broader civil rights and antipoverty movement faced daunting obstacles—any one of which was capable of derailing the project, and none of which could be overcome in short order. Organizers labored under the enormous weight of history. The social and political marginalization of poor whites—combined with decades of determined, state-sanctioned antiunionism—had left white working-class communities bereft of institutions that could articulate shared grievances and give life to an oppositional culture. For that reason, poor whites lacked the social resources available to their black counterparts, who drew on a variety of autonomous institutions, particularly the church, to survive the assault of Jim Crow and to build a civil rights movement capable of pressing their demands for justice and equality. "Whereas black people have a history of advance through organized activity and consequent belief in the benefits of organization," Boyte and Landerman observed, "in the poor white community it is each man for himself."[61]

The strictures of white supremacy compounded that weakness. "Because a disproportionate number of people in America who are poor also are black or brown, and because of the way race operates in America," Howard Fuller explained, it was often impossible "to see the class character of the [poverty] problem.... Low-income white people had this thing beaten into their heads, that no matter how bad your situation is, you're better off than those black people. 'Yeah, you're poor but you're better off than these niggers.' And so, 'Why would you be out organizing? That's stuff that these niggers do.'" Fuller appreciated the irony of the situation. "In a very strange kind of way," he reasoned, "it puts poor white people at a disadvantage, because one of the questions they've got to deal with is, 'How can I be white and poor?'"[62]

Two answers were ready in the waiting, neither of which challenged class inequalities or encouraged organization across the color line. The first, deeply rooted in an American ethic of individualism, defined the poor as failures "in a world where . . . success was the reward for merit and . . . poverty the wages of sloth and stupidity." When internalized, that theory of poverty inflicted fresh injuries on those already wounded by economic hardship. It instructed the poor to turn their anger and frustration inward, to blame their lot in life on themselves and those closest to them. Doing so produced the despair and destructive behavior that so shocked members of the North Carolina Volunteers during the summers of 1964 and 1965, and that unsettled wamy's Friendly Home Visitors as they called on their less fortunate neighbors. Durham journalist Elizabeth Tornquist described the consequences for people she met in the city's poorest white neighborhoods. "Their psyches were far more run-down than their houses," she wrote. "In nearly every family, someone had served time on the roads or lived through the brutality of the state's Central Prison. . . . [Men] used whiskey or paregoric to escape from their guilt and shame . . . [and] women, haggard from childbirths and beatings, took the brunt of male [rage]." These were the hardships that produced Durham's King Kleagle, Lloyd Jacobs, and that Jacobs himself had sought to redress by spearheading biracial protests against prisoner abuse and campaigning for public office as a sympathetic "friend to the Alcoholic."[63]

The second explanation of white poverty was equally pernicious, especially when set against the backdrop of the civil rights movement. It blamed blacks and their political allies for robbing poor whites of jobs, tax dollars, and public resources. That idea had an ancient pedigree. Charles Aycock, Democratic gubernatorial candidate and champion of white supremacy in the watershed election of 1900, had argued something similar when he attributed the economic and political turmoil of the 1890s to the corrupting influence of black voters and the traitors to the white race with whom they were allied. Aycock promised that by excluding blacks from politics and enforcing strict one-party rule, he and fellow Democrats would shield poor whites from economic competition and usher in a new era of peace and prosperity. This line of reasoning was the stock-in-trade of the Ku Klux Klan, twentieth-century southern demagogues, and the uptown segregationists who joined the White Citizens' Council and fought against civil rights. In the late 1960s, as at the turn of the century, it served tightly interlocking purposes. It rendered unthinkable the idea that poor whites might join with blacks to organize for common cause, and by affirming the solidarity of white skin, it deflected class-based critiques of real inequalities of wealth and power.[64]

John Salter and the Fund's organizing staff scolded white liberals—including some members of the Fund's board of directors—for failing to contest those ways of thinking. They spoke, in large measure, from their own growing self-awareness, cultivated in earlier encounters with entrenched power and the limitations of uplift. Most liberals, the staffers argued, neither understood nor expressed much curiosity about the ways that race and class were intertwined in the production of poverty. They instead identified prejudice and discrimination—attitudes rather than structures of inequality—as the source of economic and social wrongs, and they attributed the South's ills largely to the bigotry of poor whites. Here again were echoes of the late nineteenth century, when the architects of white supremacy had peddled segregation and disfranchisement as progressive measures aimed at protecting vulnerable blacks from violence-prone poor whites and thus averting race war. Like those self-styled reformers, many middle-class liberals were contemptuous of the white poor and dismissed them out of hand as potential agents of change. That, John Salter argued, was a tragic miscalculation. By refusing to engage poor whites with respect, liberals became unwitting accomplices in the "traditions of the blood-dimmed South" and undercut their own ardent desire for racial harmony and peaceful prosperity. They demanded that lower-class whites surrender their bigotry but offered no substitute for the racism that had long served as a "pseudo solution" to the problems of poverty. At the end of the day, liberals left their less fortunate neighbors "still poor, still powerless, still alienated."[65]

Time, too, bedeviled the project of building an "interracial coalition of the poor and powerless." In 1968, a series of events that no one could have anticipated brought a seismic shift in American politics and rearranged the terrain on which the battle against poverty was being waged. The year had begun auspiciously. Martin Luther King Jr. had recently announced his Poor People's Campaign, and in March Robert F. Kennedy put himself forward as a candidate for the Democratic presidential nomination. Kennedy made issues of poverty and economic justice the centerpiece of his campaign. He was moved to do so by the scenes of abject deprivation he had witnessed in the Mississippi Delta, which he visited in April 1967 as part of a Senate subcommittee investigation of hunger in America. Kennedy subsequently wrote an introduction to *Hunger, U.S.A.*, a stinging exposé financed by the United Auto Workers and a number of private foundations intent on forcing "the President and the United States Congress to feed starving people." Then on April 4, 1968, King was assassinated in Memphis, where he had gone to support a strike by the city's mostly black sanitation workers. Two months later, a gunman's bullet ended Kennedy's life shortly after a victory in California's Democratic primary had positioned him as a front-runner for the party's presidential nomination. In August, violence broke out in the streets of Chicago, site of the Democratic National Convention. Mayor Richard Daley, who had been an ardent foe of the OEO's policy of maximum feasible participation and was an outspoken critic of efforts to link the war in Vietnam to social problems at home, unleashed his police force on the thousands of demonstrators who had converged on the city for the purpose of calling the Democratic Party to account on issues of foreign and domestic policy. The mayhem that ensued left in tatters the Great Society alliance of middle-class liberals, blue-collar workers, and blacks.[66]

Vice President Hubert Humphrey emerged from the Chicago convention as his party's nominee, poorly positioned for the contest ahead. His candidacy had been rammed through by party bosses, despite the fact that he had not entered a single primary election. He was hobbled on the left by his support for the war in Vietnam and, on the right, by his reputation as a champion of organized labor and civil rights. In the remaining months of the campaign, Humphrey failed to steal the momentum from his rivals, former Alabama governor George Wallace, who had established his own American Independent Party, and Republican candidate Richard Nixon. In his campaign brochure, Wallace promised to defend "states rights and local government" from meddling "bureaucrats and theoreticians in Washington," to stand by the police as "the thin line" between public safety and "complete anarchy in the streets," and to "deal with [antiwar activists] as they ought to be dealt with, as traitors." Nixon tapped into the same anxieties, but he cast his campaign in more moderate, coded language. In his acceptance speech at the Republican National Convention, he offered himself as a spokesperson for the "great majority of Americans, the forgotten Americans, the non shouters, the non demonstrators" who played by the rules, worked hard, saved, and paid their taxes. These were the "good people," the "decent people," the true reservoir of America's democratic values. To counter more directly Wallace's appeal to opponents of civil rights, Nixon turned to South Carolina senator Strom Thurmond, an archsegregationist whose endorsement assured southern whites of the candidate's right thinking on matters of race. He also relied on his vice presidential running mate, Maryland governor Spiro T. Agnew, who made no secret of his hostility toward black protesters. Nixon had taken particular notice of Agnew's response to riots in Baltimore in the days after

Martin Luther King's assassination. Making no effort to hide his anger, the governor chastised prominent blacks for yielding the city to "circuit-riding[,] Hanoi-visiting . . . caterwauling, riot-inciting, burn-America-down type" agitators.[67]

Thurmond and Agnew were key players in what Nixon and his lieutenants described as their "southern strategy." In an interview published in the *New York Times* in 1970, Kevin Phillips, one of Nixon's senior campaign advisers, explained the battle plan. "Republicans are never going to get more than 10 to 20 percent of the Negro vote and they don't need any more than that," he observed. But Republicans would be shortsighted if they sought to roll back or weaken civil rights legislation, particularly the Voting Rights Act of 1965. "The more Negroes who register as Democrats in the South," Phillips reasoned, "the sooner the Negrophobe whites will quit the Democrats and become Republicans. That's where the votes are. Without that prodding from the blacks, the whites will backslide into their old comfortable arrangement with the local Democrats." Or, to put the matter more simply, the key to victory was understanding, in Phillips's words, "who hates whom." Nixon won the 1968 election by less than 1 percent of the popular vote, but postelection polling revealed just how astute he and his campaign team had been about matters of strategy. Had Wallace dropped out of the race, four out of five of his supporters would have cast their ballots for Nixon, handing the Republican Party a victory across the South.[68]

EVENTS IN NORTH CAROLINA reflected the political polarization that Nixon so deftly encouraged and exploited. He won the state—the first Republican to do so since Herbert Hoover in 1928—and George Wallace came in second with 31 percent of the vote. Democrat Robert W. Scott spoiled Jim Gardner's political ambitions by defeating him in the gubernatorial election in 1968, but Scott, as George Esser confided to colleagues at the Ford Foundation, was "no Terry Sanford." He prevailed over Gardner by talking a tough law-and-order position on social dissent. When provoked, he made good on his campaign promises. In February 1969, black food workers at the University of North Carolina campus in Chapel Hill went on strike to protest poverty-level wages and employment practices that openly flaunted state and federal labor standards. The workers called on the Foundation for Community Development, particularly its lead organizer, Howard Fuller, for assistance. After an incident in which black students overturned tables in the cafeteria, Scott ordered state highway patrolmen to occupy the campus, despite objections from the chancellor and the president of the consolidated university system.

Colleges "are not places of refuge or asylum," the governor declared, nor did he need permission from university officials to maintain order.[69]

Three months later, violent conflict erupted at the historically black North Carolina Agricultural and Technical College (A&T) campus in Greensboro. The Foundation for Community Development had been active in the city for nearly a year, helping local residents who had formed the Greensboro Association of Poor People to organize voter registration drives, protest discrimination in employment and housing, and promote equitable access to health care. In the course of those activities, members of GAPP and their student allies at A&T were involved in a number of scuffles with police. The most serious trouble broke out when the two groups rallied behind a young man named Claude Barnes, who, because of his involvement with militant advocates of Black Power, was barred from running for election as president of the student council at the all-black Dudley High School. Despite the ban, Barnes's classmates cast six hundred write-in ballots for him, three times the number of "legal" votes received by his rival. When Dudley's principal refused to acknowledge the students' will, small groups began protesting outside the school. Day by day, their number increased and the situation grew more tense.[70]

Events spun out of control on May 21, when police teargassed a group of picketers who were throwing stones at one of the high school buildings. School authorities quickly dismissed classes, but a large number of students stayed behind and joined the confrontation. The mayhem that followed quickly spilled into the streets of the adjoining black neighborhood and onto the nearby A&T campus. At the request of Greensboro's mayor, Governor Scott sent National Guard troops to occupy black sections of the city. Throughout the night, activists holed up in two A&T dormitories traded gunfire with police, guardsmen, and white toughs who circled the area looking for trouble. The standoff ended at daybreak on May 23, when the governor ordered guardsmen to clear the residence halls by force. He later praised the troops for their restraint in handling the situation, but journalists revealed that even though the guardsmen had keys, they shot the locks off the doors to most students' rooms. A sweep of the buildings turned up nine rifles, two of which were operable.[71]

In the wake of the conflict in Greensboro, the Foundation for Community Development became a lightning rod for white fears of black revolution. A report commissioned by the Ford Foundation noted that FCD stood at "the leading edge of the struggle to help poor people in the state of North Carolina achieve not simply civil rights, but a substantial power to determine their own destinies." That success made the organization "anathema to the white establishment"—including many liberals who considered themselves to be friends of the civil rights movement and the North Carolina Fund. William Snider—editor of the *Greensboro Daily News*, an early champion of the Fund, and a member of an ad hoc committee appointed by George Esser to review FCD—acknowledged that "any organization that foments change . . . will always be controversial," but he also worried that Howard Fuller and his protégés had crossed the line by advocating "unlimited revolution."[72]

In its coverage of the Greensboro violence, the *Durham Morning Herald* implied that FCD was "committed to armed rebellion" and "overthrow of the United States and state governments." The newspaper took particular notice of police reports that Howard Fuller and an associate had purchased weapons and that a gas station attendant in Greensboro had spotted firearms in the trunk of a car owned by FCD. In a press release, Nathan Garrett was quick to defend his staff. He acknowledged that they owned rifles, acquired legally and properly licensed. "Howard Fuller has likely the most dangerous job in North Carolina," Garrett explained. "He [regularly] receives threats to his own safety and to his family's safety. . . . I [told him and his coworker] that if they felt that they needed this protection, certainly with memories of Martin King and Robert Kennedy and Medgar Evers and Malcolm X and John Kennedy fresh on my mind, I could not prevent them from taking legal steps to arm themselves against the possibility of crank threats becoming real dangers."[73]

As had happened previously with PPOP, UOCI, and WAMY, the controversy over the Foundation for Community Development quickly made its way to Washington. Throughout the spring and summer of 1969, the Senate Permanent Subcommittee on Investigations—chaired by Arkansas Democrat John L. McClellan, who had assumed the post after Joseph McCarthy's ouster in 1955—held hearings on "riots, civil and criminal disorders" in major cities and on college campuses across the country. The panel focused much of its attention on militant students at historically black institutions who were pressuring faculty and administrators to take a more confrontational stand in the ongoing freedom struggle. The activists' demands ranged from the creation of new courses in black studies to the adoption of fair employment practices for campus service workers, the equalization of funding for black and white public institutions, and the development of outreach programs to serve poor communities adjacent to the campuses.[74]

Students at A&T were closely connected to that rebellion. They had brought Black Power activist Stokely Carmichael to Greensboro to speak, and they had won from the faculty and administration significant changes in academic regulations and campus life, including the suspension of mandatory participation in military ROTC programs and the establishment of a center for the study and celebration of black history and culture. When the protests at Dudley High School began in early May, A&T students were hosting a national planning conference of the Student Organization for Black Unity, later the Youth Organization for Black Unity, which had been founded in Greensboro on March 9. The keynote speaker was Cleveland Sellers, a SNCC activist who had gone to prison for his involvement in civil rights demonstrations at South Carolina State College, where, in an incident that became known as the Orangeburg Massacre, police officers opened fire on unarmed students, killing three and wounding more than two dozen others. The Student Organization for Black Unity embraced a pan-Africanist agenda. Members joined with like-minded groups in North America and the Caribbean to provide support, material as well as moral, to anticolonial and antiapartheid struggles in Africa, and, at home, they became heavily involved in labor and community organizing. The unity conference banner strung across one of the entrances to the A&T campus exclaimed, "Welcome to the Revolution."[75]

McClellan and his Senate colleagues began their investigation with the assumption that campus turmoil, at A&T and elsewhere, had been instigated by radical agitators. They put the question directly to Greensboro police chief Paul B. Calhoun and the head of his department's intelligence division, S. N. Ford. McClellan asked, "Do you believe that any of this . . . violence would have occurred . . . except for the fact that outsiders . . . [had] come in there and incited and inflamed the community?" "In my opinion, it would not have occurred," Calhoun replied. "No sir," Ford agreed, "I don't." To South Dakota senator Karl E. Mundt, who in the 1940s and 1950s had distinguished himself as an ardent anticommunist, the situation appeared disturbingly familiar. He saw in Greensboro the work of "invaders from the outside"—not only black militants, but also program officers of the Ford Foundation. The trail of money and influence seemed all too easy to follow. Nelson Johnson, an A&T undergraduate, was the founding president of the Student Organization for Black Unity. Johnson also worked part-time for GAPP, which received partial funding from FCD, and FCD had operated during its first year and a half on money from Ford Foundation grants redirected—with Ford's approval—by the North Carolina Fund. Those relationships, Mundt declared, pointed to "a Pandora's box" that was not unique to Greensboro. He suggested to fellow senators that as they dug around elsewhere they would discover that the same "mischiefmakers from the outside" were the puppet masters of campus and community unrest. In Mundt's judgment, the connection between private philanthropy and social strife was "one of the most important puzzles [yet to] be unraveled." It raised serious questions: "Are we to have these foundations with tax exempt features or not?" If so, what role were they to play in shaping social policy and civic life, and how was their participation to be policed? In the coming months, the answers to those questions would determine the fate of the War on Poverty.[76]

FOR MORE THAN A DECADE, congressional critics had bristled at what Representative B. Carroll Reece, Republican of Tennessee, labeled "tax-exempt subversion." In 1954, Reece chaired a House investigation focused on the Ford Foundation, the Carnegie Endowment for International Peace, and the Rockefeller Foundation, all of which had responded to the domestic and global challenges of the Cold War by investing heavily in what Ford officials called "the difficult and sometimes controversial task of helping to realize democracy's goals." Their support of social science research, on topics that ranged from race relations to sexual behavior and family planning, and their efforts to promote international understanding and deescalation of the nuclear arms race led Reece to charge that "tax-exempt philanthropic foundations" had become a "principle source of Communist influence . . . in the United States." In 1957 he endorsed a proposal from Senator James Eastland's Senate Internal Security Subcommittee to withdraw tax-exempt status from any foundation that "contribut[ed] funds to a Communist or Communist-front organization" or promoted vaguely defined "Communist purposes." Such decisive action, Reece explained, would impose a "death sentence" on charitable bodies that promoted dissent and encouraged "attacks upon our social and governmental systems." Such dissent included opposition to racial segregation, which Eastland defended as "the law of God."[77]

The Eastland committee's proposal never became law, but concern over the power and influence of private philanthropies did not go away. Throughout the better part of the 1960s, Texas Democrat Wright Patman carried on a crusade against the foundations' "evasion of fiscal and moral responsibility to the Nation." As chairman of the Subcommittee on Foundations of the House Select Committee on Small Business, he amassed reams of evidence to document the questionable business practices of some foundation trustees. The abuses included self-dealing, a practice that offending foundations used to reward major contributors and officers with benefits such as loans and tax-sheltered investment opportunities, and the sole ownership of businesses that, thanks to their parent foundation's tax-exempt status, held a distinct advantage over tax-paying competitors. What irked Patman the most, however, was that many foundations had begun to direct their resources to activities outside traditional investments in charity and the arts. The congressman complained that the large philanthropies—especially Ford, the wealthiest of the lot—operated as shadow governments, free from public accountability. He charged that they invested in programs that were "repugnant" to ordinary Americans who paid the taxes from which they were exempted, and that they usurped the authority of Congress and other legislative bodies by making social policy outside the political process.[78]

The foundations' critics seized an opportunity to act on those grievances early in 1969, when President Nixon moved tax reform to the front of his legislative agenda. Voters were in a sour mood. Inflation, which had risen from 1.28 percent to 4.27 percent between 1964 and 1968, was eating away at middle-class earnings; the Treasury Department had reported that hundreds of the nation's richest citizens paid no tax at all, thanks to expansive definitions of charitable giving; and, as if to add insult to injury, Lyndon Johnson had pushed through Congress in the summer of 1967 a 10 percent surcharge on corporate and individual income taxes to cover the spiraling costs of the war in Vietnam. In that context, a call for tax fairness commanded broad bipartisan support and promised the newly elected president a handsome political dividend.[79]

When Nixon addressed the nation on tax reform, he spoke primarily of closing loopholes that favored wealthy individuals and corporations. He devoted only two sentences to the regulation of foundations, but when Congress turned to the work of crafting legislation that would ultimately become the Tax Reform Act of 1969, the focus shifted quickly to the need for stricter surveillance of private philanthropy. In the Senate hearings on civil disorders under way at the same time, Karl Mundt suggested that lawmakers use federal tax policy to rein in the Ford Foundation and other tax-exempt organizations that, as he saw it, abused their privileged status. Conservatives in the House had the same idea and, in fact, had already begun working the issue in public debates and in their private conversations with colleagues.[80]

Three of the most vocal critics were Representatives Albert W. Watson of South Carolina, John R. Rarick Sr. of Louisiana, and Benjamin B. Blackburn of Georgia, all of whom staked out positions on the far right. Watson and Rarick were elected as Democrats, but in 1964 Watson followed his mentor, Senator Strom Thurmond, in publicly endorsing the presidential candidacy of Barry Goldwater, and four years later, Rarick threw his support to George Wallace. The House Democratic Caucus stripped both men of their seniority.

Watson promptly resigned his seat in 1965 and won it back by running as a Republican in a special election. Rarick remained in the House until 1975. In 1988 he was a charter member of the avowedly white supremacist Council of Conservative Citizens, and in 1980 he ran as the presidential nominee of Wallace's American Independent Party, opposing Republican Ronald Reagan as too soft on the welfare state. Blackburn, much like North Carolina's Jim Gardner, was, in the words of a contemporary observer, "a Republican of the new breed . . . handsome, vigorous, crisp and direct in speech." He won election in an affluent Atlanta suburb in 1966 and was one of the first Republicans to represent the state of Georgia since the end of Reconstruction. Blackburn remained in the House through 1974, when he lost his seat amid public anger over Nixon's Watergate scandal. He then went to work as chairman of the conservative Heritage Foundation's board of directors, and in 1976 he helped create and served as president of the Southeastern Legal Foundation, a self-described "conservative alternative to the American Civil Liberties Union."[81]

Watson and Rarick fired early shots in the tax reform debate when they commended to their colleagues two lengthy indictments of the Ford Foundation. The piece that caught Watson's eye bore the provocative title *The Financiers of Revolution*. It was written by Allan C. Brownfeld, a staff attorney for the Senate Internal Security Subcommittee, and appeared under the imprint of the American Conservative Union (ACU), where Watson served as a board member. The ACU had been founded in 1964, immediately after Barry Goldwater's defeat, with the aim of unifying disparate strands of the conservative movement. Brownfeld's pamphlet was one of a number of ACU publications that took aim at Ford for financing "pilot projects for government welfare" and supporting civil rights organizations that practiced the "politics of blackmail." Brownfeld charged that rather than doing good, as might be expected of America's leading philanthropic organization, "Ford, using tax-free funds, helped to create the conditions of serious community disorder and violence, which the government, using further tax funds, had to oppose and from which order had to be restored."[82]

Rarick entered a similar piece—in its entirety—into the *Congressional Record*. It was written by Harold Lord Varney, a onetime propagandist for the Industrial Workers of the World who renounced his leftist leanings in 1920, embraced Italian fascism, and in 1934 founded *The Awakener*, an anti–New Deal and antiunion magazine. During the 1950s and 1960s, Varney contributed regularly to the *American Mercury*, an anti-Semitic and anticommunist publication that he helped edit from 1953 to 1961, and *American Opinion*, the journal of the John Birch Society, where his essay, "How the Ford Foundation Finances Revolution," appeared in November 1968. The exposé castigated foundation leaders for violating Henry Ford's intentions and political convictions. Varney noted that Ford had been a "life-long enemy" of Jewish conspirators identified in *The Protocols of the Elders of Zion* (a publication that Ford helped popularize in America) and their modern-day allies: communists, socialists, and fellow travelers. "Mr. Ford was determined that his vast wealth should not fall into the hands of the Leftist camarilla which had subverted the foundations endowed by [Andrew] Carnegie and [John D.] Rockefeller," Varney wrote. "Above all, he was adamant that the Ford fortune should not be used by the forces of the Left to help betray America." But that, Varney charged, was precisely what had happened.[83]

The Ford Foundation's original sin was to finance a "backwash . . . against 'McCarthyism.'" Varney faulted the philanthropy for underwriting a report that criticized the federal government's loyalty oath programs and for helping rescue the reputation of J. Robert Oppenheimer, father of the atomic bomb, who had lost his security clearance when charged with past communist ties. In Varney's telling of the tale, the foundation strayed even farther to the left in the mid-1960s, when its new president, McGeorge Bundy, a former Harvard dean and national security adviser to John F. Kennedy and Lyndon Johnson, announced that "meeting the needs of the Negro Revolution" would be his first priority. That decision supposedly drove the Ford Foundation into the arms of "black 'wild men'" such as North Carolina's Floyd B. McKissick, an advocate of Black Power and the national leader of the Congress of Racial Equality. Varney described every effort at self-determination as evidence of "black racism." He denounced civil rights leaders and organizations—from the NAACP's Legal Defense Fund and Martin Luther King Jr. to Bayard Rustin, Malcolm X, and Stokely Carmichael—as a "grim phalanx" of "terrorists, pornographers, and convicted perverts," and he excoriated "white organizations [that] support[ed] racial excesses," chief among them the National League of Women Voters, the National Council of Churches, the Anti-Defamation League, the "Red-staffed Southern Regional Council," and National Educational Television. Varney's language was angry and raw, but he said nothing that had not already been said by FBI director J. Edgar Hoover, George Wallace, Vice President Spiro Agnew, and, as we know from White House tapes, President Nixon when conferring privately with his aides.[84]

In appearances before both House and Senate committees working on tax reform, Congressman Blackburn widened the attack to include tax-exempt labor and religious organizations. Blackburn was an ardent supporter of right-to-work legislation and an outspoken opponent of unions. In his testimony, he took aim at the American Federation of Labor and Congress of Industrial Organizations' Committee on Political Education (COPE), which had been heavily involved in civil rights issues since the mid-1950s. COPE was an important backer of the bus boycott in Montgomery, Alabama, in 1955–56 and a lead contributor to the Southern Regional Council's Voter Education Project, which between 1962 and 1964 spent nearly $1 million to add 688,000 black citizens to voter registration rolls in the South. Such efforts, Blackburn charged, made COPE "one of the most militant political organs in the country." In his view, the committee also violated the tax code (an assertion that the Internal Revenue Service refuted) and the individual liberties of union members whose dues had been directed to causes they would not have approved. It was true that many white trade unionists in the South (and elsewhere) opposed advances in civil rights, but a significant minority—particularly among the state and local leadership—understood that registering black voters was "the only way labor [could] ever achieve its political program." Blackburn, too, grasped that point. He offered as evidence a letter from Reed Larson, executive vice president of the National Right to Work Committee, to the commissioner of the Internal Revenue Service. Larson complained that if unions were allowed to continue contributing to political causes, they would soon succeed in their "intent to bury" the right-to-work committee and its antiunion legislative agenda.[85]

Blackburn and Rarick leveled similar criticism at liberal religious organizations' meddling in politics. The most egregious offender, they argued, was the National Council of Churches, whose constituent communions— ranging from the African Methodist Episcopal Church to the Presbyterian Church in the United States and the Russian Orthodox Greek Catholic Church of America—were "driving force[s]" in the funding of "revolutionists." The congressmen backed that claim with a 1969 report from the Church League of America, itself a tax-exempt organization that had been founded in 1937 to oppose the New Deal. The report cataloged a decade of the council's transgressions, beginning in 1959 with calls for nuclear arms control and the peaceful resolution of conflict, and continuing on through the 1960s with the endorsement of student-led sit-ins, opposition to the draft, and support for activists who openly declared their intent to "confront leaders of the private sector and the religious community with the meaning of the black revolution." Those activities, the church league contended, were "purely political" and should not be financed with tax-exempt dollars. Worse yet, such social protest had "nothing to do with the historic mission of the Christian church to preach the Gospel of our Lord and Savior Jesus Christ to the uttermost parts of the earth and to win individual souls to Him and unto Everlasting Life."[86]

Out of that broad pool of complaint, two stories — both related to the Ford Foundation — acquired iconic status in the debates around tax reform. They were told and retold in Senate and House hearings and in the press, largely because they resonated with even moderate critics of private philanthropy and social activism. The first involved a $175,000 grant that Ford made to the Cleveland chapter of the Congress on Racial Equality to support a voter registration drive, community leadership training, and economic development programs. Supporters and opponents alike credited that intervention with putting enough new black voters on the rolls to elect Carl B. Stokes as the nation's first black big-city mayor. Stokes, who was the son of a domestic worker and whose father had died when he was two years old, defeated Seth Taft, the grandson of president William Howard Taft, by a razor-thin margin.[87]

For Ford's antagonists, the Cleveland election was an egregious example of "subsidiz[ing] one political view over another." Just how dangerous such meddling could become seemed to be demonstrated by the second story, a tale of the foundation's involvement in school reform in New York. In the summer of 1967, Ford provided the city's board of education with a grant to support an experiment in community control of schools in the predominantly black Ocean Hill–Brownsville section of Brooklyn. Republican mayor John Lindsay endorsed the initiative as a means of addressing black anger at white resistance to meaningful school desegregation and as a tactic for avoiding racial unrest. The board of education gave residents of the district the opportunity to elect their own local council and, through that council, the authority to govern neighborhood schools. Ocean Hill–Brownsville residents quickly became embroiled in a battle with the United Federation of Teachers (UFT) over the question of how classroom and management posts would be staffed. Activists pressed old grievances about the meager number of blacks within the ranks of teachers and administrators, and the union held the line on its contractual control of policies governing employment, tenure, and promotion. In 1968, when the neighborhood council attempted to replace a number of union members, the UFT called for a citywide strike that lasted from September through November. The conflict pitted predominantly white, Jewish teachers, for whom employment as educators had been an important means of upward mobility, against blacks who wanted the same for themselves and their children. The UFT ultimately won the contest, but that victory did little to appease the Ford Foundation's detractors. As they saw it,

Ford had plunged the city into chaos by capitulating to the false assumption that "riots are unavoidable or that they will cease when every Negro wrong has been righted and every white heart has been cleansed of prejudice and selfishness."[88]

Foundation leaders and their allies in Congress mounted a vigorous defense. In testimony before the House Ways and Means Committee, Alan Pifer, president of the Carnegie Corporation, appealed to the value that conservatives accorded free enterprise and limited government. "If we want multiple, private centers of initiative for the public good, if we think the principle of friendly competition by private organizations with an otherwise all-powerful, all-embracing Government is a good thing," he advised lawmakers, "we must be prepared to accept the consequences of that system. Private organizations, including foundations, will at times cause irritation. They will support unpopular causes. They will assist experiments which fail. Their actions will in some measure influence the development of public policies of which some may disapprove. But, equally, they will please some people . . . and show the way to a better life for all of us."[89]

Lest the costs of hobbling a vital third force in civic life remain unclear, Representative Edward P. Boland, Democrat of Massachusetts, spelled them out. He argued that critics had it wrong when they blamed private philanthropy for civil unrest. In point of fact, foundations had not so much provoked as "worked to help the Nation survive the racial ordeal." "We benefit from suggestions from all sides and groups," Boland insisted. "That is the genius of our system. But here [in the efforts to muzzle the foundations] we are striking at the very root of the democratic, pluralistic system. We are silencing a segment of society; we are cutting off communications; we are depriving our great deliberative body, and other legislative bodies, of what might be a point of view essential to our work." "I hope," Boland pleaded, "that [the Tax Reform Act of 1969] will not be remembered as the law which began a regressive trend in American history."[90]

When the House and Senate rolls were called, such appeals made little difference. A majority in Congress, regardless of party affiliation, agreed on the need to end the fiscal abuses — real and all too common — that Wright Patman had documented, and few were willing to risk siding with intellectuals and bureaucrats who, many voters believed, were "pouring out vast sums to remake American society in their own Leftist image." The Tax Reform Act of 1969 cleared the House by a vote of 381 to 2, and the Senate by a margin of 71 to 6. President Nixon signed it into law on December 30.[91]

The legislation imposed stringent new restraints on how foundations managed their money, including a sweeping prohibition against involvement in any effort to "influence legislation either through an attempt to affect public opinion or through communication with a member or employee or a legislative body or a government official who might participate in the formulation of legislation." The law also barred foundations from attempting to influence "the outcome of any specific election." Voter registration campaigns were allowed, but only if the organizations conducting them were active in at least five states, operated with grant support from at least five different sources, and received no more than 25 percent of their funds from any single donor — stipulations that were almost impossible to meet. The penalties for violating these regulations were harsh. Foundations could be fined 10 percent of the value of grants made to offending organizations, or 100 percent if the funds were not recovered, and foundation board members and administrators could be assessed personal fines of 2.5 percent or, in the case of unrecovered funds, as much as 50 percent of the value of misappropriated awards.[92]

To civil rights and antipoverty leaders, it seemed that the floor had been cut from under their feet. Whitney Young, president of the National Urban League, had earlier shared his misgivings with the Senate Finance Committee. "It has only been in very recent years," he testified, "that we have managed to acquire in our black community the kinds of sophistication and knowledge that make it possible for us to organize and to make our requests for resources to help ourselves and to meet our needs. And to have at this point in the game suddenly to be told that the rules are changing seem[s] . . . to say to black people . . . that 'the rules are changing only when you are about to be benefitted.'" In a letter to the *New York Times*, Roy Wilkins, executive director of the NAACP, was equally blunt. "Negro citizens are not deceived by the 'tax reform' label," he wrote. "They view the move (and rightly so) as an attempt to halt the increase in Negro voting strength. The Voting Rights Act of 1965 plus grants from foundations enabled organizations like the NAACP to increase registration of Negro voters by about 800,000 before the 1968 election. The total of black registrants in the Southern states rose to slightly more than two million out of a potential of five million. Now the Congress proposes to crush the rising participation of Negro voters in the election process under the guise of regulating the foundations." A "neat business," Wilkins concluded. "At one stroke prejudice against the Negro franchise, foundations and anyone who endangers the existing *status quo* by enlarging the number of voters, is satisfied. The record does not mention race. No, sir! It is one of tax reform."[93]

IN NORTH CAROLINA, THE FATE of the Foundation for Community Development revealed how the hostilities that fueled Nixon's new majority also choked off the democratic impulses of the civil rights and antipoverty struggles. Even before Congress had settled on the details of tax reform, Ford officials had begun to second-guess their backing for FCD and their involvement in the political mobilization of the poor. They were particularly unnerved by the McClellan committee's hearings on unrest in Greensboro and the suggestion that they were the underwriters of racial violence. Ford tabled a request from FCD for more than half a million dollars in continuing financial support and in June 1969 sent a review team to Durham with instructions to report back on the advisability of awarding the new grant.

'The team produced a strikingly conflicted document. It heaped praise on FCD as a "thoroughly professional" organization and described its leader, Nathan Garrett, as "one of the most capable poverty organization directors in the country." Those strengths positioned FCD at the "leading edge of the struggle to help poor people . . . achieve not simply civil rights, but a substantial power to determine their own destinies." According to Ford's own stated principles, this was precisely the kind of return on investment that the foundation was looking for. But in practice, there were also problems inherent in the relationship. The review team spoke bluntly about the political dangers Ford faced. "First," the team noted, "it is axiomatic that in southern states the most militant and effective advocates of the blacks and the poor are, as the NAACP was for years in the black belt, anathema to the white establishment. They are both feared and disliked by most whites. Secondly, FCD's community organizing efforts have occurred during the time of a revolution in black thought which has produced a new breed of tough, intelligent, young militants and a new wave of rhetoric which white Americans across the country . . . find harsh and frightening. Thirdly, such an organization is substantially more visible in a southern state than it is in a large, populous urban center, and its activities are more widely covered in the media." This was a prescription for the kind of trouble that many at Ford were increasingly eager to avoid. In the end, the review team recommended a three-month, stop-gap award of $90,000, enough to keep FCD alive while more "appropriate relationships [could] be worked out between the Foundation" and its client.[94]

Once President Nixon signed the tax reform act into law, there was little room left for maneuvering. On January 3, 1970, George Esser submitted to FCD and Ford a memorandum in which he urged extreme caution. Both organizations were very much in the public eye, which meant that they would face intense scrutiny and, if they ran afoul of the law, certain prosecution. Many of the legal details still needed to be worked out by the courts and the Internal Revenue Service, but one point was absolutely clear: FCD would have to cease "all community organization activity" and distance itself from the forms of political agitation it had purposefully instigated. With no options at their disposal, Garrett and his board of directors immediately severed FCD's relationships with the ten poor people's associations that it had helped establish. They cut off grant payments, retroactive to January 1, and called their field staff back to the main office in Durham. This retreat from grassroots mobilization left a void in communities across North Carolina, wrote Hugh Price, a black attorney and an urban affairs consultant for Ford. "Organizations which had been effective advocates for the poor were rendered virtually helpless by the withdrawal of FCD . . . support."[95]

At the same time, FCD found itself squeezed by shifting priorities at the Office of Economic Opportunity and the White House. In April 1969, the OEO announced a $900,000 grant, supplemented by $60,000 from the Department of Commerce, to fund an FCD-sponsored plan to reclaim part of Durham's historic black business district, much of which had been razed by urban renewal and the construction of the new Durham Freeway. Months earlier, FCD had chartered a community development corporation called United Durham and had begun raising capital from local citizens and applying for federal funds to finance a variety of enterprises, including two supermarkets, a manufacturing facility for modular housing, and a black-owned industrial and office park designed to capture some of the growth spawned by the nearby Research Triangle Park. "With the solid backing of Durham's low-income people" and "federal money on the way," a contemporary observer reported, "it seemed that [United Durham] would have smooth sailing. Then the fireworks began."[96]

As soon as the federal grants were made public, Durham's newspapers — the *Herald* and the *Sun*, both owned by the same publisher — and Republican leaders launched an all-out campaign to "save" the city from FCD's brand of community investment. They sought to tar United Durham with guilt by association. The papers reminded readers that FCD employed Howard Fuller — a "'Negro activist,' 'militant,' 'Black Power Advocate,' 'Advocate of the destruction of the Capitalist system'" — and insinuated that United Durham was a front for Fuller's "revolutionary" labors. State Republican Party chairman James Holshouser joined the fray. He was a resident of Boone and a member of that city's Jaycees; from that group's tangle with WAMY, he knew all too well the sort of trouble that the North Carolina Fund and its progeny could stir up. Holshouser called on officials in Washington to take "another look at the situation." "Federal funds should be channeled through the hands of responsible organizations," he reminded them, "and should not be used to feed the fires of unrest which cross North Carolina today." From Capitol Hill, Senator Strom Thurmond and Representative John Rarick added their voices to the chorus. Thurmond scolded the OEO for providing funds to an organization that would employ "such a man as Howard Fuller" — a known instigator of "agitation, and riots, and demonstrations" — and Rarick dismissed FCD as "a band of self-declared insurrectionists."[97]

FCD's adversaries expected the Nixon administration to cut off federal funds at once, but slowing the momentum of civil rights and antipoverty organizations — in Durham and elsewhere across the nation — required a more circumspect response. The immediate curtailment of antipoverty programs was sure to reignite urban unrest; Democrats still controlled Congress and, despite the ill will that many felt toward the OEO, a majority would undoubtedly close ranks against a frontal attack; and big-city mayors wanted to control federal largesse, not stop the flow of dollars. In the face of those obstacles, President Nixon and his advisers opted for a more indirect assault, or what White House aide John Ehrlichman described as a "zig-zag" strategy. Publicly, they would affirm their concern for the poor, and at the same time, they would take advantage of every opportunity to dismantle Lyndon Johnson's Great Society.[98]

Nixon's opening gambit was to appoint Donald H. Rumsfeld, a junior congressman from Illinois, to serve as director of the OEO. The president chose Rumsfeld — a Princeton graduate and former navy flight instructor — because he seemed tough enough to take on the do-gooders within the agency and their allies in Congress. Nixon would later remark, "He's a ruthless little bastard, be sure of that." As a congressman, Rumsfeld had voted against the Economic Opportunity Act; nevertheless, he chose his words carefully in his public statements and testimony before congressional committees. He presented himself as a cautious and prudent administrator, nothing like the hatchet man liberals feared had been sent to kill the OEO. When pressed on his intentions, Rumsfeld replied that he backed the president's request to increase, not reduce, the agency's budget and offered assurances that he preferred to undertake a thorough program of review before altering antipoverty projects. Those gentle pronouncements were but a thin veil. Nixon expected Rumsfeld to get "control of all the *meshuggenehs* who were driving governors and other people crazy," a task that demanded the steely assertion of authority.[99]

In the fall of 1970, Rumsfeld became embroiled in a particularly ugly con-

President Nixon meets in the Oval Office with new OEO director Donald Rumsfeld (center) and White House aides H. R. Haldeman (left) and John Ehrlichman (right). Courtesy of White House/Handout/CNP/Corbis.

frontation with Terry F. Lenzner, director of the OEO's Legal Services Program. The trouble began five months earlier, when Rumsfeld announced his plan to delegate Lenzner's budgetary and policymaking responsibilities to the managers of the OEO's ten regional field offices, all of whom were political appointees and only two of whom were attorneys. The OEO director insisted to Senate investigators that "regionalization" was "merely an administrative shuffle, not an emasculation." That explanation was brazenly disingenuous. As *Time* magazine and the *New York Times* reported, the 850 Legal Services offices across the nation were successfully suing local and state agencies to expand poor people's access to "welfare [services,] public housing and health care." The lawsuits constituted "one of the few continuing victories in the war on poverty" and, as might be expected, "produced howls loud enough to be heard in Washington." On November 20, Rumsfeld fired Lenzner without notice. That, Lenzner charged, was an act of pure political cynicism; it laid bare the Nixon administration's willingness to "trade the right of the poor to justice for potential votes." Rumsfeld refused to take the bait. When asked whether he would proceed with the regionalization of Legal Services now that Lenzner was out of the way, he demurred: he would wait, perhaps until after the next election, for a study committee to give him a report on the matter.[100]

Rumsfeld's actions reflected a broader desire within the Nixon administration to curtail Washington's role as a broker among competing economic and political interests. The federal government had taken on that responsibility during the New Deal, and in Lyndon Johnson's Great Society the mandate for an activist state was enlarged many times over. Federal agencies became for the dispossessed and disfranchised a forceful lever for dislodging local and private power. They removed segregationists from the schoolhouse door, enforced fairness in the voting booth, and demanded justice in courts of law. Nixon aimed to restrain that intrusion into local affairs with what he called a "new federalism." The idea was to decentralize control over social welfare programs, either by moving administrative authority out of Washington, as Rumsfeld had attempted with Legal Services, or by allocating federal funds in the form of block grants awarded directly to states and municipalities with few strings attached.

In the case of antipoverty efforts, the new federalism found one of its clearest expressions in the Nixon administration's handling of the Model Cities Program, which it had inherited from the Johnson administration. Congress launched the Model Cities initiative in 1966 to help coordinate the wide range of federal programs aimed at revitalizing urban neighborhoods. In keeping with the concept of maximum feasible participation, the original plan called for "widespread citizen participation" in planning the use of government funds. By the time Nixon took office, the Model Cities project was still "in the beginning stages," thanks largely to squabbling between Congress and big-city mayors. The White House initially showed little enthusiasm for the program; after all, it served a constituency — poor urban blacks — who did not vote Republican. But as was the case with the OEO, Nixon could not afford to pull the plug immediately. He worried about a possible backlash from civil rights groups and from city leaders who desperately needed federal dollars to pay for basic municipal services and to lubricate the patronage machines that kept them in office.[101]

Nixon's aides set up five separate commissions to study the Model Cities concept. The last one, chaired by Harvard professor of government Edward C. Banfield, produced recommendations that the president could live with. The commission concluded that the "model cities program was better than what went before" but that it could be improved if local authorities were given broader discretion in deciding how federal funds were spent. That advice was hardly surprising. In the 1950s, Banfield had helped originate the concept of a culture of poverty, and in a controversial 1968 study titled *The Unheavenly City*, he had attributed the plight of the poor to "an outlook and style of life [that] attaches no value to work, sacrifice, self-improvement, or service to family, friends, or community." In light of that understanding of America's urban crisis, there had never been much of a chance that Banfield would endorse policies that aimed to involve the poor in solving their own problems.[102]

The administration embraced Banfield's report and in September 1970 announced new guidelines that gave city governments authority to determine the needs of blighted areas and to spend Model Cities grants as they thought best. Local activists in Philadelphia and across the country sued the federal government for "illegally limiting citizen participation," and by early 1972 the courts had ruled twice in their favor. But the issue was moot. Wearied by the court battles and bureaucratic foot-dragging, the neighborhood groups in Philadelphia and many other cities disbanded. A year later, the White House announced that the Model Cities program would be suspended and that its budget would be combined with other federal allocations in consolidated revenue-sharing grants to municipalities. Those changes were written into law by the Housing and Community Development Act of 1974, which achieved the core objectives of the new federalism: it limited the power of Congress to specify how federal funds were spent at the community level, returned authority to local leaders, and denied the demands of inner-city residents that they be included in the democratic administration of public resources.[103]

On a parallel front, Nixon sought to co-opt black anger at white liberalism's unfulfilled promises of equality and opportunity. By 1968, many veterans of the civil rights struggle—disillusioned by white America's continuing refusal to share the nation's bounty—gave up on integration and embraced the idea of an independent, self-sufficient black economic sphere as their only hope for opportunity and advancement. That shift occurred across a wide political spectrum that ranged from the militant socialism of the Black Panthers to a more traditional faith in self-help and self-improvement. There was no more visionary proponent of the latter values than North Carolina's Floyd McKissick, who in 1968 resigned his post as director of CORE, switched his political loyalty to the Republican Party, and endorsed Nixon's presidential candidacy. In 1972, McKissick received a $14 million Model Cities grant to build Soul City, a utopian settlement in rural Warren County—one of the blackest and poorest in the state. He envisioned a town of up to forty-six thousand inhabitants in which black-owned businesses would flourish and residents would build a community "free of racism."[104]

Nixon saw in that spirit of black enterprise an opportunity to trump the Great Society in the field of civil rights. He appropriated the virtues of thrift, individual striving, and uplift that had seen black Americans through the worst of Jim Crow and repackaged them as a political slogan, "black capitalism." As improbable as that move might have seemed, it made sense on at least two levels. First, it gave a nod to voters in Nixon's conservative base, who viewed the free market rather than government programs as the surest instrument for lifting Americans out of poverty. Second, black capitalism was the only strategy for racial advancement that Nixon could genuinely endorse. Like many—perhaps a majority—of white Americans, he believed that "blacks were *genetically inferior* to whites." White House aides John Ehrlichman and Bob Haldeman listened on more than one occasion as the president explained that "all the Federal money and programs we could devise could not change that fact. . . . Blacks could never achieve parity—in intelligence, economic success, or social qualities; but . . . we should still do what we could for them, within reasonable limits, because it was 'right' to do so." From that perspective, what the black poor needed more than empowerment was rehabilitation—and black capitalism fit the bill.[105]

In a 1968 radio address, Nixon expounded on his alternative vision for civil rights. "Black extremists are guaranteed headlines when they shout 'burn' or 'get a gun,'" he told his listeners. "But much of the black militant talk these days is actually in terms far closer to the doctrines of free enterprise than to those of the welfarist '30s—terms of 'pride,' 'ownership,' 'private enterprise,' 'capital,' 'self-assurance,' 'self-respect'—the same qualities, the same characteristics, the same ideals, the same methods that for two centuries have been at the heart of American success." Nixon claimed to understand black militants better than they understood themselves. What most were asking for, he explained, was "not separation, but to be included . . . as owners, as entrepreneurs." Nixon pledged his support for black enterprise and promised that "from this [would] flow the rest—black pride, black jobs, black opportunity and yes, black power, in the best, the most constructive sense of that often misapplied term."[106]

Nixon vigorously promoted black capitalism. In March 1969, he created in the Department of Commerce a new agency called the Office of Minority Business Enterprise. He also directed his cabinet officers to develop plans for increasing the value of procurement contracts let to black-owned businesses and for directing federal deposits to black banks. The White House expended great energy on publicizing those initiatives. In their headier moments, Nixon aides imagined that black capitalism might wean some black voters from loyalty to the Democratic Party. "We ought to be thinking of material that will make points with the Negro," advised speechwriter Patrick Buchanan. "Maybe some of them can be sold on R[ichard] N[ixon]."[107]

The Foundation for Community Development responded to these shifting political currents with its own strategy of zig and zag. Ford officials pressed hard for the organization to align itself with the new directions in poverty work. "[They] push[ed] us more and more [toward] business development and entrepreneurial stuff," one FCD staffer recalled. Nathan Garrett and his team pushed back. They adopted the mantra of economic development, but in counterpoint to black capitalism, which Nixon and others cast in individualist terms, they offered their own notion of "*community* capitalism," which affirmed — and in significant ways extended — the radical democratic project that by the late 1960s defined the North Carolina Fund and the War on Poverty.[108]

In a 1970 proposal for continuing support from the Ford Foundation, Garrett spelled out the multiple forms of capital required to meet the needs of poor communities:

Economic capital. Garrett opened with a fundamental point of fact: the poor could not "pull themselves up by their own bootstraps," as so many insisted. Historically marginalized and impoverished communities did not possess the wealth, individually or collectively, to leverage their way up — to invest in a home, send a child to college, or secure a loan to start a business. "We recognize," Garrett wrote, "that healthy injections of capital from outside the poor community are necessary to achieve economic viability and that intensive assistance in planning and managing business ventures is essential." But equally important were the terms on which those investments were offered. In the absence of inclusive decision-making, economic development schemes ran the risk of replicating existing inequalities. Poor communities needed something more than jobs; they needed employment that paid a living wage, employers who invested in community institutions, and businesses that balanced profit with the public good.

Political capital. Garrett considered it no less axiomatic that opportunity "flow[ed] only to those who [were] sanctioned by the political system." Economic injustice would not be righted through supplication, he argued. Its correction required political mobilization, fair access to the ballot box, and admission to the council chambers of government. For any group of citizens — the rich no less than poor — those were the keys to participation in American democracy. They made it possible to wield the political power poor people would need to contest "unequal treatment under the law." Garrett offered a catalog of grievances: state statutes that limited and in some cases outlawed labor organizing, the courts' disproportionate use of the death penalty to punish black offenders, and local ordinances that restricted "public assembly, voting, and delivery of government services." To right these wrongs required that the poor be included in a vigorous and open debate, and that they have a place at the table when public policy was made. With those goals in mind, Garrett proposed that FCD shake things up by filing "constitutional test cases, using the services of the NAACP Legal Defense Fund, the American Civil Liberties Union, Black attorneys," and the law schools at the University of North Carolina in Chapel Hill and North Carolina Central University in Durham.

Social and intellectual capital. Success in those struggles would require effective leadership from men and women with the "ability to identify problems, to design programs and to marshal human, financial and physical resources." To teach those skills, Garrett proposed a leadership school that would raise up "a cadre of people" trained in "problem-solving and the planning of strategy and tactics," fluent in the use of "mass media as tools of change," and knowledgeable about "Black history and culture [and the] principles of community organization." To lead effectively, representatives of poor black communities would also need a thorough understanding of "social, economic and political policy." To that end, Garrett proposed "a marriage of Black institutions of higher learning to the Black community." FCD would use Ford resources to establish a consortium among North Carolina's eleven black colleges and universities and underwrite research on a broad range of issues, from urban renewal and welfare policy to health services and school desegregation.[109]

Garrett's plan crackled with new ideas, new ways of marshaling resources against the twin scourges of economic and racial injustice. Ford supported the plan with grants of roughly half a million dollars each in 1970 and 1971. The money continued to flow, in part, because George Esser had taken a short-term job as the foundation's lead strategist for the South, and because Nathan Garrett and Ford leaders had a long relationship of mutual respect. But in 1972, Esser moved to Atlanta to work as director of the Southern Regional Council and, with Nixon's reelection, the political tide was turning

Ford away from the social experiments of the 1960s. That year, program officers from Ford insisted that FCD drop its concern for politics, leadership training, and research to "focus more sharply" on business "venture development." "In our experience," they wrote, "programmatic concentration is the best way to [build] stable organizations which lead to lasting achievement."

The patronizing tone of that directive stung Garrett and his associates. When negotiations with Ford collapsed, they voted to end FCD's work rather than surrender their principles. Garrett explained that the "great majority of FCD board members and most of its . . . staff [had] an intimate acquaintance with the problems of poverty as a result of either having lived with the problems from infancy [or] having worked at trying to solve the problems for many years." That struggle had taught the necessity of engaging poor people as equal citizens rather than as clients of public welfare or private charity. Only maximum feasible participation—the inclusion of the poor in a robust democracy—had the muscle to rearrange relationships of power that produced poverty in a land of plenty. That remained a lesson worth fighting for.[110]

In January 1973, fresh from his landslide reelection victory over Democratic opponent George McGovern, Richard Nixon began a campaign to "snuff out" the Office of Economic Opportunity (OEO). He demanded the resignation of then director Phillip V. Sanchez and other senior staff, impounded millions of dollars of congressionally appropriated funds for antipoverty work, and zeroed out the agency in his proposed budget for fiscal year 1974. The president tapped conservative activist Howard J. Phillips to serve as interim director of the agency and to manage the "wrecking operation." As a Harvard undergraduate, Phillips had been a founding member of Young Americans for Freedom (YAF), a student organization sired by William F. Buckley Jr. In the early 1960s, YAF established chapters on college campuses across the nation and mobilized a new generation of Republican youth behind the presidential candidacy of Barry Goldwater. After graduation, Phillips served as chairman of the Republican Party in Boston and from there rose rapidly through the ranks. Working for the Republican National Committee (RNC), where he ran Opportunities Unlimited, a program designed to recruit young people and minorities into the GOP, Phillips traveled widely across the country and became acquainted with "every Republican state chairman, every governor, every one of the younger members of the House on the Republican side, [and] all the Senators." In 1970, that networking landed him a job as special assistant to then OEO director Donald Rumsfeld, to whom he had been introduced by Dick Cheney, Rumsfeld's protégé and Phillips's friend from the RNC. Rumsfeld tasked Phillips with a systematic review of OEO programs, with the explicit goal of exposing "an agency awash in waste, scandal, and radicalism."[1]

When Phillips assumed the directorship, he lost no time in rejecting the basic assumptions of antipoverty programs. The OEO, he told news reporters, had been founded on "Marxist notion[s]" and from the beginning had "defended the wrong values." The idea that the poor were "a class apart," animated by shared economic and political interests, was antithetical to the conception of America as a classless society, a land of opportunity founded on free enterprise and just rewards for hard work and individual responsibility. Phillips boasted that his assignment was to set those errors right, to get the federal government "out of the business of organizing welfare rights chapters, and farm workers unions, and rent strikes, and politicizing the poor." To that end, he announced his intention to close the OEO's ten regional offices, halted payment on grant obligations to local antipoverty projects, and set in motion a plan "to spin off a few OEO functions to other Government agencies and simply kill the rest."[2]

An internal OEO memorandum that was leaked to the press in February 1973 revealed that the White House had encouraged Phillips to complete his work quickly so that the agency's supporters in Congress would have no time to respond. Predictably, the plan riled Washington liberals, but the White House was caught off guard by complaints from conservative state and local leaders who otherwise had been wary of Great Society programs. Those officials warned that nearly a decade of federal spending had created a sense of entitlement among the poor and the agencies that served them; suddenly withdrawing that support would create not only hardship but the potential for violent unrest. Raleigh mayor Robert Bradshaw worried about the consequences of federal cutbacks on "racial tranquility in the state capital." "The people on the receiving end" were likely to become "real angry," he explained, "and we [mayors] can't even call out the National Guard." In a series of decisions between April and June, the federal courts resolved the issue, at least temporarily. Judges ruled that the Nixon administration had acted illegally by appointing Phillips interim director without Senate confirmation and by attempting to disband a congressionally mandated program without first seeking lawmakers' approval. The editors of the *New York Times* saw in the president's overreach parallels with abuses of power that were being revealed in the emerging Watergate scandal. "What is most disturbing" in the OEO matter, they wrote, "is not the fate of a particular agency or set of programs. Rather, it is that the Nixon Administration shows such open contempt for Congress. . . . There has seemed to be complete failure on the part of the President and his associates to understand the meaning of the rule of law." The pressure on Congress not to pull the plug on the OEO had been building since Phillips's appointment, when four thousand protesters descended on the Capitol in a single day to lobby lawmakers, and in May the Senate began its formal investigation of the Watergate break-in and the White House cover-up. On the defensive and outflanked by the OEO's allies, Nixon and his aides declared a truce. In June, the administration and Congress worked out a deal that included Howard Phillips's resignation, the appointment of a new OEO director confirmed by the Senate, and a continuing budget appropriation of $338 million.[3]

The OEO's reprieve was short-lived. On August 9, 1974, Nixon resigned and his vice president, former Michigan congressman Gerald Ford, replaced him in the Oval Office. Five months later, Ford signed a bill that abolished the poverty agency and transferred responsibility for its most controversial program—community action—to the newly created Community Services Administration. That stroke of the pen marked the end of Lyndon Johnson's grand social experiment. For Ford, it was an accomplishment long in the making. He had voted against the Economic Opportunity Act in 1964, and as House minority leader in 1966 and 1967 had spearheaded an effort by Republicans and conservative southern Democrats to replace the War on Poverty with an "Opportunity Crusade," which, had it been successful, would have given effective control over antipoverty programs to state and local politicians and private employers. The new Community Services Administration was designed to achieve the same result—it managed block grants to state and municipal governments, which, in turn, passed the dollars on to "local programs . . . accountable to local officials [and] conducted at local option."[4]

What followed was a protracted campaign to roll back federal programs that benefited the poor and to recast the way that Americans thought about the problem of poverty. The Republican right won an early battle in 1980 with the election of Ronald Reagan to the presidency. Reagan had built his political career on opposition to the social movements of the 1960s. In his inaugural address, he declared that "government is not the solution to our problem[s], government is the problem." That line echoed the message of "A Time for Choosing," the endorsement of Barry Goldwater that first brought Reagan to the national stage in 1964. Riding the tide of a tax revolt that had begun in his home state of California, the president pushed through Congress the Omnibus Budget Reconciliation Act of 1981, which contained provisions for up to $30 billion worth of reductions in federal spending. Programs that most directly aided the poor were particularly hard-hit. Expenditures for food stamps fell by 13.8 percent; funding for Aid to Families with Dependent Children (AFDC), the federal government's largest program for the poor, was cut by 14.3 percent; the budget for unemployment insurance declined by 17.4 percent; and outlays for job training programs were slashed by 38.6 percent. Not even Social Security—the most sacred of social welfare programs—was spared the budget knife. The White House and its congressional allies raised the retirement age from sixty-five to sixty-seven, increased the payroll tax rate for employers and employees, and lowered cost-of-living adjustments. At the same time, the Reagan administration's unprecedented peacetime deficit and tripling of the national debt—driven primarily by military expenditures—created a budget environment in which it was all but impossible to shield from inflation the benefits on which the poor most heavily relied. From the late 1970s to the late 1990s, the purchasing power of food stamps dropped by 37 percent and AFDC payments lost half of their constant-dollar value. Taken together, these federal policies amounted to what critics on the left termed a "war against the poor"—a "war in which government programs and individual behavior, not the production of want and insecurity, constitute[d] the enemies."[5]

Conservatives also triumphed in the 1980s by shifting public sympathy away from the poor and redefining them as an "underclass" that threatened the moral fabric of the nation. That achievement was underwritten by newly influential think tanks, most notably the American Enterprise Institute for Public Policy Research, a once obscure business association opposed to the New Deal, and the Heritage Foundation and the Manhattan Institute for Policy Research, both established in the 1970s with backing from right-leaning philanthropies such as the John M. Olin Foundation and North Carolina's Smith Richardson Foundation. These institutions aggressively promoted the work of a loose-knit group of social scientists who contested the assumptions on which the War on Poverty had been built.[6]

First in that cohort was political scientist Charles Murray, whose 1984 book *Losing Ground* offers a sweeping indictment of post–World War II American social policy. In it, Murray surveys issues ranging from crime and juvenile delinquency to employment, education, and poverty. Even when liberals were well intentioned, Murray argues, their interventions perpetuated rather than eliminated the problems they addressed. In the case of poverty, federal welfare programs created disincentives to work, undercut mainstream values of determination and personal responsibility, and fostered dependence on the public dole that was passed from generation to generation. Murray urges soft-hearted defenders of the welfare state to "stop kidding themselves," to quit meddling, and to leave the fate of the poor to individual choice and the judgment of the marketplace. "I am proposing triage . . . by self-selection," he writes. "In triage on the battlefield, the doctor makes the decision [about who lives or dies]. In our social triage, the decision is left up to the patient. The patient always has the right to say 'I can do x' and get a chance to prove it. Society always has the right to hold him to that pledge. The patient always has the right to fail. Society always has the right to let him."[7]

Lawrence Mead, whose book *Beyond Entitlement* appeared two years later, shared many of Murray's convictions about the dysfunctional values and behaviors of the poor, but he took a different position on government intervention. "The main problem with the welfare state," he writes, "is its *permissiveness*, not its size. Today poverty often arises from the functioning problems of the poor themselves, especially difficulties in getting through school, working, and keeping their families together. But the social programs that support the needy rarely set standards for them." In his diagnosis of poverty's causes and prescription for its remedy, Mead turned a blind eye to the working poor—the millions of Americans who labored in low-wage jobs yet could not afford life's basic necessities. He built his assessment of the poor in general on his view of the chronically unemployed. Those men and women, Mead argues, had chosen not to work and to demand welfare rights instead. "Voluntary nonwork seems to be common among welfare recipients," he observes, and in many instances is a self-conscious "political act." When the problem of poverty was defined in that way, the solution seemed obvious: the state should force the poor to engage in productive labor. In that way—and in that way only—would they learn the virtues from which the nation's broad middle class derived its success. The "rhetoric of equal rights that dominates [the politics of poverty] must be turned around to justify equal obligations as well," Mead insists.[8]

Murray and Mead provoked a chorus of protest from poverty scholars who challenged their methods and derided their conclusions. But their books resonated with many politicians and policymakers, and with ordinary Americans worried about an economy that was shedding blue-collar jobs and resentful of "handouts" to those they believed were not earning their way. Mead's work in particular captured the imagination of self-styled New Democrats, represented at the top by the Democratic Leadership Council (DLC) and its chairman, former Arkansas governor Bill Clinton. Following the party's defeat in the presidential election of 1988, which marked its third consecutive loss, members of the DLC were eager to identify issues that would steal votes from Republicans. Mead's argument for moving the poor from welfare to work seemed made to order. It spoke to social conservatives who wanted to discipline the poor—especially black unwed mothers, who had "demonstrated that, on their own, they do not make the wisest decisions"—and it appealed to a broad swath of suburban, middle-class voters who believed in the power of the marketplace to educate and uplift.[9]

In 1992, candidate Clinton made "end[ing] welfare as we know it" a tenet of his presidential campaign. He pledged to "provide people with the education, training, job placement assistance and child care they need for two years—so that they can break the cycle of dependency. After two years, those who can work will be required to go to work, either in the private sector or in meaningful community service jobs." That move to the right helped

Clinton win a narrow victory over Republican incumbent George H. W. Bush. Once in the White House, the new president and his aides seriously mismanaged their legislative agenda. They led with the polarizing issue of gays in the military and then bogged down in a battle to establish a national health care system. By 1994, the administration was adrift and vulnerable to attack from conservatives. Republicans, under the leadership of Speaker of the House Newt Gingrich, rallied behind what they called the "Contract with America," which demanded a wholesale repudiation of the New Deal and the Great Society. They gave Clinton a thumping in the 1994 midterm election by winning control of both houses of Congress. Over the next year, the administration and its Republican adversaries wrestled over welfare reform. The House, in particular, pushed for draconian measures, including the denial of support to children born to unwed mothers already on public assistance. In floor debates, some congressional representatives compared welfare recipients to wild animals that lose their survival skills when people give them food. John L. Mica, Republican of Florida, carried a sign that said, "Don't Feed the Alligators," which he explained in this way: "With our current handout, non-work welfare system, we've upset the natural order. We've created a system of dependency." Clinton twice vetoed bills he judged to be too extreme, but facing intense political pressure to deliver on his campaign promise, he finally agreed to a compromise. On August 22, 1996, he signed into law the Personal Responsibility and Work Opportunity Reconciliation Act. "The President was genuinely torn between his policy advisers and his political advisers," the *New York Times* reported. "Several Cabinet officers lobbied for a veto; political advisers urged Mr. Clinton to sign the bill, to show he was in step with public opinion."[10]

The 1996 legislation was revolutionary. It dismantled the sixty-one-year-old AFDC program of direct cash payments to the poor, replaced it with Temporary Assistance for Needy Families block grants to the states, and gave local officials wide latitude to "maintain, broaden or substantially curtail eligibility" for public assistance. The law also included punitive incentives to compel the poor to find work: income support was limited to no more than two consecutive years and no more than a total of five years in an individual's lifetime. Clinton softened the impact of those restrictions by insisting on new appropriations to pay for child care and job training while welfare recipients looked for employment, but he was less effective in defending other programs on which poor people relied. Congress reduced food stamp benefits by $28 billion over six years, with half of the savings to be taken from the "poorest of the poor—those with incomes below half of the poverty line"; cut spending on child nutrition by $2.9 billion; and slashed $7 billion from benefits for disabled children who received Supplemental Security Income.[11]

Welfare reform's primary objective was to move people off the dole, and in that regard it was strikingly successful. Within four years the national welfare caseload had been cut nearly in half, and by 2001 the percentage of the total population on welfare had been rolled back to a level not seen since the beginning of the War on Poverty. What happened to people when they went off of public assistance was more complicated. By 2002, 14 percent of welfare leavers had "no employment income, no working spouse, and no cash . . . or disability benefits." They were largely on their own and "'disconnected' from both the labor market and the welfare system." A majority of leavers—roughly 60 percent—found employment, usually in low-wage, part-time jobs that provided no health insurance or other benefits. These men and women were particularly vulnerable to the ups and downs of the economy; on average, a quarter of them returned to welfare within two years. Most poor families remained trapped on the bottom rungs of the economy. Even with a full-time worker, only one in six could lift itself out of poverty.[12]

The story of poverty in North Carolina in the wake of welfare reform is equally sobering. Economic development has created dazzling prosperity in the urban Piedmont, particularly along the I-85 corridor, anchored on one end by Charlotte, the nation's second-largest banking center, and on the other by Raleigh, one of the country's fastest-growing metropolitan areas. But even there, a significant gap persists between the haves and the have-nots. According to data compiled in 2007, in Durham County, home to Duke University and some of the world's largest pharmaceutical companies, nearly 20 percent of children live in poverty. Outside of this urban crescent, many residents of the state continue to be left behind. In the western mountain counties of Watauga, Avery, Mitchell, and Yancey, 17 percent of all inhabitants—and almost 22 percent of children—live in poverty. The overall figure would be significantly higher except for the presence of an increasing number of wealthy retirees in the area. To the east, the problem becomes truly critical. In the Choanoke counties, the poverty rate for children hovers close to 35 percent, and if all forty-one counties east of I-95 were considered to be a separate state, they would rank fifty-first in the nation by most measures of wealth and general well-being.[13]

That the problems of poverty in North Carolina have persisted is not for lack of trying to put them right. As the national War on Poverty was dismantled, many of the institutions and people who had been involved with the North Carolina Fund remained at their posts. Today, the North Carolina Community Action Association, founded in 1966 with the Fund's backing, has forty-two member agencies, including all but one of the original Fund-supported community action programs. Those agencies coordinate the work of thousands of volunteers and deliver a wide array of services, most of which the Office of Economic Opportunity inaugurated more than forty years ago: Head Start, housing weatherization, water and sewer improvements, job training, and rural transportation. The Manpower Development Corporation, a Fund spin-off known today simply as MDC, has its offices in Chapel Hill and manages programs across the South that improve the lives of the unemployed and the working poor. Its regular *State of the South* reports keep policymakers and the larger public up to date on critical economic and social issues facing the region. The two North Carolina philanthropies associated with the Fund—the Z. Smith Reynolds and Mary Reynolds Babcock Foundations—have remained actively committed to issues of poverty. Over the last forty years, they have poured millions of dollars into grassroots organizations, supporting projects on community economic development, democracy, civic engagement, and social justice. Their aim has been to promote inclusiveness and to build partnerships "across race, ethnic, economic and political differences." And then there are the people — most especially the people. Veterans of the North Carolina Fund went in many directions. Some became national leaders in their professions; others took their training abroad in the Peace Corps; and still others wielded influence as politicians, policymakers, public administrators, and community activists. The vast majority have lived quiet and committed lives as teachers, ministers, social workers, and health care professionals. Nearly all remember their Fund experience as a guide star. They look to it as a reminder of how "to be tolerant, to appreciate, to respect, and to care."[14]

We, too, have found value in telling the Fund's story. We have come to understand it as a source of inspiration and instruction for a new generation of Americans charting their own ways of combating poverty. Embedded in the Fund's approach were four principles that are as salient today as they were forty years ago:

> *Poverty is political.* It arises from neither accident nor simple misfortune, but is instead a product of deliberate efforts to establish an inequitable distribution of power, wealth, and opportunity. To fight poverty, therefore, is to take democracy seriously. It requires the cultivation of citi-

zenship and inclusion of the poor and other marginalized groups in an open deliberation of our obligations to one another and the rights and resources necessary to live a life of dignity and security.

Poverty diminishes us all. It deprives the poor of opportunities to realize their potential as creative and productive contributors to society, and it denies the nonpoor the benefit of their contributions. A world that is insensitive to the plight of the poor is less prosperous, less secure, and less just.

Eradicating poverty requires activism and advocacy. The work begins in the communities of the poor with the recruitment and training of local leaders and the identification of problems to be solved. It demands the political mobilization of the poor and a coordinated plan for attacking the scourge of poverty in the halls of government, in places of worship and civic organizations, in the media, in schools and health clinics, and in the classrooms and research centers of higher education. It requires moral courage and a willingness to confront the complicity of the affluent in unjust arrangements of privilege and power.

Eradicating poverty requires alliances. Change in an unjust society cannot come from reforming attitudes alone. It demands joint problem-solving and shared responses to common challenges. The poor must find ways to bridge the historical divisions that have been used to subordinate them, those who care for justice must contest the division of society "into 'we the people' and 'they the poor,'" and all of us must make an effort to create human relationships that bridge our differences and turn them into sources of strength rather than alienation.

The North Carolina Fund fell far short of victory in its battle against poverty, but as civil rights activist Roger Wilkins said of the Great Society, it made "a good beginning and it was far from the total failure and unmitigated mess its detractors claimed it to be." Lessons were learned and a foundation was laid to "await the next cycle" of struggle.[15]

Armed with those lessons we may yet fulfill the challenge that Martin Luther King Jr. laid before the nation nearly a half century ago. "Let us march on poverty until no American parent has to skip a meal so that their children may eat. March on poverty until no starved man walks the streets of our cities and towns in search of jobs that do not exist. Let us march on poverty until wrinkled stomachs in Mississippi are filled, and the idle industries of Appalachia are realized and revitalized, and broken lives in sweltering ghettos are mended and remolded."[16]

Notes

INTRODUCTION

1. Harrington, *Other America*, 1, 7, and Carter, *Politics of Rage*, 109.

2. "Fund Directors Named," *News and Observer*, July 19, 1963; Sanford, "Poverty's Challenge to the States," 77, 81–82; "Three Years of Change: Narrative History of the North Carolina Fund," series 1.1.1, folder 1, North Carolina Fund Records, Southern Historical Collection, Wilson Library, University of North Carolina at Chapel Hill (hereafter cited as NCFR); and "Advance Guard in War on Poverty," *Business Week*, May 30, 1964. Our understanding of the Fund has been influenced by a number of recent books on the war on poverty in the South, in addition to the broader literature cited in the notes and bibliography. See especially Ashmore, *Carry It On*; Germany, *New Orleans after the Promises*; Greene, *Our Separate Ways*; Kiffmeyer, *Reformers to Radicals*; and Shepard, *Rationing Justice*.

3. Inventory of the North Carolina Fund Records, 1962–1971, ⟨http://www.lib.unc.edu/mss/inv/n/North_Carolina_Fund.html#doe73⟩; *Budget, 1965–1967*, 218–21; *Budget, 1967–1969*, 174–76; and *Budget, 1969–1971*, 194–97.

4. Esser, "Role of a State-Wide Foundation in the War on Poverty," 92. Terry Sanford shared the Fund's story with readers across the nation in his article "The Case for the New South," *Look*, December 15, 1964.

5. King, "Our God Is Marching On!," ⟨http://mlk-kpp01.stanford.edu/index.php/kingpapers/article/our_god_is_marching_on/⟩.

6. Woodward, *Tom Watson*, 220. For a survey of this period in North Carolina, see Escott, *Many Excellent People*.

7. This "awakening" is, in and of itself, fascinating. It suggests, in part, the effects of the cultural and political amnesia created by the 1950s. Southern liberals of the 1930s and 1940s often possessed incisive understandings of poverty and offered sophisticated prescriptions for change. Nevertheless, the students and liberals of the 1960s had to "discover poverty" all over again, and they did so within a Cold War and culture-of-poverty framework that was much less useful than the class framework of earlier generations.

8. Harrington, *Other America*, 2, 122.

9. Esser, "Role of a State-Wide Foundation in the War on Poverty," 96.

10. Ibid., 108, and Barnes, "The North Carolina Fund," 2–3.

11. Fairbank interview.

12. Scott interview.

13. Draft report of the executive director of the North Carolina Fund, n.d., box 28, George H. Esser Papers, Southern Historical Collection, Wilson Library, University of North Carolina at Chapel Hill (hereafter cited as Esser Papers), and Zarefsky, *President Johnson's War on Poverty*, 124–25.

14. Joseph Flora, "Poor Power," box 33, Esser Papers.

15. "Poor Mobilize in Appalachia; Talk of March," *Louisville Courier-Journal and Times*, February 19, 1967.

16. "Separate Minority Views," box 18, James Carson Gardner Congressional and Political Papers, Southern Historical Collection, Wilson Library, University of North Carolina at Chapel Hill, and Quadagno, *Color of Welfare*.

17. Hugh Price, "FCD: A Unique Experiment in Community Development," March 1972, series 1.8, folder 887, NCFR, and "HR 13270, Key Problems Affecting Foundations, and Preferred Remedies," box 15, Esser Papers.

18. Reagan, "Address before a Joint Session of Congress," ⟨http://www.presidency.ucsb.edu⟩.

19. Offprint, George Esser, "Involving the Citizen in Decision-Making," *Nation's Cities*, May 1968, 13, box 32, Esser Papers.

CHAPTER 1

1. On the late nineteenth-century transformation of North Carolina's economy, see Hall, Leloudis, Korstad, Murphy, Jones, and Daly, *Like a Family*, and Escott, *Many Excellent People*.

2. Escott, *Many Excellent People*, 253; Hanchett, *Sorting Out the New South City*, 82; and Crow and Durden, *Maverick Republican*, 50.

3. Redding, *Making Race, Making Power*, 119.

4. "Chairman F. M. Simmons Issues a Patriotic and Able Address, Summing Up the Issues, and Appealing Eloquently to the White Voters to Redeem the State," *News and Observer*, November 3, 1898. See also Gilmore, *Gender and Jim Crow*, chap. 4.

5. 1898 Wilmington Race Riot Commission, *1898 Wilmington Race Riot Report*, ⟨http://www.ah.dcr.state.nc.us/1898-wrrc/report/report.htm⟩.

6. Leloudis, *Schooling the New South*, 135.

7. Ibid., 137–38.

8. Escott, *Many Excellent People*, 261; Redding, *Making Race, Making Power*, 14; *Annual Report of the Superintendent of Public Instruction of North Carolina . . . 1880*, 4–5; and Harlan, *Separate and Unequal*, 131.

9. Escott, *Many Excellent People*, 260, and Hanchett, *Sorting Out the New South City*, 3–4.

10. Hall, Leloudis, Korstad, Murphy, Jones, and Daly, *Like a Family*, 26; Wood, *Southern Capitalism*, 65, 78, 84; Tilley, *R. J. Reynolds Tobacco Company*; and Durden, *Dukes of Durham*.

11. Durden, *Dukes of Durham*, chaps. 9 and 11; MacNeill, "Town of a Hundred Millionaires"; Hall, Leloudis, Korstad, Murphy, Jones, and Daly, *Like a Family*, 30–31, 239–48; and Hanchett, *Sorting Out the New South City*, 187.

12. Carlton and Coclanis, *Confronting Southern Poverty*, 33, 42, 54–55, 59.

13. Ashby, *Frank Porter Graham*; Singal, *War Within*, chaps. 5, 9, and 10; and Saunders, "'A New Playwright of Tragic Power and Poetic Impulse.'"

14. Morrison, *Governor O. Max Gardner*; Abrams, *Conservative Constraints*, chap. 1; and Badger, *North Carolina and the New Deal*, chap. 1.

15. Chafe, *Civilities and Civil Rights*, 339; Badger, *North Carolina and the New Deal*, chap. 3; Abrams, *Conservative Constraints*, xvi; and Morrison, *Governor O. Max Gardner*, 62.

16. Covington and Ellis, *Terry Sanford*, 3–4, 38, and Drescher, *Triumph of Good Will*, 6–7.

17. Covington and Ellis, *Terry Sanford*, 32–33, 41–42; Drescher, *Triumph of Good Will*, 9; and Abrams, *Conservative Constraints*, 218.

18. Covington and Ellis, *Terry Sanford*, chap. 5.

19. Drescher, *Triumph of Good Will*, 25.

20. Egerton, *Speak Now against the Day*, 306, and Korstad, *Civil Rights Unionism*, 202, 310. At the time of its victory at Reynolds, the union was known as the United Cannery, Agricultural, Packing, and Allied Workers of America. It soon changed its name that same year to reflect the addition of thousands of tobacco workers to its ranks.

21. Egerton, *Speak Now against the Day*, 422, and Covington and Ellis, *Terry Sanford*, 88.

22. Uesugi, "Gender, Race, and the Cold War," 269, 294, 306, and Korstad, *Civil Rights Unionism*, 363.

23. Powell, *Dictionary of North Carolina Biography*, 5:306, and Covington and Ellis, *Terry Sanford*, 112–13.

24. Wilson and Clark, "Dr. Frank"; Powell, *Dictionary of North Carolina Biography*, 5:392; and Pleasants and Burns, *Frank Porter Graham*, 2, 61, 258.

25. Covington and Ellis, *Terry Sanford*, 104, 130, and Drescher, *Triumph of Good Will*, 11–13.

26. Pleasants and Burns, *Frank Porter Graham*, 186–202.

27. President's Committee on Civil Rights, *To Secure These Rights*, ⟨http://www .trumanlibrary.org/civilrights/srights1.htm⟩, 166.

28. Pleasants and Burns, *Frank Porter Graham*, 140, 223.

29. Ibid., 212, 228–29.

30. Ibid., 244, 256–63.

31. Korstad, *Civil Rights Unionism*.

32. Griffith, *Crisis of American Labor*, and Minchin, *What Do We Need a Union For?*

33. Korstad, *Civil Rights Unionism*, 413–19; Pleasants and Burns, *Frank Porter Graham*, 247; Morgan, *Redneck Liberal*; and Bilbo, *Take Your Choice*.

34. Korstad, *Civil Rights Unionism*, 377–78, and Egerton, *Speak Now against the Day*, 556–57.

35. Egerton, *Speak Now against the Day*, 557–60, and Scales, *Cause at Heart*.

36. Pleasants and Burns, *Frank Porter Graham*, 212–13, and Drescher, *Triumph of Good Will*, 3–5.

37. Covington and Ellis, *Terry Sanford*, 159–60.

38. Drescher, *Triumph of Good Will*, 5, 21, and Covington and Ellis, *Terry Sanford*, 130.

39. *Brown v. Board of Education of Topeka*, 347 U.S. 483 (1954), and Covington and Ellis, *Terry Sanford*, 136.

40. Covington and Ellis, *Terry Sanford*, 136–38.

41. Drescher, *Triumph of Good Will*, 16–19, and Covington and Ellis, *Terry Sanford*, 136–41.

42. Chafe, *Civilities and Civil Rights*, 16, 65–66, 82; Douglas, *Reading, Writing, and Race*, 27; and Covington and Ellis, *Terry Sanford*, 137–38.

43. Covington and Ellis, *Terry Sanford*, 147–51, and Chafe, *Civilities and Civil Rights*, 66–82.

44. Lake interview; Drescher, *Triumph of Good Will*, 44–46; Kinlaw, "'Tenants and Tories,'" 15; and *Brown v. Board of Education of Topeka*, 349 U.S. 294 (1955).

45. Chafe, *Civilities and Civil Rights*, 73–74, and Covington and Ellis, *Terry Sanford*, 156.

46. Covington and Ellis, *Terry Sanford*, 174–75, and Drescher, *Triumph of Good Will*, 51–52.

47. Chafe, *Civilities and Civil Rights*, 97, 106, and Batchelor, "Rule of Law," 259, 352–55.

48. Covington and Ellis, *Terry Sanford*, 162.

49. Drescher, *Triumph of Good Will*, 67.

50. Ibid., 27.

51. Ibid., 67. On the Good Health Campaign, see Korstad, *Dreaming of a Time*, 63–66. On the Research Triangle Park and the scale of new industrial development, see Link, *Generosity of Spirit*, and Covington and Ellis, *North Carolina Century*, 493.

52. Drescher, *Triumph of Good Will*, 71–75, 98–99, and Chafe, *Civilities and Civil Rights*, 131. On Sanford's desire to avoid race as a campaign issue, see Ehle, *Free Men*, 57.

53. Lake interview, and Drescher, *Triumph of Good Will*, 46–49.

54. Drescher, *Triumph of Good Will*, 49–50.

55. Ibid., 52–54, 87–88, and Batchelor, "Rule of Law," 251–52.

56. Drescher, *Triumph of Good Will*, 162, 170–72, and Covington and Ellis, *Terry Sanford*, 250–51.

57. Drescher, *Triumph of Good Will*, 59–61, and Sanford, *But What about the People?*, 16.

58. Drescher, *Triumph of Good Will*, 142, 168–69, 194, and Covington and Ellis, *Terry Sanford*, 231.

59. Drescher, *Triumph of Good Will*, 217, and Covington and Ellis, *Terry Sanford*, 243.

60. Leloudis, *Schooling the New South*, 179.

61. Covington and Ellis, *Terry Sanford*, 238, and Drescher, *Triumph of Good Will*, 261.

62. Covington and Ellis, *Terry Sanford*, 192–94.

63. Sanford, *But What about the People?*, 7, 19, 24–25, 30–32; Lefler, *History of North Carolina*, 2:791–93; and Covington and Ellis, *Terry Sanford*, 256–57, 259.

64. Covington and Ellis, *Terry Sanford*, 262.

65. Carson et al., *Eyes on the Prize Civil Rights Reader*, 108; Houser and Rustin, *We Challenged Jim Crow!*; "Race Incidents Arise after Bus Seating Arrests," *Daily Tar Heel*, April 14, 1947; "4 Men Testing Law against Segregation Placed under Arrest," *Chapel Hill Weekly*, April 18, 1947; and Peck, "First Freedom Ride."

66. Covington and Ellis, *North Carolina Century*, 576–79, and Covington and Ellis, *Terry Sanford*, 284.

67. Covington and Ellis, *Terry Sanford*, 274–75, and Drescher, *Triumph of Good Will*, 182.

68. Manuscript containing notes for an abandoned book on Terry Sanford's term as governor, subseries 3.1, box 174, Records and Papers of Terry Sanford, Rare Book, Manuscript, and Special Collections Library, Duke University, Durham, N.C. (hereafter cited as Records and Papers of Terry Sanford).

69. Covington and Ellis, *Terry Sanford*, 275, 281–82, 284–85. John Larkins was born in Wilmington in 1913. He earned a B.A. in sociology at Shaw University and later pursued an M.A. from Atlanta University's School of Social Work, where W. E. B. Du Bois served as dean. Larkins served for three decades as a civil rights consultant to various state agencies and taught part-time at Shaw University and St. Augustine's College. John Wheeler was born in Kittrell in 1908. He graduated from Morehouse College in 1929 and began working for Mechanics and Farmers Bank that same year. Wheeler helped found the Durham Committee on Negro Affairs in 1935 and played a critical role as a liaison between Durham's black

middle-class establishment and more militant youth and working-class activists. Powell, *Dictionary of North Carolina Biography*, 4:24, 6:166–67.

70. Covington and Ellis, *Terry Sanford*, 329, and Sanford, *But What about the People?*, 3, 12, 121–23.

71. Covington and Ellis, *Terry Sanford*, 288–89, and Sanford, *But What about the People?*, 123.

72. Manuscript containing notes for an abandoned book on Terry Sanford's term as governor, subseries 3.1, box 174, Records and Papers of Terry Sanford.

73. Ibid.

74. "Excerpts from an Address by Governor Terry Sanford to Methodist Men of Gastonia District," in ibid., and Covington and Ellis, *Terry Sanford*, 290.

75. Covington and Ellis, *Terry Sanford*, 290, and "Commission on Secondary Schools of the Southern Association of Colleges and Schools," November 28, 1962, in Mitchell, *Messages, Addresses, and Public Papers of Terry Sanford*, 301–7.

76. Ehle, *Free Men*, 56–57.

77. Ibid., 56–62; Covington and Ellis, *Terry Sanford*, 295; Drescher, *Triumph of Good Will*, 172; "Observations for a Second Century," in manuscript containing notes for an abandoned book on Terry Sanford's term as governor, subseries 3.1, box 174, Records and Papers of Terry Sanford; and film of Sanford's address to the North Carolina Press Association, series 6.2, VT3531/1a, Terry Sanford Papers, Southern Historical Collection, Wilson Library, University of North Carolina at Chapel Hill.

78. Sanford, *But What about the People?*, 3–4, 13; Covington and Ellis, *Terry Sanford*, 311; and "Fraternity's Award Goes to Sanford," *Greensboro Daily News*, April 28, 1963.

79. Connor and Poe, *Life and Speeches of Charles Brantley Aycock*, 250.

CHAPTER 2

1. Harrington, *Other America*, 2, 6–7.

2. Brooks, *Dimensions of Poverty*, 3–4, and *The North Carolina Fund: Program and Policies*, series 1.1.1, folder 8, North Carolina Fund Records, Southern Historical Collection, Wilson Library, University of North Carolina at Chapel Hill (hereafter cited as NCFR). On the poverty threshold, see *Economic Report of the President, 1964*, chap. 2, 55–84, and Fisher, "Development of the Orshansky Poverty Thresholds," ⟨http://www.census.gov/hhes/www/povmeas/papers/orshansky.html#N_91⟩.

3. Lewis, *La Vida*, xliii, and Harrington, *Other America*, 12, 179. See also Lewis, *Children of Sánchez*; Lewis, "Culture of Poverty"; and Banfield, *Moral Basis of a Backward Society*.

4. Sanford, *But What about the People?*, viii, 4.

5. Covington and Ellis, *Terry Sanford*, and Sanford, *But What about the People?*, 50–51, 125. See also Covington and Ellis, *North Carolina Century*, 76–79.

6. Covington and Ellis, *Terry Sanford*, 238, and Leloudis, *Schooling the New South*.

7. Memorandum from John Ehle to Terry Sanford, November 9, 1962, reel 6P, Subject File of the Special Assistant to the Governor on Education and Cultural Affairs, 1962–1964, Official Papers of Governor Terry Sanford, North Carolina Division of Archives and History, Raleigh (hereafter cited as Sanford Governor's Papers), and Covington and Ellis, *Terry Sanford*, 301–3.

8. Terry Sanford to Henry Heald, September 21, 1962, reel 6P, Subject File of the Special Assistant to the Governor on Education and Cultural Affairs, 1962–1964, Sanford Governor's Papers.

9. Macdonald, *Ford Foundation*, 130–37.

10. Ibid., 137–59.

11. Ibid., 4, 19–35.

12. Esposito, *Conscience and Community*, xv–xxxvi, and Ylvisaker interview.

13. Ylvisaker interview, 19–23, and O'Connor, *Poverty Knowledge*, 130–31.

14. Esposito, *Conscience and Community*, xxi–xxiv, and Paul Ylvisaker, "Community Action: A Response to Some Unfinished Business," an address at the Citizens' Conference on Community Planning, Indianapolis, Ind., January 11, 1963, reel 6P, Subject File of the Special Assistant to the Governor on Education and Cultural Affairs, 1962–1964, Sanford Governor's Papers.

15. Ylvisaker interview; and Ylvisaker, "Community Action: A Response to Some Unfinished Business," an address at the Citizens' Conference on Community Planning, Indianapolis, Ind., January 11, 1963, and Terry Sanford to Henry Heald, November 29, 1962, reel 6P, Subject File of the Special Assistant to the Governor on Education and Cultural Affairs, 1962–1964, Sanford Governor's Papers.

16. Esser interview by Channing, and memorandum from George Esser to John Sanders, November 5, 1962, series 1.2.3, folder 339, NCFR.

17. "Suggestions for the Ford Foundation Conferences in North Carolina, January 15, 16, and 17, 1963," and press release, January 12, 1963, reel 6P, Subject File of the Special Assistant to the Governor on Education and Cultural Affairs, 1962–1964, Sanford Governor's Papers; and Saltzman interview.

18. "Suggestions for the Ford Foundation Conferences in North Carolina, January 15, 16, and 17, 1963," and press release, January 12, 1963, reel 6P, Subject File of the Special Assistant to the Governor on Education and Cultural Affairs, 1962–1964, Sanford Governor's Papers.

19. Ylvisaker interview.

20. "Private Schools Pushed in Caswell," *Greensboro Daily News*, February 4, 1963; Escott, *Many Excellent People*, 154; and Drescher, *Triumph of Good Will*, 262–64.

21. King, "Letter from Birmingham Jail," ⟨http://mlk-kpp01.stanford.edu/index.php/resources/article/kings_letter_from_birmingham_jail⟩.

22. Chafe, *Civilities and Civil Rights*, 166–214, quotation from 182.

23. Link, "William Friday and the North Carolina Speaker Ban Crisis," 201–3.

24. Chafe, *Civilities and Civil Rights*, 184, and Covington and Ellis, *Terry Sanford*, 313–17.

25. "Negroes Boo Gov. at Mansion," *News and Observer*, May 11, 1963, and Drescher, *Triumph of Good Will*, 265.

26. Kennedy, "Radio and Television Report to the American People on Civil Rights," ⟨http://www.jfklibrary.org/Historical+Resources/Archives/Reference+Desk/Speeches/JFK/003POF03CivilRights06111963.htm⟩.

27. Memorandum from Hargrove Bowles to Terry Sanford, June 13, 1963, General Correspondence, box 346, Sanford Governor's Papers.

28. Manuscript containing notes for an abandoned book on Terry Sanford's term as gov-

ernor, subseries 3.1, box 174, Records and Papers of Terry Sanford, Rare Book, Manuscript, and Special Collections Library, Duke University, Durham, N.C.

29. Ibid., and Covington and Ellis, *Terry Sanford*, 319–20. On the Good Neighbor Council, see Waynick, Brooks, and Pitts, *North Carolina and the Negro*.

30. Covington and Ellis, *Terry Sanford*, 321–22.

31. Drescher, *Triumph of Good Will*, 260–61; Covington and Ellis, *Terry Sanford*, 269–70, 291; and "GOP Gains Seven Seats in House," *Greensboro Daily News*, November 8, 1962.

32. Covington and Ellis, *Terry Sanford*, 305–6, 309–11, 318, and Billingsley, *Communists on Campus*, 1.

33. Covington and Ellis, *Terry Sanford*, 319; Link, "William Friday and the North Carolina Speaker Ban Crisis," 203–5; Jesse Helms, "Viewpoint" editorial 636 (June 21, 1963), North Carolina Collection, Wilson Library, University of North Carolina at Chapel Hill; and Billingsley, *Communists on Campus*, 63. See also Helms, "Viewpoint" editorials 640 (June 27, 1963) and 642 (July 1, 1963).

34. Covington and Ellis, *Terry Sanford*, 342; John P. Justice, letter to the editor, *Daily Tar Heel*, January 15, 1963, cited in McCurry, "Ideological Conflict over Race," 8; and "Chapel Hill Gets Racial Deadline," *News and Observer*, January 15, 1964.

35. Kevin Dann, "Black History: What Happens When We Forget," *Independent Weekly*, February 4, 2004; "Longtime Gay, Civil Rights Activist Dies in Boston," *Washington Blade*, June 4, 2004; biographical note, inventory of the John B. Dunne Papers, Dunne Papers, Southern Historical Collection, Wilson Library, University of North Carolina at Chapel Hill; Ehle, *Free Men*, 29; and "More Demonstrations If Law Fails, Farmer Says," *Daily Tar Heel*, January 14, 1964.

36. Ehle, *Free Men*, 262–84; Edwards, "Quest for Civil Rights in Chapel Hill," 54; and "Mississippi Law Comes to Hillsboro," *Daily Tar Heel*, April 24, 1964. See also Blanchard, "Politics of Desegregation," and Chapman, "Second Generation."

37. Biographical note, inventory of the Richardson Preyer Papers, Preyer Papers, Southern Historical Collection, Wilson Library, University of North Carolina at Chapel Hill, and Spence, *Making of a Governor*, 23.

38. Spence, *Making of a Governor*, 13–15, 85, and "700 Attend KKK Rally," *News and Observer*, March 29, 1964.

39. Luebke, *Tar Heel Politics*, 158; *News and Observer*: "Lake Booms Moore, Hits at Preyer," June 25, 1964, and "Vote for Dan Moore," June 26, 1964; and Covington and Ellis, *Terry Sanford*, 342–45.

40. Covington and Ellis, *Terry Sanford*, 342–45; Drescher, *Triumph of Good Will*, 255; and Luebke, *Tar Heel Politics*, 158.

41. Covington and Ellis, *Terry Sanford*, 216.

42. Durden, *Lasting Legacy to the Carolinas*; Wilson, *For the People of North Carolina*, 35–37, 41, 43, 47; and "$12 Million Trust Fund to Be Administered," *News and Observer*, September 13, 1953.

43. Korstad, *Civil Rights Unionism*, 61–68; Sealander, *Private Wealth and Public Life*; and Wilson, *For the People of North Carolina*, 35–36.

44. Memorandum from John Ehle to Terry Sanford, January 23, 1963, reel 6P; memorandum from Ehle to Sanford, February 1, 1963, reel 6P; Ehle to Tom Lambeth, March 19,

1963, reel 6P; and Sanford to Charles H. Babcock, May 8, 1963, reel 5P, Subject File of the Special Assistant to the Governor on Education and Cultural Affairs, 1962–1964, Sanford Governor's Papers.

45. Covington and Ellis, *North Carolina Century*, 198–201; Weare, *Black Business in the New South*, 4, 150–53; "John H. Wheeler, Political Leader," *New York Times*, July 8, 1978; and Dallek, *Flawed Giant*, 23–30.

46. John Wheeler (on behalf of the Durham Committee on Negro Affairs) to Terry Sanford, April 29, 1961, General Correspondence, box 112, Sanford Governor's Papers.

47. Ehle, *Free Men*, 59.

48. Covington and Ellis, *Terry Sanford*, 277, 328; Ylvisaker interview; Esser interview by Weaver; and notes from meeting with George Esser, February 4, 1966, series 1.1.1, folder 1, NCFR.

49. "Fund Directors Named," *News and Observer*, July 19, 1963; notes from meeting with George Esser, February 4, 1966, series 1.1.1, folder 1, NCFR; and Wilson, *For the People of North Carolina*, 73.

50. Notes from meeting with George Esser, February 4, 1966, series 1.1.1, folder 1, and Esser to John Ehle, February 4, 1963, series 1.2.3, folder 339, NCFR; and Ylvisaker interview.

51. "James A. Gray, Jr., Ex-Publisher, Leader in Old Salem Effort, Dies," *Winston-Salem Journal*, May 27, 2003.

52. "Dr. Samuel E. Duncan Succumbs En Route to Rowan Hospital," *Carolina Times*, July 13, 1968; Powell, *Dictionary of North Carolina Biography*, 2:120; and Wilson, *For the People of North Carolina*, 225–26.

53. Esser interview by Weaver, and Murchison interview.

54. Ward and Biddix, *Heritage of Old Buncombe County*, 185, and Ford, *Southern Appalachian Region*.

55. Powell, *North Carolina Lives*, 943, and Esser interview by Weaver.

56. Covington and Ellis, *North Carolina Century*, 240–43, and Wescott, "A Vision of an Open Door."

57. Notes from meeting with George Esser, February 4, 1966, series 1.1.1, folder 1, and proposal to the Ford Foundation from the North Carolina Fund, August 12, 1963, series 1.1.1, folder 2, NCFR.

58. Proposal to the Ford Foundation from the North Carolina Fund, August 12, 1963, series 1.1.1, folder 2, NCFR.

59. Ibid.

60. Ibid., 15–16.

61. Notes from meeting with George Esser, February 4, 1966, series 1.1.1, folder 1; Esser to John Ehle, February 4, 1963, series 1.2.3, folder 339; Joseph McDaniel to Terry Sanford, October 10, 1963, series 1.1.2, folder 17; and statement by North Carolina Fund executive director George Esser at the announcement of initial Fund projects, April 20, 1964, series 4.1, folder 3407, NCFR; Ylvisaker interview, 31–32, 77; and "North Carolina's Aid Fund Gets 9.5 Million to Set Up Projects," *New York Times*, October 1, 1963.

62. Notes from meeting with George Esser, February 4, 1966, 18, series 1.1.1, folder 1; statement by Governor Terry Sanford, September 30, 1963, series 1.1.2, folder 23; and clip-

ping, "Amid Pleasures and Plenty," *News and Observer*, September 22, 1963, enclosed in bulletin no. 2, Esser to board of directors, October 4, 1963, series 1.1.2, folder 23, NCFR.

63. "Man of the Year," *Goldsboro News-Argus*, February 12, 1964; "Bold Adventure," *News and Observer*, October 1, 1963; "Genesis of a Program," *Greensboro Daily News*, October 13, 1963; biographical note, inventory of the Kathrine R. Everett and R. O. Everett Papers, Everett and Everett Papers, Southern Historical Collection, Wilson Library, University of North Carolina at Chapel Hill; and R. O. Everett to George Esser, October 11, 1963, series 1.2.1, folder 135, NCFR.

64. Notes from meeting with George Esser, February 4, 1966, series 1.1.1, folder 1, and minutes of the meeting of the North Carolina Fund board of directors, August 19, 1964, series 1.1.2, folder 34, NCFR.

65. Brooks interview.

66. *The North Carolina Fund: Program and Policies*, series 1.1.1, folder 8; program proposals for dealing with the problems of poverty, February 1, 1964, series 4.1, folder 3403; and staff evaluation of proposals, n.d., series 4.1, folder 3406, NCFR.

67. *The North Carolina Fund: Program and Policies*, series 1.1.1, folder 8, and reports of on-site visits, series 4.1, folder 3400, NCFR.

68. *The North Carolina Fund: Program and Policies*, series 1.1.1, folder 8; reports of on-site visits, series 4.1, folder 3400; digest of proposals nonindexed, series 4.1, folder 3404; program proposals for dealing with the problems of poverty, February 1, 1964, series 4.1, folder 3403; and statement by North Carolina Fund executive director George Esser at the announcement of initial Fund projects, April 20, 1964, series 4.1, folder 3407, NCFR.

69. Barnes, "The North Carolina Fund"; and statement by North Carolina Fund executive director George Esser at the announcement of initial Fund projects, April 20, 1964, series 4.1, folder 3407; digest of proposals nonindexed, series 4.1, folder 3404; and Esser to Albert Coates, February 21, 1964, series 1.2.1, folder 154, NCFR.

70. Barnes interview, and "Barnes Named News Director of N.C. Fund," *Mount Holly News*, February 21, 1964.

71. William H. Koch Jr. résumé, October 3, 1963, series 4.1, folder 3372, NCFR.

72. "UNC Success Story: Trustee Draws on Wealth of Experiences," *Daily Tar Heel*, February 8, 1988, and Watts, "Carolina's First Black Ph.D. Graduate," ⟨http://fountain.unc.edu/spr_01/darity.html⟩.

73. Statement by North Carolina Fund executive director George Esser at the announcement of initial Fund projects, April 20, 1964, series 4.1, folder 3407, and reports of on-site visits, series 4.1, folder 3400, NCFR; Barnes, "The North Carolina Fund"; Brooks interview; and "N.C. Fund's Flying Squad Hard on Trail of Causes of Poverty," *Wilson Daily Times*, February 22, 1964.

74. Barnes, "The North Carolina Fund," and statement by North Carolina Fund executive director George Esser at the announcement of initial Fund projects, April 20, 1964, series 4.1, folder 3407, NCFR.

75. WAMY proposal, series 4.1, folder 3459, NCFR.

76. Ibid., and Brooks, *Dimensions of Poverty*, 6–7, 56–57.

77. Original proposals, Buncombe County, series 4.1, folder 3463, and notes on original proposals, Buncombe County, series 4.4, folder 3860, NCFR.

78. Brooks, *Dimensions of Poverty*, 64–65.

79. Nash-Edgecombe proposal, 1964, series 4.1, folder 3497, NCFR, and Brooks, *Dimensions of Poverty*, 6–7.

80. Nash-Edgecombe proposal, 1964, series 4.1, folder 3497; CADA proposal, series 4.1, folder 3484; and Craven proposal, series 4.1, folder 3472, NCFR.

81. Joint proposal to the North Carolina Fund from Richmond, Robeson, and Scotland Counties, February 1, 1964, series 4.1, folder 3508, and Craven proposal, series 4.1, folder 3472, NCFR.

82. Charlotte proposal, 1964, series 4.1, folder 3495, NCFR, and Brooks, *Dimensions of Poverty*, 6–7.

83. Charlotte proposal, 1964, series 4.1, folder 3495, and Salisbury-Rowan proposal, series 4.1, folder 3510, NCFR.

84. Charlotte proposal, 1964, series 4.1, folder 3495, NCFR.

85. Ibid., and Salisbury-Rowan proposal, series 4.1, folder 3510, NCFR.

86. *The North Carolina Fund: Program and Policies*, series 1.1.1, folder 8; "Recommended Organizational and Administrative Grants for Eleven Approved Comprehensive Community Projects," October 30, 1964, series 4.1, folder 3408; and digest of proposals nonindexed, Charlotte entry, series 4.1, folder 3404, NCFR.

87. Reginald A. Hawkins to George H. Esser, January 30, 1964, and Esser to Hawkins, February 5, 1964, series 1.2.1, folder 152, NCFR; and Esser interview by Weaver.

88. Report of the Subcommittee on the Church and Miscellaneous Organizations, series 4.1, folder 3510, NCFR.

CHAPTER 3

1. The volunteers' applications, daily activity logs, team reports, and end-of-summer questionnaires are located in series 2.1.2 and 2.1.3 of the North Carolina Fund Records, Southern Historical Collection, Wilson Library, University of North Carolina at Chapel Hill (hereafter cited as NCFR). To protect individual privacy and to comply with restrictions placed on the materials, we have changed the volunteers' names, except for those individuals who have participated in oral history interviews and have consented to the use of their records. Hereinafter, quotations and commentary by volunteers and team leaders are from the protected archival holdings, unless otherwise noted.

On the 1964 volunteers' nickname, see *The First One Hundred*, a documentary film produced by the North Carolina Fund, series 8.3, NCFR.

2. Lists of 1964 volunteers, series 2.1.2, folder 1319, and list of 1965 volunteers by hometown, series 2.1.3, folder 1500, NCFR. Ninety-two of the 100 volunteers selected in 1964 and 227 of the 250 selected in 1965 actually participated in the program. See North Carolina Volunteer Report—Summer 1965, series 2.1.3, folder 1497, NCFR.

3. Billy Barnes to Richard E. Gosswiller, July 23, 1964, series 2.1.1, folder 1239, NCFR.

4. On the Fund's determination to challenge established forms of volunteerism, see Sanford, "Poverty's Challenge to the States," 81. The best work to take up similar issues of volunteerism and social action is McAdam, *Freedom Summer*. The national program that most resembles the North Carolina Volunteers is Volunteers in Service to America (VISTA), which was modeled in part on the North Carolina experiment. The first VISTA volunteers

were trained by the Fund in 1965. See series 3.4, NCFR. Today, VISTA is part of the AmeriCorps program, which is administered by the Corporation for National and Community Service.

5. North Carolina Volunteers, Final Report, June 1, 1964–October 31, 1964, series 6.10, folder 7333, NCFR; Salmond, *Civilian Conservation Corps*; Rawick, "The New Deal and Youth"; and "'Blind Voting' Hit by Mrs. Roosevelt," *New York Times*, May 8, 1934. See also Cohen, *When the Old Left Was Young*, chap. 7.

6. Reeves, *Politics of the Peace Corps and VISTA*, 20; Peter Beinart, "A Fighting Faith: An Argument for a New Liberalism," *New Republic*, December 13, 2004, 17–19, 24, 29; and Hoffman, *All You Need Is Love*, 39–46.

7. Gregory, *Southern Diaspora*, 14–15.

8. "Conference of State and Federal Officials with the North Carolina Fund, January 14–15, 1964," series 1.3.3, folder 478, NCFR, and Harrington, *Other America*, 162, 165.

9. George Esser, untitled speech, January 1964, series 1.3.3, folder 478, NCFR.

10. Crook and Thomas, *Warriors for the Poor*, 23–43, and Reeves, *Politics of the Peace Corps and VISTA*, 25–26.

11. North Carolina Volunteers, Final Report, June 1, 1964–October 31, 1964, series 6.10, folder 7333; notes from meeting with George Esser, February 4, 1966, series 1.1.1, folder 1; "History of the Summer 1964 North Carolina Volunteers Program," series 6.10, folder 7331; and biographical sketch of James T. Beatty, series 2.1.2, folder 1272, NCFR.

12. "History of the Summer 1964 North Carolina Volunteers Program," series 6.10, folder 7331; North Carolina Volunteers, Final Report, June 1, 1964–October 31, 1964, series 6.10, folder 7333; "Student Action Corps" and untitled document, series 2.1.2, folder 1251; agenda of North Carolina Fund board of directors meeting, February 28–29, 1964, series 1.1.2, folder 26; and "Experimental Program for Mobilizing College Student Volunteer Services to Communities," series 2.1.2, folder 1252, NCFR.

13. "History of the Summer 1964 North Carolina Volunteers Program," series 6.10, folder 7331, NCFR, and Dallek, *Flawed Giant*, 24, 82, 112.

14. House Committee on Education and Labor, *Hearings before the Subcommittee on the War on Poverty Program*, 926, 933; "Three Years of Change: Narrative History of the North Carolina Fund," series 1.1.1, folder 1, NCFR; "Sanford's Political Prestige May Rise," *Charlotte Observer*, May 6, 1964; and "The President and the Fund," *Popular Government*, 7.

15. Terry Sanford to Josh L. Horne, June 29, 1964, series 1.2.1, folder 177, NCFR, and "Advance Guard in War on Poverty," *Business Week*, May 30, 1964.

16. "History of the Summer 1964 North Carolina Volunteers Program," series 6.10, folder 7331, and biographical sketch of Curtis Gans, series 2.1.2, folder 1272, NCFR.

17. McAdam, *Freedom Summer*, 14; Kennedy and Nixon, "First Joint Radio-Television Broadcast," ⟨http://www.jfklibrary.org/Historical+Resources/Archives/Reference+Desk/Speeches/JFK/JFK+Pre-Pres/1960/Senator+John+F.+Kennedy+and+Vice+President+Richard+M.+Nixon+First+Joint+Radio-Television+Broadcast.htm⟩; and Kennedy, "Inaugural Address," ⟨http://www.jfklibrary.org/Historical+Resources/Archives/Reference+Desk/Speeches/JFK/Inaugural+Address+January+20+1961.htm⟩.

18. For comparative purposes, see McAdam, *Freedom Summer*, and Hoffman, *All You Need Is Love*.

19. Quotation from Hoffman, *All You Need Is Love*, 16.

20. Miller and Draves interviews.

21. Miller interview. On existentialist concerns and student activism, see Hoffman, *All You Need Is Love*, chap. 1, and Rossinow, *Politics of Authenticity*, chap. 2.

22. Bishop interview.

23. Johnson and Entin interviews.

24. Entin interview.

25. Martha Watson survey, in authors' possession, and Miller interview.

26. Szittya interview. The phrase "citizen soldier[s]" is from Fields interview.

27. Berry, "'One Building Block in the Battle,'" 37–46, and Draves interview.

28. Draves interview.

29. Powell interview; Harrington, *Other America*, 2; and Addo interview.

30. Proposal for an Experimental Volunteer Team in Macon County, series 2.1.3, folder 1624, NCFR.

31. "Experimental Program for Mobilizing College Student Volunteer Services to Communities," series 2.1.2, folder 1252; 1965 team and team directors lists, series 2.1.3, folders 1631 and 1710–11; and Bill Darity to Jack Mansfield, February 5, 1965, series 2.1.1, folder 1242, NCFR.

32. Clifford J. Campbell to Paul Ylvisaker, July 9, 1964, Grant Files, Ford Foundation Archives, Ford Foundation, New York, and Terry Sanford to George Esser, June 20, 1964, series 2.1.1, folder 1238, NCFR.

33. Jack Mansfield to W. W. Shaw, May 7, 1964; Shaw to Mansfield, May 12, 1964; Mansfield memorandum to staff, May 27, 1964; and Russell Buxton to Mansfield, June 11, 1964, series 2.1.2, folder 1277, NCFR; and Hazirjian, "Negotiating Poverty," 496–501.

34. Miller interview.

35. Barnes, "The North Carolina Fund," 1–5, 22, and "Description of Tasks Performed by the North Carolina Volunteers, Summer, 1964," series 2.1.3, folder 1511, NCFR.

36. Fairbank interview.

37. Ibid.

38. Ibid.

39. Entin interview.

40. Untitled synopses of comments, series 2.1.2, folder 1258, NCFR, and Entin and Fields interviews.

41. Robert Seymour report, series 2.1.3, folder 1615, NCFR.

42. For a Fund veteran's latter-day perspective on the transformation that many student volunteers experienced, see Fairbank interview.

43. For a similar learning process among student antipoverty workers in eastern Kentucky, see Kiffmeyer, "From Self-Help to Sedition."

44. On the pace of desegregation in North Carolina, see U.S. Commission on Civil Rights, *Racial Isolation in the Public Schools*, 4, and Chafe, *Civilities and Civil Rights*, 105–7.

45. Draves interview.

46. Miller interview.

47. Ibid.

48. Patricia Andrews and Robert Thore surveys, in authors' possession.

49. Jones and Miller interviews.

50. Asbell, *Pill*, 167–68, and Schoen, *Choice and Coercion*, 70.

51. Jesse Helms, "Viewpoint" editorial 1071 (April 1, 1965), North Carolina Collection, Wilson Library, University of North Carolina at Chapel Hill.

52. Entin interview.

53. Jack Mansfield to George Esser, draft report on New Bern incident, n.d., series 2.1.1, folder 1249, NCFR.

54. Ibid., and Entin interview.

55. Clipping, Anne Jones, "Hollins Girl Tells of Work with Poor," *Roanoke World News*, November 29, 1965, series 2.1.3, folder 1533, NCFR, and Jones and Johnson interviews.

56. Gioia, "'How to Get Out of Hell by Raising It,'" 51–52; Davidson, *Best of Enemies*, 153–85; and Linda Pannill, Report on the North Carolina Volunteers Winter Programs, 1964 and 1965, series 2.1.4, folder 2354, and Jack Mansfield to Billy Barnes et al., position paper on North Carolina Volunteers philosophy, January 3, 1966, series 2.1.3, folder 1525, NCFR.

57. Sasson interview, and Betty Ward, untitled manuscript, January 3, 1966, series 2.1.1, folder 1250, NCFR.

CHAPTER 4

1. Moynihan, *Maximum Feasible Misunderstanding*, 87; and *The North Carolina Fund: Program and Policies*, series 1.1.1, folder 8, and clipping, "'Poor Power' Need Seen," *Fort Lauderdale News*, series 4.11, folder 4954, North Carolina Fund Records, Southern Historical Collection, Wilson Library, University of North Carolina at Chapel Hill (hereafter cited as NCFR).

2. Moynihan, *Maximum Feasible Misunderstanding*, 41, 75–101.

3. Memorandum from Charles Schultze to Bill Moyers, January 30, 1964, series 3.1, box 41, Robert Sargent Shriver Papers, John F. Kennedy Presidential Library and Museum, Boston; Sundquist, *On Fighting Poverty*, 26; "Three Years of Change: Narrative History of the North Carolina Fund," series 1.1.1, folder 1, NCFR; "Johnson Administration to Use Some Tactics of N.C. Fund," *Winston-Salem Journal*, January 17, 1964; and House Committee on Education and Labor, *Hearings before the Subcommittee on the War on Poverty Program*, 926, 933.

4. Yarmolinsky, "Beginnings of OEO," 49–51.

5. Moynihan, *Maximum Feasible Misunderstanding*, 86–87.

6. Ibid., 91, 95. See also L. H. Fountain to Paul Whitaker, August 21, 1964, and Fountain to T. J. Hackney Jr., September 4, 1964, series 2, folder 360, L. H. Fountain Papers, Southern Historical Collection, Wilson Library, University of North Carolina at Chapel Hill; and Jesse Helms, "Viewpoint" editorial 912 (August 12, 1964), North Carolina Collection, Wilson Library, University of North Carolina at Chapel Hill.

7. Barnard, *American Vanguard*, 227, and Roosevelt, "Annual Message to Congress," ⟨http://docs.fdrlibrary.marist.edu/4FREE.HTML⟩.

8. Lichtenstein, *Most Dangerous Man in Detroit*, and Boyle, *UAW and the Heyday of American Liberalism*, 5.

9. Lichtenstein, *Most Dangerous Man in Detroit*, 316, 381, and Boyle, *UAW and the Heyday of American Liberalism*, 121, 168–70.

10. Boyle, *UAW and the Heyday of American Liberalism*, 161–84, and Lichtenstein, *Most Dangerous Man in Detroit*, 385. Randolph, founder of the Brotherhood of Sleeping Car

Porters, and Rustin had first proposed such a march in 1941. They called off the protest when President Franklin Roosevelt issued an executive order that barred racial discrimination in war industries employment.

11. Boyle, *UAW and the Heyday of American Liberalism*, 162, and Lichtenstein, *Most Dangerous Man in Detroit*, 370–95.

12. Chafe, *Unfinished Journey*, 82.

13. Lichtenstein, *Most Dangerous Man in Detroit*, 389–90, and Moynihan, *Maximum Feasible Misunderstanding*, 96.

14. *Community Action Program Guide*, 7; Lichtenstein, *Most Dangerous Man in Detroit*, 390; and Moynihan, *Maximum Feasible Misunderstanding*, 97–98.

15. Moynihan, *Maximum Feasible Misunderstanding*, 98; "Economic Opportunity Act," 88th Cong., 2nd sess., *Congressional Record* 110 (August 11, 1964): 19008; Boyle, *UAW and the Heyday of American Liberalism*, 188; and Kramer, *Participation of the Poor*, 14.

16. Levitan, *Great Society's Poor Law*, 93, and North Carolina Fund, *Process Analysis Report*, part 1, p. 78, North Carolina Collection, Wilson Library, University of North Carolina at Chapel Hill (hereafter cited as North Carolina Fund, *Process Analysis Report*).

17. William Keech notes, series 4.11, folder 4963, NCFR, and North Carolina Fund, *Process Analysis Report*, part 1, pp. 78–79.

18. North Carolina Fund, *Process Analysis Report*, part 1, pp. 75, 77.

19. Ibid., 76–78.

20. Ibid., 80–81.

21. Moynihan, *Maximum Feasible Misunderstanding*, xxv; Weare, *Black Business in the New South*; and John Salter to Jim Dombrowski, April 28, 1964, folder 22, Hunter Gray (John R. Salter) Papers, Wisconsin Historical Society, Madison (hereafter cited as Gray [Salter] Papers).

22. "Operation Breakthrough, Inc.," series 4.8, folder 4352, NCFR, and Weare, "Charles Clinton Spaulding," 169. On Durham generally, see Anderson, *Durham County*.

23. Anderson, *Durham County*, 412–15, and Research Triangle Park, ⟨http://www.rtp .org/main⟩.

24. Brooks, *Dimensions of Poverty*, 6, 12; Gioia, "'How to Get Out of Hell by Raising It,'" 9; "Operation Breakthrough, Inc.," series 4.8, folder 4352, NCFR; Greene, *Our Separate Ways*, 128; and Bertie Howard and Steve Redburn, "UOCI: Black Political Power in Durham," series 4.8, folder 4563, NCFR.

25. Waynick, Brooks, and Pitts, *North Carolina and the Negro*, 63–67.

26. "Operation Breakthrough, Inc.," series 4.8, folder 4352; Paige Young, "History of the Formation of Breakthrough," series 4.8, folder 4432; and Action for Durham Development proposal addenda (board list), series 4.8, folder 4488, NCFR; and Gioia, "'How to Get Out of Hell by Raising It,'" 17.

27. Gioia, "'How to Get Out of Hell by Raising It,'" 17; and "Operation Breakthrough, Inc.," series 4.8, folder 4352, and Action for Durham Development, proposal submitted to the North Carolina Fund for Operation Breakthrough, series 4.8, folder 4487, NCFR.

28. "Operation Breakthrough, Inc.," series 4.8, folder 4352, NCFR; Gioia, "'How to Get Out of Hell by Raising It,'" 19; and Howard Fuller, "A Brief Accounting of Community Organization," series 4.8, folder 4420, NCFR.

29. "Operation Breakthrough, Inc.," series 4.8, folder 4352; Bertie Howard and Steve Redburn, "UOCI: Black Political Power in Durham," series 4.8, folder 4563; Bertie Howard, "Beginnings of Community Action in Durham," series 4.8, folder 4466; and staff biographies, series 1.4, folder 537, NCFR; and Fuller interview.

30. "An Experience in Community Organizing," series 4.8, folder 4422, NCFR.

31. Fuller interview.

32. Ibid.

33. Atwater interview, and Davidson, *Best of Enemies*, 32–36.

34. Atwater interview.

35. Ibid.

36. Fuller interview.

37. Atwater interview.

38. Ibid.

39. Bertie Howard and Steve Redburn, "UOCI: Black Political Power in Durham," series 4.8, folder 4563, NCFR, and Ruffin interview.

40. Greene, *Our Separate Ways*, 110–11, and Fuller and Nichols (Thorpe) interviews.

41. Greene, *Our Separate Ways*, 105–13, and Bertie Howard, "Beginnings of Community Action in Durham," series 4.8, folder 4466, NCFR.

42. Greene, *Our Separate Ways*, 105–13; Bertie Howard, "Beginnings of Community Action in Durham," series 4.8, folder 4466, and Patricia Wallace, "How to Get Out of Hell by Raising It: The Case of Durham," series 4.8, folder 4562, NCFR; *Thorpe v. Housing Authority of Durham*, 386 U.S. 670 (1967); and *Thorpe v. Housing Auth.*, 393 U.S. 268 (1969).

43. Greene, *Our Separate Ways*, 106–7.

44. "Negro and Community Action," series 4.8, folder 4351, and John Salter to Mike Kenney, August 31, 1966, series 1.4, folder 590, NCFR.

45. Interview with Mr. Julius Corpening, April 26, 1966, series 4.8, folder 4425, NCFR.

46. "Negro and Community Action," series 4.8, folder 4351, and "Operation Breakthrough, Inc.," series 4.8, folder 4352, NCFR; and Fuller interview.

47. Bertie Howard and Steve Redburn, "UOCI: Black Political Power in Durham," series 4.8, folder 4563, and "Negro and Community Action," series 4.8, folder 4351, NCFR.

48. Johnson, "Does the South Owe the Negro a New Deal?," 103; Weare, *Black Business in the New South*, 240–50; and Bertie Howard and Steve Redburn, "UOCI: Black Political Power in Durham," series 4.8, folder 4563, NCFR.

49. Ruffin interview; Gioia, "'How to Get Out of Hell by Raising It,'" 34; and John H. Strange, "The Politics of Protest: The Case of Durham," series 6.10, folder 7422, NCFR.

50. United Organizations for Community Improvement Planning Grant Proposal, series 4.11, folder 4951, NCFR.

51. Ibid., and Gattis interview.

52. Anderson, *Durham County*, 371–72, and "Tenement Property Owners Opposed to Slum Clearance," *Durham Herald*, September 26, 1937.

53. Anderson, *Durham County*, 411, and Davidson, *Best of Enemies*, 203.

54. Anderson, *Durham County*, 406–9.

55. "Greenberg Housing Controversy," series 6.7, folder 7120, NCFR.

56. Ibid.

57. Ibid., and "Questions Raised by Picketing," *Durham Herald*, June 26, 1966.

58. "The Landlord Just Doesn't Give a Damn," series 4.8, folder 4585; "Greenberg Housing Controversy," series 6.7, folder 7120; and Rubye Gattis to Robert Weaver, December 12, 1966, series 4.8, folder 4585, NCFR.

59. Pat Wallace, "Howard Fuller — Community Support Conference," series 4.8, folder 4427; William Pursell, "Crisis and Conflict: The Story of Operation Breakthrough," series 6.7, folder 7118; and "Greenberg Housing Controversy," series 6.7, folder 7120, NCFR.

60. "Operation Breakthrough, Inc.," series 4.8, folder 4352; "Case Study in Community Action," series 4.8, folder 4351; William Pursell, "Crisis and Conflict: The Story of Operation Breakthrough," series 6.7, folder 7118; Ernest D. Eppley to Jim McDonald, July 22, 1966, series 4.1, folder 3369; notes from North Carolina Fund staff session with Ford review team, November 4, 1966, series 4.8, folder 4431; and "Choanoke Area Development Association, Inc.," series 6.7, folder 7111, NCFR.

61. "Choanoke Area Development Association, Inc.," series 6.7, folder 7111, NCFR.

62. Ibid., and "Choanoke Area Development Association, Inc.," series 4.11, folder 4823, NCFR.

63. Untitled document, series 4.11, folder 4825, and "Choanoke Area Development Association, Inc.," series 4.11, folder 4823, NCFR.

64. "Choanoke Area Development Association, Inc.," series 4.11, folder 4823; untitled document, series 4.11, folder 4825; and People's Program on Poverty Incentive Grant Proposal and accompanying undated letter, series 4.11, folder 4947, NCFR.

65. "Choanoke Area Development Association, Inc.," series 4.11, folder 4823, NCFR.

66. Ibid.

67. Community action proposal, submitted January 28, 1964, series 4.11, folder 4883; "Choanoke Area Development Association, Inc.," series 4.11, folder 4823; and untitled document authored by John Miller, series 4.11, folder 4825, NCFR.

68. Proposal for Program Development Grant to Office of Economic Opportunity from Choanoke Area Development Association Economic Opportunities, June 8, 1965, series 4.11, folder 4886, NCFR.

69. Ibid.

70. Cofield, "Teaching Students to Read the World," 101–5; A. Reed Johnson to Wiley Branton, March 27, 1964, folder 22, Gray (Salter) Papers; Laplois Ashford to [Henry Lee] Moon, September 4, 1963, in Bracey and Meier, *Papers of the NAACP*, part 19, Youth File, series D, 1956–65, Youth Department files; "Enfield and Wilson Scenes of Trouble," *Rocky Mount Evening Telegram*, September 2, 1963; "Arrest 15 at Enfield," *Roanoke Rapids Daily Herald*, September 1, 1963; Waynick, Brooks, and Pitts, *North Carolina and the Negro*, 79–80; and John Salter to James Forman, January 29, 1964, folder 22, Gray (Salter) Papers.

71. Cofield, "Teaching Students to Read the World," 105; Salter, "Upsurge in Carolina"; 501.NC.2. *Alston v. Butts* 501 N.C. 2 (ED N.C.) (Halifax Co.) May 1964; and John Salter report to SCEF board, April 15–16, 1965, box 2, folder 1, Gray (Salter) Papers.

72. Cofield, "Teaching Students to Read the World," 105; Salter, "Upsurge in Carolina"; "Over 1,000 Attend Civil Rights Conference in Bertie County," *Carolina Times*, March 13, 1965; and CADA histories, series 4.11, folders 4823 and 4825, NCFR.

73. "Choanoke Area Development Association, Inc.," series 4.11, folder 4823; untitled

document, series 4.11, folder 4825; and Sargent Shriver to Fred Cooper, December 5, 1965, series 4.11, folder 4902, NCFR.

74. CADA press releases, August 19, 23, and 27, 1965, series 4.11, folder 4837, and Sargent Shriver to Fred Cooper, December 5, 1965, series 4.11, folder 4902, NCFR.

75. "Choanoke Area Development Association, Inc.," series 4.11, folder 4823; Sarah Herbin report on telephone conversation with Doris Cochran, September 27, 1965; and Herbin field report on CADA, September 20–21, 1965, series 4.11, folder 4938, NCFR.

76. Georgia C. Peerce, secretary, Northampton Voters Movement, to Sargent Shriver, September 30, 1965, series 4.11, folder 4879, NCFR.

77. "Choanoke Area Development Association, Inc.," series 4.11, folder 4823, NCFR, and Du Bois, *Black Reconstruction*, 721.

78. Anderson, *Race and Politics in North Carolina*, and Justesen, *George Henry White*.

79. Anderson, *Race and Politics in North Carolina*, 179, 261.

80. Justesen, *George Henry White*, 297–304; "Southern Negro's Plaint," *New York Times*, April 26, 1900; and remarks by George Henry White, 56th Cong., 2nd sess., *Congressional Record* 34 (January 29, 1901): 1638.

81. Wynne, "Historical Study of the Joseph K. Brick School." For a first-person account of the Brick School, see principal Thomas S. Inborden's "History of Brick School," Rare Book, Manuscript, and Special Collections Library, Duke University, Durham, N.C.

82. Brownlee and Morton, *Brick Rural Life School*; Brownlee, *New Day Ascending*; and "Families Re-visit Depression-Era Resettlement Farm," *Durham Herald-Sun*, September 3, 1995.

83. Biographical sketch, James A. Felton and Annie Vaughan Felton Papers, Southern Historical Collection, Wilson Library, University of North Carolina at Chapel Hill, and Felton, *Fruits of Enduring Faith*, 26–28, 32, 63, 96. On the Montford Point Marines, see McLaurin, *Marines of Montford Point*.

84. "Choanoke Area Development Association, Inc.," series 4.11, folder 4823, and John Miller, "Staff-Board Politics: Choanoke Area Development Association," series 4.11, folder 4859, NCFR.

85. John Miller, "Staff-Board Politics: Choanoke Area Development Association," series 4.11, folder 4859, and "Choanoke Area Development Association, Inc.," series 4.11, folder 4823, NCFR.

86. John Miller, "Staff-Board Politics: Choanoke Area Development Association," series 4.11, folder 4859, NCFR.

87. Ibid., and "Choanoke Area Development Association," series 4.11, folder 4825, NCFR.

88. Sarah Herbin and Arch Foster to Jim McDonald, May 25, 1966, series 4.11, folder 4911; "Choanoke Area Development Association: Autonomy from OEO, NCF and Local Community Agencies," series 4.11, folder 4859; and "Choanoke Area Development Association, Inc.," series 4.11, folder 4823, NCFR.

89. Report on Choanoke Area Development Association meeting, July 15, 1966; "Notes Taken at a Meeting in Roanoke Rapids Hospital in a Room Occupied by Fred Cooper," July 19, 1966; and A Report on the People's Conference on Poverty, series 4.11, folder 4862, NCFR.

90. People's Program on Poverty proposal, series 4.11, folder 4924; Rev. C. Melvin Creecy to Harold Bailin, August 4, 1966, series 4.11, folder 4947; and Tom Hartmann, Report on the Conference on Poverty, July 30, 1966, Woodland, N.C., series 4.11, folder 4862, NCFR.

91. "People's Conference on Poverty, July 30, 1966," and Tom Hartmann, Report on the Conference on Poverty, July 30, 1966, Woodland, N.C., series 4.11, folder 4862, NCFR.

92. Untitled transcript of Howard Fuller's speech at the People's Conference on Poverty, July 30, 1966, series 4.11, folder 4932, NCFR.

93. Ibid.

94. Transcript of a report by Mr. W. D. Debnam on WITN-TV, Wednesday, August 3, 1966, series 4.11, folder 4932, and Essie Mattison to Jim McDonald and Nathan Garrett, ca. August 8, 1966, series 4.11, folder 4881, NCFR; and Fuller interview.

95. Untitled report on Fund support for UOCI and PPOP, series 4.8, folder 4561, NCFR, and Fuller interview.

96. Piven and Cloward, *Regulating the Poor,* 271.

97. Ibid., 272; Gilbert, *Clients or Constituents,* 2, 11; and Patterson, *America's Struggle against Poverty in the Twentieth Century,* 142. See also Kramer, *Participation of the Poor,* 14.

98. Morris Cohen, "Why Should the Poor Be Involved in the War on Poverty?," 2, 9–11, series 4.2, folder 3559, NCFR.

99. Ibid., 4, 9, 11–12, 13.

100. Tom Hartmann, Report on the Conference on Poverty, July 30, 1966, Woodland, N.C., series 4.11, folder 4862, NCFR.

101. Notes used in meeting with CADA board, March 18, 1967, series 4.11, folder 4829, and field reports, series 4.11, folders 4939–40, NCFR; and King, "Letter from Birmingham Jail," ⟨http://mlk-kpp01.stanford.edu/index.php/resources/article/kings_letter_from_ birmingham_jail⟩.

102. Untitled report on Fund support for UOCI and PPOP, series 4.8, folder 4561; report on community support meeting, July 18, 1966, series 4.11, folder 4862; and Sarah Herbin report, July 26, 1966, series 4.11, folder 4829, NCFR.

103. Bertie Howard and Steve Redburn, "UOCI: Black Political Power in Durham," series 4.8, folder 4563, and "Staff Analysis of the Community Corporation Concept," series 4.11, folder 4931, NCFR.

104. Notes used in meeting with CADA board, March 18, 1967, series 4.11, folder 4829, NCFR.

105. "Choanoke Area Development Association, Inc.," series 4.11, folder 4823, and Alice Ballance to the North Carolina Fund, April 4, 1967, series 4.11, folder 4948, NCFR.

106. "People's Program on Poverty," series 4.11, folder 4924; People's Program on Poverty, Progress Report on Activities in the Choanoke Area, May 1, 1967, series 4.11, folder 4937; and Alice Murray, An Interim Report of People's Program on Poverty, October 9, 1967, series 4.11, folder 4941, NCFR; and LeMay, "Battlefield in the Backyard," 40.

107. People's Program on Poverty, Progress Report on Activities in the Choanoke Area, May 1, 1967, series 4.11, folder 4937, and People's Program on Poverty, Progress Report for Halifax County, 1 May 1967 thru 18 August 1967, in Area of Recreation and Sanitation, series 4.11, folder 4936, NCFR.

108. Letters and clippings related to James Felton's leadership, series 4.11, folder 4959;

and Felton to Reginald Durante, January 12, 1968, and PPOP fact sheet for Choanoke area, May 1, 1968, series 4.11, folder 4952, NCFR.

109. Carolyn Doggett, field report, June 21–22, 1966, series 4.11, folder 4939, and J. T. Barnet of CADA to George Esser, May 13, 1968, series 4.11, folder 4896, NCFR; and Miller, "Workers' Owned," 13–14.

110. Foner, *Reconstruction*, 104; untitled document, series 4.11, folder 4825, NCFR; and Biles, "Rise and Fall of Soul City," 58.

111. The Woodard Home-Grown Food Project: A Proposal, n.d., series 4.11, folder 4960, NCFR, and Hartman, "Seeds of Sustenance."

112. Hartman, "Seeds of Sustenance."

113. The Woodard Home-Grown Food Project: A Proposal, n.d., series 4.11, folder 4960, NCFR, and Hartman, "Seeds of Sustenance."

114. Geiger, "Unsteady March," 1, and The Woodard Home-Grown Food Project: A Proposal, n.d., series 4.11, folder 4960, NCFR.

115. Greene, *Our Separate Ways*, 128–29.

116. John H. Strange, "The Politics of Protest: The Case of Durham," series 6.10, folder 7422, and Bertie Howard and Steve Redburn, "UOCI: Black Political Power in Durham," series 4.8, folder 4563, NCFR.

117. John H. Strange, "The Politics of Protest: The Case of Durham," series 6.10, folder 7422, NCFR; "Newark, the Predictable Insurrection: Shooting War in the Streets," *Life*, July 8, 1967; Mumford, *Newark*, chap. 6; and *Durham Herald*, July 18, 1967.

118. "Narrative of the Events of Wednesday, Thursday, and Friday, July 19, 20 and 21," series 1.2.2, folder 318, NCFR.

119. "Council Moves to Cut Issues," *Durham Sun*, July 20, 1967; and Dewitt Sullivan to George Esser, July 24, 1967, and "Narrative of the Events of Wednesday, Thursday, and Friday, July 19, 20 and 21," series 1.2.2, folder 318, NCFR.

120. Bertie Howard and Steve Redburn, "UOCI: Black Political Power in Durham," series 4.8, folder 4563, and John H. Strange, "The Politics of Protest: The Case of Durham," series 6.10, folder 7422, NCFR.

121. Transcript of Rubye Gattis's testimony, series 4.8, folder 4483, NCFR, and Greene, *Our Separate Ways*, 135.

CHAPTER 5

1. Johnson, *Vantage Point*, 77–78; "Poverty Message from the President of the United States," 88th Cong., 2nd sess., *Congressional Record* 110 (March 16, 1964): 5287–89; and Spitzer, "Liberal Dilemma."

2. Weller, *Yesterday's People*, 21–23.

3. A Proposal to the North Carolina Fund, series 4.1, folder 3459, North Carolina Fund Records, Southern Historical Collection, Wilson Library, University of North Carolina at Chapel Hill (hereafter cited as NCFR), and Whisnant, *Super-Scenic Motorway*.

4. Brooks, *Dimensions of Poverty*, 6–7; and Proposals to Combat the Cycle of Poverty in Mitchell County; A Proposal to the North Carolina Fund; Proposal 2; and Community Proposal from Yancey County, series 4.1, folder 3459, NCFR.

5. "Suggestions for the Ford Foundation Conferences in North Carolina, January 15, 16, and 17, 1963," reel 6P, Subject File of the Special Assistant to the Governor on Education and Cultural Affairs, 1962–1964, Official Papers of Governor Terry Sanford, North Carolina Division of Archives and History, Raleigh.

6. Ford, *Southern Appalachian Region*, and program proposals for dealing with the problems of poverty, February 1, 1964, series 4.1, folder 3403, NCFR.

7. Community Proposal from Yancey County; A Proposal to the North Carolina Fund; and Proposals to Combat the Cycle of Poverty in Mitchell County, series 4.1, folder 3459, NCFR; and Brooks, *Dimensions of Poverty*, 18–19.

8. "A Proposed Recreation-Education Project for Mitchell County," series 4.1, folder 3459, NCFR.

9. Bob Walker, "WAMY Community Action," series 4.2, folder 3525, and Report of Personnel Committee for Avery-Mitchell-Watauga-Yancey N.C. Fund Project, series 4.2, folder 3557, NCFR.

10. North Carolina Fund, *Process Analysis Report*, part 2, p. 19, North Carolina Collection, Wilson Library, University of North Carolina at Chapel Hill; Neighborhood Youth Corps Proposal, series 4.2, folder 3728, NCFR; and Yrigoyen and Warrick, *Historical Dictionary of Methodism*, 184.

11. Ernest Eppley interview, September 27, 1966, series 4.2, folder 3626, NCFR.

12. Executive committee meeting minutes, WAMY Community Action, November 12, 1964, series 4.2, folder 3546, and Report of Review Team of WAMY's Sub-Contracting of Program to County Health and Extension Agencies, series 4.2, folder 3636, NCFR.

13. WAMY Community Action progress report, [November 1965], series 4.2, folder 3619, NCFR.

14. Review team report on WAMY Community Action, September 18–22, 1966, series 4.2, folder 3630; Gay Fox notes on interview with Dr. Tate, series 4.2, folder 3634; and Report of Review Team of WAMY's Sub-Contracting of Program to County Health and Extension Agencies, series 4.2, folder 3636, NCFR.

15. A Proposal to the North Carolina Fund, January 1, 1964, series 4.2, folder 3532, and WAMY Crafts, Quarter Report, October 1–December 31, 1967, series 4.2, folder 3678.

16. Eaton, *Handicrafts of the Southern Highlands*, 25, 328.

17. Sloop, *Miracle in the Hills*, 20, and Covington and Ellis, *North Carolina Century*, 360–62.

18. Sloop, *Miracle in the Hills*, 171.

19. Covington and Ellis, *North Carolina Century*, 87–90, and Morgan, *Gift from the Hills*, 3–9, 50.

20. Ford, *Southern Appalachian Region*, 291; Becker, *Selling Tradition*, 189–91; and Cantwell, *When We Were Good*, 19, 22, 151–52.

21. Cullum, "The Beverly Hillbillies," ⟨http://www.museum.tv/archives/etv/B/htmlB/beverlyhillb/beverlyhillb.htm⟩.

22. Ford, *Southern Appalachian Region*, 279–88; Williams, "Crafting Antipoverty Policy"; and Mountain Crafts Training and Marketing, series 4.2, folder 3660; WAMY Crafts, Quarter Report, October 1–December 31, 1967, series 4.2, folder 3678; and Narrative Progress Report, July 1–September 30, 1966, series 4.2, folder 3611, NCFR.

23. Williams, "Crafting Antipoverty Policy," and Ernest Eppley interview, June 11–12, 1968, series 6.10, folder 7270, NCFR.

24. Whitson and Elliott interview, and clipping, "Friendly Home Visitors," *Resumé*, May–June 1966, series 4.2, folder 3598, NCFR. On the origins of the term "friendly home visitors," see McVeigh and Wolfer, *Brief History of Social Problems*, 301.

25. Whitson and Elliott interview.

26. Ibid.; and "General Job Description for Neighborhood Health Visitors," "Role of Friendly Home Visitors," and "Duties and Responsibilities of the Neighborhood Health Visitors," series 4.2, folder 3557, and Narrative Progress Report, July 1–September 3, 1966, series 4.2, folder 3611, NCFR.

27. Whitson and Elliott interview, and "Additional Background Information" (on WAMY clients), series 4.2, folder 3530, NCFR. For a comparative perspective on the injuries of class, see Rubin, *Worlds of Pain*, 34.

28. Whitson and Elliott interview.

29. Ibid.

30. Ernest Eppley, Narrative Report to the North Carolina Fund, series 4.2, folder 3624, and Narrative Progress Report, October 1–December 31, 1966, series 4.2, folder 3610, NCFR.

31. Whitson and Elliott interview; and Narrative Progress Report, July 1–September 30, 1966, series 4.2, folder 3611, and Watauga County Report, mid-October to mid-December 1966, series 4.2, folder 3618, NCFR.

32. Narrative Progress Report, April 1–June 30, 1967, series 4.2, folder 3608, and Narrative Progress Report, January 1–March 31, 1967, series 4.2, folder 3609, NCFR.

33. Narrative Progress Report, January 1–March 31, 1967, series 4.2, folder 3609; Victor Waumett, "The WAMY Slide Show," series 8.3, folder 8472; and "Community Centers to Fill Many Needs," *WAMY Community Action Report*, July 1966, series 4.2, folder 3600, NCFR; and Rubin, *Worlds of Pain*, 37.

34. Ford, *Southern Appalachian Region*, 297.

35. "Use of Family Planning as an Outreach Service of Manpower" and "Family Planning as a Component in North Carolina Community Action Programs," series 7.7, folder 8016, NCFR.

36. Don Wharton, "Birth Control: The Case for the State," *The Atlantic*, October 1939, 463–67, and Schoen, "Fighting for Child Health," 96.

37. Schoen, *Choice and Coercion*, 21–61.

38. Grant request, February 7, 1967, series 4.2, folder 3681; "Starter Fund for Family Planning Clinics in Yancey, Avery and Mitchell Counties, March 1–September 30, 1967," series 4.2, folder 3681; Kenneth Sanchagrin to Richard First, July 13, 1967, series 4.2, folder 3643; and "Carolina Population Center News," Summer 1967, series 1.10, folder 1025, NCFR; "Family Planning Teams Study in Chapel Hill," North Carolina Fund Clipping Files, 1963–1969, vols. 203–7, North Carolina Collection, Wilson Library, University of North Carolina at Chapel Hill (hereafter cited as North Carolina Fund Clipping Files); and Carolina Population Center, "First Decade," ⟨http://www.cpc.unc.edu/history/history_first_decade.html⟩.

39. Family planning pamphlet, series 4.2, folder 3643, NCFR, and Whitson and Elliott interview.

40. Narrative Progress Report, July 1–September 30, 1966, series 4.2, folder 3611; "Community Centers to Fill Many Needs," *WAMY Community Action Report*, July 1966, series 4.2, folder 3600; and Narrative Progress Report, April 1–June 30, 1967, series 4.2, folder 3608, NCFR.

41. Summary of board of director's meeting, September 21, 1965, series 4.2, folder 3550, NCFR.

42. "Community Support Strategies in WAMY," series 4.2, folder 3526, and Hall, Leloudis, Korstad, Murphy, Jones, and Daly, *Like a Family*, 183–236.

43. Marguerite M. Kiely, "Community Organization through Incentive Grants," series 4.2, folder 3736, NCFR.

44. Narrative Progress Report, October 1–December 31, 1965, series 4.2, folder 3615; and Hugh Brinley Wire résumé; Wire to William Koch, November 23, 1964, March 29, 1965; and Wire to Ernest Eppley, April 12, 1965, series 4.2, folder 3555, NCFR; Wagoner interview; and Sanchagrin curriculum vitae, ⟨http://www.glenmary.org/grc/grc_sanchagrincv.htm⟩.

45. Wagoner interview, and Hugh Wire to William Koch, March 29, 1965, series 4.2, folder 3555, NCFR.

46. Untitled overview of the incentive grants program, series 4.2, folder 3734, and request for extension of incentive grants to WAMY communities, July 8, 1966, series 4.2, folder 3742, NCFR.

47. Putnam, "Bowling Alone," 67. Such arguments date back at least to the mid-nineteenth century and the work of French traveler and social observer Alexis de Tocqueville. In *Democracy in America*, published in two volumes in 1835 and 1840, Tocqueville observed that "Americans . . . constantly unite. Not only do they have commercial and industrial associations in which all take part, but they also have a thousand other kinds: religious, moral, grave, futile, very general and very particular, immense and very small." The formation of voluntary associations, he argued, was a matter of necessity in a society founded on principles of individual liberty. In such societies, individual "citizens are independent and weak; they can do almost nothing by themselves, and none of them can oblige those like themselves to lend them their cooperation. They therefore all fall into impotence if they do not learn to aid each other freely." Only by joining together around common concerns could citizens build institutions, press their interests, and accumulate wealth. "Americans," Tocqueville noted, "use associations to give fêtes, to found seminaries, to build inns, to raise churches, to distribute books, to send missionaries to the antipodes; in this manner they create hospitals, prisons, schools." See Tocqueville, *Democracy in America*, 489.

48. Untitled draft statement on incentive grants, and "Antidote to Apathy: The WAMY Incentive Grants Program," series 4.2, folder 3736, NCFR.

49. "Antidote to Apathy: The WAMY Incentive Grants Program," series 4.2, folder 3736, and "Incentive Grants Program," series 4.2, folder 3625, NCFR.

50. Marguerite M. Kiely, "Community Organization through Incentive Grants," series 4.2, folder 3736, and untitled document, series 4.2, folder 3529, NCFR.

51. Marguerite M. Kiely, "Community Organization through Incentive Grants," series 4.2, folder 3736, NCFR.

52. Chronological Report on Incentive Grants, series 4.2, folder 3742; and personal comments about the incentive grants program; "Antidote to Apathy: The WAMY Incentive

Grants Program"; and Marguerite M. Kiely, "Community Organization through Incentive Grants," series 4.2, folder 3736, NCFR.

53. "Antidote to Apathy: The WAMY Incentive Grants Program," and Marguerite M. Kiely, "Community Organization through Incentive Grants," series 4.2, folder 3736, NCFR.

54. Summary of Incentive Grants: WAMY Community Action, Inc., from the Progress Report, March 31, 1966, series 4.2, folder 3730, and Colberts Creek incentive grant evaluation, series 4.2, folder 3740, NCFR.

55. Colberts Creek incentive grant evaluation, series 4.2, folder 3740; "Youth Corps Projects Get Compliments," *WAMY Community Action Report*, November 1966, series 4.2, folder 3600; and Summary of Incentive Grants: WAMY Community Action, Inc., from the Progress Report, March 31, 1966, series 4.2, folder 3730, NCFR; and "Four Counties Wage Own Poverty Battle," *Winston-Salem Journal and Sentinel*, February 27, 1966.

56. Narrative Progress Report, January 1–March 31, 1966, series 4.2, folder 3612, and Summary of Incentive Grants: WAMY Community Action, Inc., from the Progress Report, March 31, 1966, series 4.2, folder 3730, NCFR.

57. Narrative Progress Report, January 1–March 31, 1966, series 4.2, folder 3612; Colberts Creek incentive grant evaluation, series 4.2, folder 3740; and Victor Waumett, "The WAMY Slide Show," series 8.3, folder 8472, NCFR.

58. Colberts Creek incentive grant evaluation, series 4.2, folder 3740, and Victor Waumett, "The WAMY Slide Show," series 8.3, folder 8472, NCFR.

59. "Antidote to Apathy: The WAMY Incentive Grants Program," and Marguerite M. Kiely, "Community Organization through Incentive Grants," series 4.2, folder 3736, and Victor Waumett, "The WAMY Slide Show," series 8.3, folder 8472, NCFR.

60. "Antidote to Apathy: The WAMY Incentive Grants Program," and Marguerite M. Kiely, "Community Organization through Incentive Grants," series 4.2, folder 3736; and "Programs 'Fit Together' in Avery," *WAMY Community Action Report*, January 1967, series 4.2, folder 3600, NCFR; and "Sargent Shriver and Billy Graham Visit Avery County," *Tri-County News*, May 18, 1967.

61. "Shriver Tours Mountains," *Goldsboro News-Argus*, May 14, 1967; "Programs 'Fit Together' in Avery," *WAMY Community Action Report*, January 1967, series 4.2, folder 3600; and "Antidote to Apathy: The WAMY Incentive Grants Program," and Marguerite M. Kiely, "Community Organization through Incentive Grants," series 4.2, folder 3736, NCFR; and Miller, *Billy Graham and the Rise of the Republican South*, 107–8. Shriver's office commissioned a short documentary film on his visit to Blevins Creek. See *Beyond These Hills*, RG 381.210, Records of the Community Services Administration, 1963–1981, National Archives and Records Administration, College Park, Md. The Community Services Administration was the successor agency of the OEO.

62. "Shriver Says Poor Have Voice in OEO," *Winston-Salem Journal*, May 14, 1967.

63. Narrative Progress Report, July 1–September 30, 1966, series 4.2, folder 3611; review team report on WAMY Community Action, September 18–22, 1966, series 4.2, folder 3630; and Tom Davis notes on interview with Rachel Rivers, editor of the *Watauga Democrat*, series 4.2, folder 3634, NCFR.

64. Report of the Review Team of WAMY's Sub-Contracting of Program to County Health and Extension Agencies, series 4.2, folder 3551, and review team report on WAMY Community Action, September 18–22, 1966, series 4.2, folder 3630, NCFR.

65. Review team report on WAMY Community Action, September 18–22, 1966, series 4.2, folder 3630; WAMY proposal, September 8, 1965–September 15, 1966, series 4.2, folder 3730; and George Esser to W. H. Plemmons, January 19, 1967, series 4.2, folder 3637, NCFR.

66. Handwritten notes on board of directors meeting minutes, WAMY Community Action, January 24, 1967, series 4.2, folder 3551, NCFR.

67. Robert Walker interview, June 12–13, 1968, series 6.10, folder 7282, and Ernest Eppley interview, June 11–12, 1968, series 6.10, folder 7270, NCFR.

68. Ernest Eppley interview, June 11–12, 1968, series 6.10, folder 7270, NCFR.

69. Bob Walker, "WAMY Community Action," series 4.2, folder 3525, and summary of board of directors meeting, September 21, 1965, series 4.2, folder 3550, NCFR.

70. Robert Walker interview, June 12–13, 1968, series 6.10, folder 7282; Ernest Eppley interview, June 11–12, 1968, series 6.10, folder 7270; Bob Walker, "WAMY Community Action," series 4.2, folder 3525; and Morris Cohen, "Why Should the Poor Be Involved in the War on Poverty?," series 4.2, folder 3559, NCFR.

71. Ernest Eppley interview, June 11–12, 1968, series 6.10, folder 7270, and executive committee meeting minutes, WAMY Community Action, February 9, 1967, series 4.2, folder 3548, NCFR.

72. Handwritten notes on board of directors meeting minutes, WAMY Community Action, January 24, 1967, series 4.2, folder 3551, and "Community Support Strategies in WAMY," series 4.2, folder 3526, NCFR.

73. "Antidote to Apathy: The WAMY Incentive Grants Program," and Marguerite M. Kiely, "Community Organization through Incentive Grants," series 4.2, folder 3736, and Gay Fox notes for WAMY review, series 4.2, folder 3634, NCFR.

74. Review team report on WAMY Community Action, September 18–22, 1966, series 4.2, folder 3630; Ernest Eppley interview, June 11–12, 1968, series 6.10, folder 7270; and "Explanation of Proposed Changes in the County-Level Organization of WAMY Community Action, Inc.," May 19, 1967, series 4.2, folder 3552, NCFR.

75. Bob Walker, "WAMY Community Action," series 4.2, folder 3525; Narrative Progress Report, January 1–March 31, 1967, series 4.2, folder 3609; and Robert Walker to Nathan Garrett, February 28, 1967, and Garrett to Ed Adkins, February 28, 1967, series 4.2, 3641, NCFR; and Kiffmeyer, "From Self-Help to Sedition."

76. "Poor Mobilize in Appalachia; Talk of March," *Louisville Courier-Journal and Times*, February 19, 1967; "Committee to Investigate Feasibility of a Western North Carolina Peoples Congress" and Report on Status of a Western Carolina Peoples Congress, series 4.2, folder 3703, and Robert Walker to Ernest Eppley et al., July 11, 1967, series 4.2, folder 3643, NCFR; and Whisnant, *Modernizing the Mountaineer*, 226–35. For additional background on the Council of the Southern Mountains and the Congress for Appalachian Development, see the Richard C. Austin Collection and the Congress for Appalachian Development: Gordon Ebersole Collection, Archives of Appalachia, East Tennessee State University, Johnson City.

77. "Anger Stirs Poor in Appalachians," *New York Times*, March 27, 1967; and minutes of UAC meeting, December 10, 1966, and untitled memorandum announcing UAC meeting, February 10, 1967, series 10, Council of the Southern Mountains Records, 1912–1970, Special Collections and Archives, Hutchins Library, Berea College, Berea, Ky. (hereafter cited as Council of the Southern Mountains Records).

78. Announcement of UAC meeting, January 14, 1967, Barbourville, Ky.; untitled memorandum announcing UAC meeting, February 10, 1967; and typescript quotations from the *Middlesboro Daily News*, November 18, 1966, and the *Harlan Daily Enterprise*, November 20, 1966, series 8, Council of the Southern Mountains Records; and "Poor Mobilize in Appala-·chia; Talk of March," *Louisville Courier-Journal and Times*, February 19, 1967.

79. Robert Walker to Nathan Garrett, February 28, 1967; Ernest Eppley to Ed Adkins, February 28, 1967; and Walker to James McDonald, February 21, 1967, series 4.2, folder 3641; and Mary Ann Scott and Walker, field report, March 2–4, 1967, series 4.2, folder 3625, NCFR.

80. Narrative Progress Report, January 1–March 31, 1967, series 4.2, folder 3609; Robert Walker to James McDonald, February 21, 1967, series 4.2, folder 3641; and clipping, "WAMY Talent Show Winds Up with Discussion," *Watauga Democrat*, March 2, 1967, series 4.2, folder 3625, NCFR.

81. Narrative Progress Report, January 1–March 31, 1967, series 4.2, folder 3609, and clipping, "WAMY Talent Show Winds Up with Discussion," *Watauga Democrat*, March 2, 1967, series 4.2, folder 3625, NCFR.

82. Robert Walker to James McDonald, February 21, 1967; clipping, "Yancey Aid 'Problems' Speak Out in Raleigh," *Asheville Citizen-Times*, February 15, 1967; and Carol Wilson, "Record of the Meeting of Welfare Recipients from WAMY with the State Commissioner of Welfare, February 14, 1967," series 4.2, folder 3641, NCFR.

83. Carol Wilson, "Record of the Meeting of Welfare Recipients from WAMY with the State Commissioner of Welfare, February 14, 1967," and Eugene Burris, "An Appraisal of the Trip of Welfare Recipients to the Office of the Commissioner of Public Welfare, February 14, 1967," series 4.2, folder 3641, NCFR.

84. George Esser to Robert Walker, February 14, 1967; Walker to James McDonald, February 21, 1967; Walker to Nathan Garrett, February 28, 1967; and Eugene Burris, "An Appraisal of the Trip of Welfare Recipients to the Office of the Commissioner of Public Welfare, February 14, 1967," series 4.2, folder 3641; and executive committee meeting minutes, WAMY Community Action, February 9, 1967, series 4.2, folder 3548, NCFR.

85. Robert Walker to James McDonald, February 21, 1967, series 4.2, folder 3641; board of directors meeting minutes, WAMY Community Action, March 28, 1967, series 4.2, folder 3551; Narrative Progress Report, January 1–March 31, 1967, series 4.2, folder 3609; and Mary Ann Scott and Walker, field report, March 2–4, 1967, series 4.2, folder 3625, NCFR.

86. *What WAMY Can Do*, series 4.2, folder 3597, NCFR.

87. *County Government: The Commissioners and Their Job*, series 4.2, folder 3597, NCFR.

88. Marguerite M. Kiely, "Community Organization through Incentive Grants," and untitled draft statement on incentive grants, series 4.2, folder 3736; and "Demonstration Project Plan and Supporting Data for a Community Action News Demonstration Project in Watauga, Avery, Mitchell, and Yancey Counties, North Carolina," series 4.2, folder 3698, NCFR.

89. Untitled draft statement on incentive grants, series 4.2, folder 3736; Narrative Progress Report, October 1–December 31, 1966, series 4.2, folder 3610; and Narrative Progress Report, January 1–March 31, 1967, series 4.2, folder 3609, NCFR.

90. "Barnes Wants to Help Poor Articulate Own Problems," *Charlotte Observer*, March 13, 1966.

91. Ibid., and "Demonstration Project Plan and Supporting Data for a Community Action News Demonstration Project in Watauga, Avery, Mitchell, and Yancey Counties, North Carolina," series 4.2, folder 3698, NCFR.

92. Rickie Sue Rhodarmer, "The News Demonstration Project: Evolution of an Idea," June 28, 1968, in authors' possession.

93. Ibid.

94. Ibid.

95. Ibid., and "Demonstration Project Plan and Supporting Data for a Community Action News Demonstration Project in Watauga, Avery, Mitchell, and Yancey Counties, North Carolina," series 4.2, folder 3698, NCFR.

96. Rickie Sue Rhodarmer, "The News Demonstration Project: Evolution of an Idea," June 28, 1968, in authors' possession, and "The Battle That Raged: The State Press vs. a Newspaper for the Poor," *North Carolina Anvil*, May 20, 1967.

97. Rickie Sue Rhodarmer, "The News Demonstration Project: Evolution of an Idea," June 28, 1968, in authors' possession, and board of directors meeting minutes, WAMY Community Action, April 25, 1967, series 4.2, folder 3551, NCFR.

98. "The Battle That Raged: The State Press vs. a Newspaper for the Poor," *North Carolina Anvil*, May 20, 1967, and Billy Barnes's collection of newspaper clippings related to the news demonstration project, in authors' possession.

99. "Down in Iredell," *Statesville Record and Landmark*, May 10, 1967; "Bid to Spoon-Feed," *Sanford Herald*, May 6, 1967; and "Are Seeds Being Sown for America's Pravda?," *Asheville Citizen-Times*, May 4, 1967. Similar stories and editorial denunciations ran in almost every newspaper in the state.

100. "Poverty Paper under Fire," *Asheville Citizen*, May 9, 1967; "Rep. Taylor Raps Poverty Newspaper," *Asheville Times*, May 9, 1967; "Basil Raps U.S. Subsidizing Paper," *Charlotte Observer*, May 10, 1967; "The Battle That Raged: The State Press vs. a Newspaper for the Poor," *North Carolina Anvil*, May 20, 1967; "N.C. Fund Staffer Originated Idea for Free Newspaper," *Durham Morning Herald*, May 11, 1967; "Antipoverty Newspaper Is Dropped," *Burlington Times-News*, May 13, 1967; "State's Poverty Programs on Firm Ground," *News and Observer*, May 23, 1967; and "Government Paper Objections Mount," *Durham Morning Herald*, May 10, 1967.

101. "State's Poverty Programs on Firm Ground," *News and Observer*, May 23, 1967.

102. Daniel A. Sullivan, letter to the editor, *Tri-County News*, May 18, 1967; "Antipoverty Newspaper Is Dropped," *Burlington Times-News*, May 13, 1967; and Bill Atkins, letter to the editor, *Yancey Record*, May 11, 1967.

103. "Demonstration Project Plan and Supporting Data for a Community Action News Demonstration Project in Watauga, Avery, Mitchell, and Yancey Counties, North Carolina," series 4.2, folder 3698, NCFR; Robert C. Proffit to Basil Whitener, May 11, 1967, subject series W, box 165, WAMY Community Action folder, Basil Lee Whitener Papers, Rare Book, Manuscript, and Special Collections Library, Duke University, Durham, N.C. (hereafter cited as Whitener Papers); and "Community Action News Demonstration Project in the Counties of Watauga, Mitchell, Avery, and Yancey, N.C.," 90th Cong., 1st sess., *Congressional Record* 113 (May 9, 1967): 12017.

104. *Asheville Citizen*: "Poverty Newspaper Plan Is Shelved," May 12, 1967, and "Withdrawing an Unwise Project," May 15, 1967.

105. Boone Rotary Club speech, June 1, 1967, series 4.2, folder 3955, NCFR.

106. Ibid.

107. "Jaycees Announce Anti-Poverty Plan," September 21, 1967, North Carolina Fund Clipping Files, vols. 119–20; and clipping, "Jaycees Say WAMY Felt to Be Ineffective," *Winston-Salem Journal*, December 4, 1967; Boone Jaycees press release, December 13, 1967; and "Whammy Is Put on WAMY," unidentified newspaper clipping, series 4.2, folder 3598, NCFR. On the national effort to redirect the War on Poverty, see Epilogue, note 4.

108. Boone Jaycees press release, December 13, 1967, and Ernest Eppley to Paul Smith, December 21, 1967, series 4.2, folder 3598, NCFR.

109. Transcript of *Retreat from the Hills*, series 4.2, folder 3598, NCFR.

110. Ibid., and Woodrow Anglin to Basil Whitener, August 2, 1967, subject series W, box 165, WAMY Community Action folder, Whitener Papers.

111. Transcript of *Retreat from the Hills*, series 4.2, folder 3598, NCFR. Whitener read a transcript of the WBT documentary into the *Congressional Record*; see "Retreat from the Hills," 90th Cong., 2nd sess., *Congressional Record* 114 (January 15, 1968): 15–17.

112. H. C. Moretz Jr. résumé, series 4.2, folder 3553, NCFR.

113. Robert Walker, field report, November 10, 1967, series 4.2, folder 3553, and Walker interview, June 12–23, 1968, series 6.10, folder 7282, NCFR.

114. Ernest Eppley interview, June 11–12, 1968, series 6.10, folder 7270, and Eppley to WAMY staff, April 1967, series 4.2, folder 3598, NCFR.

CHAPTER 6

1. "Recommendations concerning Future of the North Carolina Fund and Its Functions," box 28, and George Esser to Mitchell Sviridoff, February 24, 1968, box 14, George H. Esser Papers, Southern Historical Collection, Wilson Library, University of North Carolina at Chapel Hill (hereafter cited as Esser Papers).

2. "Recommendations concerning Future of the North Carolina Fund and Its Functions," box 28, Esser Papers.

3. George Esser to Mitchell Sviridoff, February 24, 1968, box 14, Esser Papers, and Esser to Terry Sanford, February 17, 1967, series 1.2.1, folder 262, North Carolina Fund Records, Southern Historical Collection, Wilson Library, University of North Carolina at Chapel Hill (hereafter cited as NCFR).

4. George Esser to Mitchell Sviridoff, undated draft, and Esser to Sviridoff, February 24, 1968, box 14, Esser Papers; and Esser to Terry Sanford, February 17, 1967, series 1.2.1, folder 262, NCFR.

5. Transcript of Southern Pines staff retreat, box 29, and George Esser to Mitchell Sviridoff, February 24, 1968, box 14, Esser Papers; and King, "Letter from Birmingham Jail," ⟨http://mlk-kpp01.stanford.edu/index.php/resources/article/kings_letter_from_birmingham_jail⟩.

6. Brennan, *Turning Right in the Sixties*, 80; Diamond, *Roads to Dominion*, 64; and Bjerre-Poulsen, *Right Face*, 286–87, 291.

7. Brennan, *Turning Right in the Sixties*, 119, and Carter, *Politics of Rage*, 307.

8. Clipping, "Irregularities in OEO," *Congressional Record*, June 14, 1967, accompanying John Strange to George Esser, August 11, 1967, series 1.2.2, folder 324, NCFR.

9. "Poverty: Progress, Protest, and Politics," *Time*, July 12, 1965; Morone, *Democratic Wish*, 240; Donovan, *Politics of Poverty*, 57; and clipping, "Political Involvement of OEO," *Congressional Record*, June 22, 1967, accompanying John Strange to George Esser, August 11, 1967, series 1.2.2, folder 324, NCFR. See also David, "Leadership of the Poor in Poverty Programs."

10. Casper, "Rise of the Republican Party in Rocky Mount, North Carolina," 36–40, and *Biographical Directory of the United States Congress, 1774–Present*, s.v. "Gardner, James Carson," ⟨http://bioguide.congress.gov/biosearch/biosearch.asp⟩ (June 19, 2009).

11. Casper, "Rise of the Republican Party in Rocky Mount, North Carolina," 38–39, and Esty, "Reinventing Southern Conservatism," 5–7.

12. Casper, "Rise of the Republican Party in Rocky Mount, North Carolina," 43, 49, and Esty, "Reinventing Southern Conservatism," 20, 22.

13. Sim DeLapp to James Gardner, September 1, 1965, box 9, Sim A. DeLapp Papers, Rare Book, Manuscript, and Special Collections Library, Duke University, Durham, N.C. (hereafter cited as DeLapp Papers).

14. Ibid.; and Sim DeLapp to George Romney, January 18, February 1, 1964, box 8, and DeLapp to Romney, July 19, 1965, box 9, DeLapp Papers. On Romney's role in establishing the Michigan Civil Rights Commission, see Fine, *"Expanding the Frontiers of Civil Rights,"* 191–213.

15. "The Republican Party in North Carolina [1968]," box 16, DeLapp Papers.

16. Reagan, "A Time for Choosing," ⟨http://www.americanrhetoric.com/speeches/ronaldreaganatimeforchoosing.htm⟩, and Sim DeLapp to Ronald Reagan, November 2, 1964, box 8, DeLapp Papers.

17. Casper, "Rise of the Republican Party in Rocky Mount, North Carolina," 37, 52–55, and Esty, "Reinventing Southern Conservatism," 30.

18. Clipping, "Political Involvement of OEO," *Congressional Record*, June 22, 1967; clipping, "Political Activities in OEO," *Congressional Record*, June 27, 1967; and clipping, "Operation Breakthrough," *Congressional Record*, June 28, 1967, all accompanying John Strange to George Esser, August 11, 1967, series 1.2.2, folder 324, NCFR.

19. Mumford, *Newark*, 98–148, and Fine, *Violence in the Model City*, 155–290.

20. National Advisory Commission on Civil Disorders, *Kerner Report*, 1, 484.

21. Ibid., 7–8, 10–11, 57, 59, 86–87, 90.

22. Ibid., 1–2, 10, 23.

23. Clipping, "OEO Political Activities Related to Violence in Newark, N.J.," *Congressional Record*, July 18, 1967; clipping, "Reasons for Riots," *Congressional Record*, July 25, 1967; clipping, "Antipoverty Workers Involvement in Newark," *Congressional Record*, July 27, 1967; and clipping, "Poverty Warriors — The Riots Are Subsidized as Well as Organized," *Congressional Record*, August 2, 1967, all accompanying John Strange to George Esser, August 11, 1967, series 1.2.2, folder 324, NCFR.

24. Clipping, "Antipoverty Workers Involvement in Newark," *Congressional Record*, July 27, 1967, accompanying John Strange to George Esser, August 11, 1967, series 1.2.2, folder 324, NCFR; *New York Times*: "Poverty — The Program Has Friends," August 13, 1967, and "Newark Jailer Says Poverty Aides Stirred Riots," August 8, 1967; and Frank Turnipseed to James Gardner, August 10, 1967, box 14, James Carson Gardner Congressional and Political Papers, Southern Historical Collection, Wilson Library, University of North Carolina at

Chapel Hill (hereafter cited as Gardner Papers). For McClellan's perspective on corruption in the labor movement, particularly within the Teamsters union, see his *Crime without Punishment*.

25. Kathryn Mills to James Gardner, July 31, 1967, box 14, Gardner Papers.

26. Doris Overman to James Gardner, n.d.; Doris Poe to Gardner, August 8, 1967; and J. C. Perkins to Gardner, n.d., box 14, Gardner Papers.

27. Doris Poe to James Gardner, August 8, 1967, and J. C. Perkins to Gardner, n.d., accompanied by transcript of Jesse Helms, "Viewpoint" editorial 1660 (August 10, 1967), box 14, Gardner Papers.

28. James Gardner to Wilbur Raynor, September 5, 1967, box 9; Doris Poe to Gardner, August 8, 1967, box 14; Mrs. Gordon [Jane] Hunt to Gardner, August 6, 1967, and Gardner to Hunt, September 8, 1967, box 18; Gardner to Doris Overman, September 7, 1967; and Gardner to Kathryn Mills, August 16, 1967, box 14, Gardner Papers.

29. Doris Poe to James Gardner, August 8, 1967, box 14; Joseph O'Neal to Gardner, May 14, 1968, box 16; Doris Overman to Gardner, n.d., box 14; and I. Beverly Lake to Gardner, August 5, 1967, box 23, Gardner Papers.

30. James Gardner press release, July 25, 1967, series 1.2.2, folder 318, NCFR.

31. Executive committee meeting minutes, July 25, 1967, box 29, Esser Papers; and H. M. Michaux Jr. to Congressman Nick Galifianakis, Sargent Shriver, and George Esser, July 25, 1967, and Charles Watts to Shriver, July 25, 1967, series 1.2.2, folder 319, NCFR.

32. Watts Hill Jr. to Sargent Shriver, July 25, 1967, series 1.2.2, folder 319, NCFR. Shriver provided Gardner with evidence that in cities across the country antipoverty workers had acted much like Howard Fuller in helping to prevent — not instigate — violence. See Shriver to Gardner, September 19, 1967, box 23, Gardner Papers.

33. An extensive collection of newspaper clippings, telegrams, and letters related to the controversy can be found in series 1.2.2, folders 317–26, NCFR.

34. "House Hearing: Its Ritual and Reality," *New York Times*, August 21, 1967, and Baker interview.

35. *New York Times*: "In the Nation: Poverty in the House," November 7, 1967, and "Still a Few Friends for Poverty Program," November 12, 1967; Moynihan, *Maximum Feasible Misunderstanding*, 158; and David, "Leadership of the Poor in Poverty Programs," 99.

36. *New York Times*: "Senate Votes $1.9 Billion Poverty Bill," December 9, 1967, and "In the Nation: Poverty in the House," November 7, 1967; and David, "Leadership of the Poor in Poverty Programs," 100.

37. Clipping, Richard Goodwin, "The Roots of Violence," *Vista Volunteer*, October 1967, box 33, Esser Papers.

38. Offprint, George Esser, "Involving the Citizen in Decision-Making," *Nation's Cities*, May 1968, box 32, Esser Papers. Esser reiterated these points in a number of speeches in late 1967 and early 1968. See, for instance, "Increasing the Individual's Involvement in Local Government" (speech delivered at the annual meeting of the International City Managers Association, New Orleans, La., October 9, 1967); "A Policy on Economic and Human Resources" (speech delivered at the annual meeting of the National League of Cities, Boston, July 31, 1967); and "The Urban Crisis" (speech delivered at the annual meeting of the National Conference of Christians and Jews, Salisbury, N.C., February, 15, 1968), box 25, Esser Papers.

39. Hugh Price, "FCD: A Unique Experiment in Community Development," March 1972, series 1.8, folder 887, NCFR, and "Foundation Investment in Solving the Problems of North Carolina and the South," box 29, Esser Papers.

40. FCD proposal, February 1968, series 1.8, folder 850, NCFR.

41. Hugh Price, "FCD: A Unique Experiment in Community Development," March 1972, series 1.8, folder 887; "Corporate Data and Early History," series 1.8, folder 831; and Steve Redburn and Bertie Howard, "The Foundation for Community Development," August 9, 1968, series 1.8, folder 886, NCFR.

42. William Darity, "An Analysis of Community Development in Some Selected Communities in North Carolina, August 11–September 1, 1968," series 1.8, folder 905, and "Corporate Data and Early History," series 1.8, folder 831, NCFR.

43. Capsule Reports on Organizations Supported by FCD, and Staff Report to the Board of Directors of the Foundation for Community Development on People's Program on Poverty, May 9, 1968, series 1.8, folder 900, NCFR.

44. John Strange to George Esser, October 19, 1967, series 1.8, folder 889; Steve Redburn and Bertie Howard, "The Foundation for Community Development," August 9, 1968, series 1.8, folder 886; Nathan Garrett, "Evaluation of Maximum Feasible Participation of the Poor," series 1.8, folder 906; and William Darity, "An Analysis of Community Development in Some Selected Communities in North Carolina," August 11–September 1, 1968, series 1.8, folder 905, NCFR.

45. "The White Poor," series 8.2, folder 8321, NCFR, and John Salter, "The Economically Deprived Southern White," box 2, folder 7, Hunter Gray (John R. Salter) Papers, Wisconsin Historical Society, Madison (hereafter cited as Gray [Salter] Papers). See also John Strange to George Esser, October 19, 1967, series 1.8, folder 889, NCFR.

46. "Dr. King Planning to Disrupt Capital in Drive for Jobs," *New York Times*, December 5, 1967; Chase, "Class Resurrection," ⟨http://etext.virginia.edu/journals/EH/EH40/chase40.html#n3.1⟩; Martin Luther King Jr., "Showdown for Non-Violence," *Look*, April 16, 1968, 23–25; King, "Beyond Vietnam," ⟨http://www.americanrhetoric.com/speeches/mlka timetobreaksilence.htm⟩; and Goodwin, *Lyndon Johnson*, 251–52.

47. King, "Beyond Vietnam," ⟨http://www.americanrhetoric.com/speeches/mlkatime tobreaksilence.htm⟩; Chase, "Class Resurrection," ⟨http://etext.virginia.edu/journals/EH/EH40/chase40.html#n3.1⟩; Rowan, "Martin Luther King's Tragic Decision," 42; "Dr. King's Disservice to His Cause," *Life*, April 21, 1967, 4; "A Tragedy," *Washington Post*, April 6, 1967; "Dr. King's Error," *New York Times*, April 7, 1967; *King Online Encyclopedia*, s.v. "Poor People's Campaign," ⟨http://mlk-kpp01.stanford.edu/index.php/encyclopedia/encyclopedia/enc_poor_peoples_campaign/⟩ (September 2, 2009); Thompson, "When God Collides with Race and Class," 264; and King, *My Life with Martin Luther King, Jr.*, 298.

48. Richard First to John Salter, November 18, 1966, series 1.4, folder 592, NCFR, and John Salter, "The Economically Deprived Southern White," box 2, folder 7, Gray (Salter) Papers.

49. John Salter, "The Economically Deprived Southern White," box 2, folder 7, Gray (Salter) Papers.

50. Greensboro Truth and Reconciliation Commission, *Final Report*, chap. 3, "North Carolina Resurgence of the Ku Klux Klan," ⟨http://www.greensborotrc.org/pre1979_kkk .pdf⟩, 101; House Committee on Un-American Activities, *Hearings on Activities of Ku Klux*

Klan Organizations in the United States, 1545–56; John Salter, "The Economically Deprived Southern White," box 2, folder 7, Gray (Salter) Papers; and Davidson, *Best of Enemies*, 187.

51. John Salter, "The Economically Deprived Southern White," box 2, folder 7, Gray (Salter) Papers.

52. John Salter, "Poor Whites and the North Carolina Leadership Training Project," series 1.4, folder 593, NCFR; Salter, "FBI Collusion with a Hard-Line Deep South Segregationist Congressman — against Hunter Gray," ⟨http://www.hunterbear.org/fbi_collusion .htm⟩; Salter, "Personal Reminiscence," ⟨http://www.hunterbear.org/personal_reminiscence .htm⟩; Salter, "Eastern North Carolina Black-Belt Followup," ⟨http://www.hunterbear .org/willacofield.htm⟩; Hunter Bear (Salter) interview, ⟨http://www.crmvet.org/nars/ hunteri.htm⟩; John Salter, "The Economically Deprived Southern White," box 2, folder 7, Gray (Salter) Papers; Lloyd Jacobs's campaign card, in authors' possession; "Protestors an Odd Concoction," *Charlotte Observer*, April 24, 1968; and Glenda Bunce, "Organizing Poor Whites: A Case Study of Patlock Park, Durham, N.C.," June 1968, series 6.10, folder 7432, NCFR.

53. Terkel, *American Dreams*, 204, and Davidson, *Best of Enemies*, 206.

54. Terkel, *American Dreams*, 205.

55. Ibid., 206–7, and Davidson, *Best of Enemies*, 245–59.

56. Terkel, *American Dreams*, 207–9.

57. Ibid., 201–3.

58. John Salter, "The Economically Deprived Southern White," box 2, folder 7, Gray (Salter) Papers.

59. Fuller interview; Tornquist, "Standing Up to America," 40; and Phyllis Freeman, "White Community Organization in Durham from 1966 to the Present," July 3, 1968, and Lawrence (Richard) Landerman and Harry Boyte, "Position Paper on White Organizing," series 6.10, folder 7432, NCFR.

60. "History of ACT," box 1, Boyte Family Papers, Rare Book, Manuscript, and Special Collections Library, Duke University, Durham, N.C., and Tornquist, "Standing Up to America," 47. For a trenchant account of the failure of white organizing in Durham, see Greene, *Our Separate Ways*, 139–64.

61. Lawrence (Richard) Landerman and Harry Boyte, "Position Paper on White Organizing," series 6.10, folder 7432, and "The White Poor," series 8.2, folder 8321, NCFR.

62. Fuller interview.

63. Tornquist, "Standing Up to America," 41; and Lawrence (Richard) Landerman and Harry Boyte, "Position Paper on White Organizing," series 6.10, folder 7432, and FCD proposal, February 1968, series 1.8, folder 850, NCFR.

64. Connor and Poe, *Life and Speeches of Charles Brantley Aycock*, 211–27.

65. Tornquist, "Standing Up to America," 44; and John Salter, "Poor Whites and the North Carolina Leadership Training Project," series 1.4, folder 593, and Lawrence (Richard) Landerman and Harry Boyte, "Position Paper on White Organizing," series 6.10, folder 7432, NCFR.

66. Tornquist, "Standing Up to America," 43–45, and Citizens' Board of Inquiry into Hunger and Malnutrition in the United States, *Hunger, U.S.A.*

67. *Stand Up for America*, Wallace campaign brochure, 1968, in authors' possession; Carter, *Politics of Rage*, 329–31, 346; Perlstein, *Nixonland*, 283–85; and Nixon, "Nomination

Acceptance Address," ⟨http://www.presidentialrhetoric.com/historicspeeches/nixon/nominationacceptance1968.html⟩.

68. "Nixon's Southern Strategy: 'It's All in the Charts,'" *New York Times*, May 17, 1970, and Carter, *Politics of Rage*, 369.

69. George Esser to Mitchell Sviridoff, August 25, 1969, series 1.8, folder 894, NCFR; Williams, "'It Wasn't Slavery Time Anymore,'" 114–24; and Chafe, *Civilities and Civil Rights*, 266.

70. Claude Barnes testimony, July 15, 2005, first public hearing of the Greensboro Truth and Reconciliation Commission, ⟨http://www.greensborotrc.org/barnes.doc⟩, and Chafe, *Civilities and Civil Rights*, 242–75.

71. Chafe, *Civilities and Civil Rights*, 265–86.

72. Mitchell Sviridoff to McGeorge Bundy, regarding Fund support for FCD, December 23, 1969, series 1.8, folder 853, and William Snider to Edward Sylvester, September 12, 1969, series 1.8, folder 894, NCFR.

73. Hugh Price, "FCD: A Unique Experiment in Community Development," March 1972, series 1.8, folder 887, and FCD press release, June 21, 1969, series 1.8, folder 893, NCFR.

74. Senate Committee on Government Operations, *Hearings before the Permanent Subcommittee on Investigations on Riots, Civil and Criminal Disorders*, 4845–48.

75. Ibid., 4851–68; Chafe, *Civilities and Civil Rights*, 242–86; Joseph, *Waiting 'til the Midnight Hour*, 196; Claude Barnes testimony, July 15, 2005, first public hearing of the Greensboro Truth and Reconciliation Commission, ⟨http://www.greensborotrc.org/barnes.doc⟩; and Wilkins, "In the Belly of the Beast," 123–28.

76. Senate Committee on Government Operations, *Hearings before the Permanent Subcommittee on Investigations on Riots, Civil and Criminal Disorders*, 4877, 4885–86, and Basil Whiting memorandum, July 23, 1969, reel 2670, Ford Foundation Archives, Ford Foundation, New York. On Mundt's background, see "House Un-American Activities Committee," ⟨http://www.departments.dsu.edu/library/archive/unamerican.htm⟩.

77. B. Carroll Reece, "Tax-Exempt Subversion," *American Mercury*, July 1957, 56–64; Bremner, *American Philanthropy*, 168; "The Supreme Court, Segregation, and the South," 83rd Cong., 2nd sess., *Congressional Record* 100 (May 27, 1954): 7251.

78. House Committee on Ways and Means, *Hearings on Tax Reform, 1969*, 12; Smith and Chiechi, *Private Foundations before and after the Tax Reform Act of 1969*, chap. 4; and "Tax-Free Dollars Are in Trouble," *New York Times*, February 23, 1969.

79. "Historical US Inflation Rate 1914–Present," ⟨http://inflationdata.com/Inflation/Inflation_Rate/HistoricalInflation.aspx⟩.

80. "Text of President Nixon's Message on Tax Reform," *New York Times*, April 22, 1969, and Senate Committee on Government Operations, *Hearings before the Permanent Subcommittee on Investigations on Riots, Civil and Criminal Disorders*, 4877.

81. *Wikipedia*, s.vv. "Albert Watson (politician)," ⟨http://en.wikipedia.org/wiki/Albert_Watson_(politician)⟩, and "John Rarick," ⟨http://en.wikipedia.org/wiki/John_Rarick⟩ (September 19, 2009); Council of Conservative Citizens, ⟨http://cofcc.org⟩; biographical note, inventory of the Ben Blackburn Congressional Papers, 1969–1974, ⟨http://russelldoc.galib.uga.edu/russell/view?docId=ead/bblack.xml⟩; Paletz, "Neglected Context of Congressional Campaigns," 200; and Cokorinos, *Assault on Diversity*, 102.

82. Excerpts from Brownfeld, *Financiers of Revolution*, 91st Cong., 1st sess., *Congressional*

Record 115 (April 30, 1969): 10888–89; Brennan, *Turning Right in the Sixties*, 114–16; and Brownfeld, *Financiers of Revolution*.

83. "The I.W.W. Exposed by Its Chief Propagandist," *New York World*, February 8, 1920; Horne, *Color of Fascism*, 47; Heidenry, *Theirs Was the Kingdom*, 125; Bjerre-Poulsen, *Right Face*, 102–4; and Harold Lord Varney, "How the Ford Foundation Finances Revolution," 91st Cong., 1st sess., *Congressional Record* 115 (March 3, 1969): 5088–92.

84. Harold Lord Varney, "How the Ford Foundation Finances Revolution," 91st Cong., 1st sess., *Congressional Record* 115 (March 3, 1969): 5088–92.

85. "Tax-Exempt Organizations Engaging in Improper Political Activities," 91st Cong., 1st sess., *Congressional Record* 115 (October 9, 1969): 29507–15; House Committee on Ways and Means, *Hearings on Tax Reform, 1969*, 951–63; and Draper, *Conflict of Interests*, 87–90.

86. "Tax-Exempt Liberal Churches Finance Revolution," 91st Cong., 1st sess., *Congressional Record* 115 (August 6, 1969): 22650–54. On the Church League of America, see Epstein and Forster, *Radical Right*, 77–79, and George and Wilcox, *Nazis, Communists, Klansmen, and Others on the Fringe*, 234–40.

87. Harold Lord Varney, "How the Ford Foundation Finances Revolution," 91st Cong., 1st sess., *Congressional Record* 115 (March 3, 1969): 5088–92; "Tax-Exempt Organizations Engaging in Improper Political Activities," 91st Cong., 1st sess., *Congressional Record* 115 (October 9, 1969): 29507–15; and Ferguson, "Organizing the Ghetto."

88. "Tax-Exempt Organizations and Foundations," 91st Cong., 1st sess., *Congressional Record* 115 (April 3, 1969): 8685, and "The Ford Foundation's Cancer," 91st Cong., 1st sess., *Congressional Record* 115 (March 4, 1969): 5301. For an account of the Ocean Hill–Brownsville conflict, see Podair, *Strike That Changed New York*.

89. House Committee on Ways and Means, *Hearings on Tax Reform, 1969*, 124.

90. Statement by Edward P. Boland, 91st Cong., 1st sess., *Congressional Record* 115 (August 6, 1969): 22608–12.

91. Harold Lord Varney, "How the Ford Foundation Finances Revolution," 91st Cong., 1st sess., *Congressional Record* 115 (March 3, 1969): 5092; and *New York Times*: "House and Senate Approve Tax Bill," December 23, 1969, and "Tax Bill Signed," December 31, 1969.

92. Summary of the Tax Reform Act of 1969, January 12, 1970, series 1.8, folder 866, NCFR; Wadsworth, "Private Foundations and the Tax Reform Act of 1969"; Labovitz, "Impact of the Private Foundation Provisions of the Tax Reform Act of 1969"; and "HR 13270, Key Problems Affecting Foundations, and Preferred Remedies," box 15, Esser Papers.

93. Senate Committee on Finance, *Hearings on the Tax Reform Act of 1969*, 5405–7, and Roy Wilkins, letter to the editor, *New York Times*, August 8, 1969.

94. Minutes of the meeting of the FCD board of directors, September 19, 1969, series 1.8, folder 843, and Mitchell Sviridoff to McGeorge Bundy, regarding Fund support for FCD, December 23, 1969, series 1.8, folder 853, NCFR.

95. George Esser to Nathan Garrett, January 3, 1970, series 1.8, folder 896; minutes of the meeting of the FCD board of directors, September 19, 1969, series 1.8, folder 843; Hugh Price, "FCD: A Unique Experiment in Community Development," March 1972, series 1.8, folder 887; and Proposal to the Ford Foundation, February 11, 1970, series 1.8, folder 857, NCFR.

96. "United Durham, Inc.," and United Durham broadside, series 1.8, folder 903, NCFR.

97. "Holshouser Asks U.S. Halt on Durham Aid," *Charlotte Observer*, May 3, 1969; Senate Committee on Labor and Public Welfare, *Hearings before the Subcommittee on Employment, Manpower, and Poverty on the Economic Opportunity Amendments of 1969*, 438; and "Subsidized Sedition," 91st Cong., 1st sess., *Congressional Record* 115 (May 26, 1969): 13839–40.

98. Klinkner and Smith, *Unsteady March*, 293; Skrentny, *Ironies of Affirmative Action*, 214; and Ehrlichman, *Witness to Power*, 212–20.

99. "President Nixon and Bob Haldeman Discuss Donald Rumsfeld, March 9, 1971," ⟨http://tapes.millercenter.virginia.edu/clips/rmn_rumsfeld.html⟩; Cockburn, *Rumsfeld*, 16–17; Senate Committee on Labor and Public Welfare, *Hearings before the Subcommittee on Employment, Manpower, and Poverty on the Economic Opportunity Amendments of 1969*, 416–19; and Mann, *Rise of the Vulcans*, 13.

100. "Politics and Poverty," *Time*, October 26, 1970; and *New York Times*: "Legal Aid Director Ousted by Rumsfeld; Aide Also Dropped," November 21, 1970; "Legal Aid and Politics," November 24, 1970; and "Federal Lawyers for the Poor," December 15, 1970.

101. *New York Times*: "Nixon Endorses Model Cities Aid with Local Rule," September 11, 1970, and "Philadelphia Groups Sue U.S. over Model Cities Participation," August 16, 1969.

102. Frieden and Kaplan, *Politics of Neglect*, 202–7, and Banfield, *Unheavenly City Revisited*, 235.

103. "Philadelphia Groups Sue U.S. over Model Cities Participation," *New York Times*, August 16, 1969; Kloman, "Citizen Participation in the Philadelphia Model Cities Program"; and Frieden and Kaplan, *Politics of Neglect*, 267.

104. Biles, "Rise and Fall of Soul City," 57–63, and "U.S. Moves to Cut Ties with Soul City," *Pittsburgh Post-Gazette*, June 29, 1979.

105. Ehrlichman, *Witness to Power*, 223, and Perlstein, *Nixonland*, 127. On Nixon and black capitalism, see Kotlowski, *Nixon's Civil Rights*, 125–56, and Skrentny, *Ironies of Affirmative Action*, 177–221.

106. Nixon radio address, quoted in Chase, "Class Resurrection," ⟨http://etext.virginia.edu/journals/EH/EH40/chase40.html#n3.1⟩.

107. Kotlowski, "Black Power—Nixon Style," 414, 420.

108. Williams, "Class Matters," 108, and Nathan Garrett to friends of FCD, May 8, 1970, series 1.8, folder 841, NCFR.

109. Proposal to the Ford Foundation, February 11, 1970, series 1.8, folder 857, NCFR.

110. Background to Ford Foundation grant to FCD, [1970], series 1.8, folder 854; Hugh Price, "FCD: A Unique Experiment in Community Development," March 1972, series 1.8, folder 887; Susan Stein to Nathan Garrett, April 12, 1972, series 1.8, folder 897; and Garrett to Ron Gault, May 24, 1971, series 1.8, folder 897, NCFR; and George Esser to Emily Wilson, January 7, 1987, box 31, Esser Papers.

EPILOGUE

1. *New York Times*: "He Has Staked Out a Conservative Course," January 28, 1973; "Poverty Programs Lag as Slump Intensifies Federal Aid Demand," April 10, 1975; "Top Officials Resign from Poverty Agency," February 1, 1973; "Judge Halts Move to Disband OEO," April 12, 1973; "Plan to Dismantle OEO," February 17, 1973; "The Good War That Might Have Been," September 29, 1974; and "Poverty Agency Chief," February 17, 1973;

Phillips interview, ⟨http://www.gwu.edu/~action/philint.html⟩; and "Scandal Stories Illustrate Why OEO Must Be Junked," *Human Events*, March 24, 1973. On Young Americans for Freedom, see Andrew, *Other Side of the Sixties*, and Schneider, *Cadres for Conservatism*.

2. *New York Times*: "Acting OEO Chief Discerns Marxism in Poverty Agency," February 4, 1973; "OEO Plans to Close 10 Regional Offices by April 28," March 13, 1973; "Poverty Chief Scored at House Hearing," February 28, 1973; and "Strategy for an Execution," February 18, 1973.

3. *New York Times*: "Plan to Dismantle OEO," February 17, 1973; "'74 Funds Sought for Poverty Unit," June 17, 1973; "Shifts in Federal Aid Alarm 'New South,'" March 19, 1973; "4 Senators Seek to Oust Head of OEO," March 15, 1973; "Judge Says Phillips Illegally Heads Poverty Agency," June 12, 1973; "Judge Halts Move to Disband OEO," April 12, 1973; "A Political Siege," April 15, 1973; "Contempt for Congress," April 21, 1973; "A Poverty Protest Mounted in Capitol," February 8, 1973; "House and Nixon Act to Aid OEO," June 27, 1973; and "Nominee to OEO Backs Aid to Poor," July 21, 1973.

4. "$4.5-Billion Fund to Aid Jobless Approved by Ford," *New York Times*, January 5, 1975; Cronin, "An Imperiled Presidency?," 58; *New York Times*: "Republicans Assail Poverty Program," May 29, 1966; "House GOP Bloc Offers a Substitute Poverty Plan," April 11, 1967; "Economy and Politics," April 16, 1967; "House Republicans Likely to Agree on a Poverty Bill, Despite Riots," August 9, 1967; "House Hearing: Its Ritual and Reality," August 21, 1967; "Whose 'Opportunity Crusade'?," November 7, 1967; "Political Moves Save the Poverty Program," November 10, 1967; and "Under Ford's Helmet," September 15, 1974; Clark, *War on Poverty*, 68–70; and "Report Praises Poverty Program Despite Officials' Negative View," *New York Times*, February 3, 1973.

5. O'Connor, "U.S. Social Welfare Policy," 39–45; Mettler, "Transformed Welfare State," 201; Gans, *War against the Poor*; and Katz, *Price of Citizenship*, 348. For an astute discussion of poverty issues over the last half century, see Katz, *Undeserving Poor*.

6. Blumenthal, *Rise of the Counter-Establishment*, and Smith, *Idea Brokers*.

7. Murray, *Losing Ground*, 234–36.

8. Mead, *Beyond Entitlement*, 3, 73, 85, 257.

9. King and Wickham-Jones, "From Clinton to Blair," 64–65, and "That Other Clinton Promise—Ending 'Welfare as We Know It,'" *Wall Street Journal*, January 18, 1993.

10. "That Other Clinton Promise—Ending 'Welfare as We Know It,'" *Wall Street Journal*, January 18, 1993; and *New York Times*: "Clinton in Political Quandary on Welfare," November 20, 1996; "Republicans Shift Strategy in Bid to Avoid Welfare Bill Veto," July 12, 1996; "Clinton Seeks New Welfare Bill, G.O.P. Plan Is Too Harsh," April 19, 1995; "House Backs Bill Undoing Decades of Welfare Policy," March 25, 1995; "Clinton to Sign Welfare Bill That Ends U.S. Aid Guarantee and Gives States Broad Power," August 1, 1996; and "Clinton Signs Bill Cutting Welfare; States in New Role," August 23, 1996.

11. National Association of Social Workers, "Personal Responsibility and Work Opportunity Reconciliation Act of 1996 (Public Law 104-193), Summary of Provisions," ⟨http://www.socialworkers.org/advocacy/welfare/legislation/summary.pdf⟩.

12. Grogger and Karoly, *Welfare Reform*, 2; Urban Institute, "A Decade of Welfare Reform," ⟨http://www.urban.org/publications/900980.html⟩; and Nichols, "Understanding Changes in Child Poverty over the Past Decade," ⟨http://www.urban.org/publications/411320.html⟩.

13. Charlotte Chamber of Commerce, ⟨http://www.charlottechamber.com⟩; U.S. Census Bureau, "Raleigh and Austin Are Fastest-Growing Metro Areas," ⟨http://www.census .gov/Press-Release/www/releases/archives/population/013426.html⟩; U.S. Census Bureau, "State and County QuickFacts," ⟨http://quickfacts.census.gov/qfd/states/37000 .html⟩; Kids Count Data Center, Annie E. Casey Foundation, "Percent of Children in Poverty—2007" (North Carolina), ⟨http://datacenter.kidscount.org/data/bystate/Map .aspx?state=NC&ind=2238⟩; and Campbell, "Which End of the Boat Are You Sitting In?," ⟨http://www.ncspin.com/spin/articles/2007_01_3_5126.php⟩.

14. North Carolina Community Action Association, ⟨http://www.nccaa.net/⟩; MDC, ⟨http://www.mdcinc.org/about/index.aspx⟩; Z. Smith Reynolds Foundation, ⟨http:// www.zsr.org/history.htm⟩; Mary Reynolds Babcock Foundation, ⟨http://www.mrbf.org/ missionAndBeliefs.aspx⟩; and Emily Coble, "Presentation on Cultural Diversity," November 16, 1995, cited in Berry, "One Building Block in the Battle," 113.

15. Townsend, *Poverty in the United Kingdom*, 57, and "The War on Poverty: Ten Years Later," *New York Times*, June 4, 1974.

16. King, "Our God Is Marching On!," ⟨http://mlk-kpp01.stanford.edu/index.php/ kingpapers/article/our_god_is_marching_on/⟩.

Bibliography

ARCHIVAL COLLECTIONS

Berea, Ky.
 Special Collections and Archives, Hutchins Library, Berea College
  Council of the Southern Mountains Records, 1912–1970
Boston, Mass.
 John F. Kennedy Presidential Library and Museum
  Robert Sargent Shriver Papers (#214)
Chapel Hill, N.C.
 North Carolina Collection, Wilson Library, University of North Carolina
  Jesse Helms "Viewpoint" editorials
  North Carolina Fund Clipping Files, 1963–1969
  North Carolina Fund, *Process Analysis Report*
 Southern Historical Collection, Wilson Library, University of North Carolina
  John B. Dunne Papers (#4391)
  George H. Esser Papers (#4887)
  Kathrine R. Everett and R. O. Everett Papers (#4735)
  James A. Felton and Annie Vaughan Felton Papers (#5161)
  L. H. Fountain Papers (#4304)
  James Carson Gardner Congressional and Political Papers (#3829)
  North Carolina Fund Records (#4710)
  Richardson Preyer Papers (#5111)
  Terry Sanford Papers (#3531)
College Park, Md.
 National Archives and Records Administration
  Records of the Community Services Administration, 1963–1981 (RG 381)
Durham, N.C.
 Rare Book, Manuscript, and Special Collections Library, Duke University
  Boyte Family Papers
  Sim A. DeLapp Papers
  Thomas S. Inborden, "History of Brick School"
  Records and Papers of Terry Sanford
  Basil Lee Whitener Papers
Johnson City, Tenn.
 Archives of Appalachia, East Tennessee State University
  Richard C. Austin Collection
  Congress for Appalachian Development: Gordon Ebersole Collection
Madison, Wisc.
 Wisconsin Historical Society
  Hunter Gray (John R. Salter) Papers

New York, N.Y.
  Ford Foundation
    Ford Foundation Archives
Raleigh, N.C.
  North Carolina Division of Archives and History
    Official Papers of Governor Terry Sanford
      Subject File of the Special Assistant to the Governor on Education and Cultural
        Affairs, 1962–1964
Winston-Salem, N.C.
  Z. Smith Reynolds Library, Wake Forest University
    Julius Corpening Papers

GOVERNMENT DOCUMENTS

Annual Report of the Superintendent of Public Instruction of North Carolina, for the Fiscal Year Ending September 1st, 1880. Raleigh: P. M. Hale and Edwards, Broughton and Co., 1881.

The Budget, 1965–1967. Vol. 1. Raleigh, N.C.: Office of State Budget and Management, 1964.

The Budget, 1967–1969. Vol. 1. Raleigh, N.C.: Office of State Budget and Management, 1965.

The Budget, 1969–1971. Vol. 1. Raleigh, N.C.: Office of State Budget and Management, 1968.

Community Action Program Guide. Washington, D.C.: Community Action Program, Office of Economic Opportunity, 1965.

Economic Report of the President, 1964. Washington, D.C.: Government Printing Office, 1964.

U.S. Commission on Civil Rights. *Racial Isolation in the Public Schools.* Vol. 1. Washington, D.C.: Government Printing Office, 1965.

U.S. Congress. House of Representatives. Committee on Education and Labor. *Hearings before the Subcommittee on the War on Poverty Program, Economic Opportunity Act of 1964.* 88th Cong., 2nd sess., 1964. Washington, D.C.: Government Printing Office, 1964.

———. Committee on Un-American Activities. *Hearings on Activities of Ku Klux Klan Organizations in the United States.* Part 1. 89th Cong., 1st sess., 1965. Washington, D.C.: Government Printing Office, 1966.

———. Committee on Ways and Means. *Hearings on Tax Reform, 1969.* 91st Cong., 1st sess., 1969. Washington, D.C.: Government Printing Office, 1969.

U.S. Congress. Senate. Committee on Finance. *Hearings on the Tax Reform Act of 1969.* 91st Cong., 1st sess., 1969. Washington, D.C.: Government Printing Office, 1969.

———. Committee on Government Operations. *Hearings before the Permanent Subcommittee on Investigations on Riots, Civil and Criminal Disorders.* 91st Cong., 1st sess., 1969. Washington, D.C.: Government Printing Office, 1969.

———. Committee on Labor and Public Welfare. *Hearings before the Subcommittee on Employment, Manpower, and Poverty on the Economic Opportunity Amendments of 1969.* 91st Cong., 1st sess., 1969. Washington, D.C.: Government Printing Office, 1969.

PERIODICALS

American Mercury
Asheville Citizen
Asheville Citizen-Times
Asheville Times
The Atlantic
Burlington Times-News
Business Week
Carolina Times
Chapel Hill Weekly
Charlotte Observer
Congressional Record
Contempo
Daily Tar Heel
   (Chapel Hill)
Durham Herald
Durham Herald-Sun
Durham Morning Herald
Durham Sun

Goldsboro News-Argus
Greensboro Daily News
Human Events
Independent Weekly
   (Durham)
Life
Look
Louisville Courier-Journal
   and Times
Mount Holly News
New Republic
News and Observer
New York Times
New York World
North Carolina Anvil
Pittsburgh Post-Gazette
Roanoke Rapids Daily
   Herald

Rocky Mount Evening
   Telegram
Sanford Herald
Statesville Record and
   Landmark
Time
Tri-County News
   (Spruce Pine)
Wall Street Journal
Washington Blade
Washington Post
Wilson Daily Times
Winston-Salem Journal
Winston-Salem Journal and
   Sentinel
Yancey Record (Burnsville)

ORAL HISTORIES

Addo, Linda Powell. Interview by Gretchen Givens, October 20, 1995. Interview O-0001, Southern Oral History Program Collection (#4007). Southern Historical Collection, Wilson Library, University of North Carolina at Chapel Hill.

Atwater, Ann. Interview by Rebecca Cerese. In authors' possession.

Baker, Donald M. Interview by Stephen Goodell, February 24, 1969. Oral History Collection, Lyndon Baines Johnson Library and Museum, Austin, Tex.

Barnes, Billy E. Interview by Rebecca Cerese. In authors' possession.

Bishop, Brenda Kay Johnson. Interview by Erin Parrish, October 14, 1995. Interview O-0007, Southern Oral History Program Collection (#4007). Southern Historical Collection, Wilson Library, University of North Carolina at Chapel Hill.

Brooks, Michael P. Interview by Rebecca Cerese. In authors' possession.

Coble, Emily R. Interview by Mary Cleary, November 11, 1995. Interview O-0009, Southern Oral History Program Collection (#4007). Southern Historical Collection, Wilson Library, University of North Carolina at Chapel Hill.

Draves, Julie Habich. Interview by Rebecca Cerese. In authors' possession.

Entin, David. Interview by Rebecca Cerese. In authors' possession.

Esser, George. Interview by Emily Berry. In authors' possession.

———. Interview by Steve Channing. In authors' possession.

———. Interview by Frances A. Weaver, June–August 1990. Interview L-0035, Southern Oral History Program Collection (#4007). Southern Historical Collection, Wilson Library, University of North Carolina at Chapel Hill.

———. "An Oral History of the North Carolina Fund by George H. Esser Executive Director 1963–69." Spring 1970. In authors' possession.

Fairbank, Alan. Interview by Rebecca Cerese. In authors' possession.

Fields, Johnette Ingold. Interview by Melynn Glusman, October 18, 1995. Interview O-0013, Southern Oral History Program Collection (#4007). Southern Historical Collection, Wilson Library, University of North Carolina at Chapel Hill.

Fuller, Howard. Interview by Rebecca Cerese. In authors' possession.

Gattis, Rubye. Interview by Rebecca Cerese. In authors' possession.

Johnson, Sandra. Interview by Rebecca Cerese. In authors' possession.

Jones, Anne. Interview by Robert Korstad. In authors' possession.

Lake, I. Beverly, Sr. Interview by Charles W. Dunn, September 8, 1987. Interview C-0043, Southern Oral History Program Collection (#4007). Southern Historical Collection, Wilson Library, University of North Carolina at Chapel Hill.

Miller, Hollis. Interview by Melynn Glusman, November 9, 1995. Interview O-0021, Southern Oral History Program Collection (#4007). Southern Historical Collection, Wilson Library, University of North Carolina at Chapel Hill.

Murchison, Wallace C. Interview by Sam Bissette, June 9, 1995. Voices of the Cape Fear, Oral History Collection, 1990–Present. Special Collections and Archives, William Madison Randall Library, University of North Carolina at Wilmington.

Nichols (Thorpe), Joyce Clayton. Interview by Rebecca Cerese. In authors' possession.

Powell, Susie R. Interview by Gretchen Givens, October 13, 1995. Interview O-0024, Southern Oral History Program Collection (#4007). Southern Historical Collection, Wilson Library, University of North Carolina at Chapel Hill.

Ruffin, Ben. Interview by Rebecca Cerese. In authors' possession.

Saltzman, Henry. Interview by Rebecca Cerese. In authors' possession.

Sasson, Diane. Interview by Emily Berry, October 28, 1995. Interview O-0025, Southern Oral History Program Collection (#4007). Southern Historical Collection, Wilson Library, University of North Carolina at Chapel Hill.

Scott, Johnny O. Interview by Rebecca Cerese. In authors' possession.

Szittya, Penn. Interview by Rebecca Cerese. In authors' possession.

Wagoner, Bobby D. Interview by Rebecca Cerese. In authors' possession.

Whitson, Betty, and True Elliott. Interview by Rebecca Cerese. In authors' possession.

Yarmolinsky, Adam. Interview by Paige Mulhollan, July 13, 1970. Oral History Collection, Lyndon Baines Johnson Library and Museum, Austin, Tex.

Ylvisaker, Paul. Interview by Charles T. Morrissey, September 27, 1973. Ford Foundation Oral History Project. Ford Foundation Archives, New York, N.Y.

BOOKS

Abrams, Douglas Carl. *Conservative Constraints: North Carolina and the New Deal.* Jackson: University Press of Mississippi, 1992.

Anderson, Eric. *Race and Politics in North Carolina, 1872–1901: The Black Second.* Baton Rouge: Louisiana State University Press, 1981.

Anderson, Jean. *Durham County: A History of Durham County, North Carolina.* Durham: Duke University Press, 1990.

Andrew, John A. *The Other Side of the Sixties: Young Americans for Freedom and the Rise of Conservative Politics*. New Brunswick, N.J.: Rutgers University Press, 1997.

Asbell, Bernard. *The Pill: A Biography of the Drug That Changed the World*. New York: Random House, 1995.

Ashby, Warren. *Frank Porter Graham, a Southern Liberal*. Winston-Salem, N.C.: J. F. Blair, 1980.

Ashmore, Susan Youngblood. *Carry It On: The War on Poverty and the Civil Rights Movement in Alabama, 1964–1972*. Athens: University of Georgia Press, 2008.

Badger, Anthony J. *North Carolina and the New Deal*. Raleigh: North Carolina Department of Cultural Resources, Division of Archives and History, 1981.

Banfield, Edward. *The Moral Basis of a Backward Society*. Glencoe, Ill.: Free Press, 1958.

———. *The Unheavenly City Revisited*. Boston: Little, Brown, 1974.

Barnard, John. *American Vanguard: The United Auto Workers during the Reuther Years, 1935–1970*. Detroit: Wayne State University Press, 2004.

Becker, Jane S. *Selling Tradition: Appalachia and the Construction of an American Folk, 1930–1940*. Chapel Hill: University of North Carolina Press, 1998.

Bilbo, Theodore. *Take Your Choice: Separation or Mongrelization*. Poplarville, Miss.: Dream House Publishing Co., 1947.

Billingsley, William J. *Communists on Campus: Race, Politics, and the Public University in Sixties North Carolina*. Athens: University of Georgia Press, 1999.

Bjerre-Poulsen, Niels. *Right Face: Organizing the American Conservative Movement 1945–65*. Copenhagen: Museum Tusculanum, 2002.

Blumenthal, Sidney. *The Rise of the Counter-Establishment: The Conservative Ascent to Political Power*. New York: Union Square Press, 2008.

Boyle, Kevin. *The UAW and the Heyday of American Liberalism, 1945–1968*. Ithaca, N.Y.: Cornell University Press, 1995.

Bracey, John H., Jr., and August Meier, eds. *Papers of the NAACP*. 21 reels. Frederick, Md.: University Publications of America, 1996.

Bremner, Robert H. *American Philanthropy*. 2nd ed. Chicago: University of Chicago Press, 1988.

Brennan, Mary C. *Turning Right in the Sixties: The Conservative Capture of the GOP*. Chapel Hill: University of North Carolina Press, 1995.

Brooks, Michael P. *The Dimensions of Poverty in North Carolina*. Durham: North Carolina Fund, 1964.

Brownfeld, Allan C. *The Financiers of Revolution: A Special Study of How Foundations and Organizations Are Using Federal "Tax Exemption" Laws to Promote Political and Social Upheaval in America*. Washington, D.C.: American Conservative Union, 1969.

Brownlee, Frederick L. *New Day Ascending*. Boston: Pilgrim Press, 1946.

Brownlee, Frederick Leslie, and Ruth A. Morton. *Brick Rural Life School, Bricks, North Carolina*. [New York?]: American Missionary Association, 1938.

Cantwell, Robert. *When We Were Good: The Folk Revival*. Cambridge, Mass.: Harvard University Press, 1996.

Carlton, David L., and Peter A. Coclanis, eds. *Confronting Southern Poverty in the Great Depression: The Report on Economic Conditions of the South with Related Documents*. Boston: Bedford Books of St. Martin's Press, 1996.

Carson, Clayborne, David J. Garrow, Gerald Gill, Vincent Harding, and Darlene Clark Hine, eds. *The Eyes on the Prize Civil Rights Reader: Documents, Speeches, and Firsthand Accounts from the Black Freedom Struggle, 1954–1990.* New York: Penguin Books, 1991.

Carter, Dan T. *The Politics of Rage: George Wallace, the Origins of the New Conservatism, and the Transformation of American Politics.* New York: Simon and Schuster, 1995.

Chafe, William Henry. *Civilities and Civil Rights: Greensboro, North Carolina, and the Black Struggle for Freedom.* New York: Oxford University Press, 1980.

———. *The Unfinished Journey: America since World War II.* New York: Oxford University Press, 1986.

Citizens' Board of Inquiry into Hunger and Malnutrition in the United States. *Hunger, U.S.A.: A Report.* Boston: Beacon Press, 1968.

Clark, Robert F. *The War on Poverty: History, Selected Programs, and Ongoing Impact.* Lanham, Md.: University Press of America, 2002.

Cobbs Hoffman, Elizabeth. *All You Need Is Love: The Peace Corps and the Spirit of the 1960s.* Cambridge, Mass.: Harvard University Press, 1998.

Cockburn, Andrew. *Rumsfeld: His Rise, Fall, and Catastrophic Legacy.* New York: Scribner, 2007.

Cohen, Robert. *When the Old Left Was Young: Student Radicals and America's First Mass Student Movement, 1929–1941.* New York: Oxford University Press, 1993.

Cokorinos, Lee. *The Assault on Diversity: An Organized Challenge to Racial and Gender Justice.* Lanham, Md.: Rowman and Littlefield, 2003.

Connor, Robert D. W., and Clarence H. Poe, eds. *The Life and Speeches of Charles Brantley Aycock.* Garden City, N.Y.: Doubleday Page, 1912.

Covington, Howard E., and Marion A. Ellis. *Terry Sanford: Politics, Progress, and Outrageous Ambitions.* Durham, N.C.: Duke University Press, 1999.

———, eds. *The North Carolina Century: Tar Heels Who Made a Difference, 1900–2000.* Charlotte, N.C.: Levine Museum of the New South, 2002.

Crook, William H., and Ross Thomas. *Warriors for the Poor: The Story of VISTA, Volunteers in Service to America.* New York: Morrow, 1969.

Crow, Jeffrey J., and Robert F. Durden. *Maverick Republican in the Old North State: A Political Biography of Daniel L. Russell.* Baton Rouge: Louisiana State University Press, 1977.

Dallek, Robert. *Flawed Giant: Lyndon Johnson and His Times, 1961–1973.* New York: Oxford University Press, 1998.

Davidson, Osha Gray. *The Best of Enemies: Race and Redemption in the New South.* New York: Scribner, 1996.

Diamond, Sara. *Roads to Dominion: Right-Wing Movements and Political Power in the United States.* New York: Guilford Press, 1995.

Donovan, John C. *The Politics of Poverty.* Washington, D.C.: University Press of America, 1980.

Douglas, Davison M. *Reading, Writing, and Race: The Desegregation of the Charlotte Schools.* Chapel Hill: University of North Carolina Press, 1995.

Draper, Alan. *Conflict of Interests: Organized Labor and the Civil Rights Movement in the South, 1954–1968.* Ithaca, N.Y.: ILR Press, 1994.

Drescher, John. *Triumph of Good Will: How Terry Sanford Beat a Champion of Segregation and Reshaped the South.* Jackson: University Press of Mississippi, 2000.

Du Bois, W. E. Burghardt. *Black Reconstruction: An Essay toward a History of the Part Which Black Folk Played in the Attempt to Reconstruct Democracy in America, 1860–1880*. New York: Russel and Russel, 1935.

Durden, Robert F. *The Dukes of Durham, 1865–1929*. Durham, N.C.: Duke University Press, 1975.

———. *Lasting Legacy to the Carolinas: The Duke Endowment, 1924–1994*. Durham, N.C.: Duke University Press, 1998.

Eaton, Allen H. *Handicrafts of the Southern Highlands*. New York: Russell Sage Foundation, 1937.

Egerton, John. *Speak Now against the Day: The Generation before the Civil Rights Movement in the South*. Chapel Hill: University of North Carolina Press, 1995.

Ehle, John. *The Free Men*. New York: Harper & Row, 1965.

Ehrlichman, John. *Witness to Power: The Nixon Years*. New York: Simon and Schuster, 1982.

Epstein, Benjamin R., and Arnold Forster. *The Radical Right: Report on the John Birch Society and Its Allies*. New York: Random House, 1967.

Escott, Paul D. *Many Excellent People: Power and Privilege in North Carolina, 1850–1900*. Chapel Hill: University of North Carolina Press, 1985.

Esposito, Virginia M. *Conscience and Community: The Legacy of Paul Ylvisaker*. New York: Peter Lang, 1999.

Everett, Robinson O., ed. *Anti-Poverty Programs*. Dobbs Ferry, N.Y.: Oceana Publications, 1966.

Felton, James A. *Fruits of Enduring Faith: A Story of Racial Unity*. New York: Exposition Press, 1965.

Fine, Sidney. *"Expanding the Frontiers of Civil Rights": Michigan, 1948–1968*. Detroit: Wayne State University Press, 2000.

———. *Violence in the Model City: The Cavanagh Administration, Race Relations, and the Detroit Riot of 1967*. Ann Arbor: University of Michigan Press, 1989.

Foner, Eric. *Reconstruction: America's Unfinished Revolution, 1863–1877*. New York: Harper & Row, 1988.

Ford, Thomas R., ed. *The Southern Appalachian Region: A Survey*. 1962. Reprint, Lexington: University of Kentucky Press, 1967.

Frieden, Bernard J., and Marshall Kaplan. *The Politics of Neglect: Urban Aid from Model Cities to Revenue Sharing*. Cambridge, Mass.: MIT Press, 1975.

Gans, Herbert J. *The War against the Poor: The Underclass and Antipoverty Policy*. New York: Basic Books, 1995.

George, John, and Laird M. Wilcox. *Nazis, Communists, Klansmen, and Others on the Fringe: Political Extremism in America*. Buffalo, N.Y.: Prometheus Books, 1992.

Germany, Kent B. *New Orleans after the Promises: Poverty, Citizenship, and the Search for the Great Society*. Athens: University of Georgia Press, 2007.

Gilbert, Neil. *Clients or Constituents*. San Francisco: Jossey-Bass, 1970.

Gilmore, Glenda Elizabeth. *Gender and Jim Crow: Women and the Politics of White Supremacy in North Carolina, 1896–1920*. Chapel Hill: University of North Carolina Press, 1996.

Goodwin, Doris Kearns. *Lyndon Johnson and the American Dream*. New York: St. Martin's Press, 1991.

Greene, Christina. *Our Separate Ways: Women and the Black Freedom Movement in Durham, North Carolina*. Chapel Hill: University of North Carolina Press, 2005.

Gregory, James N. *The Southern Diaspora: How the Great Migrations of Black and White Southerners Transformed America*. Chapel Hill: University of North Carolina Press, 2005.

Griffith, Barbara S. *The Crisis of American Labor: Operation Dixie and the Defeat of the CIO*. Philadelphia: Temple University Press, 1988.

Grogger, Jeff, and Lynn A. Karoly. *Welfare Reform: Effects of a Decade of Change*. Cambridge, Mass.: Harvard University Press, 2005.

Hall, Jacquelyn Dowd, James Leloudis, Robert Korstad, Mary Murphy, Lu Ann Jones, and Christopher B. Daly. *Like a Family: The Making of a Southern Cotton Mill World*. Chapel Hill: University of North Carolina Press, 1987.

Hanchett, Thomas W. *Sorting Out the New South City: Race, Class, and Urban Development in Charlotte, 1875–1975*. Chapel Hill: University of North Carolina Press, 1998.

Harlan, Louis R. *Separate and Unequal: Public School Campaigns and Racism in the Southern Seaboard States, 1901–1915*. New York: Atheneum, 1968.

Harrington, Michael. *The Other America: Poverty in the United States*. New York: Macmillan, 1962.

Heidenry, John. *Theirs Was the Kingdom: Lila and Dewitt Wallace and the Story of the Reader's Digest*. New York: W. W. Norton, 1993.

Horne, Gerald. *The Color of Fascism: Lawrence Dennis, Racial Passing, and the Rise of Right-Wing Extremism in the United States*. New York: New York University Press, 2006.

Houser, George M., and Bayard Rustin. *We Challenged Jim Crow!: A Report on the Journey of Reconciliation, April 9–23, 1947*. [New York]: Fellowship of Reconciliation and Congress of Racial Equality, 1947.

Johnson, Lyndon Baines. *The Vantage Point: Perspectives of the Presidency, 1963–1969*. New York: Holt, Rinehart and Winston, 1971.

Joseph, Peniel E. *Waiting 'til the Midnight Hour: A Narrative History of Black Power in America*. New York: Henry Holt, 2006.

Justesen, Benjamin. *George Henry White: An Even Chance in the Race of Life*. Baton Rouge: Louisiana State University Press, 2001.

Katz, Michael B. *The Price of Citizenship: Redefining the American Welfare State*. New York: Metropolitan Books, 2001.

———. *The Undeserving Poor: From the War on Poverty to the War on Welfare*. New York: Pantheon Books, 1989.

Kiffmeyer, Thomas. *Reformers to Radicals: The Appalachian Volunteers and the War on Poverty*. Lexington: University Press of Kentucky, 2008.

King, Coretta Scott. *My Life with Martin Luther King, Jr.* New York: Holt, Rinehart and Winston, 1969.

Klinkner, Philip A., and Philip Smith. *The Unsteady March: The Rise and Decline of Racial Equality in America*. Chicago: University of Chicago Press, 1999.

Korstad, Robert Rodgers. *Civil Rights Unionism: Tobacco Workers and the Struggle for Democracy in the Mid-Twentieth-Century South*. Chapel Hill: University of North Carolina Press, 2003.

———. *Dreaming of a Time: The School of Public Health, the University of North Carolina at Chapel Hill, 1939–1989.* Chapel Hill: School of Public Health, University of North Carolina at Chapel Hill, 1990.

Kotlowski, Dean J. *Nixon's Civil Rights: Politics, Principle, and Policy.* Cambridge, Mass.: Harvard University Press, 2001.

Kramer, Ralph M. *Participation of the Poor: Comparative Community Case Studies in the War on Poverty.* Englewood Cliffs, N.J.: Prentice-Hall, 1969.

Lawson, Steven F., ed. *To Secure These Rights: The Report of Harry S. Truman's Committee on Civil Rights.* Boston: Bedford/St. Martin's, 2004.

Lefler, Hugh T. *History of North Carolina.* 2 vols. New York: Lewis Historical Publishing Co., 1956.

Leloudis, James L. *Schooling the New South: Pedagogy, Self, and Society in North Carolina, 1880–1920.* Chapel Hill: University of North Carolina Press, 1996.

Levitan, Sar A. *The Great Society's Poor Law: A New Approach to Poverty.* Baltimore: Johns Hopkins Press, 1969.

Lewis, Oscar. *The Children of Sánchez: Autobiography of a Mexican Family.* New York: Random House, 1961.

———. *La Vida: A Puerto Rican Family in the Culture of Poverty—San Juan and New York.* New York: Random House, 1966.

Lichtenstein, Nelson. *The Most Dangerous Man in Detroit: Walter Reuther and the Fate of American Labor.* New York: Basic Books, 1995.

Link, Albert N. *A Generosity of Spirit: The Early History of the Research Triangle Park.* Research Triangle Park: Research Triangle Foundation of North Carolina, 1995.

Luebke, Paul. *Tar Heel Politics: Myths and Realities.* Chapel Hill: University of North Carolina Press, 1990.

Macdonald, Dwight. *The Ford Foundation: The Men and the Millions.* New York: Reynal, 1956.

Mann, Jim. *Rise of the Vulcans: The History of Bush's War Cabinet.* New York: Viking, 2004.

McAdam, Doug. *Freedom Summer.* New York: Oxford University Press, 1988.

McClellan, John L. *Crime without Punishment.* New York: Duell Sloan and Pearce, 1962.

McLaurin, Melton A. *The Marines of Montford Point: America's First Black Marines.* Chapel Hill: University of North Carolina Press, 2007.

McVeigh, Frank J., and Loreen Therese Wolfer. *Brief History of Social Problems: A Critical Thinking Approach.* Dallas: University Press of America, 2004.

Mead, Lawrence M. *Beyond Entitlement: The Social Obligations of Citizenship.* New York: Free Press, 1986.

Meyer, David S. *The Politics of Protest: Social Movements in America.* New York: Oxford University Press, 2007.

Minchin, Timothy J. *What Do We Need a Union For?: The TWUA in the South, 1945–1955.* Chapel Hill: University of North Carolina Press, 1997.

Miller, Steven P. *Billy Graham and the Rise of the Republican South.* Philadelphia: University of Pennsylvania Press, 2009.

Mitchell, Memory F., ed. *Messages, Addresses, and Public Papers of Terry Sanford, Governor of North Carolina, 1961–1965.* Raleigh: Council of State, State of North Carolina, 1966.

Morgan, Chester M. *Redneck Liberal: Theodore G. Bilbo and the New Deal.* Baton Rouge: Louisiana State University Press, 1985.

Morgan, Lucy, with LeGette Blythe. *Gift from the Hills: Miss Lucy Morgan's Story of Her Unique Penland School*. Chapel Hill: University of North Carolina Press, 1971.

Morone, James A. *The Democratic Wish: Popular Participation and the Limits of American Government*. Rev. ed. New Haven: Yale University Press, 1998.

Morrison, Joseph L. *Governor O. Max Gardner: A Power in North Carolina and New Deal Washington*. Chapel Hill: University of North Carolina Press, 1971.

Moynihan, Daniel. *Maximum Feasible Misunderstanding: Community Action in the War on Poverty*. New York: Free Press, 1969.

Mumford, Kevin J. *Newark: A History of Race, Rights, and Riots in America*. New York: New York University Press, 2007.

Murray, Charles A. *Losing Ground: American Social Policy, 1950–1980*. New York: Basic Books, 1984.

National Advisory Commission on Civil Disorders. *The Kerner Report: The 1968 Report of the National Advisory Commission on Civil Disorders*. New York: Pantheon Books, 1988.

O'Connor, Alice. *Poverty Knowledge: Social Science, Social Policy, and the Poor in Twentieth-Century U.S. History*. Princeton: Princeton University Press, 2002.

Patterson, James T. *America's Struggle against Poverty in the Twentieth Century*. Cambridge, Mass.: Harvard University Press, 2000.

Perlstein, Rick. *Nixonland: The Rise of a President and the Fracturing of America*. New York: Scribner, 2008.

Piven, Frances Fox, and Richard A. Cloward. *Regulating the Poor: The Functions of Public Welfare*. Rev. ed. New York: Vintage Books, 1993.

Pleasants, Julian M., and Augustus M. Burns. *Frank Porter Graham and the 1950 Senate Race in North Carolina*. Chapel Hill: University of North Carolina Press, 1990.

Podair, Jerald E. *The Strike That Changed New York: Blacks, Whites, and the Ocean Hill–Brownsville Crisis*. New Haven: Yale University Press, 2002.

Powell, William S. *North Carolina Lives: The Tar Heel Who's Who*. Hopkinsville, Ky.: Historical Record Association, 1962.

———, ed. *Dictionary of North Carolina Biography*. 6 vols. Chapel Hill: University of North Carolina Press, 1979–96.

Quadagno, Jill. *The Color of Welfare: How Racism Undermined the War on Poverty*. New York: Oxford University Press, 1994.

Redding, Kent. *Making Race, Making Power: North Carolina's Road to Disfranchisement*. Urbana: University of Illinois Press, 2003.

Reeves, Richard. *President Kennedy: Profile of Power*. New York: Simon & Schuster, 1993.

Reeves, T. Zane. *The Politics of the Peace Corps and VISTA*. Tuscaloosa: University of Alabama Press, 1988.

Rossinow, Douglas C. *The Politics of Authenticity: Liberalism, Christianity, and the New Left in America*. New York: Columbia University Press, 1998.

Rubin, Lillian B. *Worlds of Pain: Life in the Working-Class Family*. New York: Basic Books, 1976.

Salmond, John A. *The Civilian Conservation Corps, 1933–1942: A New Deal Case Study*. Durham, N.C.: Duke University Press, 1967.

Sanford, Terry. *But What about the People?* New York: Harper & Row, 1966.

Scales, Junius. *Cause at Heart: A Former Communist Remembers*. Athens: University of
   Georgia Press, 1987.

Schneider, Gregory L. *Cadres for Conservatism: Young Americans for Freedom and the Rise of
   the Contemporary Right*. New York: New York University Press, 1999.

Schoen, Johanna. *Choice and Coercion: Birth Control, Sterilization, and Abortion in Public
   Health and Welfare*. Chapel Hill: University of North Carolina Press, 2005.

Sealander, Judith. *Private Wealth and Public Life: Foundation Philanthropy and the Reshaping
   of American Social Policy from the Progressive Era to the New Deal*. Baltimore: Johns
   Hopkins University Press, 1997.

Shepard, Kris. *Rationing Justice: Poverty Lawyers and Poor People in the Deep South*. Baton
   Rouge: Louisiana State University Press, 2007.

Singal, Daniel Joseph. *The War Within: From Victorian to Modernist Thought in the South,
   1919–1945*. Chapel Hill: University of North Carolina Press, 1982.

Skrentny, John David. *The Ironies of Affirmative Action: Politics, Culture, and Justice in
   America*. Chicago: University of Chicago Press, 1996.

Sloop, Mary T. Martin. *Miracle in the Hills*. New York: McGraw-Hill, 1953.

Smith, James Allen. *The Idea Brokers: Think Tanks and the Rise of the New Policy Elite*. New
   York: Free Press, 1991.

Smith, William H., and Carolyn P. Chiechi. *Private Foundations before and after the Tax
   Reform Act of 1969*. Washington, D.C.: American Enterprise Institute for Public Policy
   Research, 1974.

Spence, James T. *The Making of a Governor: The Moore-Preyer-Lake Primaries of 1964*.
   Winston-Salem, N.C.: J. F. Blair, 1968.

Sundquist, James L., ed. *On Fighting Poverty: Perspectives from Experience*. New York: Basic
   Books, 1969.

Terkel, Studs. *American Dreams: Lost and Found*. New York: Pantheon Books, 1980.

Tilley, Nannie M. *The R. J. Reynolds Tobacco Company*. Chapel Hill: University of North
   Carolina Press, 1985.

Tocqueville, Alexis de. *Democracy in America*. Translated, edited, and with an introduction
   by Harvey C. Mansfield and Debra Winthrop. Chicago: University of Chicago Press,
   2000.

Townsend, Peter. *Poverty in the United Kingdom: A Survey of Household Resources and
   Standards of Living*. Berkeley: University of California Press, 1979.

Ward, Doris Cline, and Charles D. Biddix. *The Heritage of Old Buncombe County*. Asheville,
   N.C.: Old Buncombe County Genealogical Society, 1981.

Waynick, Capus M., John C. Brooks, and Elsie W. Pitts. *North Carolina and the Negro*.
   Raleigh: North Carolina Mayors' Co-operating Committee, 1964.

Weare, Walter B. *Black Business in the New South: A Social History of the North Carolina
   Mutual Life Insurance Company*. Durham, N.C.: Duke University Press, 1993.

Weller, Jack E. *Yesterday's People: Life in Contemporary Appalachia*. Lexington: University
   of Kentucky Press, 1965.

Whisnant, Anne Mitchell. *Super-Scenic Motorway: A Blue Ridge Parkway History*. Chapel
   Hill: University of North Carolina Press, 2006.

Whisnant, David E. *Modernizing the Mountaineer: People, Power, and Planning in
   Appalachia*. Rev. ed. Knoxville: University of Tennessee Press, 1994.

Wilson, Emily Herring. *For the People of North Carolina: The Z. Smith Reynolds Foundation at Half-Century, 1936–1986.* Chapel Hill: Published for the Z. Smith Reynolds Foundation by the University of North Carolina Press, 1988.

Wood, Phillip. *Southern Capitalism: The Political Economy of North Carolina, 1880–1980.* Durham, N.C.: Duke University Press, 1986.

Woodward, C. Vann. *Tom Watson, Agrarian Rebel.* New York: Macmillan, 1938.

Yrigoyen, Charles, Jr., and Susan E. Warrick, eds. *Historical Dictionary of Methodism.* 2nd ed. Lanham, Md.: Scarecrow Press, 2005.

Zarefsky, David. *President Johnson's War on Poverty: Rhetoric and History.* University: University of Alabama Press, 1986.

ARTICLES

Barnes, Billy E. "The North Carolina Fund: A Progress Report." *Popular Government* 30 (June 1964): 1–5, 22.

Biles, Roger. "The Rise and Fall of Soul City: Planning, Politics, and Race in Recent America." *Journal of Planning History* 4 (February 2005): 52–72.

Cofield, Willa. "Teaching Students to Read the World." In *Seeding the Process of Multicultural Education,* edited by Cathy L. Nelson and Kim A. Wilson, 101–10. Plymouth: Minnesota Inclusiveness Program, 1998.

Cronin, Thomas E. "An Imperiled Presidency?" *Society* 16 (November 1978): 57–64.

David, Stephen M. "Leadership of the Poor in Poverty Programs." *Proceedings of the Academy of Political Science* 29, no. 1 (1968): 86–100.

Esser, George H. "The Role of a State-Wide Foundation in the War on Poverty." In *Anti-Poverty Programs,* edited by Robinson O. Everett, 90–113. Dobbs Ferry, N.Y.: Oceana Publications, 1966.

Ferguson, Karen. "Organizing the Ghetto: The Ford Foundation, CORE, and White Power in the Black Power Era, 1967–1969." *Journal of Urban History* 34 (November 2007): 67–100.

Geiger, H. Jack. "The Unsteady March." *Perspectives in Biology and Medicine* 48 (Winter 2005): 1–9.

Johnson, Guy B. "Does the South Owe the Negro a New Deal?" *Social Forces* 13 (May 1934): 100–103.

Kiffmeyer, Thomas J. "From Self-Help to Sedition: The Appalachian Volunteers in Eastern Kentucky, 1964–1970." *Journal of Southern History* 64 (February 1998): 65–94.

King, Desmond, and Mark Wickham-Jones. "From Clinton to Blair: The Democratic (Party) Origins of Welfare to Work." *Political Quarterly* 70 (January 1999): 62–74.

Kloman, Erasmus. "Citizen Participation in the Philadelphia Model Cities Program: Retrospect and Prospect." *Public Administration Review* 32 (September 1972): 402–8.

Kotlowski, Dean. "Black Power—Nixon Style: The Nixon Administration and Minority Business Enterprise." *Business History Review* 72 (Autumn 1998): 409–45.

Labovitz, John R. "The Impact of the Private Foundation Provisions of the Tax Reform Act of 1969: Early Empirical Measurements." *Journal of Legal Studies* 3 (January 1974): 63–105.

Lewis, Oscar. "The Culture of Poverty." In *Poor Americans: How the White Poor Live,* edited by Marc Pilisuk and Phyllis Pilisuk, 20–28. New Brunswick, N.J.: Transaction Publishers, 1973.

Link, William A. "William Friday and the North Carolina Speaker Ban Crisis, 1963–1968." *North Carolina Historical Review* 72 (April 1995): 198–228.

MacNeill, Ben Dixon. "The Town of a Hundred Millionaires." *North American Review* 232 (August 1931): 101–10.

McAdam, Doug. "Gender as a Mediator of the Activist Experience: The Case of Freedom Summer." *American Journal of Sociology* 97 (March 1992): 1211–40.

Mettler, Suzanne. "The Transformed Welfare State and the Redistribution of Political Voice." In *The Transformation of American Politics: Activist Government and the Rise of Conservatism*, edited by Paul Pierson and Theda Skocpol, 191–222. Princeton: Princeton University Press, 2007.

Miller, Marc. "Workers' Owned." *Southern Exposure* 8 (Winter 1980): 12–21.

O'Connor, John. "U.S. Social Welfare Policy: The Reagan Record and Legacy." *Journal of Social Policy* 27 (January 1998): 37–61.

Paletz, David L. "The Neglected Context of Congressional Campaigns." *Polity* 4 (Winter 1971): 195–217.

Peck, Jim. "The First Freedom Ride, 1947." *Southern Exposure* 9 (Spring 1981): 36–37.

"The President and the Fund." *Popular Government* 30 (June 1964): 6–8.

Putnam, Robert D. "Bowling Alone: America's Declining Social Capital." *Journal of Democracy* 6, no. 1 (1995): 65–78.

Rowan, Carl T. "Martin Luther King's Tragic Decision." *Reader's Digest* 91 (September 1967): 37–42.

Salter, John R. "An Upsurge in Carolina." *Southern Patriot* 22 (June 1964): 1–2.

Sanford, Terry. "Poverty's Challenge to the States." In *Anti-Poverty Programs*, edited by Robinson O. Everett, 77–89. Dobbs Ferry, N.Y.: Oceana Publications, 1966.

Saunders, Frances Wright. "'A New Playwright of Tragic Power and Poetic Impulse': Paul Eliot Green at UNC–Chapel Hill in the 1920s." *North Carolina Historical Review* 72 (July 1995): 277–300.

Schoen, Johanna. "Fighting for Child Health: Race, Birth Control, and the State in the Jim Crow South." *Social Politics* 4 (Spring 1997): 90–113.

Thompson, Mark R. "When God Collides with Race and Class: Working-Class America's Shift to Conservatism." *University of Pittsburgh Law Review* 68 (2006–7): 243–66.

Tornquist, Elizabeth. "Standing Up to America: Poor Whites in Durham." *New South* 24 (Fall 1969): 40–48.

Uesugi, Sayoko. "Gender, Race, and the Cold War: Mary Price and the Progressive Party in North Carolina, 1945–1948." *North Carolina Historical Review* 77 (July 2000): 269–311.

Wadsworth, Homer C. "Private Foundations and the Tax Reform Act of 1969." *Law and Contemporary Problems* 39 (Autumn 1975): 255–62.

Weare, Walter B. "Charles Clinton Spaulding: Middle-Class Leadership in the Age of Segregation." In *Black Leaders of the Twentieth Century*, edited by John Hope Franklin and August Meier, 167–89. Urbana: University of Illinois Press, 1982.

Williams, Jeffrey J. "Class Matters: An Interview with Adolph Reed, Jr." *Minnesota Review* 65–66 (Fall 2006): 103–19.

Yarmolinsky, Adam. "The Beginnings of OEO." In *On Fighting Poverty: Perspectives from Experience*, edited by James L. Sundquist, 34–51. New York: Basic Books, 1969.

THESES AND DISSERTATIONS

Batchelor, John E. "Rule of Law: North Carolina School Desegregation from *Brown* to *Swain*, 1954–1974." Ed.D. diss., North Carolina State University, 1992.

Berry, Emily. "'One Building Block in the Battle': The North Carolina Volunteers and the Legacy of Idealism." Senior honors thesis, Department of History, University of North Carolina at Chapel Hill, 1996.

Blanchard, Gary F. "The Politics of Desegregation: A Case Study of Desegregation and Municipal Decision-Making in Chapel Hill, North Carolina." Senior honors thesis, Department of Political Science, University of North Carolina at Chapel Hill, 1964.

Casper, Craven Randall. "The Rise of the Republican Party in Rocky Mount, North Carolina, 1948–1972." Senior honors thesis, Department of History, University of North Carolina at Chapel Hill, 2005.

Chapman, John K. "Second Generation: Black Youth and the Origins of the Black Civil Rights Movement in Chapel Hill, N.C., 1937–1963." M.A. thesis, Department of History, University of North Carolina at Chapel Hill, 1995.

Edwards, Jennifer Anne. "The Quest for Civil Rights in Chapel Hill, North Carolina." Senior honors thesis, Department of History, University of North Carolina at Chapel Hill, 1989.

Esty, Amos. "Reinventing Southern Conservatism: The North Carolina Republican Party and the Ideology of Reactionary Progress, 1963–1968." M.A. thesis, Department of History, University of North Carolina at Chapel Hill, 2003.

Gioia, Chris. "'How to Get Out of Hell by Raising It': Race and Politics in Durham's War on Poverty." Senior honors thesis, Department of History, University of North Carolina at Chapel Hill, 1996.

Hazirjian, Lisa Gayle. "Negotiating Poverty: Economic Insecurity and the Politics of Working-Class Life in Rocky Mount, North Carolina, 1929–1969." Ph.D. diss., Department of History, Duke University.

Kinlaw, Patrick F. "'Tenants and Tories': North Carolina's Pearsall Plan and Its Legacies." Senior honors thesis, Department of History, University of North Carolina at Chapel Hill, 2000.

LeMay, Erika. "Battlefield in the Backyard: A Local Study of the War on Poverty." M.A. thesis, Department of History, University of North Carolina at Chapel Hill, 1997.

McCurry, Douglas S. "The Ideological Conflict over Race: Chapel Hill in 1963–64, 1968–69, and 1991–93." Senior honors thesis, Department of History, University of North Carolina at Chapel Hill, 1994.

Rawick, George. "The New Deal and Youth: The Civilian Conservation Corps, the National Youth Administration and the American Youth Congress." Ph.D. diss., Department of History, University of Wisconsin.

Spitzer, Scott. "The Liberal Dilemma: Welfare and Race, 1960–1975." Ph.D. diss., Columbia University, 2000.

Wescott, Joseph. "A Vision of an Open Door: The Establishment and Expansion of the

North Carolina Community College System." Ed.D. thesis, North Carolina State
University, 2005.

Wilkins, Fanon Che. "In the Belly of the Beast: Black Power, Anti-Imperialism, and the
African Liberation Solidarity Movement, 1968–1975." Ph.D. diss., Department of
History, New York University, 2001.

Williams, J. Derek. "'It Wasn't Slavery Time Anymore': Foodworkers' Strike at Chapel
Hill, Spring 1969." M.A. thesis, Department of History, University of North Carolina at
Chapel Hill, 1979.

Williams, Lauren. "Crafting Antipoverty Policy: WAMY Community Action, Inc.,
Mountain Crafts, and Maximum Feasible Participation Unrealized." Unpublished
paper, Duke University, 2002.

Wynne, Robert Lee. "A Historical Study of the Joseph K. Brick School, the Brick Rural
Life School, and the Franklinton Center at Bricks, North Carolina." M.A. thesis, Sacred
Theology, Union Theological Seminary, 1969.

WEB SOURCES

Campbell, Tom. "Which End of the Boat Are You Sitting In?" *NC Spin*, January 3, 2007,
⟨http://www.ncspin.com/spin/articles/2007_01_3_5126.php⟩. June 19, 2009.

Carolina Population Center. "First Decade: Focus on Technical Assistance." CPC History.
⟨http://www.cpc.unc.edu/history/history_first_decade.html⟩. June 19, 2009.

Charlotte Chamber of Commerce. ⟨http://www.charlottechamber.com⟩. June 19, 2009.

Chase, Robert T. "Class Resurrection: The Poor People's Campaign of 1968 and
Resurrection City." *Essays in History* 40 (1998), ⟨http://etext.virginia.edu/journals/
EH/EH40/chase40.html#n3.1⟩. June 19, 2009.

Council of Conservative Citizens. ⟨http://cofcc.org⟩. September 19, 2009.

Cullum, Paul. "The Beverly Hillbillies." Museum of Broadcast Communications. ⟨http://
www.museum.tv/archives/etv/B/htmlB/beverlyhillb/beverlyhillb.htm⟩. June 19, 2009.

1898 Wilmington Race Riot Commission. *1898 Wilmington Race Riot Report*. May 31, 2006.
⟨http://www.history.ncdcr.gov/1898-wrrc/report/report.htm⟩. June 19, 2009.

Fisher, Gordon M. "The Development of the Orshansky Poverty Thresholds and Their
Subsequent History as the Official U.S. Poverty Measure." Working paper, Poverty
Measurement Studies and Alternative Measures, U.S. Census Bureau, May 1992
(partially revised September 1997). ⟨http://www.census.gov/hhes/www/povmeas/
papers/orshansky.html#N_91⟩. June 19, 2009.

Greensboro Truth and Reconciliation Commission. *Final Report*. May 25, 2006. ⟨http://
www.greensborotrc.org⟩. June 19, 2009.

———. "First Public Hearing." July 15–16, 2005. Statement Archives. Public Hearings.
⟨http://www.greensborotrc.org/hear_statements.php⟩. September 19, 2009.

"Historical US Inflation Rate 1914–Present." InflationData.com. ⟨http://inflationdata
.com/Inflation/Inflation_Rate/HistoricalInflation.aspx⟩. September 19, 2009.

"House Un-American Activities Committee." Mundt Archives. ⟨http://www.departments
.dsu.edu/library/archive/unamerican.htm⟩. June 19, 2009.

Hunter Bear (John Salter). Interview, July 2005. Civil Rights Movement Veterans. ⟨http://
www.crmvet.org/nars/hunteri.htm⟩. June 19, 2009.

Inventory of the Ben Blackburn Congressional Papers, 1969–1974. Richard B. Russell
Library for Political Research and Studies. University of Georgia Libraries. ⟨http://
russelldoc.galib.uga.edu/russell/view?docId=ead/bblack.xml⟩. September 19, 2009.

Inventory of the North Carolina Fund Records, 1962–1971. Southern Historical Collection,
Wilson Library, University of North Carolina at Chapel Hill. ⟨http://www.lib.unc.edu/
mss/inv/n/North_Carolina_Fund.html#doe73⟩. June 19, 2009.

Kennedy, John F. "Inaugural Address." January 20, 1961. John F. Kennedy Presidential
Library and Museum. ⟨http://www.jfklibrary.org/Historical+Resources/Archives/
Reference+Desk/Speeches/JFK/Inaugural+Address+January+20+1961.htm⟩.
September 3, 2009.

———. "Radio and Television Report to the American People on Civil Rights."
June 11, 1963. John F. Kennedy Presidential Library and Museum. ⟨http://www
.jfklibrary.org/Historical+Resources/Archives/Reference+Desk/Speeches/JFK/
003POF03CivilRights06111963.htm⟩. June 19, 2009.

Kennedy, John F., and Richard M. Nixon. "First Joint Radio-Television Broadcast."
September 26, 1960. John F. Kennedy Presidential Library and Museum. ⟨http://www
.jfklibrary.org/Historical+Resources/Archives/Reference+Desk/Speeches/JFK/
JFK+Pre-Pres/1960/Senator+John+F.+Kennedy+and+Vice+President+Richard+M.+
Nixon+First+Joint+Radio-Television+Broadcast.htm⟩. September 3, 2009.

Kids Count Data Center. Annie E. Casey Foundation. "Percent of Children in Poverty—
2007" (North Carolina). ⟨http://datacenter.kidscount.org/data/bystate/Map
.aspx?state=NC&ind=2238⟩. June 19, 2009.

King, Martin Luther, Jr. "Beyond Vietnam—A Time to Break Silence." April 4, 1967.
American Rhetoric. ⟨http://www.americanrhetoric.com/speeches/mlkatimeto
breaksilence.htm⟩. June 19, 2009.

———. "Letter from Birmingham Jail." April 16, 1963. Martin Luther King Jr. Research
and Education Institute. ⟨http://mlk-kpp01.stanford.edu/index.php/resources/
article/kings_letter_from_birmingham_jail⟩. June 19, 2009.

———. "Our God Is Marching On!" March 25, 1965. Martin Luther King Jr. Research
and Education Institute. ⟨http://mlk-kpp01.stanford.edu/index.php/kingpapers/
article/our_god_is_marching_on/⟩. November 3, 2009.

Mary Reynolds Babcock Foundation. ⟨http://www.mrbf.org/missionAndBeliefs.aspx⟩.
June 19, 2009.

MDC. ⟨http://www.mdcinc.org/about/index.aspx⟩. June 19, 2009.

National Association of Social Workers. "Personal Responsibility and Work Opportunity
Reconciliation Act of 1996 (Public Law 104-193), Summary of Provisions." August 1996.
⟨http://www.socialworkers.org/advocacy/welfare/legislation/summary.pdf⟩. June 19,
2009.

Nichols, Austin. "Understanding Changes in Child Poverty over the Past Decade." May 11,
2006. Urban Institute. ⟨http://www.urban.org/publications/411320.html⟩. June 19,
2009.

Nixon, Richard. "Nomination Acceptance Address." August 8, 1958. PresidentialRhetoric
.com. ⟨http://www.presidentialrhetoric.com/historicspeeches/nixon/
nominationacceptance1968.html⟩. September 18, 2009.

North Carolina Community Action Association. ⟨http://www.nccaa.net/⟩. June 19, 2009.

Phillips, Howard. Interview, May 2000. Democracy in Action. ⟨http://www.gwu.edu/
~action/philint.html⟩. June 19, 2009.

"President Nixon and Bob Haldeman Discuss Donald Rumsfeld, March 9, 1971." Nixon
Tapes. Presidential Recordings Program. Miller Center of Public Affairs. ⟨http://tapes
.millercenter.virginia.edu/clips/rmn_rumsfeld.html⟩. September 19, 2009.

President's Committee on Civil Rights. "To Secure These Rights: The Report of the
President's Committee on Civil Rights." Harry S. Truman Library and Museum.
⟨http://www.trumanlibrary.org/civilrights/srights1.htm⟩. June 19, 2009.

Reagan, Ronald. "Address before a Joint Session of Congress on the State of the Union."
January 25, 1988. American Presidency Project. ⟨http://www.presidency.ucsb.edu/ws/
index.php?pid=36035⟩. June 19, 2009.

———. "A Time for Choosing (aka 'The Speech')." October 27, 1964. American Rhetoric.
⟨http://www.americanrhetoric.com/speeches/ronaldreaganatimeforchoosing.htm⟩.
June 19, 2009.

Research Triangle Park. ⟨http://www.rtp.org/main⟩. September 15, 2009.

Roosevelt, Franklin D. "Annual Message to Congress." January 6, 1941. "The 'Four
Freedoms' Speech." Franklin D. Roosevelt Presidential Library and Museum. ⟨http://
docs.fdrlibrary.marist.edu/4FREE.HTML⟩. September 3, 2009.

Salter, John R. "Eastern North Carolina Black-Belt Followup: Dr. Willa Johnson Cofield
and Clemency Letter to North Carolina Governor." Lair of Hunter Bear. ⟨http://www
.hunterbear.org/willacofield.htm⟩. June 19, 2009.

———. "FBI Collusion with a Hard-Line Deep South Segregationist Congressman—
against Hunter Gray." Lair of Hunter Bear. ⟨http://www.hunterbear.org/fbi_collusion
.htm⟩.

———. "Personal Reminiscence: North Carolina and Jesse Helms." Lair of Hunter Bear.
⟨http://www.hunterbear.org/personal_reminiscence.htm⟩. June 19, 2009.

Sanchagrin, Kenneth, Ph.D. Curriculum vitae. Glenmary Research Center. ⟨http://www
.glenmary.org/grc/grc_sanchagrincv.htm⟩. June 19, 2009.

Urban Institute. "A Decade of Welfare Reform: Facts and Figures." July 26, 2006. ⟨http://
www.urban.org/publications/900980.html⟩. June 19, 2009.

U.S. Census Bureau. "Raleigh and Austin Are Fastest-Growing Metro Areas." News
release, March 19, 2009. ⟨http://www.census.gov/Press-Release/www/releases/
archives/population/013426.html⟩. June 19, 2009.

———. "State and County QuickFacts." ⟨http://quickfacts.census.gov/qfd/states/37000
.html⟩. November 3, 2009.

Watts, Nadia R. "Carolina's First Black Ph.D. Graduate." The Fountain, Spring 2001,
⟨http://fountain.unc.edu/spr_01/darity.html⟩. June 19, 2009.

Z. Smith Reynolds Foundation. ⟨http://www.zsr.org/history.htm⟩. June 19, 2009.

FILM AND RADIO DOCUMENTARIES

Hartman, Leda. "Seeds of Sustenance and a Harvest of Change: The Story of the North
Carolina Fund." WUNC-FM, 2005.

Wilson, John, and Martin Clark. "Dr. Frank: The Life and Times of Frank Porter Graham."
North Carolina Public Television, 1994.

Acknowledgments

This book has been a collaborative project from start to finish. We owe our greatest debt to the hundreds of men and women affiliated with the North Carolina Fund and the anti-poverty initiatives it supported across the state. They did the hard work of translating big ideas into action and building community institutions that to this day address the needs of the poor and advocate for a more just society. We could not recount all of their stories, but the record they left behind has influenced everything that we have written. They helped us recover a largely forgotten moment of democratic upheaval and experimentation. In constructing our narrative, we have tried to remain mindful of labors untold and to put down markers to stories that other scholars might explore.

We also enjoyed the good fortune of working with students who have been our partners in discovery. A number of them—Emily Berry, David Biggs, Tim Caldwell, Chris Gioia, Lisa Hazirjian, and Erika LeMay—wrote honors, master's, and doctoral theses on the Fund that stand as important works of scholarship in their own right. Dozens more produced research papers in courses we taught on public policy and oral history. They include Katherine Adkins, David Allen, Mollie Allick, Sara Appel, Aaron Augustino, Margaret Bellis, Alice Bonner, Victoria Cantore, Mary Cleary, Brian Clemmons, Ashely Davis, Laura Duke, Henry Eng, Naomi Feaste, Jennifer Fiumara, John Flickinger, Christopher Fregiato, Gretchen Givens, Melynn Glusman, Larissa Goodwin, Samuel Hellebush, Christina Hsu, Lauren Jarvis, Jillian Johnson, Shelia Jordan, Stephen Keadey, Michael Lamb, Andrew Lang, David Lee, Erica Lee, Maegan Lobo-Berg, Natalie Lowe, Gordon Mantler, Leandra Marin, Jason Matthews, Richard McCray, Kelly Meshaw, Sally Meyerhoff, Paige Miller, Alexis Morant, Ryan Morton-Wurst, Sean O'Keefe, Frederick Parker, Erin Parrish, Susan Patrick, Neal Perlmutter, Kevin Perry, Kyle Peterson, Marcus Peterson, Karen Raley, Sarah Rankin, Noah Raper, Elise Richards, Stacie Richardson, Ross Rocklin, Andrea Russo, David Segall, Evan Shoop, Elizabeth Smith, Jennifer Smith, Hye Seung Suh, Michele Sutton, Kathryn Tamblyn, Claire Thompson, Jenna Turner, Stacy Vlasits, Madeline Walter, William Weir, William Wilson, Jennifer Whytock, and Shiyi Zhao. Drawing on her experience as a member of the Fund staff, Lucy Rodgers Wadkins helped prepare many of the students' papers for online publication.

Other former students deserve special mention. Karen Thomas worked with Lisa Hazirjian and Robin Turner to read carefully through the applications and field notes of the young people who served in the Fund's volunteer program during the summers of 1964 and 1965. Sarah Thuesen's research on the Fund's beginning provided the scaffolding for Chapters 1 and 2. Jennifer Whytock pored through newspaper coverage of the political battles that embroiled the Fund during the late 1960s. And at the end, Ken Zogry located the images that illustrate our story.

Several projects grew up alongside our work on the Fund and informed our understanding of the battle against poverty. In 1996, a group of young community activists — J. B. Buxton, Scott Cooper, Tony Deifell, Claudia Horwitz, Charles McKinney, Julia Scatliff, and Jason Scott—organized a conference they called "No Easy Walk," which brought Fund veterans together with a new generation of student antipoverty workers to discuss how knowledge of the past might contribute to progressive social action. During the closing session, Terry Sanford, George Esser, and Howard Fuller shared the stage in a passionate reaffirmation of the political values that guided their actions decades earlier. Transcripts from that conference provided the foundation for a collection of interviews undertaken by the University of North Carolina's Southern Oral History Program and supported by its Walter R. Davis research fund. Our collaboration with the oral history program continues today as part of the Long Civil Rights Movement research initiative, which seeks to understand the origins and aftermath of the upheavals of the 1960s. In 2005, producer Emily Hanford and reporter Leda Hartman at WUNC radio created a documentary series, *North Carolina Voices: Understanding Poverty*, inspired in part by one of the Fund's promotional films. Their effort to situate contemporary poverty issues within a broad historical framework won the Alfred I. duPont–Columbia University Award, the broadcast equivalent of a Pulitzer Prize. Most recently, Rebecca Cerese and Steve Channing at Video Dialog have examined the Fund in a film called *Change Comes Knocking*, which was named best documentary at the 2008 Appalachian Film Festival. Interviews they conducted and shared with us provide many of the voices heard in this book.

Scholarship itself would be impoverished without the contributions, often hidden, of archivists and librarians. We are particularly indebted to Linda Sellers, who processed the North Carolina Fund Records, a collection that occupies more than three hundred linear feet of shelf space. Without the clarity of organization she brought to those materials and the expert catalog she prepared, we would have been hopelessly lost. We are also indebted to Tim West, Laura Clark Brown, Matt Turi, and Stephanie Stewart at the Southern Historical Collection; Robert Anthony, Harry McKown, Jason Tomberlin, Nicholas Graham, Stephen Fletcher, Keith Longiotti, and Patrick Cullom at the North Carolina Collection; and Kim Cumber at the North Carolina State Archives.

Over the years, many colleagues have read our work, shared their own research, and asked questions that challenged us to sharpen our thinking. They include Jack Boger, William Chafe, Charles Clotfelter, James Clotfelter, Sandy Darity, Linda Gordon, Elna Green, Sherman James, Gordon Mantler, Gene Nichol, Charles Payne, John Rubin, Rachel Seidman, and Aiden Smith. Christina Greene, William Link, and Howard Sitkoff offered thoughtful suggestions as readers of our manuscript for the University of North Carolina Press, and Greene's scholarship has been invaluable for our understanding of the struggles of poor whites and blacks in Durham. Jacquelyn Hall also provided incisive commentary at points all along the way. Jacquelyn has been a colleague and mentor since our time in graduate school. Her insistence on intellectual rigor and her conviction that scholarship can be a force for justice in the world have guided our work. Our universities have also been generous in providing time and research funds to help us write this book. We are especially grateful to Bruce Jentleson, Bruce Kuniholm, and the Arts and Sciences Research Council at Duke, and at Carolina, to Bernadette Gray-Little, Holden Thorp, Bobbi Owen, the late Richard Soloway, Lloyd Kramer, and the Institute for the Arts and Humanities.

At the UNC Press, editor in chief David Perry quickly recognized the Fund's historical significance and its value to contemporary debates. He encouraged us and championed our work for many years. Paul Betz and Zach Read shepherded the book through production, and Mark Simpson-Vos, Sylvia Miller, Kenneth Reed, Adam Constabaris, and Russ Damian developed it as a prototype for Publishing the Long Civil Rights Movement, an innovative project in scholarly communication supported by the Andrew W. Mellon Foundation. Our copyeditor, Katie Haywood, is a master of that craft. She saved us from embarrassing errors of fact and infelicities of style.

Finally, we owe thanks to the late George Autry, longtime director of MDC, an offshoot of the Fund that continues to promote economic development in the rural South. Autry offered encouragement at the beginning of this project and assured George Esser and Billy Barnes of the seriousness of our intentions. We could not have undertaken this project without the rich documentary and photographic record Esser and Barnes labored to preserve. They also gave generously of their time, memories, and insights, but always respected our responsibility to tell the North Carolina Fund story as we saw it.

Index

Durham Manifesto, 22

Durham Merchants Association, 228

Durham Morning Herald, 192, 194, 226, 326

Durham Sun, 337

Earley, Mrs., 258

Eastland, James O., 290, 300, 328

Economic capital, 343

Economic development: 1880–1900, 11; 1940s–1950s investment in, 37; Hodges administration, 46; school improvement plan for, 46; Sanford's program for, 52–53, 198–99; race element in, 88; N.C. Fund projects for, 97, 99–100; in Choanoke region, 198–99; social capital role in, 254–55

Economic equity, fight for, 6, 191–92

Economic Opportunity Act, 1–2, 115, 158, 349; requirement to include participation by the poor, 6; N.C. Fund role in drafting, 87, 166; participation requirement for CAPs, 165, 166–67; goals of, 167; North Carolina's response to, 167; National Labor Relations Act (Wagner Act) compared, 172; Shriver on, 172; congressional hearings on antipoverty programs, 215–16; Work Experience and Training Program, 268

Economy: 1960s, 3–4; 1899–1927 growth in, 17–18; timber and mining industry declines, 65, 97, 99. *See also* Agriculture industry; Textile industry; Tobacco industry

Edgemont Community Council, 194–95

Edison, Thomas, 60

Edmund Pettis Bridge, 149

Education: funding for, 16, 46–47, 59–60, 72, 99; 1930s investment in, 18–19; Sanford's focus on, 42–46, 49–50, 58–60; teacher salaries, 47; Aycock's public school campaign, 55, 59, 89; illiteracy rates, 58, 86; dropout rates, 58, 158, 234; 1902–10 school-building campaign and, 59; poverty and, 92; literacy programs, 160, 202; early childhood, 174–75, 189,

190, 202–4, 222, 300; for self-help and racial advancement, 207; school lunch funding and, 237; New York City school reform efforts, 333; New York City teachers' strike, 333. *See also* School desegregation

Ehle, John, 53, 59–60, 76, 81–82, 88, 93

Ehringhaus, John C. B., 20, 46–47

Ehrlichman, John, 338, 342

Eisenhower, Dwight D., 114

Elizabeth City State College, 123

Elliott, True, 243, 244, 245–46, 249–50

Ellis, C. P. (Claiborne Paul), 192, 316–18

Ellis, Marion, 47

Ellis, Tom, 40

Embree, Edwin R., 61

Enfield, N.C., 201, 207

Entin, David, 124, 135, 158

Eppley, Anita, 235

Eppley, Ernest, 235–36; WAMY hiring of, 235–36; Blue Ridge Hearthside Crafts, position on, 241; on mountaineer's life, 242; WAMY staff and, 252–54, 267; WAMY tenure, 256, 264–67; Adkins and, 269, 271–72; media project and, 280, 281, 282; resignation, 281–82, 284; criticism of, 283, 284; H.C. Moretz Jr., concerns about, 284; poverty activists, concerns about, 284–85

Equal employment opportunity, 22, 25–26, 28, 54, 72, 158, 167–70, 214, 222, 228–29. *See also* Labor

Equal opportunity, 44–45, 168

Ervin, Sam J., Jr., 204, 279–80

Esser, George H., Jr., 88, 297, 326; on N.C. Fund's purpose, 2, 7, 10; background, 64; North Carolina Foundation plan, 64–65; Ford funding, involvement in, 66, 82, 85–87; N.C. Fund and, 92–93, 95, 96–97, 105–6, 287–88; Hawkins letter to, 105; on breaking cycle of poverty, 113–14; Volunteers program, 115–16, 117, 130, 159; Johnson administration and, 116; Economic Opportunity Act, role in drafting, 166; CADA OEO application

233; race element in, 88; Esser on importance of, 113–14; social capital in, 254–55. *See also* Antipoverty programs; North Carolina Fund; War on Poverty
Poverty of self-sufficiency, 237–39
Poverty-segregation complex, 223
Poverty warriors, 254, 255, 258, 286, 289, 299, 318–19. *See also* North Carolina Volunteers
"Poverty Warriors — The Riots Are Subsidized as Well as Organized" (*Barron's*), 299
Powell, Susie, 109
Presbyterian Church in the United States, 332
Presnell, Max, 258
Preyer, L. Richardson, 77–79, 130, 290
Price, Hugh, 337
Price, Julian, 232
Price's Creek, N.C., 134
Prison reform, 315
Progressive Party, 23
Protestant Christian Church, 106
The Protocols of the Elders of Zion, 331
Public housing, 157, 187–88, 192–93, 225–26, 228
Public housing activism, 194–96, 225–28
Public services, 220–21
Puerto Rico, 63
Pupil Assignment Act, 34, 35
Putnam, Robert, 254

Racial capitalism, 3, 29, 311
Racial equality, 27–29, 52–55
Racial intermarriage, 34–35, 40
Racialized language of inferiority and separation, 266
Racial justice, 50–54, 70
Racial unrest: Newark, N.J., 226; 1967, Newark and Detroit, 297–300, 303, 305–6; presidential commission to investigate, 298–99; Agnew's response to, 323–24; violence used to quell, 325
Racism, Salter on, 313–14

Radio. *See* Media
Raleigh, N.C., 48, 49, 66, 68–69, 89, 296, 315, 353
Raleigh jail lock-out, 69
Raleigh News and Observer. See *News and Observer*
Ramsey, D. Hiden, 29
Randolph, A. Philip, 169
Rape, black-on-white, 12–13
Rarick, John R., Sr., 329–30, 332, 338
Reader's Digest, 312
Reagan, Ronald, 8–9, 296, 329, 349–50
Reconstruction, 2, 13–14, 54, 205, 278, 295
Red Book (NCF), 90, 92, 105
Redding, Kent, 12
Reece, B. Carroll, 328
Religion-poverty relationship, 280–81
Religious organizations, Blackburn/Rarick attack on, 332–33
Republican National Convention, 323
Republican Party: conservative control of, 8–9, 290, 292–97, 302, 305; OEO's dismantling by, 9, 338–40, 347–49; 1900–1910, 16; 1963 legislative session gains, 72–73; black political power, 206–7; 1966 elections to Congress, 290–91, 306; growth strategies, 324, 343; youth recruitment, 347
Republican-Populist (biracial) Fusionist alliance, 11–14, 16, 43, 54, 67, 168–69
Research Triangle Park, 37, 176, 192, 337
Retreat from the Hills (WBT), 283–85
Reuther, Walter, 168–69, 170, 171, 305
Reynolds, Richard Joshua (R. J.), 79
Reynolds, R. J., Jr., 80
Reynolds, Zachary Smith, 79
Reynolds family, 18
Reynolds Foundation. *See* Z. Smith Reynolds Foundation
Richardson, H. Smith, 77
Richardson, Lunsford, 77
Riots. *See* Racial unrest
R. J. Reynolds Tobacco Company, 17, 22, 28, 80

University of North Carolina at Greensboro. *See* Woman's College

University of North Carolina Institute of Government, 64, 66

University of North Carolina Medical School, 37

University of North Carolina School of Law, 48, 75

UOCI confederation. *See* United Organizations for Community Improvement

Urban migration. *See* Migration

Urban renewal, 192–93, 299, 302–3, 337, 340

Vance, Rupert, 247–48

Vanderbilt, Cornelius, 99

Vanderbilt, George W., II, 99

Varney, Harold Lord, 330–31

Vick Chemical Company, 77

Vicks VapoRub, 77

Vietnam War, 312, 323, 329

Vista Volunteer, 306–7

Volunteers in Service to America, 5, 247

Voter registration: Freedom Summer campaign, 5, 119; post–World War II, 22; drives for, 190, 310, 332; Halifax Voters Movement, 201–2; federal restrictions on, 335

Voters movement, 211

Voting rights: literacy tests to limit, 14–15, 44; disfranchisement amendment, 14–16, 206; black North Carolinians demand for, 22; movement for, 38–39

Voting Rights Act, 7, 278, 295, 311–12, 324, 335

Waddell, Alfred Moore, 13, 15–16

Wage and workplace protections, 169, 188–89, 222, 310, 324

Wagner, Robert F., Jr., 215–16

Wagner Act, 22, 168, 172

Wagoner, Bobby, 252–53

Wake Forest College, 39

Walker, Robert, 263–64, 268, 269, 271, 284

Wallace, George C., 1, 70, 114, 302, 323, 324, 329–30, 331

Wallace, Henry, 23

Walsh, William, 291

WAMY Community Action program: beginnings, 97, 233–35; community improvement projects, 134–35, 257–71; hostility to, 134–35, 321; steering committee, 233–34; staff, 235, 236, 251, 252–53, 267, 277, 284; vision, 235, 242, 264; OEO funding, 235, 277; subcontracting relationships with welfare agencies, 236–37, 264, 266; antipoverty crafts project, 237–39, 241–42, 246; women volunteers, 242–46, 249–51, 255, 256, 266–67, 269, 274, 283, 321; family planning project, 249–51; maximum feasible participation by, 251–52, 256, 265, 277; incentive grants program, 253–61; community development advisory councils, 256; N.C. Fund review, 261–63; board of directors, dissent and changes, 263–65, 272, 277–78; reforms, 264–67, 272–74; citizen education campaign, 267; community speak-outs, 269–70; publications, 272–73; media project, 275–82; Jaycees review, 283; public criticism of, 283–84; WBT program on, 283–85

—the poor and: process of empowering, 252–61, 265, 267, 269–72; mobilizing as political force, 271–72, 274–75; educating, 272–74, 277; communicating with, 275–82

WAMY region: history of activism in, 7, 251–52; poverty in, 57, 128, 134, 244–45, 257, 259, 270, 283, 353; education in, 99, 234, 239; tourism in, 232; identified needs in, 234–35; health census, 243–44; blacks, percent of population, 252, 266; geographic and social isolation, 252, 280–81; racialized language of inferiority and separation, 266; health care in, 266–67. *See also* Appalachia

Ward, Betty, 151, 163

War on Poverty: agenda, 6–7; dismantling of, 8–9, 338–40, 347–49; Sanford and, 55; beginnings, 87, 115–16, 166–67, 171–72;

N.C. Fund model for, 115–16, 166, 172; citizen soldiers in, 126; role of birth control in, 147, 247–48; winning, requirements for, 171, 216–25, 311; architects of, 171–72; unexpected consequences of, 188; black vision for, 208; struggle for control in, 215–18; white power structure expectations of controlling, 215–16; purpose, 216; successes, 231, 288; guiding principles of, 260–61; Johnson's hopes for, 290; Monte protest of, 297; bipartisan effort to contain, 305; weaknesses, 311; failure, causes of, 312. *See also* North Carolina Fund; Office of Economic Opportunity; Poverty—battle against

Washington, D.C., 63
Washington Post, 312
Watauga Democrat, 269–70
Watergate, 330, 348
Watkins, Lucy Rodgers, 288
Watkins, Mary, 23
Watson, Albert W., 329–30
Watson, Martha, 125
Watson, Tom, 3
Watt, Mel, 207
Watts, Charles D., 303–4
WBT-TV, 283–85
Weaver, Robert, 194
Webster, Noah, 60
Welch, Robert W., Jr., 292
Welfare clients, empowering, 184, 214, 246–47, 271
Welfare leavers, 353
Welfare policies, arbitrary enforcement of, 271
Welfare reform, 349–53
What WAMY Can Do (WAMY), 272
Wheeler, John H., 49, 81–82, 89, 176–77
White, George H., 206
White flight, 34–35, 63, 192, 298
White Government Unions, 13, 206
Whitener, Basil L., 279, 281, 284
White poverty, 231, 321–22. *See also* Poverty
White privilege, 16, 25–26
Whites: racial fears, 30, 34–35, 40, 147–49,

300–303, 325, 336; middle class, 42–43, 45–46, 279–80, 300–301; attitudes toward the poor, 279–80, 300–301; blacks characterized by, 295, 301; working class, 320

White supremacy/supremacists, 2–3, 41, 43, 206, 313–14, 318, 322, 342. *See also individual organizations*

Whitson, Betty, 242–43, 245–46
Wicker, Tom, 306
Wildcat Hollow, N.C., 253–54
Wilkins, Roger, 355
Wilkins, Roy, 335
Wilson, French, 181
Wilson, N.C., 96, 100, 310
Winston, Francis D., 206–7
Winston-Salem, N.C., 18, 103, 142
Winston-Salem Journal, 29
Winston-Salem State College, 142, 147–48
Winters, John, 49, 69
Wire, Hugh Brinley, 252, 253, 270, 282
WITN-TV, 214
Woman's College, 23
Women poor, empowering, 242–50, 255–56, 266–67, 269, 321
Woodard, N.C., 223
Woodward Enterprises, 223–24
Work Experience and Training Program, 268
Working class, 27–28, 320
Working poor, 351, 353
Works Progress Administration, 20
World War II, 37, 208
Worst, Edward F., 240
WRAL radio, 25
WRAL-TV, 73, 78, 149, 179, 301
Wright, Richard, 30
Wright brothers, 60

Yancey Record, 280
Yarmolinsky, Adam, 166, 167
Ylvisaker, Paul, 60, 62–66, 82, 83, 87, 165, 174
YMCA, Chapel Hill, 124
Young, Andrew, 207

About the DVD *Change Comes Knocking*

The North Carolina-based production company Video Dialog Inc. produced the documentary *Change Comes Knocking: The Story of the North Carolina Fund*. The film tells the tumultuous story of the biracial antipoverty organization called the North Carolina Fund that boldly confronted the explosive issues of race, class, and politics during the turbulent 1960s.

For over two decades, Video Dialog has been creating documentary and educational films to help teach and inspire. Our core belief is that history matters, that from the past we can better understand our world today and work toward creating a better future. We've told many southern stories, from the "Lost Colony" in the founding era to the PBS broadcast *February One: The Story of the Greensboro Four*, which helped restore to national memory the 1960 Woolworth lunch counter sit-in.

It was therefore natural to approach historians Robert Korstad and James Leloudis about producing a film on the North Carolina Fund. We followed the path of Fund workers as they worked across the state, from the mountains to the Black Belt in the Northeast, to find and interview the individuals who made up the organizations spawned by the Fund. We also spoke with some of the North Carolina Volunteers, who as college students during the summers of 1964 and 1965 had worked to improve the lives of low-income families. The story of the North Carolina Fund is as rich and diverse as the people that shared in its creation.

We are especially grateful for the skills and generous spirit of Billy Barnes, who took thousands of photographs that document the story of the North Carolina Fund and the communities it reached out to and helped. The documentary features many of these archival images, as well as excerpts from Fund-produced promotional films, to present an authentic visual palette of North Carolina during this critical period of time. *Change Comes Knocking* won Best Documentary film at the Appalachian Film Festival in 2008.

Producer Rebecca Cerese is an award-winning filmmaker who graduated from the University of North Carolina at Chapel Hill, with a degree in communications and English. Her first documentary, *February One*, has been screened at the Martin Luther King, Jr. Center, the Smithsonian Museum of American History, and the National Archives and has won numerous awards at film festivals around the country.

With a Ph.D. from the University of North Carolina at Chapel Hill, Executive Producer Steven Channing brings a long career as historian, teacher, writer, and filmmaker to the challenge of creating a fresh look at this classic American story. Channing first taught at the University of Kentucky, Stanford University, and Duke University. Prior to his work as documentary filmmaker, he published the Allen Nevins Award–winning *Crisis of Fear: Secession in South Carolina* and, for Time-Life's Civil War series, *The Confederate Ordeal*.